1993 GUIDE
TO
COUNTY CRICKET

1993 GUIDE TO COUNTY CRICKET

Edited by Rob Steen
Introduction by Mike Atherton,
Lancashire and England

BOXTREE

Acknowledgements

The preparation of this guide would have been impossible without the assistance of Jeremy Novick, Michael Henderson, Huw Richards, Paul Filer, David Frith and Steven Lynch at *Wisden Cricket Monthly*, *The Cricketers' Who's Who*, *The Wisden Guide to Cricket Grounds*, *The Cricketer Quarterly*, anyone and everyone at a county headquarters who answered my calls and queries, and, above all, Britannic Assurance, to whom England's greatest sporting institution owes so much.

Rob Steen, April 1993

First published in the UK 1993 by BOXTREE LIMITED,
Broadwall House, 21 Broadwall, London SE1 9PL.

10 9 8 7 6 5 4 3 2 1

© Boxtree Limited 1993

Design of text and cover by Design 23

Cover and text pictures courtesy of DAVID MUNDEN/PORTSLINE

ISBN 1-85283-803-5

Printed and bound in Great Britain by Cox & Wyman Ltd, Reading

Except in the United States of America, this book is sold subject to the condition that it shall not, by way of trade or otherwise, be lent, resold, hired out or otherwise circulated without the publisher's prior consent in any form of binding or cover other than that in which it is published and without a similar condition including this condition being imposed on a subsequent purchaser.

A catalogue record for this book is available from the British Library

Contents

Introduction — 2

Foreword — 3

Editorial Preface — 5

Competition — 7

Roll of Honour 1992 — 8

1992 First Class Averages — 11

1992 Leading One-Day Averages — 19

England First-Class Career Records — 21

1992 BAC Scores — 35

BAC FIXTURES 1993 — 71
  Fixtures
  BACflashes

WHAT, WHERE AND HOW — 92
  Ground information, admissions/directions
  Membership information

WHO'S WHO – County-by-county guide — 131
  Points system
  County record
  Playing staff 1993
  BAC Averages 1992
  Prospects
  Overseas Player   profiles

ENGLAND IN 1992–93 — 198
  1992-3 averages
  Test career averages

A–Z of Cricket — 201

1993 Fixtures — 206

Introduction

Cricket, thank heaven, remains our national summer sport even in these days of ridiculously frenetic change. The County Championship lies at the heart of the game, well placed between the countless club and village matches and the international fixtures. The Championship is fundamental to the sport, and its welfare is surely a barometer for the game as a whole. In this sense Britannic's sponsorship, begun in 1983, provides essential finance for its continuation and therefore has an altruistic value for a worthwhile cause – as all readers would surely agree!

However, sponsorship – especially over the long-term – must be justified commercially. For us this principally means improved name awareness, and the fact that cricket appeals to a wide cross-section of people is clearly an advantage, in addition to the goodwill it generates. Without commercial justification, either the sponsorship cannot be undertaken or it will quickly finish. My belief is that the best sponsorships are those which combine proper commercial justification with a feel and understanding of the sport by the management of the sponsoring business.

If you query the latter need, the simplest explanation would be to point out that if the business concerned understands the game and its traditions then it is much more likely to be able to work in close harmony with the management and players of the sport. Thus the common purposes of supporting and promoting the sport most effectively will be more easily and effectively established to the mutual benefit of both parties. Additional resources – time and money – are needed on top of the sponsorship fee.

The media are the third vital ingredient to a sport (and its sponsor). Thinking of this, what a pleasure it is to welcome this initiative on the part of Boxtree, whereby we can re-live memories of the past season and look forward to an exciting new season under a new format. With best wishes for happy hours of reading (and days of watching).

B. H. Shaw
Director and General Manager
Britannic Assurance PLC

Foreword by Michael Atherton, Lancashire, England

Despite the fact that four-day cricket has been present on the cricket calendar for five years, 1993 marks a watershed. The ill-judged mixture of three- and four-day cricket has given way to a full four-day programme for the first time in the history of the Championship. The new format follows hard on the heels of the Murray Report which also incorporates a 50-over Sunday League and a new-fangled knockout Benson & Hedges Cup competition.

Those sceptical of the changes point to the perceived financial consequences. David Lemmon for example has argued that the changes could be the death knell of first-class county cricket in England and within a few years five or six counties could disappear. Certainly the festival weeks will be less lucrative. Counties may find the last two days of a four-day game (Saturday and Monday) more difficult to sell. Corporate entertainment is notoriously difficult to obtain for Saturdays whilst people may be unenthusiastic for a Monday for fear that a game may finish early. The fact that Saturday will no longer be the first day of a game may have a discouraging effect on the paying spectators.

Some also have doubts in pure cricketing terms. It is argued that teams will slow the pace of the game down and play a three-day game in four days, the net result being negative fare and, as has happened in Australia, pitiful crowds. The entertaining festival weeks will be reduced. At Essex for example, the weeks at Ilford, Colchester and Southend form an integral part of their programme, the advantages being not only financial but in the variety and spice of cricket offered. They are still with us, but others, such as those at Uxbridge, Worksop, Bournemouth and Coventry, are not. The old-fashioned turners encountered at many of these grounds are scarcely found on main county grounds. The fear is that the inherent variety of county cricket will become moribund and replaced by a bland sameness.

Jim Cumbes, marketing manager at Lancashire, is sceptical of the financial argument against four-day cricket. To him, there will merely have to be adjustments to the new programme, for example, as counties get used to one four-day game in a week as opposed to two three-day games. Thursdays and Fridays will be excellent corporate days while any net loss at the gate is offset by the knowledge that Championship gate receipts are not a money-spinner in any case.

While county cricket in England is inherently valuable, it is not financially viable without the Test and County Cricket Board handout which results from international matches. The continued existence, therefore, of a fully professional first-class game in England is inextricably linked to the success of the national side. County cricket needs an entertaining, marketable and successful England team. If four-day cricket is likely to produce better cricketers, and a potentially better Test side, then it is surely financially defensible.

What seems to be undeniable is the better quality cricket that a four-day Championship will bring. When three-day games were played on uncovered wickets, the emphasis was largely on bowling sides out in more helpful bowling conditions. With the advent of covered wickets and the increase in one-day cricket, the emphasis has switched to containment. Generally unresponsive wickets and continual cricket leave bowlers tired and dispirited and there are often occasions when batsmen are aware that bowlers are just going through the motions waiting for a third-innings declaration and a run chase.

This will not be permissible in four-day cricket. Teams with aspirations to win the Championship will have to bowl sides out twice. An inability to do so will lead to being batted out of the game. At the moment, England do not possess the strike bowlers that, say, Pakistan and the West Indies have. At a stroke, four-day cricket switches the emphasis to taking wickets and, it is to be hoped, in time, more and more matchwinning bowlers will appear. Declaration bowling will thankfully disappear as games will be allowed to reach a natural conclusion with the better side having more chance of forcing a win.

Four-day cricket will enable younger players who often bat at five or six to play longer innings. It ought to encourage conditions in which spinners can thrive, once again a crucial part of a captain's armoury and not just a last resort as in recent years. There will be more time for quality practice, match planning and preparation. For too long, too many players have hidden behind a veneer of mediocrity in the knowledge that they can do enough to get by. The new programme could revive the flagging reputation of county cricket as the toughest finishing school: no easy runs and, as fewer innings make each one more valuable, no easy wickets. The new conditions will help to differentiate between those who can play and those who can't and revive the Championship as a tough and quality-controlled competition.

In general, a greater gulf exists between county cricket and Test cricket than, for example, Sheffield Shield cricket and Test cricket. This is not due to quality as there is certainly equal, if not more quality within England than elsewhere. It concerns mental toughness: the quantity of cricket in England dulls both quality and competitive edge. Four-day cricket, it is to be hoped, will bring a new edge, an edge that is crucial to success at the highest levels of the game.

Much depends upon the state of wickets. Four-day cricket needs wickets that will last and yet that will provide an equal contest between bat and ball. There *is* enough quality in the English game to sustain a four-day structure and most judges expect a beneficial net result: a fairer Championship, tougher, higher quality cricket with, crucially, the emphasis shifted to attack through bowling sides out, thus bringing greater, not less entertainment.

Down the Track

There is no crisis in cricket, there is only the next ball. W. G. GRACE

If Britannia no longer rules the waves, we can at least console ourselves that these decreasingly green and pleasant lands still command a few lagoons. Along with good ale, lake districts, male voice choirs and seaside piers, County Championship cricket ranks high on the Made in Britain scroll of honour. And nothing that happened on the road from Calcutta to Colombo during the early months of 1993 can change that. Those besotted with bottom lines regard the longer form of the county game as an anachronism and an indulgence. Fortunately, there are many more of the same persuasion as J. H. Hardy, who once admitted that 'if I knew I was going to die today I'd still like to hear the cricket scores'. Despite the advent of the limited-overs lash, the 'scores' still signify the Championship close of play scoreboard and its attendant sense of a life in progress, its promise of a tomorrow.

Like so many of life's delights, the County Championship was never formally planned. For years, the only references were in the form of tables printed in newspapers from time to time. In 1837, for example, one Maidstone journal insisted that a match between Kent and Nottinghamshire was for a so-called 'county championship', on the less than convincing grounds that the protagonists had both previously beaten Sussex. By 1864 Middlesex, Surrey, Yorkshire and Lancashire had swelled this embryonic circuit, hence the customary appearance in *Wisden* of a list detailing the champion county from that year on. Yet although 1873 is deemed to have marked the starting point for the official Championship, *Wisden* wisely declined to publish a table until 1888, the year in which the first (unofficial) scoring system was introduced. The cricketing *Hansard* now lists Championship positions dating back to 1890, when the competition was officially constituted.

The County Championship has since become synonymous with that beastly beauty we call the English summer. The smell of damp, newly-mown outfields, of leather and wood. The sound of leather on wood, and raindrops on wood. The sight of cream, of pristine flannels and starched shirts. The touch of a Gower or a Woolley or a Bedi. The taste of history. The overwhelming sense of intimacy, and, better still, of an international community.

The image also has a place in reality. Without domestic first-class cricket, Test cricket, as Groucho Marx once observed of something quite different, would be a travesty of a travesty. Admittedly, the crowds who went – or rather, didn't go – to the South Africa-India series at the end of last year confirmed that Test cricket itself is in more than a bit of bother. At the same time, thank goodness, there is a fervent desire among the members of the International Cricket Council to preserve, for all its comparative lack of profitability, the unique fascination and rich traditions of the five-day chess match.

This, inevitably, has meant compromise. There are too many one-day biff-and-bangs for several tastes, yet without these abridged imitations the genuine article could not hope to survive. Neither could Test cricket carry on without the aid of a university to sift through the students and turn out graduates worthy of flying the flag. Together, the Britannic Assurance County Championship, Sheffield Shield, Red Stripe Cup, Shell Trophy, Currie Cup, Quaid-e-Azam Trophy, Ranji Trophy and Singer Inter-Provincial Tournament form a transcontinental old boys' association of global renown.

That there appeared to be so few Englishmen worthy of bearing the standard on the subcontinent (henceforth to be known as the sob-continent) is symptomatic of a long-standing, deeper-rooted malaise. Since no other domestic structure demands anything like so much of its players' physical and mental capacities, should we wonder at the lack of drive and enthusiasm shown by Graham Gooch and company? Quantity and quality are not normally found sharing the same bed.

A sensible balance appears to have been achieved via the package of changes recommended by the Murray Report, adopted by the counties on a three-season, suck-it-and-see trial basis. Reactions have been mixed to say the least. Some club chairmen were understandably aggrieved to have to vote for a package as opposed to individual reforms. The players, moreover, are less than delirious either about having to give up their Sunday morning lie-in or playing for an extra couple of hours.

The most significant development has attracted a more positive sense of unanimity. And, since our doughty shirehorses like nothing better than a good whinny, anything that finds them in contented accord, as Mike Atherton's persuasive foreword on the four-day Championship indicates, can only be a good thing. The prospect of more days off, far from unwarranted, has much to do with this, but then so has the desire for a bona fide test of ability. The extra day should meet it, reducing drastically (Pluvius permitting) the frequency of third-day phoney wars and prefab finishes, enhancing the quality of play if not the speed at which it is conducted. Since when, though, has speed been a guarantee of good cricket? The appeal of the first-class game centres on individual craftsmanship and drama that unfolds through subtle twists and turns. A novel to absorb rather than a comic to skim, which is how the abbreviated game strikes the SOPs (snotty old purists) among us.

The new Thursday-to-Monday programme has also been roundly attacked for shortcomings in commercial awareness. This conveniently ignores the fact that, these days, what the counties take at their own gates has little or nothing to do with whether they make a profit or not. Much as the more independently-minded bemoan this, domestic first-class cricket is scarcely a crowd-puller. Spurred on by postwar euphoria, eager to celebrate survival by embracing tradition, more than two million customers poured through the gates in 1947; spoilt in their choice of leisure pursuits, fewer than 50,000 watched Lancashire's first-class home dates in 1990.

Not even the most devoted TCCB marketing bod would claim that today's average audience deserves to be called a crowd. In fact, it would probably destroy the whole appeal if the turnstiles were to click any faster. God help us if the *Sun* ever tried to raise the profile of Championship cricket in the way it has peddled domestic football. So long as the major matches can generate enough income to feed each club – the 1992 dividend was nearly £½m a head – the county game now geared primarily towards unearthing and grooming top-class entertainers, can afford to retain its intimacy.

International cricket, though, is not the be-all and end-all, as was summed up by Andy Lloyd, the former Warwickshire captain whose Test career, terminated by a blow to the temple from Malcom Marshall in 1984, lasted precisely 33 minutes. 'I reckon I lost 30% of my right-eye vision,' he said after announcing his retirement last winter. 'I was happy enough to be able to play county cricket, but I suppose I knew I could never play for England again. It doesn't matter. I have had a good career and enjoyed it all. The game was good to me.'

For the game to be as beneficial to Lloyd's successors – not to mention ourselves – it would seem sensible to divide the Championship into two divisions and institute promotion and relegation. Not only would this reduce the workload still further while investing greater meaning for a greater number of counties in the preponderantly anticlimactic latter months, it would also pep up those sickly gate receipts. All the same, only those with an overt flair for the dramatic – and an underdeveloped awareness of current happenings in Bosnia, Kashmir, Ulster and Moscow – would say county cricket is in the midst of a crisis. A state of flux, perhaps, but there is no crisis, merely the next season. Speaking of which, welcome, as Elvis Costello might say, to this year's model. Enjoy.

ROB STEEN

Britannic Assurance Championship Competition 1993

Readers of the *BAC 1993 Guide to County Cricket* are invited to take part in a competition to win a year's free full membership to the county of their choice – by being a selector for the day. To do so, choose two teams in correct batting order drawn from the 300–odd players on the county circuit in 1993. One should be an imaginary World XI, the other a collection of the best young England-qualified players, none of whom must have played in a Test match prior to June 3, 1993, the opening day of the first Test. The closing date is September 30, 1993 and all entries should be sent to: The Editor, *BAC Guide to County Cricket*, Boxtree Ltd, Second floor, Broadwall House, 21 Broadwall, London SE1 9PL. The reader sending in the best selections in the view of the editor will win the prize. Tie-breaker: in no more than 25 words, describe your favourite county ground.

To help you on your way, the following teams might have been selected had we been publishing last year:

WORLD XI *(selected from those playing county cricket in 1992):*

GOOCH (Essex & Eng, capt)
HAYNES (Middx & WI)
WAUGH (Essex & Aus)
GOWER (Hants & Eng)
JONES (Durham & Aus)
HOOPER (Kent & WI)
RUSSELL (Gloucs & Eng, wkt)
BISHOP (Derbys & WI)
AMBROSE (Northants & WI)
WALSH (Gloucs & WI)
TUFNELL (Middx & Eng)

12th man: LEWIS (Notts & Eng)
Squad members: Richards (Glam & WI), Marshall (Hants & WI), Morrison (Lancs & NZ), Gatting (Middx & Eng).

YOUNG ENGLAND

FORDHAM (Northants)
WARD (Kent)
ROSEBERRY (Middx, capt)
CRAWLEY (Lancs)
THORPE (Surrey)
BROWN (Surrey)
HEGG (Lancs, wkt)
CORK (Derbys)
MARTIN (Lancs)
ILOTT (Essex)
KENDRICK (Surrey)
12th man: FLEMING (Kent)

Squad members: Boiling (Surrey), Speight (Sussex), Crawley (Notts), Lathwell (Somerset).

1992 ROLL OF HONOUR

BRITANNIC ASSURANCE CHAMPIONSHIP

		P	W	L	D	T	Bt	Bl	Pts
1	Essex (1)	22	11	6	5	0	60	64	300
2	Kent (6)	22	9	3	10	0	60	55	259
3	Northamptonshire (10)	22	8	4	10	0	62	58	248
4	Nottinghamshire (4)	22	7	7	8	0	54	58	224
5	Derbyshire (3)	22	7	6	9	0	47	63	222
6	Warwickshire (2)	22	6	8	8	0	55	68	219
7	Sussex (11)	22	6	7	9	0	60	61	217
8	Leicestershire (16)	22	7	7	8	0	40	59	211
9	Somerset (17)	22	5	4	13	0	64	62	206
10	Gloucestershire (13)	22	6	6	9	0	48	58	202
11	Middlesex (15)	22	5	3	14	0	62	60	202
12	Lancashire (8)	22	4	6	12	0	75	49	188
13	Surrey (5)	22	5	7	10	0	56	50	186
14	Glamorgan (12)	22	5	4	13	0	53	49	182
15	Hampshire (9)	22	4	6	12	0	61	57	182
16	Yorkshire (14)	22	4	6	12	0	56	52	172
17	Worcestershire (6)	22	3	4	14	0	54	65	167
18	Durham (-)	22	2	10	10	0	46	53	131

1991 positions shown in brackets

SUNDAY LEAGUE

		P	W	L	T	NR	Away	Pts	Run Rate
1	Middlesex (11)	17	14	2	0	1	6	58	93.91
2	Essex (6)	17	11	5	0	1	4	46	83.33
3	Hampshire (17)	17	10	6	0	1	3	42	76.71
4	Surrey (8)	17	10	7	0	0	7	40	90.46
5	Somerset (9)	17	9	6	0	2	3	40	81.23
6	Kent (10)	17	8	5	0	4	5	40	89.84
7	Worcestershire (4)	17	7	6	1	3	3	36	74.48
8	Gloucestershire (12)	17	8	8	0	1	3	34	76.04
9	Durham (-)	17	7	7	0	3	4	34	89.11
10	Warwickshire (5)	17	7	7	1	2	2	34	82.55
11	Sussex (13)	17	7	8	0	2	3	32	82.54
12	Lancashire (2)	17	6	7	0	4	3	32	84.07
13	Northamptonshire (3)	17	7	9	0	1	3	30	83.21
14	Derbyshire (15)	17	7	9	0	1	1	30	81.06
15	Yorkshire (7)	17	6	9	0	2	3	28	79.53
16	Glamorgan (16)	17	4	10	0	3	3	22	86.21
17	Nottinghamshire (1)	17	3	11	0	3	1	18	81.17
18	Leicestershire (14)	17	3	12	0	2	2	16	81.08

1991 positions shown in brackets

BENSON & HEDGES CUP

Winners: Hampshire
Runners-up: Kent
Losing semi-finalists: Somerset and Surrey

NATWEST TROPHY

Winners: Northamptonshire
Runners-up: Leicestershire
Losing semi-finalists: Essex and Warwickshire

1992 FIRST-CLASS TOP-TENS
INDIVIDUAL SCORES

241*	P. D. Bowler	Derbyshire v Hampshire	Portsmouth
233	M. R. Ramprakash	Middlesex v Surrey	Lord's
233	R. G. Twose	Warwickshire v Leicestershire	Edgbaston
232	N. J. Speak	Lancashire v Leicestershire	Leicester
228*	T. S. Curtis	Worcestershire v Derbyshire	Derby
222*	N. J. Lenham	Sussex v Kent	Hove
221	T. C. Middleton	Hampshire v Surrey	Southampton
219*	M. E. Waugh	Essex v Lancashire	Ilford
216	G. P. Thorpe	Surrey v Somerset	The Oval
213*	G. A. Hick	Worcestershire v Nottinghamshire	Trent Bridge
213	D. M. Smith	Sussex v Essex	Southend

INNINGS BOWLING

8–26	M. J. McCague	Kent v Hampshire	Canterbury
8–47	K. J. Shine	Hampshire v Lancashire	Old Trafford
8–50	S. D. Udal	Hampshire v Sussex	Southampton
8–66	R. D. B. Croft	Glamorgan v Warwickshire	Swansea
8–75	N. F. Williams	Middlesex v Gloucestershire	Lord's
8–107	A. M. Babington	Gloucestershire v Kent	Bristol
8–111	P. J. Hartley	Yorkshire v Sussex	Hove
7–23	J. P. Taylor	Northamptonshire v Hampshire	Bournemouth
7–27	C. A. Walsh	Gloucestershire v Essex	Bristol
7–29	F. D. Stephenson	Sussex v Worcestershire	Worcester

MATCH BOWLING

14–104	H. R. J. Trump	Somerset v Gloucestershire	Gloucester
14–169	R. D. B. Croft	Glamorgan v Warwickshire	Swansea
13–105	K. J. Shine	Hampshire v Lancashire	Old Trafford
12–110	T. A. Munton	Warwickshire v Leicestershire	Edgbaston
12–138	I. D. K. Salisbury	Sussex v Yorkshire	Hove
12–139	N. F. Williams	Middlesex v Gloucestershire	Lord's
11–76	Wasim Akram	Pakistan v Gloucestershire	Bristol
11–83	I. D. K. Salisbury	Sussex v Lancashire	Old Trafford
11–104	C. A. Walsh	Gloucestershire v Yorkshire	Headingley
11–107	F. D. Stephenson	Sussex v Worcestershire	Worcester

PARTNERSHIPS

347*	3rd	M. E. Waugh & N. Hussain	Essex v Lancashire	Ilford
322	4th	Javed Miandad & Salim Malik	Pakistan v England	Edgbaston
290	1st	T. R. Ward & M. R. Benson	Kent v Warwickshire	Edgbaston
285	1st	A. J. Moles & R. G. Twose	Warwickshire v Leicestershire	Leicester
267	1st	V. P. Terry & T. C. Middleton	Hampshire v Surrey	Southampton
266	1st	D. L. Haynes & M. A. Roseberry	Middlesex v Nottinghamshire	Trent Bridge
265	3rd	R. J. Harden & C. J. Tavaré	Somerset v Nottinghamshire	Taunton
263	3rd	N. J. Lenham & A. P. Wells	Sussex v Lancashire	Old Trafford
259	2nd	P. D. Bowler & J. E. Morris	Derbyshire v Somerset	Taunton
259	3rd	P. D. Bowler & T. J. G. O'Gorman	Derbyshire v Hampshire	Portsmouth

HIGHEST TOTALS

616–7 dec	Somerset v Nottinghamshire	Taunton
603–8 dec	Kent v Warwickshire	Edgbaston
563	Sussex v Lancashire	Old Trafford
562	Lancashire v Durham	Gateshead Fell
557	Surrey v Somerset	The Oval
552–9 dec	Hampshire v Surrey	Southampton
526	Essex v Kent	Chelmsford
521–9 dec	Durham v Glamorgan	Cardiff
510–2 dec	Essex v Lancashire	Ilford
507	Kent v Gloucestershire	Bristol

LOWEST TOTALS

70	Hampshire v Kent	Canterbury
74	Derbyshire v Yorkshire	Harrogate
75	Essex v Leicestershire	Leicester
75	Cambridge University v Essex	Fenner's
76	Surrey v Kent	Guildford
80	Hampshire v Essex	Bournemouth
83	Essex v Yorkshire	Headingley
85	Derbyshire v Warwickshire	Edgbaston
93	Pakistan v Worcestershire	Worcester
95	Middlesex v Northamptonshire	Northampton

1992 FIRST-CLASS AVERAGES

BATTING

Qualification: 8 innings, average 10.00.
*denotes not out

	M	I	NO	Runs	HS	Av	100	50
Salim Malik	15	21	6	1184	165	78.93	2	8
M. E. Waugh	16	24	7	1314	219*	77.29	4	6
D. M. Jones	14	23	7	1179	157	73.69	4	5
G. A. Gooch	18	29	3	1850	160	71.15	8	7
M. W. Gatting	24	36	6	2000	170	66.67	6	10
P. D. Bowler	24	38	7	2044	241*	65.94	6	11
N. H. Fairbrother	12	18	7	689	166*	62.64	1	5
A. J. Lamb	18	28	4	1460	209	60.83	6	5
Javed Miandad	12	17	3	809	153*	57.79	2	4
N. J. Speak	22	36	3	1892	232	57.33	4	12
R. J. Turner	7	10	5	286	101*	57.20	1	1
M. A. Roseberry	25	41	5	2044	173	56.78	9	8
Asif Mujtaba	16	25	6	1074	154*	56.53	2	6
R. T. Robinson	19	33	5	1547	189	55.25	4	8
N. R. Taylor	21	35	7	1508	144	53.86	1	11
G. A. Hick	17	27	2	1337	213*	53.48	4	5
M. D. Moxon	19	28	2	1385	183	53.27	5	5
T. L. Penney	16	24	7	904	151	53.18	3	4
K. J. Barnett	19	29	5	1270	160	52.92	4	4
Inzamam-ul-Haq	15	21	7	736	200*	52.57	1	5
G. R. Cowdrey	21	31	6	1291	147	51.64	3	7
M. A. Atherton	21	37	6	1598	199	51.55	5	7
G. D. Lloyd	23	37	10	1389	132	51.44	4	10
G. P. Thorpe	24	41	4	1895	216	51.22	3	13
V. P. Terry	11	17	2	766	141	51.07	3	3
T. S. Curtis	23	41	5	1829	228*	50.81	4	7
R. J. Harden	20	33	5	1387	187	49.54	3	6
T. C. Middleton	24	40	4	1780	221	49.44	6	7
A. D. Brown	11	16	1	740	175	49.33	3	3
R. J. Bailey	23	39	7	1572	167*	49.13	2	8
A. P. Wells	22	35	5	1465	165*	48.83	5	4
T. R. Ward	21	37	3	1648	153	48.47	5	9
C. White	19	26	8	859	79*	47.72	0	7
G. F. Archer	7	13	3	475	117	47.50	1	4
C. L. Hooper	21	32	4	1329	131	47.46	5	7
D. I. Gower	20	33	7	1225	155	47.12	1	8
H. Morris	23	37	3	1597	146	46.97	6	6
P. A. Cottey	20	28	5	1076	141	46.78	2	6
J. J. B. Lewis	13	20	4	746	133	46.63	1	7
S. R. Tendulkar	16	25	2	1070	100	46.52	1	7
R. J. Blakey	21	32	9	1065	125*	46.30	2	5
P. Johnson	19	29	4	1147	107*	45.88	2	10
D. L. Haynes	20	35	2	1513	177	45.85	3	10
J. P. Crawley	17	29	3	1175	172	45.19	2	7
M. R. Benson	21	35	2	1482	139	44.91	4	6
Shoaib Mohammad	12	21	4	761	105*	44.76	1	7
P. Bainbridge	17	30	9	923	92*	43.95	0	8
A. Fordham	23	41	2	1710	192	43.85	4	7
J. P. Stephenson	21	37	5	1401	159*	43.78	3	8
P. J. Prichard	23	38	4	1485	136	43.68	4	9

	M	I	NO	Runs	HS	Av	100	50
B. C. Broad	14	27	3	1040	159*	43.33	5	0
Ramiz Raja	16	26	2	1036	172	43.17	2	6
M. A. Lynch	23	40	6	1465	107	43.09	3	8
R. C. Russell	20	34	11	985	75	42.83	0	5
Aamir Sohail	17	28	2	1110	205	42.69	2	4
T. M. Moody	11	19	2	724	178	42.59	4	1
A. J. Stewart	19	33	4	1234	190	42.55	2	8
D. Ripley	22	31	10	891	107*	42.43	2	4
D. R. Pringle	16	17	5	509	112*	42.42	2	2
A. Dale	22	33	5	1159	150*	41.39	2	7
J. E. Morris	23	33	0	1358	120	41.15	3	12
C. J. Adams	23	33	6	1109	140*	41.07	4	4
C. L. Cairns	21	30	6	984	107*	41.00	2	6
R. J. Twose	23	38	3	1412	233	40.34	1	10
P. W. G. Parker	20	35	2	1331	124	40.33	3	8
M. R. Ramprakash	20	33	3	1199	233	39.97	3	5
R. R. Montgomerie	9	15	3	477	103*	39.75	1	1
S. P. James	24	39	4	1376	152*	39.31	3	6
J. W. Hall	20	34	5	1125	140*	38.79	1	8
C. J. Tavaré	21	32	2	1157	125	38.57	3	6
P. N. Weekes	17	21	7	539	95	38.50	0	3
M. Saxelby	8	13	1	462	73	38.50	0	5
J. D. Carr	25	39	7	1228	114	38.38	2	8
N. E. Briers	24	42	6	1372	123	38.11	3	9
T. J. Boon	24	41	3	1448	139	38.11	2	10
M. P. Maynard	23	36	4	1219	176	38.09	2	7
M. P. Speight	20	33	2	1180	179	38.06	5	0
R. A. Smith	17	28	3	950	127	38.00	2	5
C. C. Lewis	17	26	4	836	134*	38.00	2	5
S. A. Kellett	22	36	1	1326	96	37.89	0	9
N. Hussain	20	26	3	866	172*	37.65	1	5
W. P. C. Weston	14	23	5	675	66*	37.50	0	5
W. Larkins	22	41	0	1536	143	37.46	4	8
P. W. Jarvis	15	14	4	374	80	37.40	0	3
M. C. J. Nicholas	21	32	5	1003	95*	37.15	0	6
M. A. Crawley	25	44	9	1297	160*	37.06	4	5
N. D. Burns	22	33	12	772	73*	36.76	0	4
M. N. Lathwell	19	33	1	1176	114	36.75	1	11
N. J. Lenham	20	34	2	1173	222*	36.66	4	3
D. M. Ward	18	30	6	879	138	36.63	3	1
W. K. Hegg	18	24	7	618	80	36.35	0	4
D. J. Bicknell	24	42	5	1340	120*	36.22	2	7
A. J. Moles	23	41	3	1359	122	35.76	1	12
T. J. G. O'Gorman	24	37	8	1031	95	35.55	0	8
S. J. Rhodes	24	34	11	815	116*	35.43	2	2
F. A. Griffith	7	10	3	248	81	35.43	0	1
G. B. T. Lovell	9	13	1	422	110*	35.17	1	2
D. P. Ostler	22	37	2	1225	192	35.00	3	4
G. D. Hodgson	21	36	1	1224	147	34.97	2	8
D. M. Smith	19	33	2	1076	213	34.71	2	5
D. A. Reeve	17	28	4	833	79	34.71	0	7
G. Fowler	11	20	2	623	106	34.61	1	4
S. A. Marsh	22	30	4	896	125	34.46	1	6
S. C. Goldsmith	10	11	3	273	100*	34.13	1	1
P. Moores	21	30	5	851	109	34.04	1	3
D. W. Randall	19	29	3	882	133*	33.92	1	5
J. T. C. Vaughan	11	18	4	473	99	33.79	0	4

	M	I	NO	Runs	HS	Av	100	50
M. A. Feltham	13	19	6	437	50	33.62	0	1
A. N. Hayhurst	23	38	2	1197	102	33.25	1	9
K. D. James	23	37	2	1149	116	32.83	1	8
F. D. Stephenson	18	25	4	680	133	32.38	1	2
M. W. Alleyne	22	36	3	1065	93	32.27	0	7
N. V. Knight	20	30	6	774	109	32.25	2	3
C. W. J. Athey	20	32	0	1022	181	31.94	2	4
S. P. Titchard	14	24	3	668	74	31.81	0	6
N. A. Felton	22	37	3	1076	103	31.65	1	9
I. V. A. Richards	14	23	0	722	127	31.39	1	4
J. E. R. Gallian	9	15	0	468	112	31.20	1	3
G. D. Rose	22	34	4	930	132	31.00	1	6
I. T. Botham	17	25	2	713	105	31.00	1	4
J. P. Arscott	10	14	3	341	79	31.00	0	3
V. J. Wells	17	23	6	526	56	30.94	0	3
S. G. Hinks	10	16	3	402	88*	30.92	0	3
D. G. Cork	19	21	2	578	72*	30.42	0	3
D. Byas	20	30	4	784	100	30.15	1	6
P. R. Pollard	19	33	3	900	75	30.00	0	5
D. J. Capel	23	34	4	892	103	29.73	1	5
D. B. D'Oliveira	13	19	1	535	100	29.72	1	2
P. A. Nixon	16	25	7	529	107*	29.39	1	1
I. Smith	12	16	1	435	110	29.00	1	2
I. D. Austin	8	10	2	230	115*	28.75	1	1
N. Shahid	15	21	1	561	132	28.05	1	3
R. M. Wight	10	17	3	388	62*	27.71	0	2
P. J. Martin	22	24	6	492	133	27.33	1	2
D. A. Leatherdale	23	40	4	983	112	27.31	1	5
P. D. Atkins	7	14	0	382	99	27.29	0	2
T. H. C. Hancock	10	17	1	436	102	27.25	1	2
R. P. Snell	16	20	4	436	81	27.25	0	3
R. D. B. Croft	24	34	10	650	60*	27.08	0	3
R. J. Bartlett	8	13	0	352	72	27.08	0	2
S. Hutton	8	15	0	406	78	27.07	0	2
R. J. Scott	19	31	3	751	73	26.82	0	4
J. J. Whitaker	22	34	3	830	74	26.77	0	2
K. H. MacLeay	12	19	3	427	74	26.69	0	3
M. V. Fleming	21	32	2	797	100*	26.57	1	4
A. C. H. Seymour	11	21	0	556	133	26.48	1	1
J. E. Emburey	23	27	6	554	102	26.38	1	3
A. A. Metcalfe	11	17	1	422	73	26.38	0	1
G. R. Haynes	9	13	2	288	66	26.18	0	2
R. S. M. Morris	5	9	1	209	74	26.13	0	2
L. Potter	23	36	4	834	96	26.06	0	4
B. F. Smith	15	20	3	441	100*	25.94	1	3
K. R. Brown	25	37	7	776	106	25.87	1	3
A. J. Wright	19	33	3	772	128	25.73	1	3
C. L. Keey	8	13	1	308	64	25.67	0	3
M. D. Marshall	19	25	5	513	70	25.65	0	2
K. Greenfield	6	10	2	205	48	25.63	0	0
J. D. Robinson	9	17	5	307	65*	25.58	0	2
N. M. K. Smith	12	20	2	454	67	25.22	0	1
K. M. Curran	21	30	1	730	82	25.17	0	5
P. A. J. DeFreitas	13	14	1	325	72	25.00	0	3
T. A. Lloyd	23	39	2	919	84*	24.84	0	5
M. P. Bicknell	19	26	8	447	88	24.83	0	2
P. J. Newport	22	25	6	467	75*	24.58	0	3

	M	I	NO	Runs	HS	Av	100	50
D. W. Headley	17	14	3	270	91	24.55	0	1
J. R. Wood	10	13	1	294	57	24.50	0	1
R. J. Parks	7	10	3	169	33	24.14	0	0
R. P. Davis	18	24	11	312	54*	24.00	0	1
J. R. Ayling	18	26	1	593	121	23.72	1	2
M. A. Garnham	24	28	4	569	82*	23.71	0	4
Moin Khan	13	14	4	237	53	23.70	0	1
N. G. B. Cook	17	11	6	118	37	23.60	0	0
S. R. Lampitt	19	29	5	565	71*	23.54	0	4
R. E. Bryson	11	13	2	257	76	23.36	0	1
N. A. Foster	11	14	0	326	54	23.29	0	2
J. D. R. Benson	18	28	1	623	122	23.07	1	1
R. M. Ellison	19	22	9	323	64	23.07	0	1
Zahid Fazal	6	8	3	115	51	23.00	0	1
C. W. Scott	18	24	5	433	57*	22.79	0	2
G. T. J. Townsend	7	13	1	272	49	22.67	0	0
Rashid Latif	8	8	2	136	50	22.67	0	1
J. D. Glendenen	17	28	1	607	117	22.48	1	3
B. T. P. Donelan	16	25	6	421	68*	22.16	0	2
E. E. Hemmings	7	11	5	132	52*	22.00	0	1
K. P. Evans	19	24	4	438	104	21.90	1	2
N. V. Radford	22	19	7	261	73*	21.75	0	2
D. L. Hemp	12	17	2	326	84*	21.73	0	2
C. C. Remy	7	9	0	192	47	21.33	0	0
S. D. Udal	23	29	10	400	44	21.05	0	0
R. K. Illingworth	20	20	6	294	43	21.00	0	0
G. W. Jones	6	12	0	249	44	20.75	0	0
G. D. Mendis	5	8	1	145	45	20.71	0	0
W. K. M. Benjamin	20	25	3	453	72	20.59	0	4
M. A. Ealham	17	27	5	452	67*	20.55	0	4
I. R. Bishop	20	21	2	388	90	20.42	0	1
K. J. Piper	19	25	8	345	72	20.29	0	2
R. P. Gofton	5	8	1	142	75	20.29	0	1
M. Watkinson	20	25	1	482	96	20.08	0	1
A. R. Caddick	20	19	6	261	54*	20.08	0	1
C. E. L. Ambrose	18	20	10	200	49*	20.00	0	0
A. N. Aymes	18	23	5	359	65	19.94	0	2
Wasim Akram	14	18	3	299	45*	19.93	0	0
C. P. Metson	23	28	6	437	46*	19.86	0	0
A. A. Donald	21	22	10	234	41	19.50	0	0
J. P. Carroll	5	9	0	175	92	19.44	0	1
J. D. Fitton	8	9	2	136	48*	19.43	0	0
J. D. Ratcliffe	7	14	0	272	50	19.43	0	1
M. P. Briers	16	28	4	460	62*	19.17	0	4
N. M. Kendrick	17	21	5	306	55	19.13	0	2
A. R. Roberts	14	19	3	304	62	19.00	0	1
J. Boiling	19	21	11	190	29	19.00	0	0
Waqar Younis	10	9	4	95	23*	19.00	0	0
P. A. Smith	19	27	5	416	45	18.91	0	0
A. M. Smith	12	14	5	169	51*	18.78	0	1
S. W. Johnson	9	13	2	201	50	18.27	0	1
R. A. Pick	10	12	4	145	52	18.13	0	1
A. M. Brown	7	8	0	144	43	18.00	0	0
S. J. E. Brown	20	24	13	197	47*	17.91	0	0
M. I. Gidley	5	10	2	143	39	17.88	0	0
P. J. Hartley	20	23	3	353	69	17.65	0	2
J. P. Taylor	23	19	8	188	74*	17.09	0	1

	M	I	NO	Runs	HS	Av	100	50
P. J. Berry	9	15	3	205	76	17.08	0	1
A. R. C. Fraser	18	20	7	218	33	16.77	0	0
D. A. Graveney	21	29	9	333	36	16.65	0	0
G. C. Small	17	17	6	181	31*	16.45	0	0
C. S. Pickles	6	9	1	131	49	16.38	0	0
S. Bramhall	8	10	3	114	37*	16.29	0	0
B. N. French	17	20	4	260	55	16.25	0	1
A. E. Warner	17	15	2	210	55	16.15	0	1
K. M. Krikken	23	27	3	383	57*	15.96	0	2
A. C. S. Pigott	17	19	7	191	27*	15.92	0	0
C. A. Connor	16	13	5	127	51	15.88	0	1
O. H. Mortensen	15	13	10	47	13*	15.67	0	0
M. B. Loye	10	14	1	195	46	15.00	0	0
A. M. Hooper	10	19	1	268	48	14.89	0	0
R. J. Maru	8	11	3	119	27	14.88	0	0
C. M. Tolley	13	10	4	89	27	14.83	0	0
I. D. K. Salisbury	20	22	3	279	50	14.68	0	1
S. N. Warley	7	10	2	117	35	14.63	0	0
D. J. Millns	19	19	9	144	33*	14.40	0	0
J. D. Batty	18	15	4	155	49	14.09	0	0
H. R. J. Trump	18	18	7	154	28	14.00	0	0
M. C. J. Ball	12	21	6	201	54	13.40	0	2
N. F. Williams	17	17	3	186	46*	13.29	0	0
P. Carrick	19	25	5	261	46	13.05	0	0
A. L. Penberthy	10	14	1	164	33	12.62	0	0
A. C. Storie	7	10	1	113	29	12.56	0	0
C. M. Pitcher	6	8	3	62	32*	12.40	0	0
P. N. Hepworth	10	15	1	173	381	12.36	0	0
T. A. Munton	19	19	7	148	47	12.33	0	0
J. H. Childs	22	17	8	110	43	12.22	0	0
R. M. Pearson	11	13	5	96	33*	12.00	0	0
N. A. Mallender	17	21	5	190	29*	11.88	0	0
G. J. Parsons	14	14	2	142	35	11.83	0	0
N. F. Sargeant	14	19	4	176	30	11.73	0	0
R. C. Williams	7	11	1	117	44	11.70	0	0
C. A. Walsh	18	27	3	280	51	11.67	0	1
J. E. Benjamin	18	18	8	116	42	11.60	0	0
S. P. Hughes	20	25	5	229	42	11.45	0	0
M. Davies	19	23	10	148	32*	11.38	0	0
P. M. Such	15	13	3	113	35*	11.30	0	0
A. N. Jones	10	9	4	56	17	11.20	0	0
P. A. Booth	8	11	4	78	22*	11.14	0	0
R. I. Dawson	6	8	0	88	29	11.00	0	0
A. M. Babington	9	11	4	75	24	10.71	0	0
C. W. Taylor	18	14	7	75	14	10.71	0	0
A. P. van Troost	11	9	5	42	12	10.50	0	0
D. K. Morrison	14	12	1	113	30	10.27	0	0
A. R. Fothergill	6	8	1	71	23	10.14	0	0
D. E. Malcolm	19	19	4	150	26	10.00	0	0
T. D. Topley	11	12	2	100	29	10.00	0	0
A. A. Barnett	22	17	10	70	17	10.00	0	0

BOWLING

Qualification: 10 wickets

	O	M	R	W	Av	BB	5i	10m
C. A. Walsh	587.2	138	1469	92	15.97	7–27	8	2
Wasim Akram	499.5	127	1330	82	16.22	6–32	7	2
I. R. Bishop	483	116	1118	64	17.47	7–34	4	0
J. R. Ayling	356.2	78	989	48	20.60	5–12	1	0
D. J. Millns	468.5	107	1526	74	20.62	6–87	6	1
R. P. Davis	582	150	1609	74	21.74	7–64	5	0
A. A. Donald	576.2	139	1647	74	22.26	7–37	6	0
S. D. Thomas	113.2	18	404	19	22.44	5–79	2	0
M. A. Robinson	413.5	79	1134	50	22.68	6–57	3	1
V. J. Wells	301	93	751	33	22.76	4–26	0	0
N. A. Mallender	436.3	94	1282	55	23.31	5–29	4	0
G. J. Parsons	343.2	92	955	39	24.49	6–70	2	0
Mushtaq Ahmed	614.4	158	1620	66	24.55	5–46	4	0
Waqar Younis	287.1	50	913	37	24.68	5–22	4	0
N. G. B. Cook	325.1	90	939	38	24.71	7–34	1	1
F. A. Griffith	113	31	373	15	24.87	4–33	0	0
D. R. Pringle	423.5	99	1177	47	25.04	5–63	1	0
D. J. Capel	446	92	1214	48	25.29	5–61	1	0
P. M. Such	411.5	126	1015	40	25.38	6–17	3	0
J. E. Emburey	854.5	249	2069	81	25.54	5–23	3	0
Tanvir Mehdi	94	21	307	12	25.58	3–24	0	0
M. P. Bicknell	628.5	116	1823	71	25.68	6–107	4	0
P. J. Newport	618.2	130	1770	68	26.03	5–22	4	0
R. J. Maru	204.2	75	444	17	26.12	4–8	0	0
C. E. L. Ambrose	543.4	151	1307	50	26.14	4–53	0	0
J. D. Robinson	93.4	14	341	13	26.23	3–22	0	0
N. F. Williams	437	86	1283	48	26.73	8–75	2	1
Aqib Javed	292	58	966	36	26.83	5–34	1	0
M. J. McCague	457.2	86	1430	53	26.98	8–26	5	1
A. R. Caddick	587.4	98	1918	71	27.01	6–52	3	1
J. H. Childs	678.2	205	1822	67	27.19	6–82	3	0
I. J. Turner	182.4	51	519	19	27.32	5–81	1	0
M. D. Marshall	529	134	1348	49	27.51	6–58	1	0
K. M. Curran	452.4	96	1376	50	27.52	6–45	1	0
C. S. Pickles	120.1	27	387	14	27.64	4–40	0	0
E. S. H. Giddins	247.5	52	857	31	27.65	5–32	2	0
N. V. Radford	532.2	99	1670	60	27.83	6–88	4	1
R. G. Twose	249.3	48	794	28	28.36	6–63	1	0
D. G. Cork	450.4	74	1366	48	28.46	5–36	2	0
I. D. K. Salisbury	772.4	176	2520	87	28.97	7–54	6	2
M. V. Fleming	245	46	696	24	29.00	4–63	0	0
P. W. Jarvis	393.4	89	1164	40	29.10	4–27	0	0
P. Carrick	630.1	202	1375	47	29.26	6–58	1	0
M. Davies	560.5	143	1661	56	29.66	4–73	0	0
J. A. North	96.3	14	331	11	30.09	3–51	0	0
N. A. Foster	256	63	724	24	30.17	4–47	0	0
P. J. Hartley	549.5	101	1690	56	30.18	8–111	3	0
J. P. Taylor	648.2	119	2072	68	30.47	7–23	3	1
M. E. Waugh	184.4	31	671	22	30.50	3–38	0	0
A. E Warner	367.5	87	888	29	30.62	4–52	0	0
A. P. Igglesden	480.4	95	1413	46	30.72	5–41	3	0
N. M. Kendrick	595.1	171	1567	51	30.73	6–61	3	0
C. C. Lewis	594.3	119	1633	53	30.81	6–90	2	1

	O	M	R	W	Av	BB	5i	10m
S. L. Watkin	689.3	148	2126	68	31.26	6–97	1	0
J. A. Afford	509.1	128	1599	51	31.35	6–68	2	1
G. W. Mike	90.2	17	314	10	31.40	3–48	0	0
J. Wood	134.2	17	534	17	31.41	5–68	1	0
R. D. B. Croft	657.1	124	2152	68	31.65	8–66	5	1
W. K. M. Benjamin	489	102	1498	47	31.87	4–34	0	0
P. A. J. DeFreitas	349.5	65	1091	34	32.09	6–94	1	0
A. Dale	234	62	644	20	32.20	3–30	0	0
K. J. Shine	333.5	49	1290	40	32.25	8–47	3	1
C. M. Wells	119	26	323	10	32.30	3–26	0	0
H. R. J. Trump	558	134	1584	49	32.33	7–52	2	1
P. A. Smith	373	57	1362	42	32.43	6–91	4	0
T. D. Topley	240.4	54	779	24	32.46	5–15	1	0
J. T. C. Vaughan	202.4	44	588	18	32.67	3–46	0	0
M. Watkinson	660	140	2178	66	33.00	6–62	4	1
G. C. Small	367.2	83	1003	30	33.43	3–43	0	0
E. E. Hemmings	259.5	95	602	18	33.44	4–30	0	0
D. K. Morrison	335.4	52	1209	36	33.58	6–48	1	0
M. A. Ealham	406.1	70	1243	37	33.59	4–67	0	0
T. A. Munton	640.4	176	1725	51	33.82	7–64	3	1
S. J. E. Brown	509.1	75	1973	58	34.02	7–105	3	0
M. A. Crawley	221.4	56	647	19	34.05	3–18	0	0
F. D. Stephenson	467.2	93	1375	40	34.38	7–29	1	1
Ata-ur-Rehman	159.1	29	621	18	34.50	3–69	0	0
O. H. Mortensen	338.4	87	795	23	34.57	2–22	0	0
S. D. Udal	692.2	177	2012	58	34.69	8–50	2	0
A. M. Smith	249.2	35	835	24	34.79	3–53	0	0
J. E. R. Gallian	208	41	628	18	34.89	4–29	0	0
J. Boiling	591.1	156	1579	45	35.09	6–84	1	1
C. L. Cairns	592.3	110	1974	56	35.25	6–70	2	0
A. D. Mullally	518.2	125	1485	42	35.36	5–119	1	0
S. J. W. Andrew	265	45	849	24	35.38	4–54	0	0
M. C. Ilott	675.3	145	2264	64	35.38	6–87	3	0
J. D. Fitton	171.1	38	465	13	35.77	4–81	0	0
R. W. Sladdin	499.3	138	1396	39	35.79	6–58	1	0
M. W. Alleyne	138.1	31	502	14	35.86	3–25	0	0
K. P. Evans	595.4	132	1723	48	35.90	5–27	1	0
S. R. Lampitt	369.3	44	1257	35	35.91	4–57	0	0
P. C. R. Tufnell	596.2	144	1559	43	36.26	5–83	2	0
D. Gough	255.1	53	910	25	36.40	4–43	0	0
A. P. van Troost	175.4	20	766	21	36.48	6–48	2	0
D. E. Malcolm	451.1	64	1648	45	36.62	5–45	2	0
D. J. Foster	191.3	27	820	22	37.27	5–87	1	0
C. L. Hooper	500.5	114	1307	35	37.34	4–57	0	0
R. K. Illingworth	635.3	185	1580	42	37.62	4–43	0	0
R. D. Stemp	331.5	80	1054	28	37.64	6–67	3	1
D. B. Pennett	296.2	51	981	26	37.73	4–58	0	0
Naved Anjum	107.1	24	379	10	37.90	3–73	0	0
P. J. Berry	178.3	27	649	17	38.18	7–113	1	1
M. C. J. Ball	322	61	1072	28	38.29	5–101	1	0
J. P. Stephenson	251.5	51	854	22	38.82	6–54	1	0
A. C. S. Pigott	363	74	1063	27	39.37	3–34	0	0
R. M. Wight	231.3	39	748	19	39.37	3–65	0	0
J. E. Benjamin	582.2	94	1780	45	39.56	6–30	2	0
L. Potter	360.1	80	1075	27	39.81	4–73	0	0
P. J. Bakker	162	48	441	11	40.09	4–38	0	0
P. J. Martin	520.2	129	1490	37	40.27	4–45	0	0

	O	M	R	W	Av	BB	5i	10m
C. M. Tolley	239	56	726	18	40.33	3-38	0	0
P. W. Henderson	96	14	405	10	40.50	3-59	0	0
D. W. Headley	385	74	1258	31	40.58	3-31	0	0
P. Bainbridge	188.1	39	569	14	40.64	5-100	1	0
C. W. Taylor	409.2	82	1425	35	40.71	4-50	0	0
R. M. Ellison	401.5	80	1204	29	41.52	6-95	2	0
J. D. Batty	426	87	1408	33	42.67	4-34	0	0
P. A. Booth	279.4	74	814	19	42.84	4-29	0	0
D. A. Graveney	380.4	87	1201	28	42.89	3-22	0	0
C. A. Connor	417.2	69	1386	32	43.31	5-58	1	0
I. D. Austin	164.5	41	522	12	43.50	3-44	0	0
I. T. Botham	346	70	1144	26	44.00	4-72	0	0
R. P. Snell	339.1	60	1194	27	44.22	3-29	0	0
A. M. Babington	188	21	753	17	44.29	8-107	1	0
G. D. Rose	392.1	84	1250	28	44.64	4-59	0	0
M. A. Feltham	326.1	61	1125	25	45.00	4-75	0	0
S. R. Barwick	602	155	1627	36	45.19	4-67	0	0
S. M. McEwan	229	44	800	17	47.06	3-52	0	0
A. A. Barnett	595	84	2165	46	47.07	5-78	2	0
B. T. P. Donelan	404	85	1323	28	47.25	6-77	1	0
R. A. Pick	254.1	50	862	18	47.89	3-33	0	0
R. J. Scott	267.4	39	959	20	47.95	2-9	0	0
A. R. Roberts	323.2	60	1056	22	48.00	4-101	0	0
A. J. Murphy	178.4	34	531	11	48.27	3-97	0	0
D. A. Reeve	267	80	632	13	48.62	2-4	0	0
N. M. K. Smith	332.3	63	1178	24	49.08	5-61	1	0
S. P. Hughes	548.3	98	1672	34	49.18	5-25	1	0
P. N. Weekes	222	51	595	12	49.58	3-61	0	0
M. P. W. Jeh	233.5	38	846	17	49.76	3-44	0	0
S. Bastien	305.3	73	954	19	50.21	5-95	1	0
M. P. Briers	144.3	22	621	12	51.75	3-109	0	0
M. B. Abington	146.4	23	530	10	53.00	3-33	0	0
D. B. D'Oliveira	153.4	29	536	10	53.60	2-44	0	0
M. G. Field-Buss	169	29	590	11	53.64	4-71	0	0
S. W. Johnson	164	27	541	10	54.10	3-62	0	0
R. E. Bryson	333.4	41	1256	23	54.61	5-48	2	0
A. R. C. Fraser	426.4	90	1273	23	55.35	3-16	0	0
K. D. James	264.3	65	781	14	55.79	2-23	0	0
R. M. Pearson	402.3	64	1279	20	63.95	5-108	1	0
M. Frost	198.1	29	833	13	64.08	3-100	0	0
A. N. Jones	161.5	17	745	11	67.73	3-76	0	0

FIELDING

71 D. Ripley (66ct/5st). 57 K. M. Krikken (52/5). 54 C. P. Metson (49/5). 52 S. A. Marsh (44/8), S. J. Rhodes (47/5). 51 A. N. Aymes (47/4). 50 K. R. Brown (39/11). 49 R. J. Blakey (44/5). 45 P. A. Nixon (40/5), B. N. French (41/4), N. D. Burns (42/3). 44 M. A. Garnham (41/3). 43 K. J. Piper (41/2), R. C. Russell (40/3). 41 J. D. Carr, N. F. Sargeant (35/6). 39 W. K. Hegg (33/6), P. Moores (32/7). 32 G. A. Hick. 30 J. D. R. Benson, D. Byas. 29 Moin Khan (28/1), Rashid Latif (27/2), C. W. Scott (27/2). 27 M. E. Waugh. 25 C. L. Hooper, T. R. Ward. 24 M. A. Atherton, M. A. Lynch, N. Hussain, A. P. Wells. 23 R. J. Parks (21/2), S. A. Kellett, M. W. Alleyne. 22 R. J. Bailey, A. J. Stewart, Inzamam-ul-Haq. 21 G. D. Lloyd, J. E. Emburey, M. A. Crawley, S. Bramhall (16/5). 20 C. J. Adams, P. R. Pollard, D. P. Ostler, S. P. James.

1992 LEADING ONE-DAY AVERAGES

BATTING AVERAGES – Including fielding

Name	M	I	NO	Runs	HS	Av	100s	50s	Ct	St
D. L. Haynes	21	21	4	1210	101	71.17	1	13	5	–
V. P. Terry	14	14	3	637	109	57.90	2	4	6	–
R. A. Smith	23	23	2	1151	109	54.81	1	10	13	–
M. E. Waugh	20	19	5	766	105*	54.71	2	3	5	–
D. J. Bicknell	23	23	3	1082	135	54.10	3	6	7	–
A. P. Wells	23	22	6	865	119	54.06	2	7	11	–
D. M. Jones	17	16	2	752	114	53.71	2	5	7	–
G. A. Gooch	23	23	2	1089	127	51.85	3	5	10	–
T. M. Moody	16	16	2	721	80*	51.50	–	9	5	–
J. D. Carr	25	20	5	731	104*	48.73	1	5	15	–
T. C. Middleton	20	20	2	857	98	47.61	–	7	7	–
R. J. Bailey	26	24	7	806	109*	47.41	1	6	7	–
A. J. Stewart	24	24	3	995	105*	47.38	3	7	31	4
R. J. Harden	22	20	4	746	108*	46.62	1	6	8	–
P. D. Bowler	24	24	6	837	111	46.50	1	8	9	–
J. J. Whitaker	25	24	2	977	118*	44.40	1	7	6	–
M. R. Ramprakash	22	19	4	649	108*	43.26	1	3	9	–
M. P. Maynard	23	22	1	898	122*	42.76	1	6	12	–
H. Morris	23	22	3	808	104*	42.52	1	6	4	–
P. R. Pollard	15	14	4	420	76*	42.00	–	2	2	–
G. A. Hick	23	23	4	794	83*	41.78	–	7	11	–
N. J. Speak	22	22	3	788	102*	41.47	1	7	4	–
M. A. Roseberry	25	25	3	912	112	41.45	1	7	6	–
T. S. Curtis	21	20	1	774	78	40.73	–	8	9	–
I. V. A. Richards	17	17	3	569	109*	40.64	1	3	4	–
C. J. Adams	23	21	4	684	141*	40.23	2	4	15	–
K. M. Curran	23	19	7	481	80*	40.08	–	3	4	–
D. M. Ward	23	20	7	519	101*	39.92	1	2	10	–
K. R. Brown	25	20	9	438	73*	39.81	–	1	18	12
P. E. Robinson	15	15	0	595	104	39.66	1	4	4	–
A. J. Lamb	27	26	4	858	120	39.00	2	4	7	–
A. Fordham	25	24	0	925	103	38.54	1	8	6	–
K. J. Barnett	19	19	2	641	84*	37.70	–	5	11	–
A. N. Hayhurst	24	23	3	747	95	37.35	–	6	2	–
R. G. Twose	25	25	1	895	107*	37.29	2	5	5	–
J. D. Glendenen	22	20	2	670	78	37.22	–	5	5	–
N. H. Fairbrother	18	18	4	520	79	37.14	–	4	6	–
P. Johnson	18	18	3	551	90	36.73	–	4	3	–
D. W. Randall	17	16	3	477	91*	36.69	–	5	6	–
A. J. Wright	24	21	2	697	107*	36.68	1	5	7	–
G. D. Hodgson	23	23	2	767	103*	36.52	1	4	5	–
G. P. Thorpe	24	24	5	686	84	36.10	–	6	11	–
S. R. Tendulkar	17	17	2	540	107	36.00	1	1	3	–
A. D. Brown	24	24	3	755	113	35.95	2	2	4	–
I. T. Botham	24	22	3	678	86	35.68	–	6	10	–
B. C. Broad	16	15	0	535	83	35.66	–	5	3	–
C. White	17	15	5	356	63	35.60	–	2	4	–
M. W. Alleyne	25	23	3	706	134*	35.30	1	4	8	–
M. W. Gatting	23	22	2	703	96	35.15	–	5	11	–

Qualification: 6 completed innings

BOWLING AVERAGES

Qualification 20 wickets

Name	Overs	Mdns	Runs	Wkts	Avge	Best	5wI
M. J. McCague	162.4	0	772	48	16.08	5–43	1
A. A. Donald	129.5	16	395	24	16.45	5–28	1
C. A. Walsh	133.5	17	486	29	16.75	6–21	1
M. C. Ilott	135	11	558	32	17.43	4–15	–
S. D. Udal	208	8	956	51	18.74	4–40	–
P. W. Jarvis	92.3	8	386	20	19.30	5–29	1
G. D. Rose	110.5	12	453	22	20.59	3–21	–
F. D. Stephenson	168.4	21	667	32	20.84	4–22	–
A. F. Warner	186.3	15	711	34	20.91	4–23	–
D. W. Headley	129.2	11	600	28	21.42	5–20	1
S. P. Hughes	177.2	11	774	36	21.50	4–41	–
S. R. Lampitt	114.5	6	560	26	21.53	4–40	–
P. J. Newport	159.3	11	611	28	21.82	5–31	1
M. D. Marshall	197	21	702	31	22.64	4–20	–
M. A. Feltham	174	10	726	32	22.68	5–30	1
A. R. Caddick	162.3	13	636	28	22.71	6–30	1
C. E. L. Ambrose	146	22	501	22	22.77	4–7	–
I. R. Bishop	177.2	15	637	27	23.59	4–30	–
M. P. Bicknell	186.5	14	807	34	23.73	4–48	–
D. J. Millns	102	7	479	20	23.95	4–51	–
T. A. Munton	168.5	22	534	22	24.27	4–16	–
K. M. Curran	162	5	754	31	24.32	4–21	–
D. Gough	148	16	614	25	24.56	3–30	–
C. A. Connor	210	24	795	32	24.84	4–32	–
D. R. Pringle	185.2	22	722	29	24.89	4–42	–
R. K. Illingworth	221	19	798	32	24.93	3–30	–
W. K. M. Benjamin	140.2	16	528	21	25.14	5–32	1
K. H. MacLeay	157.3	5	606	24	25.25	5–20	1
A. M. Babington	174.1	19	660	26	25.38	4–21	–
M. V. Fleming	153	3	738	29	25.44	3–34	–
P. A. J. DeFreitas	183.2	14	821	32	25.65	5–16	1
J. P. Stephenson	150.5	6	719	28	25.67	5–58	1
J. P. Taylor	180.2	18	696	27	25.77	3–38	–
I. D. K. Salisbury	142.3	12	570	22	25.90	5–30	1
J. E. Emburey	194.4	15	840	32	26.25	3–14	–
P. N. Weekes	164	15	759	28	27.10	4–37	–
N. F. Williams	181.2	15	761	28	27.17	3–25	–

These combined one-day averages include Texaco Trophy, Sunday League, NatWest Trophy and Benson & Hedges Cup matches.

ENGLAND FIRST-CLASS CAREER RECORDS UPDATED

BATTING AVERAGES – Including fielding

Name	Matches	Inns	NO	Runs	HS	Avge	100s	50s	Ct	St
M. B. Abington	7	7	0	20	6	2.85	–	–	4	–
C. J. Adams	69	103	13	3014	140*	33.48	8	11	71	–
J. A. Afford	115	99	41	208	22*	3.58	–	–	36	–
Aftab Habib	1	2	1	19	12	19.00	–	–	–	–
R. I. Alikhan	101	173	14	4547	138	28.59	2	31	56	–
M. W. Alleyne	124	194	25	5082	256	30.07	5	28	103	2
C. E. L. Ambrose	110	140	37	1603	59	15.56	–	3	26	–
D. J. Anderson	8	8	3	18	9	3.60	–	–	3	–
S. J. W. Andrew	100	69	31	292	35	7.68	–	–	21	–
G. F Archer	7	13	3	475	117	47.50	1	4	6	–
J. P. Arscott	21	30	5	573	79	22.92	–	4	18	8
Asif Din	199	326	44	8423	158*	29.86	8	39	108	–
M. A. Atherton	123	211	26	8424	199	45.53	26	34	108	–
C. W. J. Athey	387	639	62	20129	184	34.88	42	99	369	2
P. D. Atkins	17	32	3	853	114*	29.41	1	3	5	–
I. D. Austin	51	66	17	1249	115*	25.49	2	5	7	–
J. R. Ayling	56	84	11	1993	121	27.30	1	11	14	–
A. N. Aymes	50	63	17	1402	75*	30.47	–	8	121	9
A. M. Babington	87	92	37	475	58	8.63	–	1	31	–
R. J. Bailey	233	390	60	13725	224*	41.59	29	73	166	–
P. Bainbridge	274	454	69	13276	169	34.48	22	77	118	–
P. J. Bakker	69	54	19	333	22	9.51	–	–	9	–
M. C. J. Ball	32	44	9	379	54	10.82	–	2	23	–
A. A. Barnett	25	20	12	92	17	11.50	–	–	7	–
K. J. Barnett	333	533	47	18495	239*	38.05	38	98	216	–
R. J. Bartlett	51	82	6	1856	117*	24.42	2	8	35	–
S. R. Barwick	173	162	62	724	30	7.24	–	–	37	–
S. J. Base	103	130	33	1135	58	11.70	–	2	45	–
S. Bastien	44	33	13	152	36*	7.60	–	–	5	–
J. D. Batty	45	41	13	403	51	14.39	–	1	16	–
A. W. Bee	3	3	3	41	29*	–	–	–	1	–
M. A. V. Bell	3	5	2	10	5	3.33	–	–	–	–
J. E. Benjamin	43	40	16	341	42	14.20	–	–	12	–
W. K. M. Benjamin	124	148	34	2630	101*	23.07	1	14	60	–
J. D. R. Benson	50	76	8	1854	133*	27.26	3	5	52	–
M. R. Benson	248	419	31	16035	257	41.32	42	88	120	–
P. J. Berry	16	22	9	281	76	21.61	–	1	6	–
D. J. Bicknell	122	213	22	7364	186	38.55	17	36	45	–
M. P. Bicknell	119	133	40	1563	88	16.80	–	4	38	–
I. R. Bishop	88	115	32	1342	103*	16.16	1	1	19	–
J. Bishop	1	1	1	51	51*	–	–	1	4	–
R. J. Blakey	157	254	35	7242	221	33.06	9	38	252	25
D. J. P. Boden	2	1	0	5	5	5.00	–	–	2	–
J. Boiling	28	34	15	250	29	13.15	–	–	27	–
T. J. Boon	208	350	39	10117	144	32.53	12	59	106	–
P. A. Booth	52	69	15	686	62	12.70	–	3	15	–
I. T. Botham	392	600	45	18983	228	34.20	37	94	346	–
M. N. Bowen	3	3	2	26	13*	26.00	–	–	–	–
P. D. Bowler	128	223	22	8256	241*	41.07	18	49	82	1
S. Bramhall	10	13	5	115	37*	14.37	–	–	16	6
M. P. Briers	16	28	4	460	62*	19.16	–	4	7	–

21

Name	Matches	Inns	NO	Runs	HS	Avge	100s	50s	Ct	St
N. E. Briers	335	547	55	15977	201*	32.47	26	84	144	-
B. C. Broad	311	557	38	20147	227*	38.81	47	95	174	-
A. D. Brown (Ess)	14	16	4	99	30	8.25	-	-	28	5
A. D. Brown (Sur)	11	16	1	740	175	49.33	3	3	6	-
A. M. Brown	22	31	3	815	139*	29.10	1	3	19	-
D. R. Brown	3	3	2	54	44*	54.00	-	-	2	-
G. K. Brown	6	10	1	345	103	38.33	1	1	5	-
K. R. Brown	136	212	36	6059	200*	34.42	10	31	180	11
S. J. E. Brown	35	38	19	267	47*	14.05	-	-	9	-
R. E. Bryson	39	43	11	745	100	23.28	1	2	9	-
M. Burns	2	3	0	85	78	28.33	-	1	7	1
N. D. Burns	143	211	50	4870	166	30.24	4	24	278	28
A. R. Butcher	401	682	60	22633	216*	36.38	46	123	185	-
M. A. Butcher	2	2	1	52	47	52.00	-	-	-	-
D. Byas	99	161	17	4488	153	31.16	8	22	99	-
A. R. Caddick	22	20	6	261	54*	18.64	-	1	7	-
C. L. Cairns	59	77	14	1945	110	30.87	3	11	24	-
D. J. Capel	261	394	58	10068	134	29.96	12	62	126	-
J. D. Carr	138	223	28	6623	156	33.96	12	33	123	-
P. Carrick	441	568	102	10255	131*	22.00	3	41	196	-
J. P. Carroll	5	9	0	175	92	19.44	-	1	1	-
C. A. Chapman	3	5	1	55	20	13.75	-	-	3	-
R. J. Chapman	1	0	0	0	0	-	-	-	-	-
G. Chapple	2	2	1	19	18	19.00	-	-	-	-
J. H. Childs	326	290	136	1391	43	9.03	-	-	103	-
C. A. Connor	160	129	38	889	51	9.76	-	1	47	-
N. B. G. Cook	337	344	94	2989	75	11.95	-	4	191	-
K. E. Cooper	273	281	67	2141	46	10.00	-	-	85	-
D. G. Cork	42	56	12	1022	72*	23.22	-	3	23	-
A. C. Cottam	6	8	1	43	31	6.14	-	-	1	-
P. A. Cottey	88	136	22	3582	156	31.42	5	21	46	-
N. G. Cowans	221	228	61	1531	66	9.16	-	1	59	-
C. S. Cowdrey	299	452	68	12252	159	31.90	21	58	295	-
G. R. Cowdrey	124	193	27	6009	147	36.19	11	33	66	-
R. M. F. Cox	9	12	2	287	104*	28.70	1	-	5	-
J. P. Crawley	32	52	6	2127	172	46.23	3	16	25	-
M. A. Crawley	62	94	19	2900	160*	38.66	8	13	51	-
P. M. Crawley	4	6	2	118	45	29.50	-	-	-	-
R. D. B. Croft	73	100	27	1902	91*	26.05	-	8	28	-
K. M. Curran	210	320	53	9441	144*	35.36	18	42	118	-
T. S. Curtis	249	423	54	15311	248	41.49	27	82	139	-
A. Dale	53	83	12	2509	150*	35.33	4	13	23	-
J. A. Daley	2	4	1	190	88	63.33	-	2	2	-
S. S. K. Das	3	5	1	38	24*	9.50	-	-	1	-
H. R. Davies	17	20	6	178	39	12.71	-	-	-	-
M. Davies	20	24	11	153	32*	11.76	-	-	11	-
R. P. Davis	110	136	37	1620	67	16.36	-	4	94	-
R. I. Dawson	6	8	0	88	29	11.00	-	-	2	-
P. A. J. DeFreitas	167	224	4	4295	113	21.47	4	22	43	-
W. A. Dessaur	2	3	0	164	148	54.66	1	-	1	-
G. R. Dilley	234	252	93	2339	81	14.71	-	4	75	-
M. C. Dobson	10	15	3	211	52	17.58	-	2	2	-
D. B. D'Oliveira	212	331	22	8667	237	28.04	10	41	188	-
A. A. Donald	151	178	69	1282	46*	11.76	-	-	53	-
B. T. P. Donelan	49	62	20	1026	68*	24.42	-	5	13	-
A. R. Dunlop	2	3	0	108	56	36.00	-	1	1	-
M. A. Ealham	25	39	8	656	67*	21.16	-	4	7	-

Name	Matches	Inns	NO	Runs	HS	Avge	100s	50s	Ct	St
P. H. Edmonds	391	495	91	7651	142	18.93	3	22	345	–
R. M. Ellison	204	280	71	4954	108	23.70	1	20	85	–
J. E. Emburey	446	562	112	10316	133	22.92	5	45	403	–
K. P. Evans	89	123	30	2374	104	25.52	2	11	69	–
J. Everett	1	2	0	53	33	26.50	–	–	3	–
N. Fairbrother	221	345	55	12177	366	41.99	26	70	140	–
P. Farbrace	38	48	11	694	79	18.75	–	4	86	12
M. A. Feltham	114	142	38	2526	101	24.28	1	7	48	–
N. A. Felton	183	312	18	8771	173*	29.83	13	52	101	–
M. G. Field-Buss	18	18	4	136	34*	9.71	–	–	7	–
J. D. Fitton	52	61	15	872	60	18.95	–	1	11	–
M. V. Fleming	68	108	14	2898	116	30.83	4	15	34	–
S. D. Fletcher	113	96	32	476	28*	7.43	–	–	27	–
N. A. Folland	2	4	1	212	82*	70.66	–	2	1	–
A. Fordham	103	182	16	6759	206*	40.71	14	33	65	–
D. J. Foster	45	39	15	201	20	8.37	–	–	8	–
N. A. Foster	222	257	56	4108	107*	20.43	2	11	115	–
A. R. Fothergill	7	9	1	74	23	9.25	–	–	10	1
G. Fowler	274	464	27	15803	226	36.16	35	79	143	5
A. G. J. Fraser	10	10	5	137	52*	27.40	–	1	1	–
A. R. C. Fraser	119	134	34	1240	92	12.40	–	1	19	–
B. N. French	340	444	88	6721	105*	18.87	1	24	772	95
M. Frost	62	48	16	87	12	2.71	–	–	7	–
D. P. Fulton	1	2	0	58	42	29.00	–	–	2	–
J. E. R. Gallian	10	16	1	485	112	32.33	1	3	7	–
M. A. Garnham	171	221	46	4956	123	28.32	4	26	362	31
M. W. Gatting	432	676	107	28512	258	50.10	72	144	376	–
M. J. Gerrard	16	19	7	81	42	6.75	–	–	4	–
E. S. H. Giddins	13	9	7	29	14*	14.50	–	–	4	–
M. I. Gidley	21	32	7	559	80	22.36	–	3	11	–
J. D. Glendenen	17	28	1	607	117	22.48	1	3	5	–
R. P. Gofton	5	8	1	142	75	20.28	–	1	2	–
S. C. Goldsmith	75	118	12	2646	127	24.96	2	12	37	–
G. A. Gooch	484	816	66	36126	333	48.16	98	178	478	–
D. Gough	41	47	14	532	72	16.12	–	2	6	–
J. W. Govan	10	13	1	87	17	7.25	–	–	6	–
D. I. Gower	432	699	69	25203	228	40.00	49	131	269	1
S. Graham	1	2	0	62	35	31.00	–	–	–	–
D. A. Graveney	425	530	158	6501	119	17.47	2	15	224	–
A. P. Grayson	14	18	5	291	57	22.38	–	1	7	–
K. Greenfield	25	42	5	995	127*	26.89	3	2	27	–
F. A. Griffith	20	31	4	467	81	17.29	–	1	12	–
C. M. Gupte	13	15	2	236	55*	18.15	–	1	3	–
J. W. Hall	55	97	9	2951	140*	33.53	4	17	21	–
T. H. C. Hancock	15	26	3	529	102	23.00	1	3	15	–
R. Hanley	5	7	0	52	28	7.42	–	–	–	–
A. R. Hansford	10	11	3	109	29	13.62	–	–	3	–
R. J. Harden	155	245	411	7902	187	38.73	15	42	100	–
P. J. Hartley	125	140	36	2279	127*	21.91	1	8	42	–
C. J. Hawkes	4	6	2	65	18	16.25	–	–	2	–
A. N. Hayhurst	106	168	21	4851	172*	33.00	9	22	31	–
D. L. Haynes	298	510	58	21176	255*	46.84	50	113	162	1
G. R. Haynes	13	17	3	339	66	24.21	–	2	5	–
D. W. Headley	29	29	4	472	91	18.88	–	2	10	–
W. K. Hegg	127	179	34	3698	130	25.50	2	16	284	35
E. E. Hemmings	482	627	146	9297	127*	19.32	1	27	196	–
D. L. Hemp	13	19	3	338	84*	21.12	–	2	7	–

Name	Matches	Inns	NO	Runs	HS	Avge	100s	50s	Ct	St
P. W. Henderson	5	7	0	119	46	17.00	–	–	1	–
P. N. Hepworth	46	75	7	1672	115	24.58	2	6	28	–
G. A. Hick	226	364	41	19083	405*	59.08	67	72	271	–
J. E. Hindson	1	0	0	0	0	–	–	–	–	–
S. G. Hinks	164	283	18	7971	234	30.07	11	38	99	–
G. D. Hodgson	71	119	7	3705	147	33.08	5	25	30	–
C. J. Hoey	2	3	1	16	8	8.00	–	–	–	–
P. C. L. Holloway	11	17	6	436	102*	39.63	1	2	25	1
A. M. Hooper	24	41	2	848	125	21.74	1	3	2	–
C. L. Hooper	118	178	21	6528	196	41.58	15	35	120	–
S. P. Hughes	199	218	68	1738	53	11.58	–	1	49	–
N. Hussain	99	142	22	5163	197	43.02	10	24	121	–
S. Hutton	8	15	0	406	78	27.06	–	2	3	–
A. P. Igglesden	103	106	37	670	41	9.71	–	–	29	–
R. K. Illingworth	243	264	70	4094	120*	21.10	3	10	105	–
M. C. Ilott	42	39	11	331	42*	11.82	–	–	10	–
R. Irani	7	7	1	99	31*	16.50	–	–	4	–
K. D. James	140	197	36	5379	162	33.41	8	24	47	–
S. P. James	77	131	11	4067	152*	33.89	10	17	53	–
M. E. D. Jarrett	9	13	2	106	27	9.63	–	–	2	–
P. W. Jarvis	143	162	51	1896	80	17.08	–	4	36	–
M. Jean-Jacques	53	66	14	587	73	11.28	–	1	13	–
M. P. W. Jeh	9	11	2	81	23	9.00	–	–	2	–
R. H. J. Jenkins	17	21	6	123	20	8.20	–	–	4	–
P. Johnson	215	353	37	11467	165*	36.28	22	67	143	1
R. L. Johnson	1	1	0	1	1	1.00	–	–	1	–
S. W. Johnson	22	27	9	321	50	17.83	–	1	9	–
A. N. Jones	170	147	61	998	43*	11.60	–	–	42	–
D. M. Jones	157	255	28	11780	248	51.89	34	52	119	–
G. W. Jones	9	17	1	268	44	16.75	–	–	1	–
C. L. Keey	8	13	1	308	64	25.66	–	3	1	–
S. A. Kellett	66	111	9	3422	125*	33.54	2	23	58	–
T. R. Kemp	2	1	0	0	0	0.00	–	–	1	–
N. M. Kendrick	36	41	12	513	55	17.69	–	3	35	–
G. J. Kersey	4	3	2	69	27*	69.00	–	–	14	1
S. Kirnon	1	0	0	0	0	–	–	–	–	–
N. V. Knight	27	40	7	1215	109	36.81	3	6	21	–
K. M. Krikken	74	104	16	1676	77*	19.04	–	6	175	12
A. J. Lamb	412	684	101	28495	294	48.87	79	146	320	–
S. R. Lampitt	89	99	22	1665	93	21.62	–	8	35	–
W. Larkins	436	762	48	24384	252	34.15	53	104	260	–
M. N. Lathwell	21	36	1	1239	114	35.40	1	11	14	–
D. A. Leatherdale	49	75	6	1864	157	27.01	2	9	38	–
R. P. Lefebvre	43	44	10	715	100	21.02	1	2	20	–
N. J. Lenham	128	218	21	6467	222*	32.82	13	28	53	–
C. C. Lewis	91	132	17	3282	189*	28.53	3	15	65	–
D. A. Lewis	5	9	1	260	122*	32.50	1	–	1	–
J. J. B. Lewis	16	23	5	935	133	51.94	2	7	6	–
D.G.C. Ligertwood	4	7	0	63	28	9.00	–	–	7	1
N. J. Llong	9	12	2	200	92	20.00	–	1	9	–
G. D. Lloyd	63	101	13	3478	132	39.52	7	24	44	–
T. A. Lloyd	312	547	45	17211	208*	34.28	29	87	147	–
J. I. Longley	7	12	0	211	110	17.58	1	–	4	–
G. B. T. Lovell	18	26	4	672	110*	30.54	1	2	13	–
M. B. Loye	11	15	2	198	46	15.23	–	–	8	–
M. A. Lynch	300	483	58	15377	172*	36.18	34	74	289	–
R. H. MacDonald	10	9	4	54	20	10.80	–	–	–	–

Name	Matches	Inns	NO	Runs	HS	Avge	100s	50s	Ct	St
K. H. Macleay	129	173	34	3750	114*	26.97	3	19	79	–
D. E. Malcolm	130	143	39	826	51	7.94	–	1	25	–
H. S. Malik	1	1	0	4	4	4.00	–	–	–	–
N. A. Mallender	307	343	107	3868	100*	16.39	1	9	103	–
S. A. Marsh	172	240	45	5492	125	28.16	6	30	368	31
M. D. Marshall	366	464	62	9863	117	24.53	6	49	131	–
P. J. Martin	50	46	17	641	133	22.10	1	2	15	–
R. J. Maru	200	190	46	2353	74	16.34	–	6	210	–
M. P. Maynard	188	306	36	11362	243	42.08	25	63	161	2
A. McBrine	4	6	0	155	102	25.83	1	–	1	–
M. J. McCague	35	41	10	386	34	12.45	–	–	20	–
C. McCrum	1	2	0	109	70	54.50	–	1	–	–
P. McCrum	2	3	1	0	0*	0.00	–	–	–	–
S. M. McEwan	65	48	17	407	54	13.12	–	1	24	1
G. D. Mendis	348	609	61	20337	209*	37.11	40	101	140	1
A. A. Metcalfe	177	307	18	10163	216*	35.16	23	48	66	–
C. P. Metson	166	212	46	3001	96	18.07	–	6	387	30
T. C. Middleton	78	130	13	4522	221	38.65	12	18	56	–
G. W. Mike	10	13	4	246	61*	27.33	–	2	6	–
S. M. Milburn	1	2	1	7	5	7.00	–	–	–	–
D. J. Millns	63	68	28	509	44	12.72	–	–	30	–
A. J. Moles	164	296	31	10814	230*	40.80	22	62	117	–
R. R. Montgomerie	18	28	5	786	103*	34.17	1	5	12	–
T. M. Moody	130	213	18	9424	210	48.32	31	39	102	–
P. D. Moore	1	1	1	0	0*	–	–	–	2	–
P. Moores	136	188	25	3933	116	24.12	4	17	270	34
H. Morris	217	367	38	12579	160*	38.23	31	61	126	–
J. E. Morris	218	359	26	12806	191	38.45	29	66	92	–
R. S. M. Morris	5	9	1	209	74	26.12	–	2	7	–
D. K. Morrison	93	90	28	495	36	7.98	–	–	33	–
O. H. Mortensen	145	159	89	639	74*	9.12	–	1	43	–
M. D. Moxon	236	401	28	15234	218*	40.84	33	80	185	–
A. D. Mullally	57	55	17	314	34	8.26	–	–	13	–
T. A. Munton	147	151	59	892	47	9.69	–	–	52	–
A. J. Murphy	72	71	28	225	38	5.23	–	–	12	–
P. A. Neale	354	571	93	17445	167	36.49	98	89	134	–
M. Newell	102	178	26	4636	203*	30.50	6	24	93	1
P. J. Newport	194	212	66	3720	98	25.47	–	12	55	–
M. C. J. Nicholas	321	526	76	14952	206*	33.22	29	66	195	–
P. A. Nixon	45	59	19	1081	107*	27.02	1	1	109	9
W. M. Noon	12	16	2	150	37	10.71	–	–	23	3
J. A. North	16	20	3	285	63*	16.76	–	2	2	–
T. J. G. O'Gorman	71	120	16	3228	148	31.03	5	17	45	–
R. D. Oliphant-Callum	3	2	1	28	19*	28.00	–	–	1	–
D. A. Orr	1	1	1	23	23*	–	–	–	1	1
D. P. Ostler	55	96	9	3019	192	34.70	4	19	50	–
B. Parker	1	2	0	37	30	18.50	–	–	1	–
P. W. G. Parker	352	601	78	18495	215	35.36	44	86	244	–
R. J. Parks	255	284	82	3944	89	19.52	–	14	638	72
G. J. Parsons	260	341	77	4929	76	18.67	–	22	78	–
K. A. Parsons	1	2	0	1	1	0.50	–	–	–	–
B. M. W. Patterson	5	8	0	462	108	57.75	2	3	8	–
T. J. T. Patterson	4	6	1	211	84	42.20	–	2	3	–
A. Payne	1	1	1	51	51*	–	–	1	–	–
R. M. Pearson	21	25	6	166	33*	8.73	–	–	6	–
A. L. Penberthy	39	56	7	905	101*	18.46	1	4	25	–
C. Penn	123	141	36	1985	115	18.90	1	6	54	–

Name	Matches	Inns	NO	Runs	HS	Avge	100s	50s	Ct	St
D. B. Pennett	12	11	1	69	29	6.90	–	–	3	–
T. L. Penney	22	33	10	1146	151	49.82	3	5	6	–
I. L. Philip	7	11	1	574	145	57.40	3	2	7	–
R. A. Pick	138	135	39	1430	63	14.89	–	3	32	–
C. S. Pickles	58	76	21	1336	66	24.29	–	7	24	–
A. C. S. Pigott	234	282	63	4452	104*	20.32	1	19	115	–
K. J. Piper	64	85	14	1388	111	19.54	1	4	158	9
C. M. Pitcher	6	8	3	62	32*	12.40	–	–	–	–
P. R. Pollard	81	143	7	153	4056	29.82	6	16	76	–
J. C. Pooley	17	30	2	628	88	22.42	–	4	9	–
L. Potter	211	337	40	8623	165*	29.03	7	49	178	–
P. J. Prichard	194	306	38	9610	245	35.85	16	57	125	–
D. R. Pringle	281	383	74	8633	128	27.93	10	42	142	–
N. V. Radford	257	253	62	3140	76*	16.44	–	7	121	–
M. R. Ramprakash	117	193	32	6327	233	39.29	12	33	48	–
D. W. Randall	483	817	81	28176	237	38.28	52	159	255	–
J. D. Ratcliffe	54	102	8	2715	127*	28.88	2	14	33	–
M. P. Rea	6	12	1	307	89	27.90	–	2	1	–
D. A. Reeve	189	248	61	6492	202*	35.09	5	42	128	–
C. C. Remy	10	11	1	196	47	19.60	–	–	2	–
S. J. Rhodes	213	277	87	5939	116*	31.25	3	30	503	62
I. V. A. Richards	490	764	56	34977	322	49.40	112	155	448	1
A. W. Richardson	1	1	0	5	5	5.00	–	–	–	–
M. S. Richardson	1	0	0	0	0	–	–	–	1	–
D. Ripley	178	229	57	4268	134*	24.81	6	9	372	55
A. R. Roberts	33	42	13	577	62	19.89	–	1	15	–
J. D. Robinson	31	49	10	898	79	23.02	–	5	12	–
M. A. Robinson	100	95	42	126	19*	2.37	–	–	22	–
P. E. Robinson	133	219	31	6687	189	35.56	7	44	96	–
R. T. Robinson	312	544	71	20209	220*	42.72	46	100	200	–
A. G. Robson	7	7	3	3	3	0.75	–	–	1	–
R. J. Rollins	1	2	0	19	13	9.50	–	–	2	–
G. D. Rose	122	159	36	3726	132	30.29	3	20	58	–
M. A. Roseberry	120	201	25	6782	173	38.53	15	36	83	–
A. B. Russell	6	8	1	200	51	28.57	–	1	10	–
R. C. Russell	251	351	80	7334	128*	27.06	4	31	567	84
I. D. K. Salisbury	80	87	29	939	68	16.19	–	2	52	–
G. Salmond	2	3	0	279	118	93.00	1	2	2	–
D. C. Sandiford	10	11	1	210	83	21.00	–	1	11	1
N. F. Sargeant	41	52	9	612	49	14.23	–	–	91	16
M. Saxelby	24	40	7	982	73	29.75	–	7	4	–
C. W. Scott	81	96	23	1696	78	23.23	–	7	162	11
R. J. Scott	66	111	8	2516	127	24.42	3	12	33	–
A. C. Seymour	25	45	4	1253	157	30.56	2	5	17	–
N. Shahid	49	68	11	1966	132	34.49	2	11	42	–
K. L. P. Sheridan	1	0	0	0	0	–	–	–	–	–
K. J. Shine	41	33	16	204	26*	12.00	–	–	3	–
R. J. Sims	1	1	0	3	3	3.00	–	–	–	–
R. W. Sladdin	21	25	6	199	39	10.47	–	–	12	–
G. C. Small	272	351	82	4033	70	14.99	–	7	83	–
A. M. Smith	26	27	7	229	51*	11.45	–	1	3	–
B. F. Smith	32	45	9	1134	100*	31.50	1	6	13	–
D. M. Smith	297	476	87	14137	213	36.34	27	69	183	–
I. Smith	74	97	14	2109	116	25.41	4	7	28	–
N. M. K. Smith	40	61	10	1399	161	27.43	1	5	14	–
P. A. Smith	193	311	38	7377	140	27.02	4	44	53	–
R. A. Smith	230	390	68	14227	209*	44.18	33	76	153	–

Name	Matches	Inns	NO	Runs	HS	Avge	100s	50s	Ct	St
J. N. Snape	1	0	0	0	0	–	–	–	1	–
R. P. Snell	41	53	10	724	81	16.83	–	3	11	–
N. J. Speak	53	92	7	3380	232	39.76	6	18	35	–
M. P. Speight	80	130	12	4164	179	35.28	8	23	58	–
N. A. Stanley	21	35	4	1019	132	32.87	1	7	9	–
J. Stanworth	44	40	11	266	50*	9.17	–	1	63	10
R. D. Stemp	22	16	11	103	16*	20.60	–	–	5	–
F. D. Stephenson	142	215	28	5108	165	27.31	6	27	60	–
J. P. Stephenson	155	265	29	8684	202*	36.79	15	48	84	–
A. J. Stewart	222	366	45	12608	206*	39.27	21	74	273	6
A. C. Storie	53	86	13	1495	106	20.47	1	6	34	–
P. M. Such	132	105	40	315	35*	4.84	–	–	50	–
S. A. Sylvester	5	2	1	0	0*	0.00	–	–	2	–
C. J. Tavaré	418	692	74	24277	219	39.28	47	136	396	–
C. W. Taylor	27	21	8	147	21	11.30	–	–	5	–
J. P. Taylor	43	37	14	239	74*	10.39	–	1	16	–
N. R. Taylor	264	450	61	15623	204	40.16	38	74	143	–
S. R. Tendulkar	60	97	11	4708	159	54.74	10	30	28	–
V. P. Terry	227	379	38	12281	190	36.01	27	67	250	–
S. D. Thomas	6	7	2	25	10	5.00	–	–	1	–
K. Thomson	1	0	0	0	0	–	–	–	–	–
G. P. Thorpe	96	157	26	5650	216	43.13	10	34	60	–
M. J. Thursfield	3	0	0	0	0	–	–	–	–	–
G. E. Thwaites	4	6	0	68	32	11.33	–	–	2	–
S. P. Titchard	25	44	4	1343	135	33.57	1	9	16	–
C. M. Tolley	33	32	11	432	37	20.57	–	–	14	–
T. D. Topley	111	125	28	1536	66	15.83	–	4	67	–
C. J. Townsend	5	4	1	8	8	2.66	–	–	8	–
G. T. J. Townsend	12	22	2	414	53	20.70	–	1	10	–
H. R. J. Trump	66	66	18	429	48	8.93	–	–	42	–
P. C. R. Tufnell	114	113	45	722	37	10.61	–	–	49	–
I. J. Turner	20	22	7	142	39*	9.46	–	–	9	–
R. J. Turner	41	64	14	1245	101*	24.90	1	4	42	12
A. Tutt	1	0	0	0	0	–	–	–	–	–
T. A. Tweats	1	1	0	24	24	24.00	–	–	1	–
R. G. Twose	56	96	12	2900	233	34.52	3	18	36	–
S. D. Udal	32	36	12	479	44	19.95	–	–	6	–
A. P. van Troost	15	10	6	42	12	10.50	–	–	4	–
J. T. C. Vaughan	33	53	12	1462	106*	35.55	1	8	32	–
A. Walker	96	91	45	664	41*	14.43	–	–	37	–
C. A. Walsh	252	306	72	2969	63*	12.68	–	6	68	–
D. M. Ward	121	192	31	6430	263	39.93	14	22	100	3
I. J. Ward	1	1	0	0	0	0.00	–	–	1	–
T. R. Ward	93	160	12	5683	235*	38.39	13	32	71	–
S. J. S. Warke	11	20	2	832	144*	46.22	2	4	7	–
S. N. Warley	9	13	2	132	35	12.00	–	–	3	–
A. E. Warner	163	221	40	3164	91	17.48	–	14	39	–
R. J. Warren	2	3	1	27	19	13.50	–	–	–	–
S. L. Watkin	117	122	33	738	41	8.29	–	–	24	–
M. Watkinson	200	292	36	6192	138	24.18	3	33	99	–
M. E. Waugh	139	217	33	10448	229*	56.78	35	45	175	–
P. N. Weekes	26	35	8	863	95	31.96	–	6	23	–
A. P. Wells	234	386	64	12481	253*	38.76	26	59	131	–
C. M. Wells	276	436	69	12203	203	33.25	20	58	86	–
V. J. Wells	31	48	7	1008	58	24.58	–	6	13	–
M. J. Weston	154	245	23	5320	145*	23.96	3	26	73	–
W. P. C. Weston	16	26	5	703	66*	33.47	–	5	2	–

Name	Matches	Inns	NO	Runs	HS	Avge	100s	50s	Ct	St
J. J. Whitaker	225	357	43	12003	200*	38.22	24	59	142	-
C. White	32	41	10	1045	79*	33.71	-	7	20	-
P. Whitticase	129	169	39	2963	114*	22.79	1	15	302	13
J. M. S. Whittington	1	0	0	0	0	-	-	-	-	-
R. M. Wight	10	17	3	388	62*	27.71	-	2	3	-
J. R. Wileman	1	1	0	109	109	109.00	1	-	2	-
N. F. Williams	198	232	46	3629	77	19.51	-	12	54	-
R. C. Williams	8	13	1	130	44	10.83	-	-	-	-
R. C. J. Williams	23	25	8	278	55*	16.35	-	2	53	12
R. G. Williams	284	447	65	11817	175*	30.93	18	55	99	-
M. G. N. Windows	1	1	0	71	71	71.00	-	1	1	-
B. S. Wood	13	10	2	37	13	4.62	-	-	-	-
J. Wood	8	6	1	80	28	16.00	-	-	1	-
J. R. Wood	26	35	3	935	96	29.21	-	5	13	-
T. N. Wren	7	5	2	23	16	7.66	-	-	4	-
A. J. Wright	205	352	26	9337	161	28.64	12	49	140	-

BOWLING AVERAGES

Name	Balls	Runs	Wkts	Avge	Best	5wI	10wM
M. B. Abington	880	530	10	53.00	3-33	-	-
C. J. Adams	598	375	10	37.50	4-29	-	-
J. A. Afford	20748	9900	296	33.44	6-68	9	2
R. I. Alikhan	347	274	7	39.14	2-19	-	-
M. W. Alleyne	4103	2505	62	40.40	4-48	-	-
C. E. L. Ambrose	22238	9293	420	22.12	8-45	19	3
D. Anderson	989	511	9	56.77	2-68	-	-
S. J. W. Andrew	15066	8349	260	32.11	7-92	5	-
J. P. Arscott	288	252	7	36.00	1-17	-	-
Asif Din	6273	4256	73	58.30	5-100	1	-
M. A. Atherton	8813	4666	106	44.01	6-78	3	-
C. W. J. Athey	4318	2339	45	51.97	3-3	-	-
I. D. Austin	6144	2919	78	37.42	5-79	1	-
J. R. Ayling	7086	3254	131	24.84	5-12	1	-
A. N. Aymes	42	75	1	75.00	1-75	-	-
A. M. Babington	13002	6911	194	35.62	8-107	3	-
R. J. Bailey	4231	2361	55	42.92	3-27	-	-
P. Bainbridge	21022	10554	287	36.77	8-53	8	-
P. J. Bakker	11525	5406	193	28.01	7-31	7	-
M. C. J. Ball	4554	2449	70	34.98	5-101	2	-
A. A. Barnett	4378	2559	56	45.69	5-78	2	-
K. J. Barnett	10752	5324	137	38.86	6-28	2	-
R. J. Barlett	180	145	4	36.25	1-9	-	-
S. R. Barwick	27850	12931	378	34.20	8-42	9	1
S. J. Base	16948	8915	323	27.60	7-60	12	1
S. Bastien	7058	3715	96	38.69	6-75	5	-
J. D. Batty	7080	3864	99	39.03	6-48	2	-
A. W. Bee	427	219	3	73.00	2-20	-	-
M. A. V. Bell	476	247	8	30.87	3-78	-	-
J. E. Benjamin	7449	3800	109	34.86	6-30	6	-
W. K. M. Benjamin	18715	8946	343	26.08	7-54	17	2
J. D. R. Benson	769	488	8	61.00	2-24	-	-
M. R. Benson	467	493	5	98.60	2-55	-	-
P. J. Berry	1886	1050	24	43.75	7-113	1	1
D. J. Bicknell	255	265	3	88.33	2-62	-	-
M. P. Bicknell	22000	10298	383	26.88	9-45	13	-
I. R. Bishop	14472	6659	325	20.48	7-34	18	1

Name	Balls	Runs	Wkts	Avge	Best	5wI	10wM
R. J. Blakey	63	68	1	68.00	1–68	–	–
D. J. P. Boden	185	68	4	17.00	4–11	–	–
J. Boiling	5126	2286	62	36.87	6–84	1	1
T. J. Boon	619	525	11	47.72	3–40	–	–
P. A. Booth	8817	3804	91	41.80	5–98	1	–
I. T. Botham	62432	31386	1159	27.08	8–34	59	8
M. N. Bowen	408	247	2	123.50	1–23	–	–
P. D. Bowler	2283	1449	20	72.45	3–41	–	–
M. P. Briers	867	621	12	51.75	3–109	–	–
N. E. Briers	2047	988	32	30.87	4–29	–	–
B. C. Broad	1625	1036	16	64.75	2–14	–	–
A. D. Brown (Sur)	96	78	0	–	–	–	–
A. M. Brown	18	9	0	–	–	–	–
D. R. Brown	445	204	8	25.50	3–27	–	–
G. K. Brown	108	103	1	103.00	1–39	–	–
K. R. Brown	231	162	5	32.40	2–7	–	–
S. J. E. Brown	4783	2787	83	33.57	7–105	3	–
R. E. Bryson	7025	3735	136	27.46	7–68	10	2
N. D. Burns	3	8	0	–	–	–	–
A. R. Butcher	10008	5433	141	38.53	6–48	1	–
M. A. Butcher	264	115	1	115.00	1–95	–	–
D. Byas	948	612	10	61.20	3–55	–	–
A. R. Caddick	3915	2169	76	28.53	6–52	3	1
C. L. Cairns	10062	5619	187	30.04	7–34	6	2
D. J. Capel	27091	14350	439	32.68	7–46	12	–
J. D. Carr	6622	2866	64	44.78	6–61	3	–
P. Carrick	77839	32115	1078	29.79	8–33	47	5
R. J. Chapman	78	77	2	38.50	1–38	–	–
G. Chapple	288	128	5	25.60	3–40	–	–
J. H. Childs	58220	25095	840	29.87	9–56	45	8
C. A. Connor	25834	13326	405	32.90	7–31	10	1
N. G. B. Cook	61569	24380	854	28.54	7–34	31	4
K. E. Cooper	42994	19332	711	27.19	8–44	25	1
D. G. Cork	6301	3135	115	27.26	8–53	3	1
A. C. Cottam	697	280	6	46.66	1–1	–	–
P. A. Cottey	492	303	6	50.50	2–42	–	–
N. G. Cowans	30440	15241	620	24.58	6–31	23	1
C. S. Cowdrey	14524	7962	200	39.81	5–46	2	–
G. R. Cowdrey	1087	749	11	68.09	1–5	–	–
R. M. F. Cox	6	1	0	–	–	–	–
J. P. Crawley	72	104	1	104.00	1–90	–	–
M. A. Crawley	5313	2682	57	47.05	6–92	1	–
P. M. Crawley	396	236	3	78.66	2–36	–	–
R. D. B. Croft	11710	6076	143	42.49	8–66	6	1
K. M. Curran	20381	10589	409	25.89	7–47	12	4
T. S. Curtis	926	657	11	59.72	2–17	–	–
D. B. D'Oliveira	2894	1712	37	46.27	2–17	–	–
A. Dale	2899	1547	38	40.71	3–21	–	–
H. R. Davies	1846	1377	13	105.92	3–93	–	–
M. Davies	3413	1677	56	29.94	4–73	–	–
R. P. Davis	20976	10010	280	35.75	7–64	11	1
P. A. J. DeFreitas	30652	14847	542	27.39	7–21	27	2
G. R. Dilley	34418	17395	648	26.48	7–63	34	3
M. C. Dobson	886	486	9	54.00	2–20	–	–
A. A. Donald	25891	12586	546	23.05	8–37	30	3
B. T. P. Donelan	7969	4118	96	42.89	6–62	3	1
A. R. Dunlop	240	143	2	71.50	1–8	–	–

Name	Balls	Runs	Wkts	Avge	Best	5wI	10wM
M. A. Ealham	3526	1835	58	31.63	5-39	2	-
P. H. Edmonds	86116	31981	1246	25.66	8-53	47	9
R. M. Ellison	29680	13604	471	28.88	7-33	18	2
J. E. Emburey	96355	35599	1366	26.06	7-27	63	9
K. P. Evans	12325	6405	182	35.19	5-27	3	-
N. H. Fairbrother	656	423	5	84.60	2-91	-	-
P. Farbrace	25	64	1	64.00	1-64	-	-
M. A. Feltham	17724	9266	292	31.73	6-53	6	-
N. A. Felton	288	345	2	172.50	1-48	-	-
M. G. Field-Buss	1913	1004	22	45.63	4-33	-	-
J. D. Fitton	8391	4359	82	53.15	6-59	3	-
M. V. Fleming	5963	2786	68	40.97	4-63	-	-
S. D. Fletcher	15168	8375	240	34.89	8-58	5	-
A. Fordham	362	238	3	79.33	1-25	-	-
D. J. Foster	6064	3844	96	40.04	6-84	2	-
N. A. Foster	44330	21473	896	23.96	8-99	49	8
G. Fowler	407	366	10	36.60	2-34	-	-
A. G. J. Fraser	745	386	12	32.16	3-46	-	-
A. R. C. Fraser	22309	9376	355	26.41	7-77	16	2
B. N. French	90	70	1	70.00	1-37	-	-
M. Frost	9569	5825	162	35.95	7-99	4	2
J. E. R. Gallian	1374	693	19	36.47	4-29	-	-
M. A. Garnham	24	39	0	-	-	-	-
M. W. Gatting	9731	4466	154	29.00	5-34	2	-
M. J. Gerrard	1973	1016	26	39.07	6-40	1	1
E. S. H. Giddins	1825	1043	33	31.60	5-32	2	-
M. I. Gidley	2303	1116	16	69.75	3-51	-	-
R. P. Gofton	490	348	6	58.00	4-81	-	-
S. C. Goldsmith	2898	1571	29	54.17	3-42	-	-
G. A. Gooch	17872	8034	231	34.77	7-14	3	-
D. Gough	5327	3105	79	39.30	5-41	1	-
J. W. Govan	1906	846	35	24.17	6-70	2	-
D. I. Gower	260	227	4	56.75	3-47	-	-
D. A. Graveney	63285	27314	912	29.95	8-85	38	7
A.P. Grayson	960	523	3	174.33	1-3	-	-
K. Greenfield	159	133	0	-	-	-	-
F. A. Griffith	1773	1017	33	30.81	4-33	-	-
C. M. Gupte	313	253	4	63.25	2-41	-	-
J. W. Hall	12	14	0	-	-	-	-
T. H. C. Hancock	202	136	4	34.00	2-43	-	-
A. R. Hansford	1921	991	30	33.03	5-79	1	-
R. J. Harden	1397	952	19	50.10	2-7	-	-
P. J. Hartley	18719	10863	318	34.16	8-111	12	-
C. J. Hawkes	336	162	5	32.40	4-18	-	-
A. N. Hayhurst	7047	3918	86	45.55	4-27	-	-
D. L. Haynes	416	201	7	28.71	1-2	-	-
G. R. Haynes	388	210	0	-	-	-	-
D. W. Headley	4287	2516	60	41.93	5-46	2	-
W. K. Hegg	6	7	0	-	-	-	-
E. E. Hemmings	93989	41461	1404	29.53	10-175	66	14
P. W. Henderson	576	405	10	40.50	3-59	-	-
P. N. Hepworth	1332	902	19	47.47	3-51	-	-
G. A. Hick	11314	5575	142	39.26	5-37	4	1
J. E. Hindson	202	74	8	9.25	5-42	1	-
S. G. Hinks	597	381	8	47.62	2-18	-	-
G. D. Hodgson	24	65	0	-	-	-	-
C. J. Hoey	266	144	5	28.80	3-38	-	-

Name	Balls	Runs	Wkts	Avge	Best	5wI	10wM
A. M. Hooper	402	275	6	45.83	1-5	-	-
C. L. Hooper	13555	6039	181	33.36	5-33	5	-
S. P. Hughes	27715	14587	458	31.84	7-35	10	-
N. Hussain	207	198	1	198.00	1-38	-	-
S. Hutton	1	4	0	-	-	-	-
A. P. Igglesden	17601	9275	328	28.27	6-34	14	2
R. K. Illingworth	41141	16749	525	31.90	7-50	19	4
M. C. Ilott	7448	3980	117	34.01	6-87	5	-
R. Irani	524	292	5	58.40	2-21	-	-
K. D. James	14509	7228	219	33.00	6-22	7	-
P. W. Jarvis	23798	12571	457	27.50	7-55	18	3
M. Jean-Jacques	6916	4091	115	35.57	8-77	2	1
M. P. W. Jeh	1403	846	17	49.76	3-44	-	-
R. H. J. Jenkins	2782	1610	24	67.08	5-100	1	-
P. Johnson	478	510	5	102.00	1-9	-	-
R. L. Johnson	84	71	1	71.00	1-25	-	-
S. W. Johnson	2449	1601	16	100.06	3-62	-	-
A. N. Jones	22408	13143	408	32.21	7-30	12	1
D. M. Jones	1886	966	15	64.40	1-0	-	-
S. A. Kellett	30	19	0	-	-	-	-
T. R. Kemp	174	128	1	128.00	1-35	-	-
N. M. Kendrick	6834	3259	95	34.30	6-61	5	1
S. Kirnon	84	21	1	21.00	1-14	-	-
N. V. Knight	30	32	0	-	-	-	-
K. M. Krikken	36	40	0	-	-	-	-
A. J. Lamb	305	199	8	24.87	2-29	-	-
S. R. Lampitt	10595	5673	186	30.50	5-32	8	-
W. Larkins	3463	1858	42	44.23	5-59	1	-
M. N. Lathwell	552	323	5	64.60	1-9	-	-
D. A. Leatherdale	114	59	1	59.00	1-12	-	-
R. P. Lefebvre	7065	2945	74	39.79	6-53	2	-
N. J. Lenham	2652	1395	29	48.10	4-85	-	-
C. C. Lewis	15849	7757	271	28.62	6-22	13	3
D. A. Lewis	306	232	4	58.00	2-39	-	-
N. J. Llong	402	264	7	37.71	3-50	-	-
G. D. Lloyd	151	186	1	186.00	1-57	-	-
T. A. Lloyd	2333	1682	23	73.13	3-7	-	-
G. B. T. Lovell	192	141	1	141.00	1-13	-	-
M. A. Lynch	2117	1360	26	52.30	3-6	-	-
R. H. MacDonald	1420	645	15	43.00	3-66	-	-
K. H. MacLeay	22122	9080	300	30.26	6-93	6	-
D. E. Malcolm	21746	12500	394	31.72	7-74	10	1
H. S. Malik	150	88	0	-	-	-	-
N. A. Mallender	47929	22368	842	26.56	7-27	33	5
S. A. Marsh	154	227	2	113.50	2-20	-	-
M. D. Marshall	66634	28511	1524	18.70	8-71	83	13
P. J. Martin	7761	3814	96	39.72	4-30	-	-
R. J. Maru	34810	15538	479	32.43	8-41	15	1
M. P. Maynard	774	566	5	113.20	3-21	-	-
A. McBrine	595	221	6	36.83	3-64	-	-
M. J. McCague	5713	2997	101	29.67	8-26	7	1
C. McCrum	168	97	3	32.33	3-57	-	-
P. McCrum	282	173	1	173.00	1-80	-	-
S. M. McEwan	9028	4869	156	31.21	6-39	3	-
G. D. Mendis	177	158	1	158.00	1-65	-	-
A. A. Metcalfe	392	316	4	79.00	2-18	-	-
C. P. Metson	6	0	0	-	-	-	-

Name	Balls	Runs	Wkts	Avge	Best	5wI	10wM
T. C. Middleton	234	237	5	47.40	2–41	–	–
G. W. Mike	1072	684	14	48.85	3–48	–	–
S. M. Milburn	168	115	1	115.00	1–54	–	–
D. J. Millns	9148	5227	195	26.80	9–37	11	2
A. J. Moles	3270	1763	36	48.97	3–21	–	–
R. R. Montgomerie	60	31	0	–	–	–	–
T. M. Moody	5433	2365	73	32.39	7–43	1	1
P. Moores	12	16	0	–	–	–	–
H. Morris	348	380	2	190.00	1–6	–	–
J. E. Morris	771	753	5	150.60	1–13	–	–
D. K. Morrison	15665	8795	266	33.06	7–82	9	–
O. H. Mortensen	22215	9673	411	23.53	6–27	15	1
M. D. Moxon	2626	1474	28	52.64	3–24	–	–
A. D. Mullally	9809	4701	119	39.50	5–119	1	–
T. A. Munton	24148	10839	392	27.65	8–89	15	3
A. J. Murphy	12797	6841	174	39.31	6–97	5	–
P. A. Neale	472	369	2	184.50	1–15	–	–
M. Newell	363	282	7	40.28	2–38	–	–
P. J. Newport	29646	15757	568	27.74	8–52	27	3
M. C. J. Nicholas	5783	3208	72	44.55	6–37	2	–
J. A. North	2017	1164	37	31.45	4–47	–	–
T. J. G. O'Gorman	260	207	3	69.00	1–7	–	–
D. P. Ostler	90	90	0	–	–	–	–
P. W. G. Parker	985	699	11	63.54	2–21	–	–
R. J. Parks	189	166	0	–	–	–	–
G. J. Parsons	35977	18436	606	30.42	9–72	18	1
D. N. Patel	120	72	2	36.00	2–72	–	–
T. J. T. Patterson	216	96	3	32.00	2–54	–	–
A. Payne	162	71	7	71.00	1–71	–	–
R. M. Pearson	4407	2377	35	67.91	5–108	1	–
A. L. Penberthy	3402	1909	50	38.18	4–91	–	–
C. Penn	17681	9493	283	33.54	7–70	12	–
D. B. Pennett	1778	981	26	37.73	4–58	–	–
T. L. Penney	36	39	0	–	–	–	–
R. A. Pick	20505	11521	352	32.73	7–128	11	3
C. S. Pickles	6441	3638	83	43.83	4–40	–	–
A. C. Pigott	33484	18426	600	30.71	7–74	23	1
K. J. Piper	28	57	1	57.00	1–57	–	–
C. M. Pitcher	786	445	3	148.33	1–35	–	–
P. R. Pollard	178	113	1	113.00	1–46	–	–
J. C. Pooley	12	11	0	–	–	–	–
L. Potter	12524	6121	153	40.00	4–52	–	–
P. J. Prichard	247	409	1	409.00	1–28	–	–
D. R. Pringle	42846	19189	732	26.21	7–18	25	3
N. V. Radford	44822	23469	900	26.07	9–70	45	7
M. R. Ramprakash	991	583	6	97.16	1–0	–	–
D. W. Randall	489	413	13	31.76	3–15	–	–
J. D. Ratcliffe	180	96	1	96.00	1–15	–	–
D. A. Reeve	24180	10424	373	27.94	7–37	6	–
C. C. Remy	992	593	12	49.41	4–63	–	–
S. J. Rhodes	6	30	0	–	–	–	–
I. V. A. Richards	15107	9835	219	44.90	5–88	1	–
A. W. Richardson	78	38	2	19.00	2–38	–	–
M. S. Richardson	144	64	2	32.00	2–49	–	–
D. Ripley	60	103	2	51.50	2–89	–	–
A. R. Roberts	4801	2571	61	42.14	6–72	1	–
J. D. Robinson	1923	1152	28	41.14	3–22	–	–

Name	Balls	Runs	Wkts	Avge	Best	5wI	10wM
M. A. Robinson	15429	7624	227	33.58	6-57	3	1
P. E. Robinson	209	238	1	238.00	1-10	-	-
R. T. Robinson	240	254	3	84.66	1-22	-	-
A. G. Robson	948	508	9	56.44	4-37	-	-
G. D. Rose	15803	8340	264	31.59	6-41	4	-
M. A. Roseberry	483	382	4	95.50	1-1	-	-
A. B. Russell	198	98	3	32.66	2-27	-	-
R. C. Russell	27	38	1	38.00	1-4	-	-
I. D. K. Salisbury	15128	8168	210	38.89	7-54	9	2
N. F. Sargeant	30	88	1	88.00	1-88	-	-
M. Saxelby	1086	765	9	85.00	3-41	-	-
C. W. Scott	6	10	0	-	-	-	-
R. J. Scott	3179	1830	40	45.75	3-43	-	-
A. C. Seymour	24	27	0	-	-	-	-
N. Shahid	1395	947	24	39.45	3-91	-	-
K. L. P. Sheridan	210	104	1	104.00	1-62	-	-
K. J. Shine	5200	3384	95	35.62	8-47	5	1
R. W. Sladdin	5210	2361	66	35.77	6-58	2	-
G. C. Small	43396	21497	750	28.66	7-15	27	2
A. M. Smith	3358	1818	53	34.30	4-41	-	-
B. F. Smith	78	91	1	91.00	1-5	-	-
D. M. Smith	2797	1574	30	52.46	3-40	-	-
I. Smith	4252	2692	60	44.86	3-48	-	-
N. M. K. Smith	5058	2763	57	48.47	5-61	1	-
P. A. Smith	13578	8768	243	36.08	6-91	7	-
R. A. Smith	918	691	12	57.58	2-11	-	-
J. N. Snape	156	62	1	62.00	1-20	-	-
R. P. Snell	6856	3402	124	27.43	6-48	5	-
N. J. Speak	67	92	2	46.00	1-0	-	-
M. P. Speight	21	32	2	16.00	1-2	-	-
N. A. Stanley	60	19	0	-	-	-	-
R. D. Stemp	3324	1602	46	34.82	6-67	3	1
F. D. Stephenson	26265	12884	536	24.03	8-47	32	8
J. P. Stephenson	5354	2903	89	32.61	6-54	2	-
A. J. Stewart	407	352	3	117.33	1-7	-	-
A. C. Storie	390	199	2	99.50	1-17	-	-
P. M. Such	20284	9034	301	30.01	6-17	9	-
S. A. Sylvester	624	320	4	80.00	2-34	-	-
C. J. Tavaré	789	720	5	144.00	1-3	-	-
C. W. Taylor	3625	2044	59	34.64	5-33	1	-
J. P. Taylor	6480	3479	105	33.13	7-23	4	1
N. R. Taylor	1575	891	16	55.68	2-20	-	-
S. R. Tendulkar	2118	1172	16	73.25	3-60	-	-
V. P. Terry	95	58	0	-	-	-	-
S. D. Thomas	680	404	18	22.44	5-79	2	-
K. Thomson	156	82	2	41.00	1-27	-	-
G. P. Thorpe	1228	738	13	56.76	2-31	-	-
M. J. Thursfield	348	165	4	41.25	1-11	-	-
C. M. Tolley	3390	1641	42	39.07	4-69	-	-
T. D. Topley	18266	9473	351	26.98	7-75	15	2
H. R. J. Trump	12272	6038	158	38.21	7-52	6	1
P. C. R. Tufnell	27979	11975	377	31.76	7-47	19	2
I. J. Turner	3629	1628	46	35.39	5-81	1	-
R. J. Turner	13	26	0	-	-	-	-
A. Tutt	114	53	0	-	-	-	-
R. G. Twose	3590	1802	55	32.76	6-63	1	-
S. D. Udal	5783	3050	82	37.19	8-50	2	-

Name	Balls	Runs	Wkts	Avge	Best	5wI	10wM
A. P. van Troost	1574	1033	27	38.25	6–48	2	–
J. T. C. Vaughan	3063	1462	43	34.00	5–72	1	–
A. Walker	13465	6871	221	31.09	6–50	2	–
C. A. Walsh	46379	22244	989	22.49	9–72	55	11
D. M. Ward	107	113	2	56.50	2–66	–	–
I. J. Ward	48	35	0	–	–	–	–
T. R. Ward	934	535	6	89.16	2–48	–	–
A. E. Warner	21170	10591	326	32.48	5–27	2	–
S. L. Watkin	22728	11532	374	30.83	8–59	16	3
M. Watkinson	29449	15486	460	33.66	7–25	21	1
M. E. Waugh	6764	3882	105	36.97	5–37	1	–
P. N. Weekes	2152	1047	23	45.52	3–57	–	–
A. P. Wells	961	690	9	76.66	3–67	–	–
C. M. Wells	28494	13410	392	34.20	7–42	7	–
V. J. Wells	2620	1165	51	22.84	5–43	1	–
M. J. Weston	6439	3108	80	38.85	4–24	–	–
W. P. C. Weston	444	237	2	118.50	2–39	–	–
J. J. Whitaker	176	268	2	134.00	1–29	–	–
C. White	1140	700	15	46.66	5–74	1	–
P. Whitticase	5	7	0	–	–	–	–
J. M. S. Whittington	114	44	0	–	–	–	–
R. M. Wight	1389	748	19	39.36	3–65	–	–
N. F. Williams	28088	15141	515	29.40	8–75	16	2
R. C. Williams	621	381	6	63.50	3–44	–	–
R. G. Williams	27016	12722	376	33.83	7–33	9	–
B. S. Wood	1639	1017	16	63.56	2–24	–	–
J. Wood	806	534	17	31.41	5–68	1	–
J. R. Wood	63	38	1	38.00	1–5	–	–
T. N. Wren	993	629	15	41.93	3–14	–	–
A. J. Wright	74	68	1	68.00	1–16	–	–

Correct to end 1992 English season; includes only those playing first class cricket in 1992.

KEY TO 1992 MATCH SCORECARDS

Condensed scores and highlights from last season's 198 (including one abandonment) Britannic Assurance County Championship matches, reproduced by kind permission of *Wisden Cricket Monthly*. Individual innings of 40+ are listed according to a player's place in the batting order; bowlers claiming four or more wickets are listed according to the order in which they came on to bowl. HS (highest scores) and BB (best bowling) in a player's first-class career are noted in the summary following the match scores.

The points system in operation was as follows: Win = 16 pts plus bonus points gleaned from the first 100 overs of each side's first innings, up to a maximum of four for batting and four for bowling; Tie = 8 points to both sides; Drawn with the scores level = 8 points to side batting last. Bonus points were awarded as follows: BATTING 1 pt – 150 to 199 runs; 2 pts – 200 to 249; 3 pts – 250 to 299; 4pts – 300+. BOWLING 1pt – 3 to 4 wickets; 2 pts – 5 to 6; 3 pts – 7 to 8; 4 pts – 9 to 10. 21:3/2 therefore indicates that a side has won and gained 21 points: 16 for victory plus 3 batting and 2 bowling points.

BRITANNIC ASSURANCE CHAMPIONSHIP
1992 SCORES

April 25, 26, 27, 28
OLD TRAFFORD: LANCASHIRE 397 (123.3 overs) (N. J. Speak 47, G. D. Lloyd 132, P. A. J. DeFreitas 55*, A. P. Igglesden 4 for 85, M. A. Ealham 4 for 81) and 213 for 5 dec (G. Fowler 66); KENT 300 for 7 dec (97 overs) (M. R. Benson 53, T. R. Ward 40, N. R. Taylor 40, S.A. Marsh 78, R.P. Davis 54*, M. Watkinson 4 for 60) and 192 for 8. DRAWN (Lancs 7:4/3, Kent 7:4/3).
Lloyd (HS) 100 in 211 mins, 14x4. 1st inns Kent were 167 for 6, then Marsh/Davis 115 for 7th wkt. A. A. Barnett's 1st delivery saw Ward 'ct' off no-ball. Kent target 311 in 75 overs; rain cost 7 overs; were 133 for 6, then Ealham (33)/Davis (24*) 58 for 7th wkt.

TRENT BRIDGE: WARWICKSHIRE 249 (104.1 overs) (A. J. Moles 51, M. Asif Din 40, R. G. Twose 55) and 263 (T. A. Lloyd 41, D. P. Ostler 102); NOTTINGHAMSHIRE 311 (102.2 overs) (C. L. Cairns 48, E. E. Hemmings 52*, R. A. Pick 52, P. A. Smith 5 for 79) and 202 for 2 (B. C. Broad 104, M. A. Crawley 64*). NOTTINGHAMSHIRE WON BY 8 WICKETS (Notts 23:4/3, Warwicks 6:2/4).
T. A. Munton (Warwicks) broke left-hand middle finger attempting catch; batted in 2nd inns (0*) with hand behind back as 10 added for 10th wkt. Notts were 202 for 9, then Hemmings (7x4)/Pick 109 for 10th wkt in 25 overs, best 10th-wkt stand for Notts since B. Dooland/A. K. Walker 123 v Som, 1956; Pick 2x6 in 100th over (P. A. Booth) to raise 300 & 4th batting pt. Ostler 251 mins, 13x4. Notts target 202 in 73 overs, reached with 14.1 to spare; Broad 17x4, Crawley 1st BAC 50.

TAUNTON: GLOUCESTERSHIRE 344 (145.2 overs) (C. W. J. Athey 65, T. H. C. Hancock 102, M. C. J. Ball 54, A. R. Caddick 4 for 96); SOMERSET 348 for 9 dec (136.4 overs) (A. N. Hayhurst 54, G. T. J. Townsend 40, G. D. Rose 85, A. Payne 51*, M. C. J. Ball 4 for 103). DRAWN (Som 5:3/2, Gloucs 4:1/3).
Fc debut A. Payne (Som). Athey 4.5 hrs. Hancock (155 mins, 11x4; maiden fc 100)/Ball (maiden fc 50) 95 for 8th wkt. Caddick BB on BAC debut. 147 overs lost to rain during match.

April 25, 27, 28, 29
DURHAM UNIVERSITY: DURHAM 164 (82.1 overs) (P. W. G. Parker 77) and 318 (P. W. G. Parker 117, I. T. Botham 105, D. J. Millns 5 for 69); LEICESTERSHIRE 342 (130 overs) (T. J. Boon 110, B. F. Smith 100*, V. J. Wells 42) and 142 for 3 (N. E. Briers 43). LEICESTERSHIRE WON BY 7 WICKETS (Leics 23:3/4, Durham 3:1/2).
Durham's 1st BAC match. 1st inns A. D. Mullally (Leics) 21.1–10–29–3. Boon 236 balls, 15x4; Smith maiden fc 100 in 321 mins, 235 balls, 12x4 (later inj tendons in ankle while fielding); Wells HS for Leics. Botham (7x4, 5x6) hit Durham's 1st BAC 100 in 98 balls after car broken into prev night (phone & radio stolen); Parker 117 in 6 hrs on BAC debut for Durham after 103 on fc debut for them v OU. Parker/Botham 178 for 5th wkt, then Durham lost last 6 wkts for 28, Millns 5 for 12 in 7 overs. Leics target 141 in min 51 overs.

SOUTHAMPTON: HAMPSHIRE 468 for 2 dec (145.2 overs) (V. P. Terry 141, T. C. Middleton 153, R. A. Smith 107*, D. I. Gower 55*) and forfeited second innings; SUSSEX 169 for 2 dec (40 overs) (D. M. Smith 61, B. T. P. Donelan 68*) and 149 (S. D. Udal 8 for 50). HAMPSHIRE WON BY 150 RUNS (Hants 20:4/0, Sussex 1:1/0).
Sx debut A. G. Robson (Sy). Sx won toss, put Hants in; Terry (25th fc 100; 16x4)/Middleton (HS; 445 mins, 367 balls, 11x4) 246 for 1st wkt; Smith 15x4; Gower 9x4. No play 3rd day. HS Donelan. A. N. Aymes (Hants wkpr) 7–0–75–1 (wkt of Smith). Udal BB in 1st BAC match since 1990.

LORD'S: MIDDLESEX 341 (95.4 overs) M. W. Gatting 170, J. E. Emburey 57, S. Bastien 5 for 95) and 179 for 2 dec (M. A. Roseberry 86, M. W. Gatting 48*); GLAMORGAN 255 for 3 dec (103.4 overs) (H. Morris 146, R. D. B. Croft 51) and 237 for 6 (S. P. James 94, H. Morris 40, M. P. Maynard 40, J. E. Emburey 4 for 77). DRAWN (Middx 5:4/1, Glam 6:2/4).
Middx were 129 for 6, then Gatting (339 mins, 27x4)/Emburey 148 for 7th wkt. Morris (300 mins, 19x4)/Croft (1st time at No. 3) 173 for 2nd wkt. No play 3rd day. Glam target 266 in 65 overs; HSBAC James.

THE OVAL: YORKSHIRE 495 for 9 dec (167.4 overs) (M. D. Moxon 141, A. A. Metcalfe 73, S. A. Kellett 49, P. W. Jarvis 62, A. P. Grayson 57, C. S. Pickles 49, N. M. Kendrick 4 for 89); SURREY 164 (67.5 overs) (D. Gough 4 for 43, P. Carrick 4 for 60) and 64 for 2. DRAWN (Surrey 2:1/1, Yorks 8:4/4).
Moxon (rt-hand index finger broken by R. E. Bryson/Metcalfe 221 for 1st wkt. Jarvis (HS) 8x4. Grayson (1st fc 50)/Pickles 104 for 7th wkt. Carrick (6) passed career total of 10,000 fc runs; 2nd current county player (after I. T. Botham) to achieve 10,000 run/1,000-wkt double. No play 3rd day; Surrey 6 for 2 (3.2 overs) at 2nd-day close. HS of Sy inns was A. J. Murphy's 32 from No. 11; he added 60 for 10th wkt with Kendrick (31*), hitting 3x6 (1st of career) off Carrick.*

WORCESTER: WORCESTERSHIRE 345 (136.1 overs) (T. S. Curtis 43, G. A. Hick 92, D. J. Capel 5 for 61) and 282 for 9 dec (D. A. Leatherdale 60, S. J. Rhodes 45, A. R. Roberts 4 for 101); NORTHAMPTONSHIRE 354 (127.1 overs) (A. J. Lamb 101, D. Ripley 60*, P. J. Newport 5 for 102) and 180 for 7 (A. J. Lamb 66, R. K. Illingworth 4 for 43). DRAWN (Worcs 6:3/3, Northants 5:3/2).
All Worcs players to double figs in 1st inns except No. 11 R. D. Stemp (7). Hick 15x4. Lamb 100 in 176 balls, 11x4, 2x6. Ripley/A. Walker (39) 82 for 9th wkt. G. R. Dilley (Worcs) bowled 11 overs before inj Achilles tendon; out 6 weeks. Leatherdale 9x4. Northants target 274 in 53 overs; Lamb 8x4, 1x6; were 155 for 7, then Ripley (14*)/R. J. Bailey (14*; batted No. 9 after inj hamstring) survived last 17 overs to draw.*

May 7, 8, 9, 10
LORD'S: LANCASHIRE 343 (127.3 overs) (N. J. Speak 93, P. A. J. DeFreitas 69, W. K. Hegg 63) and 113 for 3 dec (M. A. Atherton 51*); MIDDLESEX 493 for 8 dec (139.5 overs) (D. L. Haynes 62, M. W. Gatting 103, M. R. Ramprakash 108, J. E. Emburey 78, D. W. Headley 40*). DRAWN (Middx 7:4/3, Lancs 5:3/2).
Speak/DeFreitas (11x4) 137 for 5th wkt. Hegg 11x4. Gatting 192 mins, 143 balls, 16x4. No play 3rd day. Emburey 10x4. Atherton 7x4.

HEADINGLEY: YORKSHIRE 250 (81.5 overs) (S. R. Tendulkar 86, R. J. Blakey 72) and 74 for 1; HAMPSHIRE 397 for 8 dec (130.1 overs) (T. C. Middleton 55, D. I. Gower 68, K. D. James 116, C. A. Connor 51, M. D. Marshall 46*). DRAWN (Yorks 5:3/2, Hants 7:3/4).
M. D. Marshall capt Hants. Yorks were 27 for 3, then Tendulkar (HS for Yorks; 12x4)/Blakey 139 for 4th wkt. M. A. Robinson (Yorks; 12) passed career total of 100 fc runs in 84th match. Middleton 186 balls, 2x4. Gower 77 balls, 12x4 (4x4 in D. Gough over). No play 3rd day. James 326 mins 16x4. Connor 8x4, 1x6) maiden fc 50 in 63 balls.

May 7, 8, 9, 11
CHELMSFORD: LEICESTERSHIRE 223 (111.4 overs) (N. E. Briers 51, L. Potter 70) and 312 for 7 (T. J. Boon 82, N. E. Briers 99); ESSEX 424 for 4 dec (111 overs) (G. A. Gooch 160, J. P. Stephenson 91, P. J. Prichard 102). DRAWN (Essex 7:4/3, Leics 3:2/1).
1st inns J. J. Whitaker (Leics) ret hurt (33) after cheekbone fractured by D. R. Pringle delivery. Leics were 134 for 2, 163 for 7. Gooch (92nd fc 100, 100 before lunch; 212*

mins, 193 balls, 25x4, 1x6)/Stephenson (285 mins) 238 for 1st wkt. Prichard 135 mins, 122 balls, 15x4, 1x6. 21 overs 3rd day (only fc cricket anywhere in country on May 9). Boon/Briers 147 for 1st wkt.

CANTERBURY: KENT 244 (80 overs) (M. R. Benson 75, N. R. Taylor 57, S. J. E. Brown 7 for 105) and 253 for 3 dec (N. R. Taylor 78*, C. L. Hooper 115*); DURHAM 239 (109.4 overs) (W. Larkins 40, R. M. Ellison 5 for 77) and 145 for 3 (J. D. Glendenen 57*, P. Bainbridge 61*). DRAWN (Kent 5:2/3, Durham 6:2/4).
Kent were 240 for 6, 244 all out. BB Brown. D. M. Jones (Durham) 34 in 157 mins 1st inns. No play 3rd day. Taylor/Hooper (fastest 100 of season to date in 82 balls; in all 89 balls, 13x4, 5x6) 197* for 4th wkt in 28 overs. Durham target 259 in min 50 overs; Bainbridge HS for Durham.

NORTHAMPTON: NORTHAMPTONSHIRE 375 (107.2 overs) (A. Fordham 192, D. Ripley 49) and 147 for 3 dec (D. J. Capel 41*); SURREY 279 for 6 dec (110 overs) (D. J. Bicknell 99, G. P. Thorpe 64) and 142 for 5 (G. P. Thorpe 42, M. A. Feltham 42*). DRAWN (Northants 6:4/2, Surrey 6:3/3).
Fc debut M. N. Bowen (Northants). Fordham 311 mins, 28x4, 2x6. Bicknell (played on) 12x4, 1x6. No play 3rd day. Surrey target 244 in min 56 overs; were 51 for 4.

HOVE: SOMERSET 264 (113.1 overs) (R. J. Bartlett 41, G. D. Rose 65, A. G. Robson 4 for 37) and 253 for 5 (A. N. Hayhurst 55, R. J. Bartlett 72); SUSSEX 346 (116.3 overs) (D. M. Smith 47, A. P. Wells 61, F. D. Stephenson 133, I. D. K. Salisbury 42, N. A. Mallender 5 for 86). DRAWN (Sussex 6:3/3, Som 6:3/3).
Fc debut A. C. Cottam (Som). Rose 7x4, 1x6. BB Robson. Sx were 128 for 7, then Stephenson (1st 100 for Sx; HS in UK; 250 mins, 17x4) 105 for 8th wkt with A. C. S. Pigott (27), 102 for 9th with Salisbury. No play 3rd day. C. J. Tavaré (Som capt) absent 4th day (wife ill).

EDGBASTON: WARWICKSHIRE 235 (92.2 overs) (A. J. Moles 50, J. D. Ratcliffe 50, D. E. Malcolm 4 for 83) and 178 for 1 (A. J. Moles 86*, J. D. Ratcliffe 45); DERBYSHIRE 85 (31.2 overs) (A. A. Donald 4 for 22, T. A. Munton 5 for 44) and 327 (K. J. Barnett 57, J. E. Morris 69, D. G. Cork 72*, P. A. Smith 6 for 91). WARWICKSHIRE WON BY 9 WICKETS (Warwicks 22:2/4, Derbys 4:0/4).
1st inns Derbys were 9 for 5 (21 for 5 at 1st-day close), then 48 for 8, before No. 10 D. E. Malcolm top-scored with 26 (4x4, 1x6). No play 3rd day. Derbys 2nd inns No. 11 O. H. Mortensen (0) batted one-handed (disloc finger), adding 8 with Cork (HS) before run out; BB Smith. T. J. G. O'Gorman (Derbys) 'pair', bowled by Donald in both inns. Warwicks target 178 in 48 overs, reached with 9 to spare; Moles/Ratcliffe 120 for 1st wkt.

May 14, 15, 16
CHELMSFORD: KENT 166 (53.2 overs) (C. L. Hooper 46, M. C. Ilott 4 for 56) and 274 (M. R. Benson 53, N. R. Taylor 42 ret hurt, C. L. Hooper 74, G. R. Cowdrey 82*, J. H. Childs 5 for 69); ESSEX 526 (141 overs) (G. A. Gooch 43, M. E. Waugh 120, N. Hussain 77, N. Shahid 132, M. A. Garnham 43, D. R. Pringle 80, R. M. Ellison 6 for 95). ESSEX WON BY AN INNINGS AND 86 RUNS (Essex 24:4/4, Kent 3:1/2).
Pringle 17–7–33–3 1st inns, inc 500th wkt for Essex. Waugh (100 inc 13x4)/Hussain 142 for 3rd wkt. Ellison 3 for 0 in 16 balls. Shahid (HS; 238 balls, 17x4, 1x6)/Pringle 152 for 7th wkt, during which both warned (& later reported) by umpire D. O. Oslear, for running down centre of pitch. Taylor ret hurt after hit on left thumb by Ilott. Essex won with over a day to spare.

CARDIFF: GLAMORGAN 224 (71.5 overs) (H. Morris 46, M.P. Maynard 88)

and 193 (P. A. Cottey 112*, S. J. E. Brown 5 for 66); DURHAM 521 for 9 dec (166.5 overs) (W. Larkins 143, D. M. Jones 94, P. W. G. Parker 124, I. T. Botham 40, P. W. Henderson 45, R. D. B. Croft 5 for 105). DURHAM WON BY AN INNINGS AND 104 RUNS (Durham 24:4/4, Glam 3:2/1).
Fc debut P. W. Henderson (Durham; aged 17); wkts of Test players Morris, Maynard (10x4) & I. V. A. Richards (1) in 1st-inns 17–4–61–3. Larkins (50th fc 100, 1st for Durham; 24x4)/Jones (HS for Durham) 206 for 2nd wkt. Parker (HS for Durham) 3rd fc 100 of season. Botham 30 balls, 7x4. Cottey 265 mins, 12x4. Durham completed their 1st BAC win with over a day to spare.

LEICESTER: LANCASHIRE 485 (129.3 overs) (N. J. Speak 232, N. H. Fairbrother 65, G. D. Lloyd 56, D. J. Millns 4 for 123); LEICESTERSHIRE 258 (86.1 overs) (T. J. Boon 139, A. A. Barnett 5 for 78) and 182 (W. K. M. Benjamin 72). LANCASHIRE WON BY AN INNINGS AND 45 RUNS (Lancs 24:4/4, Leics 4:3/1).
G. D. Mendis (Lancs) finger broken by Millns delivery during inns of 31 (out 6 weeks). Speak (his 1st 200, and 1st of 1992 season) 251 balls, 38x4, 2x6; 160 for 3rd wkt with Fairbrother, 139 for 4th with Lloyd. BB Barnett. D. K. Morrison (Lancs) 2 consec accidental beamers to Leics capt N. E. Briers; 2nd called no-ball. 2nd inns Leics were 84 for 8, then Benjamin 52 balls, 5x4, 5x6 (to 50 in 23 balls); last 2 wkts added 98 in 13 overs. Lancs won with over a day to spare.

May 14, 15, 16, 17
HEADINGLEY: GLOUCESTERSHIRE 411 (149.2 overs) (G. D. Hodgson 124, A. J. Wright 51, M. W. Alleyne 88*, C. A. Walsh 51) and 142 (R. C. Russsell 48*, P. J. Hartley 5 for 48); YORKSHIRE 272 (89.3 overs) (S. R. Tendulkar 92, R. J. Blakey 66, C. A. Walsh 4 for 77) and 134 (C. A. Walsh 7 for 27). GLOUCESTERSHIRE WON BY 147 RUNS (Gloucs 23:3/4, Yorks 5:3/2).
Gloucs debut M. Davies (SLA; 1 match for Glam 1990). Hodgson (HSBAC) 17x4; 104 for 1st wkt with S. G. Hinks (31), 113 for 2nd with Wright. Walsh 3x4, 4x6. Tendulkar (11x4, 1x6) HS for Yorks. 15 wkts 3rd day. Yorks target 282, from 105 for 4 needed 177 more on 4th day, but lost last 6 wkts in 70 mins (Walsh 5 for 9 in 9 overs). Umpires G. I. Burgess/J. H. Hampshire reported pitch to TCCB as substandard.

May 14, 15, 16, 18
DERBY: DERBYSHIRE 251 (103.4 overs) (P. D. Bowler 91, J. E. Morris 55, N. V. Radford 5 for 67) and 433 for 7 dec (P. D. Bowler 112, C. J. Adams 121, S. C. Goldsmith 100*, N. V. Radford 6 for 88); WORCESTERSHIRE 470 for 9 dec (168 overs) (T. S. Curtis 228*, P. J. Newport 42). DRAWN (Derbys 4:2/2, Worcs 6:24).
Curtis 570 mins, 477 balls, 23x4; HS for Worcs v Derbys (prev 182, G. M. Turner, 1980). G. A. Hick (Worcs) ct at slip 1st ball off I. R. Bishop. R. W. Sladdin (Derbys; SLA) 62–15–148–3, inc 36 consec overs 2nd day. Bowler (100 inc 9x4)/Adams (HSBAC; 16x4, 3x6) 218 for 4th wkt. Goldsmith 1st BAC 100.

NORTHAMPTON: NORTHAMPTONSHIRE 282 (82.2 overs) (A. Fordham 88, N. A. Felton 64, A. J. Lamb 44, K. P. Evans 5 for 27) and 296 (R. J. Bailey 40, A. J. Lamb 46, D. J. Capel 52, J. P. Taylor 74*, C. C. Lewis 5 for 74); NOTTINGHAMSHIRE 342 (100.2 overs) (D. W. Randall 49, C. C. Lewis 134*) and 237 for 7 (B. C. Broad 40, P. Johnson 95, J. P. Taylor 4 for 76). NOTTINGHAMSHIRE WON BY 3 WICKETS (Notts 24:4/4, Northants 6:3/3).
Fordham 15x4. Evans (BB) 4 for 4 in 13 balls. 1st inns P. R. Pollard (Notts) ret hurt (13), finger broken by C. E. L. Ambrose delivery. Lewis (1st 100 for Notts) 275 mins, 18x4, 1x6. 2nd inns Northants were 152 for 8, then Taylor HS (prev HS 11; in 21 prev fc matches had scored total of 61 runs). Capel 3 consec 4s off R. A. Pick, hit on helmet by next delivery. M. B. Loye (Northants) 'pair' – also injured nose while fielding. Notts target 237; completed 1st win at Northampton since 1966 after 90 mins 4th day. Johnson 14x4.*

May 19, 20, 21, 22
SOUTHAMPTON: HAMPSHIRE 552 for 9 dec (164.5 overs) (V. P. Terry 131, T. C. Middleton 221, N. M. Kendrick 6 for 164) and 2 for 0; SURREY 184 (60.3 overs) (D. M. Ward 45, M. D. Marshall 6 for 58) and 369 (D. J. Bicknell 71, G. P. Thorpe 50, M. P. Bicknell 88). HAMPSHIRE WON BY 10 WICKETS (Hants 24:4/4, Surrey 1:1/0).

Terry (298 mins, 262 balls, 19x4, 1x6)/Middleton (maiden 200; 3rd 100 in 4 fc inns 1992; 540 mins, 447 balls, 19x4, 1x6) 267 for 1st wkt. BB Kendrick (ct 4, inc 3 c&bs). 1st inns Ward 6 over pavilion off S. D. Udal; Terry badly disloc thumb catching J. D. Robinson (out 3–4 weeks). Hants claimed extra half-hour 3rd day, but took no further wkts. M. P. Bicknell (HS; 195 mins, 201 balls, 10x4)/Kendrick (26) 103 for 8th wkt.

LEICESTER: MIDDLESEX 467 (159.5 overs) (M. A. Roseberry 51, M. W. Gatting 86, J. E. Emburey 102, D. W. Headley 91) and 6 for 0; LEICESTERSHIRE 248 (100.3 overs) (J. D. R. Benson 122, J. E. Emburey 4 for 44) and 224 (N. E. Briers 53, J. D. R. Benson 58, V. J. Wells 50*, J. E. Emburey 4 for 45). MIDDLESEX WON BY 10 WICKETS (Middx 23:3/4, Leics 5:2/3).

Gatting 11x4. Emburey (14x4, 1x6)/Headley (HS; 10x4, 1x6) 160 for 8th wkt. Benson 273 mins, 15x4. Wells (HS for Leics) 6x4. T. J. Boon (Leics) 'pair'.

May 19, 20, 21
GLOUCESTER: WORCESTERSHIRE 270 (99.3 overs) (T. M. Moody 118, D. A. Leatherdale 56, M. Davies 4 for 75) and 145 (M. C. J. Ball 4 for 47); GLOUCESTERSHIRE 206 (79.5 overs) (C. W. J. Athey 42, R. D. Stemp 6 for 67) and 210 for 7 (R. C. Russell 72*, R. D. Stemp 5 for 79). GLOUCESTERSHIRE WON BY 3 WICKETS (Gloucs 22:2/4, Worcs 7:3/4).

T. S. Curtis lbw to 1st ball of match (C. A. Walsh) after on field throughout prev game. Worcs were 8 for 2, then Moody (15x4, 3x6)/Leatherdale (8x4) 181 for 3rd wkt. BB Davies (16–10–19–2 in 2nd inns); Stemp (5 for 16 in 47 balls: omitted from next match when R. K. Illingworth back from 1-day intls). Gloucs target 210; were 169 for 7, then Russell (10x4)/Walsh (30*, 2x4, 3x6) 41* for 8th wkt to win with over a day to spare.

May 20, 21, 22
SWANSEA: GLAMORGAN 346 for 5 dec (100 overs) (M. P. Maynard 62, I. V. A. Richards 127, P. A. Cottey 42*) and 167 for 6 dec (A. Dale 67*); WARWICKSHIRE 248 (86.4 overs) (A. J. Moles 66, N. M. K. Smith 67, R. D. B. Croft 6 for 103) and 172 (D. A. Reeve 79, R. D. B. Croft 8 for 66). GLAMORGAN WON BY 93 RUNS (Glam 24:4/4, Warwicks 4:2/2).

Richards 112th fc 100; 129 balls, 15x4, 4x6; 111 for 4th wkt with Maynard, 108 for 5th with Cottey. N. M. K. Smith 10x4, 1x6. Richards pulled hamstring while fielding, dnb 2nd inns (out 3–4 weeks). Warwicks target 26 in 72 overs; R. G. Twose (31) 4 consec 4s off Croft; Croft improved BB for 2nd time in match, taking wkts of P. A. Booth/T. A. Munton with 4th & 5th balls of last over of match to win.

CANTERBURY: KENT 480 for 7 dec (110 overs) (T. R. Ward 53, M. R. Benson 78, G. R. Cowdrey 127, S. A. Marsh 125) and 153 for 2 dec (T. R. Ward 53, N. R. Taylor 83*); YORKSHIRE 340 for 7 (110 overs) (S. A. Kellett 90, D. Byas 51, C. White 63*, P. J. Hartley 61*) and 292 for 8 (D. Byas 82, R. J. Blakey 95*). DRAWN (Kent 7:4/3, Yorks 6:4/2).

Fc debut B. Parker (Yorks). Byas capt Yorks for 1st time (M. D. Moxon inj, A. A. Metcalfe dropped). Kent were 192 for 5, then Cowdrey (16x4, 5x6; from 85–109 in 5 balls – 66444)/Marsh (HS; 17x4) 235 for 6th wkt. Byas 8x4, 1x6. White (HS)/Hartley 96* for 8th wkt. Yorks target 294 in 72 overs; Hartley run out from last ball, going for 2nd run which would have tied scores (& given Yorks 8 extra pts).

BLACKPOOL: LANCASHIRE 327 for 7 dec (99.4 overs) (N. J. Speak 61, W. K. Hegg 59, I. D. Austin 115*, M. Jean-Jacques 4 for 46) and 273 for 2 dec (M. A. Atherton 140*, S. P. Titchard 54, N. J. Speak 64); DERBYSHIRE 300 for 9 dec (93.3 overs) (P. D. Bowler 53, C. J. Adams 72, S. C. Goldsmith 60*, K. M. Krikken 44) and 301 for 5 (K. J. Barnett 44, P. D. Bowler 104, J. E. Morris 98, T. J. G. O'Gorman 42). DERBYSHIRE WON BY 5 WICKETS (Derbys 23:4/3, Lancs 8:4/4).
BAC debut R. C. Irani (Lancs). Lancs were 139 for 5, then Hegg/Austin (HS) 178 for 6th wkt in 48 overs. Adams 11x4. 1st inns Derbys were 257 for 9, then Goldsmith/ O. H. Mortensen (13) 43* for 10th wkt to earn 4th batting pt. Derbys target 301 in 69 overs; Bowler/Morris (out 1st ball 1st inns; 94 balls, 11x4, 4x6) 149 for 2nd wkt in 31 overs; won with 11 balls to spare.*

TRENT BRIDGE: SUSSEX 365 (107.2 overs) (N. J. Lenham 60, M. P. Speight 166, J. A. Afford 4 for 117) and 208 for 8 dec (M. P. Speight 41, J. A. Afford 6 for 68); NOTTINGHAMSHIRE 249 (78.4 overs) (M. A. Crawley 43, B. N. French 46, K. P. Evans 50, I. D. K. Salisbury 5 for 69) and 294 for 8 (M. A. Crawley 76, K. Saxelby 54, P. Johnson 42, I. D. K. Salisbury 4 for 122). DRAWN (Notts 5:2/3, Sussex 8:4/4).
1st inns Sussex were 186 for 6, then Speight (HS; 230 balls, 23x4, 2x6)/B. T. P. Donelan (33) 145 for 7th wkt. BB Afford. Notts target 325 in 80 overs.

TAUNTON: ESSEX 259 (70.1 overs) (J. P. Stephenson 113*, N. Hussain 43, A. P. van Troost 6 for 48) and 314 for 2 dec (P. J. Prichard 55, J. P. Stephenson 159*, N. V. Knight 47); SOMERSET 275 (95.2 overs) M. N. Lathwell 76, R. J. Harden 72, R. J. Bartlett 46, M. C. Ilott 4 for 76) and 302 for 6 (A. N. Hayhurst 43, M. N. Lathwell 79, R. J. Harden 68, J. H. Childs 4 for 91). SOMERSET WON BY 4 WICKETS (Som 23:3/4, Essex 7:3/4).
Stephenson on field entire match; carried bat 1st inns (11x4, 4x6); 205 balls, 21x4, 2x6 2nd. BB van Troost (5 for 17 in 39 balls). Lathwell 15x4, 1x6 1st inns, 14x4, 1x6 in 2nd-inns HS, inc 4x4 in A. G. J. Fraser over. 1st inns M. E. Waugh (Essex) warned after beamer to No. 11 van Troost. Som target 299 in 77 overs; reached with 26 balls to spare with R. P. Snell (16) 6 off Childs; Ilott (groin inj) unable to complete 3rd over.*

May 23, 25, 26
DERBY: DERBYSHIRE 500 for 9 dec (120.3 overs) (K. J. Barnett 71, P. D. Bowler 155, J. E. Morris 120, C. C. Lewis 4 for 88); NOTTINGHAMSHIRE 347 (96 overs) (R. T. Robinson 97, P. Johnson 75, I. R. Bishop 4 for 70, D. E. Malcolm 4 for 71) and 341 for 1 (B. C. Broad 117, M. A. Crawley 160*). DRAWN (Derbys 8:4/4, Notts 5:4/1).
Lewis given 'stern warning' by Notts after arriving 50 mins late for start after delayed driving from London day after Oval 1–day intl. Barnett/Bowler (3rd BAC 100 in 6 days; 19x4, 1x6) 126 for 1st wkt, Bowler/Morris (22x4, 1x6; 103 between lunch & tea) 194 for 2nd wkt, Robinson/Johnson 161 for 3rd wkt in 30 overs. 2nd inns Broad (44th fc 100)/Crawley (HS; 1st BAC 100) 230 for 1st wkt.

STOCKTON: NORTHAMPTONSHIRE 420 for 9 dec (110 overs) (A. J. Lamb 58, M. B. Loye 46, K. M. Curran 82, D. Ripley 104, S. J. E. Brown 5 for 124) and 95 for 2; DURHAM 258 (85.3 overs) (W. Larkins 46, P. Bainbridge 92*) and 253 (D. M. Jones 157). NORTHAMPTONSHIRE WON BY 8 WICKETS (Northants 24:4/4, Durham 5:3/2).
HS Loye. Curran/Ripley 161 for 7th wkt. Bainbridge (HS for Durham)/Brown (19) 61 for 10th wkt. Following on, Durham were 112 for 7, then Jones (1st 100 for Durham; 338 mins, 271 balls) 41 for 8th wkt with D. A. Graveney (5), 87 for 9th with S. P. Hughes (20). Northants target 92 in 9 overs; R. J. Bailey (8) 4 off I. T. Botham's last ball of match to win.*

GLOUCESTER: SOMERSET 257 (103.4 overs) A. N. Hayhurst 97, C. J. Tavaré 74, C. A. Walsh 5 for 55 and 140 (R. J. Harden 56, C. A. Walsh 5 for 30); GLOUCESTERSHIRE 177 (64.5 overs) (R. C. Russell 58*, H. R. J. Trump 7 for 52) and 203 (S. G. Hinks 60, R. C. Russell 41, H. R. J. Trump 7 for 52). SOMERSET WON BY 17 RUNS (Som 22:2/4, Gloucs 5:1/4).
Hayhurst (15x4)/Tavaré 131 for 3rd wkt. 1st inns Gloucs were 88 for 9, then Russell/ A. M. Smith (34; HS) 89 for 10th wkt. M. N. Lathwell (Som) 'pair'. Gloucs target 221; Hinks (HS for Gloucs) 7x4. BB Trump; best match figs of season to date; hat-trick (Russell, M. C. J. Ball, Walsh).

OLD TRAFFORD: HAMPSHIRE 349 for 5 dec (101 overs) (T. C. Middleton 73, K. D. James 98, D. I. Gower 74) and 316 for 4 dec (T. C. Middleton 138*, D. I. Gower 71, M. C. J. Nicholas 45); LANCASHIRE 322 for 6 dec (73.5 overs) (S. P. Titchard 47, N. J. Speak 58, G. D. Lloyd 102*, W. K. Hegg 80, K. J. Shine 5 for 58) and 171 (M. A. Atherton 52, S. P. Titchard 73, K. J. Shine 8 for 47). HAMPSHIRE WON BY 172 RUNS (Hants 22:4/2, Lancs 6:4/2).
Middleton (4x4)/James 164 for 1st wkt. Atherton ret hurt after hit on wrist by Shine's 1st ball of 1st inns; resumed later & scored 13. Lloyd (14x4)/Hegg 169 for 6th wkt in 132 mins. Lancs target 344 in min 62 overs; Atherton/Titchard (11x4, 1x6) 132 for 1st wkt; Shine (BB; best inns analysis of season to date) 8 for 13 in 38 balls, inc hat-trick (Lloyd, Hegg, I. D. Austin) & 4 wkts in 5 balls (hat-trick + P. J. Martin 2nd ball); Lancs lost all 10 wkts for 39 in 90 mins after tea; Hants won with 8.5 overs to spare. M. Watkinson (Lancs) 'pair'.

LORD'S: MIDDLESEX 486 for 7 dec (122.1 overs) (M. A. Roseberry 63, M. R. Ramprakash 233, J. D. Carr 52, P. N. Weekes 89*); SURREY 188 (85.3 overs) (M. A. Lynch 51, N. F. Williams 4 for 31) and 227 for 9 (N. M. Kendrick 55, M. A. Lynch 42, C. W. Taylor 4 for 50). DRAWN (Middx 8:4/4, Surrey 3:1/2).
Middx were 12 for 2, then Ramprakash (maiden 200) 401 mins, 319 balls, 31x4, 2x6; 128 for 3rd wkt with Roseberry, 111 for 5th wkt with Carr, 206 for 6th wkt with Weekes (HSBAC). Kendrick (HS) batted for 68 overs after opening in follow-on; prev HS (52) also v Middx at Lord's (1990). Last-wkt pair R. E. Bryson (11*)/J. E. Benjamin (8*) survived last 13 balls of match to draw.*

HOVE: SUSSEX 335 (111.4 overs) (A. P. Wells 144, P. Moores 47, M. A. Ealham 4 for 67) and 368 for 1 dec (J. W. Hall 99, N. J. Lenham 222*); KENT 368 for 7 dec (80 overs) (M. R. Benson 45, N. R. Taylor 47, C. L. Hooper 121, G. R. Cowdrey 62) and 338 for 6 (T. R. Ward 44, M. R. Benson 45, N. R. Taylor 61, C. L. Hooper 43*). KENT WON BY 4 WICKETS (Kent 22:4/2, Surrey 7:4/3).
Wells 294 balls, 18x4. Hooper (HS for Kent) 15x4, 2x6; one 6 off I. D. K. Salisbury onto press-box roof. Cowdrey 8x4. 3rd morning Kent bowled 63 overs before lunch; Ward 34-4-90-0, Cowdrey 36-6-147-1. After lunch S. A. Marsh bowled (5-0-53-0) while M. V. Fleming kept wkt. Hall 9x4, 1x6. Lenham (maiden 200) 302 balls, 26x4, 4x6. Kent target 336; Sussex bowled only 34 overs in 150 mins before start of last 20 overs; Benson (11x4, 3x6) 100 in 82 balls, equalling Hooper's fastest 100 of season to date; Hooper 6 off Salisbury to win match with 4 balls remaining.

EDGBASTON: WARWICKSHIRE 313 for 8 dec (102 overs) (R. G. Twose 43, P. C. L. Holloway 102*, T. M. Moody 4 for 50) and 189 (D. A. Reeve 49, P. J. Newport 5 for 45); WORCESTERSHIRE 208 (70 overs) (T. S. Curtis 40, T. M. Moody 54) and 242 (T. S. Curtis 54, G. A. Hick 70, A. A. Donald 5 for 69). WARWICKSHIRE WON BY 52 RUNS (Warwicks 24:4/4, Worcs 5:2/3).
Warwicks were 119 for 6; Holloway (batting No. 8) reached maiden fc 100 with reverse-swept 4 off Hick; 98 for 9th wkt with Donald (33*). Moody BB for Warwicks. Worcs target 295 in min 80 overs. A. C. H. Seymour (38) played and missed at 1st 5 balls of Donald over, dropped at slip off 6th; Hick 13x4; all out with 11 overs remaining.*

May 29, 30, June 1
SWANSEA: LEICESTERSHIRE 246 for 6 (80.2 overs) (T. J. Boon 69, L. Potter 65, J. D. R. Benson 49) v GLAMORGAN. DRAWN (Glam 2:0/2, Leics 2:2/0).
C. S. Cowdrey BAC debut for Glam. Boon (19 in prev 5 inns) 11x4, 1x6. Potter (10x4) 50 in 175 mins. Benson 10x4. 8 balls 2nd day, no play 3rd.

SOUTHAMPTON: DURHAM 306 (94.4 overs). (W. Larkins 45, P. W. G. Parker 41, J. D. Glendenen 64, I. T. Botham 51, S. P. Hughes 40, C. A. Connor 5 for 58) and 87 for 2; HAMPSHIRE 210 (66.4 overs) (K. D. James 62, J. R. Wood 57, J. Wood 5 for 68). DRAWN (Hants 6:2/4, Durham 8:4/4).
Wood (BB) wkt of T. C. Middleton with 1st ball on BAC debut; also dismissed D. I. Gower with 6th ball of 1st over (Hants were 0 for 2). Glendenen (HSBAC; 8x4, 2x6) batted at No. 5 after scratching retina in rt eye. Botham 7x4, 1x6. Hughes HS for Durham. No play 3rd day.

OLD TRAFFORD: SOMERSET 376 for 9 dec (97.5 overs) (M. N. Lathwell 74, C. J. Tavaré 49, R. J. Bartlett 43, N. D. Burns 73*, R. P. Snell 55); LANCASHIRE 313 for 7 (75 overs) (G. Fowler 56, M. Watkinson 96, N. J. Speak 102). DRAWN (Lancs 8:4/4, Som 7:4/3).
Lathwell 77 balls, 11x4 (out for 74 out of 92). Burns/Snell (HS for Som; 8x4, 1x6) 88 for 7th wkt. P. A. J. DeFreitas (Lancs) no-balled for 2 consec bouncers at Burns. Former Lancs capt D. P. Hughes fielded as sub for part of 2nd day after injuries to Speak/P. J. Martin. Lancs were 115 for 5, then Watkinson (16x4, 1x6)/Speak (13x4, 2x6) 163 for 6th wkt in 34 overs.

NORTHAMPTON: DERBYSHIRE 180 for 0 dec (34.2 overs) (K. J. Barnett 82*, P. D. Bowler 90*) and forfeited second innings; NORTHAMPTONSHIRE forfeited first innings and 181 for 2 (N. A. Felton 58*, R. J. Bailey 72). NORTHAMPTONSHIRE WON BY 8 WICKETS (Northants 16:0/0, Derbys 1:1/0).
No play 1st day, 11 overs 2nd. Bowler's 6th consec fc 50 (eq T. S. Worthington's 1935 Derbys record). Northants target 181 in 50 overs; reached with 13.3 to spare; Felton 7x4; A. J. Lamb 23 in 12 balls, inc 4x4.*

THE OVAL: SUSSEX 300 for 6 dec (87.2 overs) (A. P. Wells 165*, J. A. North 53*, M. P. Bicknell 4 for 47); SURREY 396 for 8 dec (101.3 overs) (A. J. Stewart 140, G. P. Thorpe 53, M. A. Lynch 71). DRAWN (Surrey 6:4/2, Sussex 7:4/3.
Fc debut D. G. C. Ligertwood (Surrey wkpr). Wells (17x4, 2x6)/North 134 for 7th wkt, after M. P. Bicknell banned from bowling by ump D. O. Oslear for persistent running down pitch (D. J. Bicknell completed over). Ligertwood (28)/Stewart (100 in 97 balls) 153 for 2nd wkt. F. D. Stephenson warned for short-pitched bowling at Ligertwood after confident slip-catch appeal rejected.*

WORCESTER: WORCESTERSHIRE v GLOUCESTERSHIRE – ABANDONED.
No play 1st, 2nd or 3rd day. 1st completely-abandoned Ch'ship match at New Road since Sept 1969 (Worcs v Derbys).

June 2, 3
NORTHAMPTON: NORTHAMPTONSHIRE 117 (53.1 overs) (V. J. Wells 4 for 26) and 238 (R. J. Bailey 42, V. J. Wells 4 for 68); LEICESTERSHIRE 77 (32.3 overs) and 112 (K. M. Curran 4 for 20). NORTHAMPTONSHIRE WON BY 166 RUNS (Northants 20:0/4, Leics 4:0/4).
22 wkts 1st day; N. A. Felton (Northants; 28 in 117 mins) only player past 20 in either 1st inns. Wells BB for Leics. Bailey 151 mins. Leics target 279; all out in 24 overs, to lose with over a day to spare.

June 2, 3, 4
DARLINGTON: SOMERSET 270 (93.5 overs) (A. N. Hayhurst 76, M. N. Lathwell 53, G. D. Rose 47, S. J. E. Brown 4 for 71) and 192 for 6 dec (M. N.

Lathwell 50); DURHAM 250 for 8 dec (84.2 overs) (P. W. G. Parker 42, P. Bainbridge 45, C. W. Scott 57*) and 213 for 2 (W. Larkins 92, D. M. Jones 78). DURHAM WON BY 8 WICKETS (Durham 23:3/4, Som 6:3/3).
Fc debut M. P. Briers (Durham). J. D. Glendenen (Durham) dnb either inns after suffering breathing difficulties, apparently in reaction to medicine prescribed for leg inj. Scott (7x4) HS for Durham. Durham target 213 in 42 overs; reached with 3 overs to spare; Larkins/Jones 175 for 1st wkt in 113 mins.

CHELMSFORD: ESSEX 313 for 7 dec (98 overs) (M. E. Waugh 52, N. V. Knight 70, N. Shahid 96, S. L. Watkin 4 for 80) and 102 for 4 (J. P. Stephenson 60): GLAMORGAN 289 (83.4 overs) (S. P. James 45, M. P. Maynard 82, I. V. A. Richards 51, J. H. Childs 6 for 82). DRAWN (Essex 8:4/4, Glam 6:3/3).
Knight/Shahid (14x4) 147 for 5th wkt. No play 3rd day.

BASINGSTOKE: YORKSHIRE 210 (100.3 overs) (P. J. Hartley 46, P. J. Bakker 4 for 38) and 222 for 7; HAMPSHIRE 351 for 9 dec (119.4 overs) (K. D. James 59, D. I. Gower 155, J. D. Batty 4 for 75). DRAWN (Hants 7:3/4, Yorks 3:2/1).
Bakker spell of 4 for 5, inc S. R. Tendulkar 2nd ball for 0 (only his 2nd duck of fc career). Gower HS for Hants; 49th fc 100: 300 mins, 18x4. 5 Yorks players passed 30 2nd ins, none reached 40.

TUNBRIDGE WELLS: WORCESTERSHIRE 327 for 6 dec (117.4 overs) (T. S. Curtis 140*, D. A. Leatherdale 91, M. A. Ealham 4 for 78) and 210 for 6 dec (A. C. H. Seymour 62, T. M. Moody 100); KENT 250 for 1 dec (81.4 overs) (T. R. Ward 140*, N. R. Taylor 67*) and 190 for 3 (T. R. Ward 59, M. R. Benson 84*). DRAWN (Kent 4:3/1, Worcs 3:3/0).
Curtis (100 in 297 balls)/Leatherdale (12x4) 164 for 4th wkt. Ward (18x4)/Taylor (5x4, 3x6) 171 for 2nd wkt. 2nd inns Worcs were 0 for 1, then Seymour/Moody (11x4) 155 for 2nd wkt. Kent target 288 in 69 overs; needed 98 from 18 overs when rain ended play.*

TRENT BRIDGE: MIDDLESEX 401 for 2 dec (110 overs) (D. L. Haynes 114, M. A. Roseberry 148, J. D. Carr 47*, M. W. Gatting 65*); NOTTINGHAMSHIRE 211 (86.2 overs) (D. W. Randall 63, P. H. Edmonds 4 for 48, J. E. Emburey 4 for 55) and 53 for 0. DRAWN (Notts 2:2/0, Middx 8:4/4).
Edmonds (now 41) 1st fc match since 1987. Haynes (12x4)/Roseberry (HS; 15x4, 2x6/ 266 for 1st wkt, Carr/Gatting 120 for 3rd. No play 3rd day.*

THE OVAL: DERBYSHIRE 249 (111 overs) (P. D. Bowler 40, D. G. Cork 44, M. P. Bicknell 4 for 56) and 244 for 1 dec (K. J. Barnett 140*, T. J. G. O'Gorman 63*); SURREY 253 for 9 dec (99.1 overs) (G. P. Thorpe 70, M. A. Feltham 43*) and 69 for 3. DRAWN (Surrey 6:3/3, Derbys 6:2/4).
Fc debut A. D. Brown (Surrey). 1st inns J. Boiling (Surrey) 15–11–8–2. Thorpe 210 mins, 6x4. Feltham ret hurt after hit under eye by Cork delivery, resumed later. Surrey target 241 in 49 overs; rain ended play with 19.4 remaining; Cork 5.2–1–9–3; D. J. Bicknell ret hurt (14) after hit on rt elbow by I. R. Bishop delivery.*

HOVE: WARWICKSHIRE 340 for 5 dec (96 overs) (A. J. Moles 122, D. P. Ostler 108, D. A. Reeve 57) and 224 for 6 dec (D. A. Reeve 46); SUSSEX 315 (101.1 overs) (D. M. Smith 77, A. P. Wells 115, A. A. Donald 5 for 82) and 250 for 8 (D. M. Smith 82, J. W. Hall 54, N. M. K. Smith 4 for 101). SUSSEX WON BY 2 WICKETS (Sussex 22:4/2, Warwicks 8:4/4).
1st inns R. G. Twose (Warwicks) ret hurt (7), needed stitches in mouth after hit through faceguard by F. D. Stephenson delivery. Moles (275 mins, 13x4)/Ostler (16x4) 193 for 2nd wkt. Wells 3rd consec 100. K. J. Piper (Warwicks wkpr) damaged finger; Ostler deputised. Sussex target 250 in 49 overs; reached in semi-darkness with legbye from 5th ball of N. M. K. Smith's last over of match.*

June 5, 6, 8
CHESTERFIELD: DURHAM 241 for 3 dec (D. M. Jones 93*, P. W. G. Parker 75, P. Bainbridge 48*); DERBYSHIRE 31 for 0. DRAWN (Derbys 0, Durham 0).
No play 1st or 2nd days; 1-inns match played on 3rd day (12pts to winner; no bonus pts). Jones/Parker 137 for 3rd wkt in 21 overs. I. R. Bishop (Derbys) no-balled for 2nd bouncer in over. Derbys target 242 in min 50 overs; violent thunderstorm stopped play after 11 overs.

TUNBRIDGE WELLS: ESSEX 342 for 4 dec (95 overs) (P. J. Prichard 133, N. Hussain 75*) and forfeited second innings; KENT forfeited first innings and 343 for 6 (M. R. Benson 67, N. R. Taylor 90, C. L. Hooper 86, G. R. Cowdrey 57*). KENT WON BY 4 WICKETS (Kent 17:0/1, Essex 4:4/0).
4.2 overs 1st day. A. P. Igglesden (sore shins) off field after bowling 10 balls 2nd day. S. A. Marsh (Kent wkpr) inj leg; Benson then Cowdrey deputised. Prichard (12x4, 1x6)/Hussain 145 for 3rd wkt. Kent target 343 in 92 overs; reached with 3.2 to spare; Taylor 16x4; Hooper (9x4, 1x6)/Cowdrey 125 for 4th wkt in 20 overs.

OLD TRAFFORD: LANCASHIRE 298 (100 overs) (N. J. Speak 144, M. Watkinson 42, W. K. Hegg 41, C. A. Walsh 6 for 42) and 70 for 0 dec; GLOUCESTERSHIRE 29 for 1 dec (7 overs) and 148 for 1 (G. D. Hodgson 50, S. G. Hinks 88*). DRAWN (Lancs 3:3/0, Gloucs 4:0/4).
No play 1st day. Speak (100 inc 10x4) last out, to last ball of 100th over, trying for 4th batting pt. Gloucs target 340 in 94 overs; rain ended play after 46; Hinks HS for Gloucs; N. H. Fairbrother (Lancs captain) carried off after aggravating hamstring injury while fielding (out 2–3 weeks).

LORD'S: MIDDLESEX 102 (41.1 overs) (M. W. Gatting 45, V. J. Wells 4 for 27) and 265 for 2 dec (D. L. Haynes 94, M. A. Roseberry 102); LEICESTERSHIRE 128 for 5 dec (39 overs) (J. D. R. Benson 46, N. F. Williams 4 for 45) and 141 for 5 (B. F. Smith 67*). DRAWN (Middx 2:0/2, Leics 4:0/4).
No play 1st day. 1st inns Middx were 67 for 2, 67 for 6. Haynes (13x4)/Roseberry (12x4, 2x6; 6s in consec balls from D. J. Millns, then 3 successive 4s in his next over) 195 for 1st wkt. Leics target 240 in min 43 overs.

MIDDLESBROUGH: YORKSHIRE 317 for 7 dec (110 overs) (M. D. Moxon 117, S. A. Kellett 87); SOMERSET 167 (64 overs) (R. J. Bartlett 56, P. Carrick 6 for 58) and 57 for 0. DRAWN (Yorks 7:3/4, Som 3:1/2).
No play 1st day. Moxon (16x4, 2x6)/Kellett 203 for 1st wkt (Yorks record for any wkt at Acklam Park). All Som 1st-inns wkts fell to catches (D. Byas ct 4 at slip, S. R. Tendulkar 3 at silly mid-off).

June 12, 13
LEICESTER: SUSSEX 171 (62 overs) (P. Moores 46, D. J. Millns 4 for 35) and 103; LEICESTERSHIRE 251 (74.5 overs) (J. J. Whitaker 74, B. F. Smith 56) and 24 for 0. LEICESTERSHIRE WON BY 10 WICKETS (Leics 23:3/4, Sussex 5:1/4).
Sussex were 65 for 6 at lunch 1st day. Leics 1st inns T. J. Boon ret hurt (24) after struck fearful blow in lower abdomen by A. C. S. Pigott delivery. 18 wkts 2nd day (10 before lunch). Leics won with over a day to spare.*

June 12, 13, 15
HARTLEPOOL: ESSEX 360 (93 overs) (G. A. Gooch 113, M. E. Waugh 75, N. A. Foster 54) and 309 for 6 dec (G. A. Gooch 86, J. P. Stephenson 81, P. J. Prichard 66); DURHAM 300 for 7 dec (83.4 overs) (S. Hutton 43, D. M. Jones 57, P. W. G. Parker 55, P. Bainbridge 60, I. T. Botham 55*, J. H. Childs 4 for 85) and 179 (S. Hutton 40, N. A. Foster 4 for 49). ESSEX WON BY 190 RUNS (Essex 23:4/3, Durham 8:4/4).

Fc debut Hutton (LHB). 1st fc match at Park Drive. Gooch (21x4)/Waugh 157 for 3rd wkt. Foster 36 balls. Parker 11x4. Botham (given police escort to and from ground at tea 1st day, after news of his OBE leaked out) 8x4, 2x6. Gooch (79 balls, 12x4, 2x6)/ Stephenson 152 for 1st wkt in 24 overs. Durham target 370 in 87 overs; all out in 50.2; Bainbridge ret hurt (6*), rt forearm broken by M. C. Ilott delivery (out 5–6 weeks).

COLWYN BAY: GLAMORGAN 296 (94.2 overs) (I. V. A. Richards 68, C. P. Metson 46*, D. K. Morrison 4 for 55) and 298 for 2 dec (S. P. James 152*, H. Morris 104); LANCASHIRE 295 (99.4 overs) (M. A. Atherton 48, N. J. Speak 71, P. A. J. DeFreitas 72) and 242 for 7 (M. A. Atherton 69, G. D. Lloyd 52). DRAWN (Glam 7:3/4, Lancs 7:3/4).
W. K. Hegg (Lancs wkpr) ct 4, st 1 in 1st inns; later inj hamstring (G. Fowler kept wkt 2nd inns). Morrison (BB for Lancs) 3 wkts in 4 balls. DeFreitas 53 balls, 6x4, 6x6, inc 3 consec 6s off S. L. Watkin. James (HS; 1st BAC 100; 19x4, 2x6)/Morris 250 for 1st wkt. Lancs target 300 in 58 overs. 22x6 hit in match.

THE OVAL: SURREY 301 for 9 dec (99.1 overs) (A. J. Stewart 42, M. A. Lynch 107, N. M. Kendrick 51) and 169 for 5 dec (G. P. Thorpe 69*); WORCESTERSHIRE 195 for 7 dec (108 overs) (S. R. Lampitt 71*) and 219 for 7 (T. S. Curtis 48, G. A. Hick 73, N. M. Kendrick 4 for 60). DRAWN (Surrey 7:4/3, Worcs 5:1/4).
Lynch (15x4, inc 4x4 in R. K. Illingworth over)/Kendrick 131 for 7th wkt. Worcs were 157 for 7 after 100 overs; had been 91 for 7, then Lampitt (196 mins, 9x4, 1x6)/ Illingworth (39) 104* for 8th wkt. N. V. Radford took 500th fc wkt for Worcs (D. G. C. Ligertwood in 2nd inns). Thorpe 76 balls, 6x4, 2x6. Worcs target 276 in 68 overs.*

EDGBASTON: HAMPSHIRE 290 (104.4 overs) T. C. Middleton 124, R. A. Smith 49, P. A. Smith 5 for 63) and 182 for 3 dec (T. C. Middleton 77); WARWICKSHIRE 216 for 9 dec (97 overs) (A. J. Moles 95) and 198 for 8 (D. P. Ostler 65, R. G. Twose 51). DRAWN (Warwicks 5:2/3, Hants 7:3/4).
Middleton (5th 100 in 10 fc inns 1992; 2nd inns 8th score over 50 in 11 inns) 375 mins, 297 balls, 9x4. Moles 283 mins. A. N. Aymes (Hants wkpr) inj knee (K. D. James deputised 1st inns, R. A. Smith 2nd). Warwicks target 257 in 62 overs.

HARROGATE: DERBYSHIRE 227 (94.3 overs) (P. D. Bowler 60, D. G. Cork 47, P. Carrick 4 for 58, J. D. Batty 4 for 84) and 74 (J. D. Batty 4 for 34); YORKSHIRE 305 (118.5 overs) (M. D. Moxon 64, S. R. Tendulkar 89, C. White 53, I. R. Bishop 5 for 37). YORKSHIRE WON BY AN INNINGS AND 4 RUNS (Yorks 22:2/4, Derbys 3:1/2).
Tendulkar 212 balls. Yorks were 303 for 6, lost last 4 wkts for 2 (Bishop 4 wkts in 11 balls). R. W. Sladdin (Derbys; SLA) 45 consec overs (2 for 119). Derbys' 74 lowest total yet by fc county in 1992; Carrick 18–13–15–3; C. J. Adams batted No. 10 after straining neck in June 14 SL match.

June 16, 17, 18
BRISTOL: KENT 507 (116 overs) (C. L. Hooper 52, G. R. Cowdrey 147, M. V. Fleming 65, S. A. Marsh 86, M. A. Ealham 58, A. M. Babington 8 for 107) and 96 for 0 dec (M. A. Ealham 67*); GLOUCESTERSHIRE 263 for 6 dec (103.3 overs) (S. G. Hinks 50, A. J. Wright 128) and 272 for 9 (G. D. Hodgson 75, M. W. Alleyne 69, R. P. Davis 7 for 99). DRAWN (Gloucs 5:3/2, Kent 6:4/2).
Hooper 39 mins on 0. Cowdrey (HS; 302 mins, 255 balls, 16x4, 2x6)/Marsh 137 for 6th wkt. Ealham 1st fc 50 (improved HS in 2nd inns). BB Babington. Hinks 53 overs. Wright 13x4, 2x6. Gloucs target 341 in 102 overs; BB Davis; last pair R. C. J. Williams (11*)/A. M. Smith (4*) survived last 6 overs to draw.*

LEICESTER: LEICESTERSHIRE 450 for 7 dec (117 overs) (N. E. Briers 63, L. Potter 96, P. A. Nixon 107*, W. K. M. Benjamin 71) and 140 for 5 dec (J. D. R. Benson 47*); HAMPSHIRE 282 for 3 dec (102 overs) (V. P. Terry 99, K. D. James 67) and 294 for 9 (V. P. Terry 69, D. I. Gower 80, M. C. J. Nicholas 46*, G. J. Parsons 5 for 79). DRAWN (Leics 5:4/1, Hants 5:3/2).
Briers 50 in 163 balls; Potter 50 in 39 balls, inc 7x4, 1x6; Nixon maiden fc 100 in 157 balls; Benjamin 61 balls, 8x4, 3x6. T. C. Middleton (18, 1st inns) scored 16 in 79 balls to become (June 17) 1st player to 1000 runs in 1992 season (12 inns). Hants target 309 in 68 overs; Gower 82 balls, 11x4, 1x6.

TRENT BRIDGE: NOTTINGHAMSHIRE 199 (71.5 overs) (K. P. Evans 43) and 392 for 5 dec (P. Johnson 62, D. W. Randall 133*, C. L. Cairns 102*); LANCASHIRE 292 (107.4 overs) (P. J. Martin 80, C. L. Cairns 6 for 70) and 103 for 3. DRAWN (Notts 4:1/3, Lancs 7:3/4).
14 wkts 1st day, inc N. J. Speak (Lancs) for 23 (8 short of becoming 1st to 1000 fc runs in season). B. N. French (Notts) inj finger while batting, kept wkt for only 3 overs (Johnson deputised). Martin (8x4, 1x6) HS. Cairns BB for Notts. Randall (18x4, 1x6)/Cairns (1st 100 for Notts; 114 balls, 5x6) 203 for 6th wkt in 37 overs. Lancs target 300 in 44 overs.*

BATH: NORTHANTS 307 for 8 dec (96 overs) (K. M Curran 61, D. Ripley 107*) and 266 (A. Fordham 71, N. A. Felton 86, A. R. Caddick 4 for 56); SOMERSET 250 for 3 dec (79.2 overs) (A. N. Hayhurst 53, M. N. Lathwell 86, G. D. Rose 55*) and 147 for 3. DRAWN (Som 6:3/3, Northants 5:4/1).
Curran 7x4, 1x6. Ripley 191 mins, 184 balls, 10x4. Hayhurst/Lathwell (HS; 13x4) 133 for 1st wkt. Fordham/Felton 125 for 1st wkt. Som target 324 in 69 overs.

COVENTRY: MIDDLESEX 304 (94.3 overs) (D. L. Haynes 67, M. W. Gatting 117, R. G. Twose 6 for 63) and 299 for 2 dec (D. L. Haynes 72, M. W. Gatting 163*); WARWICKSHIRE 251 for 3 dec (77.5 overs) (A. J. Moles 55, T. A. Lloyd 84*, D. P. Ostler 49) and 126 (T. A. Lloyd 43, C. W. Taylor 4 for 50, J. E. Emburey 5 for 23). MIDDLESEX WON BY 226 RUNS (Middx 21:4/1, Warwicks 7:3/4).
Haynes/Gatting (22x4, 1x5; 50th Ch'ship 100 for Middx, 69th in all) 161 for 2nd wkt. Middx were 177 for 1, 225 for 8, then P. N. Weekes (39)/A. R. C. Fraser (33) 72 for 9th wkt; no one else into double figs. BB Twose, inc spell of 6 for 11 in 64 balls. Lloyd (15x4, 1x6)/Ostler 135 for 2nd wkt in 27 overs. Gatting (2x100 in match for 1st time; 150 mins, 169 balls, 18x4, 6x6)/M. R. Ramprakash (33) 155* for 3rd wkt; Ramprakash (3) & Gatting (64662) 27 off P. A. Booth over. Warwicks target 353 in min 74 overs; all out in 36.3 (from 118 for 4 lost last 6 wkts in 19 balls).*

WORCESTER: WORCESTERSHIRE 407 for 5 dec (122.1 overs) (T. S. Curtis 124, G. R. Haynes 66, D. A. Leatherdale 66, S. R. Lampitt 66, S. J. Rhodes 46*) and 83 for 2 (T. S. Curtis 43*); GLAMORGAN 150 (45 overs) (P. J. Newport 4 for 34) and 339 (H. Morris 123, S. L. Watkin 41, R. D. B. Croft 40*, P. J. Newport 5 for 101). WORCESTERSHIRE WON BY 8 WICKETS (Worcs 24:4/4, Glam 2:1/1).
Curtis 356 mins, 289 balls, 13x4; in 2nd inns became 2nd player (after T. C. Middleton of Hants) to pass 1000 runs in season. Haynes (maiden fc 50) & Leatherdale both 118 balls, 11x4. T. M. Moody (Worcs) ret hurt (12) after turning ankle while running. HS Watkin.*

HEADINGLEY: ESSEX 223 (85.3 overs) (M. E. Waugh 46, N. Hussain 47, M. A. Robinson 5 for 48) and 83 (M. A. Robinson 4 for 20); YORKSHIRE 361 (114.4 overs) (D. Byas 55, S. R. Tendulkar 93, C. White 69, J. D. Batty 49). YORKSHIRE WON BY AN INNINGS AND 55 RUNS (Yorks 23:3/4, Essex 5:2/3).

Hussain back after 2-match suspension for dressing-room incident. White (HS)/Batty (HSBAC) 92 for 9th wkt. Tendulkar HS for Yorks (4th score over 85). 2nd inns Essex were 40 for 8, then M. C. Ilott (22)/S. J. W. Andrew (14*) 41 for 9th wkt. Yorks 2nd consec inns victory (1st instance since 1974).

June 19, 20, 22
BRISTOL: WARWICKSHIRE 253 (84.3 overs) (D. P. Ostler 83, T. L. Penney 55) and 205 for 9 dec (D. A. Reeve 72, C. A. Walsh 4 for 60); GLOUCESTERSHIRE 199 (79 overs) (C. W. J. Athey 43, M. W. Alleyne 55, R. J. Scott 50, A. A. Donald 5 for 44) and 184 (A. M. Smith 51*, T. A. Munton 4 for 60). WARWICKSHIRE WON BY 75 RUNS (Warwicks 23:3/4, Gloucs 5:1/4).
BAC debut Penney. Ostler 12x4. M. Davies (Gloucs; SLA) 37 consec overs 1st inns (3 for 102). Gloucs target 260 in 72 overs; were 123 for 9, then Smith (maiden fc 50)/ A. M. Babington (9; out with 9 overs left) 61 for 10th wkt.

BOURNEMOUTH: HAMPSHIRE 300 for 8 dec (98.3 overs) (D. I. Gower 41, M. C. J. Nicholas 81) and 80 (M. C. Ilott 4 for 19); ESSEX 149 (56.1 overs) (N. Hussain 63) and 310 (N. Shahid 48, M. A. Garnham 60*, D. R. Pringle 51). ESSEX WON BY 79 RUNS (Essex 19:0/3, Hants 8:4/4).
Gower 9x4. Nicholas 14x4. R. J. Parks (wkpr) made 689th dismissal for Hants (J. P. Stephenson, 1st inns), to break county rec of N. T. McCorkell (1932–51). Following on, Essex were 164 for 7 (only 13 ahead), then Garnham (9x4)/Pringle (11 overs on 0*; 9x4) 107 for 8th wkt. Hants target 160 in 31 overs; all out in 27.5.

OLD TRAFFORD: LANCASHIRE 456 for 3 dec (133 overs) (M. A. Atherton 135, N. J. Speak 111, G. D. Lloyd 103*, S. P. Titchard 68*) and 190 for 2 dec (M. A. Atherton 43, N. J. Speak 74*); MIDDLESEX 306 for 3 dec (84 overs) (M. W. Gatting 126 ret hurt, M. R. Ramprakash 69) and 309 for 9 (M. R. Ramprakash 63, J. D. Carr 80, K. R. Brown 56, P. J. Martin 4 for 45). DRAWN (Lancs 5:4/1, Middx 5:4/1).
Atherton (315 mins, 17x4)/Speak (14x4) 233 for 2nd wkt. Speak 3rd to 1000 fc runs in season when 8* (all scored in Ch'ship). Lloyd/Titchard 169* for 4th wkt. Gatting (19x4) 3rd consec 100; ret hurt after hit on forehead by S. D. Fletcher delivery; 2nd inns scored 27 from No. 7, despite 8 stitches in forehead, Middx target 341 in 66 overs; last pair A. R. C. Fraser (2*)/C. W. Taylor (0*) survived M. Watkinson's last over of match to win.

TRENT BRIDGE: NORTHAMPTONSHIRE 326 for 9 dec (110 overs) (N. A. Felton 64, R. J. Bailey 54, D. Ripley 54, A. R. Roberts 62) and 272 for 5 dec (A. Fordham 119, N. A. Felton 41, R. J. Bailey 46); NOTTINGHAMSHIRE 302 for 4 dec (87 overs) (B. C. Broad 159*, R. T. Robinson 52, P. Johnson 44) and 297 for 8 (P. R. Pollard 69, R. T. Robinson 100). NOTTINGHAMSHIRE WON BY 2 WICKETS (Notts 23:4/3, Northants 4:3/1).
Fc debut W. A. Dessaur (Notts). Roberts maiden fc 50. Broad 310 mins, 264 balls, 22x4. Fordham 139 balls, 21x4. Notts target 297 in 68 overs; reached with 1 ball to spare; Robinson 100 in 97 balls.

BATH: SOMERSET 376 for 9 dec (103 overs) (A. N. Hayhurst 41, M. N. Lathwell 114, R. J. Harden 73, G. D. Rose 41) and 20 for 1; SURREY 116 (55.2 overs) (N. A. Mallender 5 for 29) and 276 (G. P. Thorpe 48, J. D. Robinson 53, M. P. Bicknell 49*). SOMERSET WON BY 9 WICKETS (Som 24:4/4, Surrey 3:0/3).
Lathwell maiden fc 100; 163 balls, 12x4; 7th 50 in 11 fc inns 1992; 1st 100 for Som in 92. Following on Surrey were 160 for 7 (still 100 behind), then Robinson (160 mins, 7x4)/M. P. Bicknell (batted for much of inns with brother D. J. as runner) 87 for 8th wkt.

HORSHAM: DURHAM 300 for 8 dec (95.4 overs) (W. Larkins 53, S. Hutton 78, P. W. G. Parker 44, C. W. Scott 48, F. D. Stephenson 4 for 65) and 190 for 3 dec (D. M. Jones 89*, M. P. Briers 62*); SUSSEX 151 for 4 dec (39.1 overs) (J. W. Hall 82*) and 340 for 6 (D. M. Smith 67, N. J. Lenham 118, M. P. Speight 49, A. P. Wells 65). SUSSEX WON BY 4 WICKETS (Sussex 20:1/3, Durham 5:4/1).
33 overs 1st day. HS Hutton. Jones/Briers (maiden fc 50) 139 for 4th wkt. Sussex target 340 in 65 overs; needed 12 from S. P. Hughes's last over, 2 from last ball, achieved by Stephenson (after 6 earlier in over). Lenham (165 balls, 19x4) batted with runner (Hall) throughout inns (twisted ankle). Wells 37 balls.*

WORCESTER: WORCESTERSHIRE 386 for 9 dec (125.1 overs) (T. S. Curtis 197, P. J. Newport 61) and 144 for 4 dec; YORKSHIRE 234 for 9 dec (91 overs) (M. D. Moxon 47, S. R. Tendulkar 42, R. J. Blakey 57, N. V. Radford 4 for 41) and 207 (S. R. Tendulkar 46, C. White 79*, P. J. Newport 4 for 69). WORCESTERSHIRE WON BY 89 RUNS (Worcs 23:3/4, Yorks 5:2/3).
Fc debut S. M. Milburn (Yorks). P. A. Neale (ex-Worcs capt) 1st fc match since July 1991. Curtis (4th BAC 100 of season)/Newport 136 for 8th wkt, Worcs record v Yorks (prev 125, B. L. D'Oliveira/N. Gifford, Hull, 1974). R. K. Illingworth (Worcs) 19–12–23–2 1st inns. Yorks target 296 in 71 overs; all out in 68; HS White.

June 26, 27
DERBY: WARWICKSHIRE 121 (46.2 overs) (I. R. Bishop 4 for 32, D. G. Cork 4 for 41) and 174 (D. A. Reeve 60, S. J. Base 5 for 35); DERBYSHIRE 343 (109 overs) (J. E. Morris 74, T. J. G. O'Gorman 75, S. C. Goldsmith 40, P. A. Smith 4 for 67). DERBYSHIRE WON BY AN INNINGS AND 48 RUNS (Derbys 24:4/4, Warwicks 3:0/2).
Warwicks were 18 for 4, 34 for 5 1st inns; 11 for 4, 28 for 5 2nd (Base 5 for 15 in 12 overs). Derbys won with over a day to spare.

ILFORD: ESSEX 510 for 2 dec (97.1 overs) (G. A. Gooch 46, P. J. Prichard 50, M. E. Waugh 219*, N. Hussain 172*); LANCASHIRE 212 (58.2 overs) (G. Fowler 45, G. D. Lloyd 61, J. H. Childs 5 for 50) and 261 (G. D. Lloyd 76, S. P. Titchard 74). ESSEX WON BY AN INNINGS AND 37 RUNS (Essex 24:4/4, Lancs 2:2/0).
Waugh (HS for Essex; 34x4, 1x6)/Hussain (24x4) county rec 347 for 3rd wkt in 64 overs (prev rec 343, P. A. Gibb/R. Horsfall, v Kent, Blackheath, 1951; Hussain now shares 3 of Essex's record stands). D. K. Morrison 10–0–83–0. 19 Lancs wkts fell 2nd day as Essex won with over a day to spare after claiming extra ½ hour. 2nd inns Lloyd (8x4, 2x6)/Titchard (9x4) 132 for 4th wkt.*

June 26, 27, 29
BRISTOL: GLOUCESTERSHIRE 352 for 9 dec (120 overs) (G. D. Hodgson 68, C. W. J. Athey 57, A. J. Wright 47, M. W. Alleyne 46, R. C. Russell 47, M. C. J. Ball 53*, J. Boiling 4 for 119) and 178 (M. W. Alleyne 49, J. Boiling 6 for 84); SURREY 300 for 5 dec (91.3 overs) (D. J. Bicknell 81, G. P. Thorpe 75, J. D. Robinson 65*) and 232 for 6 (A. J. Stewart 41, D. M. Ward 82). SURREY WON BY 4 WICKETS (Surrey 22:4/2, Gloucs 5:3/2).
Fc debut M. A. Butcher (Surrey; son of Glam capt A. R.). Hodgson 10x4. Athey 50 in 204 mins, 2x4. D. J. Bicknell 228 mins, 10x4. Alleyne 10x4. Boiling BB in inns & match. Surrey target 231 in 46 overs; reached with 5 balls to spare; Ward 8x4, 3x6.

LORD'S: MIDDLESEX 355 for 5 dec (113 overs) (D. L. Haynes 54, M. A. Roseberry 85, M. W. Gatting 90, M. R. Ramprakash 68) and 234 for 6 dec (D. L. Haynes 84, M. A. Roseberry 67); SOMERSET 270 for 7 dec (98.4 overs) (A. N. Hayhurst 97, C. J. Tavaré 53) and 144 for 5 (R. J. Harden 58, K. H. MacLeay 50). DRAWN (Middx 7:4/3, Som 4:3/1).

P. C. R. Tufnell (Middx) 1st fc match since appendix operation; 24.4–3–63–3 1st inns, 24–9–37–0 2nd. Gatting 4x4 in R. P. Snell over. J. E. Emburey (Middx; 3 for 76) became 9th bowler to 1000 wkts for Middx 1st inns (wkt of Harden). Hayhurst 256 mins. Tavaré 10x4. Som target 320 in 68 overs; 17 for 3 after 9 overs; Harden 171 mins.

LUTON: NORTHAMPTONSHIRE 499 for 5 dec (119.5 overs) (A. Fordham 137, R. J. Bailey 165, A. J. Lamb 109 ret ill); GLAMORGAN 176 (70.2 overs) (I. V. A. Richards 49, C. E. L. Ambrose 4 for 53) and 139 (A. R. Butcher 59*, D. J. Capel 4 for 41). NORTHANTS WON BY AN INNINGS AND 184 RUNS (Northants 24:4/4, Glam 1:1/0).
Fordham (2nd consec 100 inc 19x4)/Bailey 206 for 2nd wkt. Lamb 14x4, 1x6; ret ill (hay fever) at overnight score; Northants added 83 in 35 mins 2nd morning. 20 wkts 2nd day (Glam 98 for 7 in follow-on at close). 40 mins 3rd day. S. P. James & S. R. Barwick (Glam) both 'pairs'.

WORCESTER: SUSSEX 289 (95 overs) (J. W. Hall 59, F. D. Stephenson 87*, N. V. Radford 4 for 77) and 194 for 7 dec (A. P. Wells 46, P. Moores 61*); WORCESTERSHIRE 208 (85.4 overs) (W. P. C. Weston 56, G. A. Hick 40, S. J. Rhodes 51, F. D. Stephenson 4 for 78) and 195 (G. A. Hick 131, F. D. Stephenson 7 for 29). SUSSEX WON BY 80 RUNS (Sussex 23:3/4, Worcs 6:2/4).
Sussex were 180 for 7, last 3 wkts added 109. Weston maiden fc 50. Worcs target 273 in 72 overs; were 5 for 3; Hick 64th fc 100 (1st in 31 inns in all cricket in 1992 season) out of 130; 187 mins, 147 balls, 13x4, 5x6, inc 3x6 in I. D. K. Salisbury over. Stephenson BB for Sussex; scored 29 in 2nd inns to complete 'match double'.

June 27, 28 29
GATESHEAD FELL: KENT 392 (99.4 overs) (M. R. Benson 46, C. L. Hooper 87, G. R. Cowdrey 115, M. V. Fleming 49, J. Wood 4 for 92) and 235 for 6 dec (N. J. Llong 92, G. R. Cowdrey 46, N. R. Taylor 50*); DURHAM 329 for 8 dec (106.1 overs) (W. Larkins 90, S. Hutton 76, P. W. G. Parker 72*, R. P. Davis 7 for 64) and 216 for 5 (W. Larkins 41, M P. Briers 56*, G. K. Brown 48). DRAWN (Durham 8:4/4, Kent 6:4/2).
1st fc match at Gateshead. Cowdrey 100 in 201 balls, 12x4, 1x6. Fleming 65 mins, 7x4, 1x6. D. A. Graveney (Durham capt) took 900th fc wkt (S. A. Marsh 1st inns). Larkins/Hutton 169 for 1st wkt. D. M. Jones (Durham) ret hurt (6) after hit in face by M. J. McCague delivery; dnb 2nd inns. Davis (BB) 5 for 13 in 37 balls. HS Llong. Durham target 299 in 56 overs; G. K. Brown HS for Durham. 3rd day tea interval dispensed with (2 150-min sessions played) to allow Kent early departure for next day's match at Maidstone.*

June 30, July 1, 2
DERBY: GLOUCESTERSHIRE 281 (91.5 overs) (G. D. Hodgson 50, M. W. Alleyne 78*, A. M. Smith 40, A. E. Warner 4 for 52, D. G. Cork 5 for 103) and 29 for 0 dec; DERBYSHIRE forfeited first innings and 303 for 9 (P. D. Bowler 77, J. E. Morris 50, T. J. G. O'Gorman 70*). DRAWN (Derbys 4:0/4, Gloucs 3:3/0).
C. W. J. Athey (Gloucs) 39 in 53 overs. No play 2nd day. Derbys target 311 in 72 overs.

ILFORD: MIDDLESEX 273 (90.4 overs) (J. D. Carr 102, T. D. Topley 4 for 67) and 185 for 3 dec (M. A. Roseberry 70*, M. W. Gatting 69); ESSEX 204 for 8 dec (82.4 overs) (P. J. Prichard 53) and 255 for 2 (N. V. Knight 109, M. E. Waugh 94*). ESSEX WON BY 8 WICKETS (Essex 22:2/4, Middx 6: 6:3/3).
Carr 217 mins, 175 balls, 16x4. In Essex 1st inns J. J. B. Lewis (31) hit 4 from Tufnell 'misbowl' which rolled out towards midwicket. Essex target 255 in 43 overs; reached with 1 over to spare; Knight (HS)/Waugh (9x4, 2x6) 152 for 2nd wkt.*

MAIDSTONE: KENT 359 (88 overs) (M. R. Benson 131, N. R. Taylor 40, M. V. Fleming 63, C. L. Cairns 5 for 75) and 55 for 1 dec; NOTTINGHAMSHIRE 113 for 3 dec (36 overs) (R. T. Robinson 42*) and 266 (D. W. Randall 66, M. A. Crawley 102*, A. P. Igglesden 4 for 32). KENT WON BY 35 RUNS (Kent 21:4/1, Notts 4:0/4).
68 overs 1st day (Kent 311 for 5). Benson 225 mins, 16x4, 3x6; to 100 with 3x4, 1x6 in D. B. Pennett (BAC debut) over. Fleming 79 balls, 10x4, 1x6 in 63* 1st day, using borrowed kit after leaving his at Gateshead after previous match v Durham; out 1st ball next morning when own kit returned. Notts target 302 in 70 overs; Crawley 10x4; last man Pennett out with 8 balls left.

LEICESTER: WORCESTERSHIRE 232 for 9 dec (93 overs) (P. J. Newport 75*, D. J. Millns 6 for 87) and forfeited second innings; LEICESTERSHIRE forfeited first innings and 234 for 1 (T. J. Boon 97, N. E. Briers 122*). LEICESTERSHIRE WON BY 9 WICKETS (Leics 20:0/4, Worcs 2:2/0).
59.2 overs 1st day (Worcs 141 for 6). W. P. C. Weston (Worcs) ret hurt (27*), after hit on forearm by W. K. M. Benjamin delivery. No play 2nd day. Leics target 233 in 77 overs; reached with 7.4 to spare; Boon (213 balls)/Briers (100 inc 10x4) 213 for 1st wkt.

THE OVAL: NORTHAMPTONSHIRE 312 for 8 dec (95 overs) (R. J. Bailey 40, A. J. Lamb 56, D. J. Capel 103, M. P. Bicknell 6 for 107) and 102 for 6 dec (R. J. Bailey 45*); SURREY 164 for 2 dec (49 overs) (M. A. Lynch 69*) and 252 for 5 (P. D. Atkins 48, D. M. Ward 103*). SURREY WON BY 5 WICKETS (Surrey 20:1/3, Northants 4:4/0).
Lamb 9x4, 1x6. Capel 222 mins, 204 balls, 14x4. 40.3 overs 2nd day. 1st inns D. J. Bicknell (Surrey) ret hurt (14*) with back strain. Surrey target 251 in 48 overs; reached with 7 balls left; Ward (50 in 29 balls) fastest 100 of season to date in 70 balls; 70 mins, 14x4, 2x6.

ARUNDEL: HAMPSHIRE 271 for 9 dec (105 overs) (K. D. James 59) and forfeited second innings; SUSSEX forfeited first innings and 141 (R. J. Maru 4 for 8). HAMPSHIRE WON BY 130 RUNS (Hants 18:2/0, Sussex 4:0/4).
64 overs 1st day, 41 2nd. Sussex target 272 in min 76 overs; at tea 3rd day were 84 for 3; lost 7 wkts for 57 after interval; Maru 15.4–10–8–4; M. D. Marshall (Hants; 16–3–44–3) took 1500th fc wkt (D. M. Smith).

July 3, 4, 6
STOCKTON: GLOUCESTERSHIRE 259 for 4 dec (A. J. Wright 83*, R. J. Scott 51*); DURHAM 227 for 7 (W. Larkins 74, P. W. G. Parker 43, M. Davies 4 for 73). DRAWN (Durham 0, Gloucs 0).
No play 1st & 2nd days; 1-inns match played (12 pts to winner; no bonus pts). Durham target 260 in 46 overs; Larkins 101 balls, 13x4; BB Davies. R. C. J. Williams (Gloucs wkpr) ct 2, st 3 of 7 wkts to fall.

NEATH: SURREY 316 for 6 dec (85.4 overs) (G. P. Thorpe 93, D. M. Ward 138) and 232 for 5 dec (P. D. Atkins 49, G. P. Thorpe 69*); GLAMORGAN 250 for 6 dec (78 overs) (S. P. James 105, H. Morris 58) and 248 (H. Morris 59, M. P. Maynard 66, P. A. Cottey 45, M. P. Bicknell 5 for 43). SURREY WON BY 50 RUNS (Surrey 22:4/2, Glam 5:3/2).
Thorpe/Ward (159 mins, 25x4; 96 in lunch-tea session shortened by 10 mins by rain) 211 for 4th wkt in 46.4 overs. James (to 100 with 6 off J. Boiling onto roof of nearby swimming-pool)/Morris (7x4) 147 for 1st wkt. 2 wkts fell in 1st over after tea 2nd day to different bowlers: A. J. Murphy had A. Dale ct behind, 2 balls later went off with leg injury; J. D. Robinson completed over, dismissing I. V. A. Richards (0) with 1st ball. Thorpe 10x4 (2nd inns). Glam target 299 in 68 overs; Maynard 11x4; were 247 for 6, then M. P. Bicknell 4 for 0 in 11 balls, as Surrey won with 9 balls remaining.

SOUTHAMPTON: HAMPSHIRE 261 for 6 dec (82 overs) (V. P. Terry 52, T. C. Middleton 71, M. C. J. Nicholas 46) and forfeited second innings; NOTTINGHAMSHIRE forfeited first innings and 262 for 5 (R. T. Robinson 95, D. W. Randall 93). NOTTINGHAMSHIRE WON BY 5 WICKETS (Notts 18:0/2, Hants 3:3/0).
No play 1st day, 37 overs 2nd. Terry 'ct' at slip off C. L. Cairns no-ball; out 2 balls later. S. D. Udal (Hants) ret ill (0*) with stomach upset on 3rd morning. Notts target 262 in 57 overs; reached with 14 balls to spare; Robinson (142 balls, 10x4)Randall (92 balls, 14x4) 153 for 4th wkt in 25 overs).

MAIDSTONE: KENT 193 (61.3 overs) (G. R. Cowdrey 77, S. A. Marsh 42, D. K. Morrison 6 for 48) and 113 for 1 dec (T. R. Ward 55*, M. A. Ealham 54); LANCASHIRE 11 for 0 dec (5.1 overs) and 242 for 6 (G. Fowler 52, S. P. Titchard 71). DRAWN (Kent 1:1/0, Lancs 4:0/4).
32 overs 1st day; Kent were 5 for 0, 5 for 3 (lost 3 wkts in 8 balls). 34.4 overs 2nd day. Cowdrey 11x4. Morrison BB for Lancs. Kent 2nd inns lasted 9 overs; Fowler 5–0–60–1; Ealham 50 in 17 balls (6x4, 4x6), Ward 50 in 26 balls (10x4, 1x6). Lancs target 296 in 90 overs.

NORTHAMPTON: SUSSEX 251 for 8 dec (92.2 overs) (M. P. Speight 42, K. Greenfield 48); NORTHAMPTONSHIRE 0 for 0 dec (0.1 overs). DRAWN (Northants 3:0/3, Susex 3:3/0).
No play 1st day, 7.3 overs 2nd.

TAUNTON: SOMERSET 299 for 5 dec (106 overs) (R. J. Harden 166*, C. J. Tavaré 59) and forfeited second innings; DERBYSHIRE forfeited first innings and 301 for 4 (P. D. Bowler 147*, J. E. Morris 109). DERBYSHIRE WON BY 6 WICKETS (Derbys 18:0/2, Som 3:3/0).
No play 1st day. HS Harden (prev HS 134 v Derbys, 1991). Derbys target 300 in 85 overs; reached with 32.1 overs to spare; Bowler (100 inc 17x4, 1x6)/Morris (4th 100 in consec BAC inns at Taunton inc 11x4, 2x6) 259 for 2nd wkt in 44 overs.

EDGBASTON: ESSEX 275 for 7 dec (79 overs) (P. J. Prichard 74, J. J. B. Lewis 60*, N. A. Foster 53) and forfeited second innings; WARWICKSHIRE forfeited first innings and 204 for 7 (D. A. Reeve 54*, T. L. Penney 41). DRAWN (Warwicks 3:3/0, Essex 3:3/0).
No play 1st day, 35 overs 2nd. A. A. Donald's first ball of Essex inns to Prichard rolled onto stumps without dislodging bail. Warwicks target 276 in 66 overs. M. A. Garnham (Essex wkpr) ill, did not take field (M. E. Waugh/N. Shahid deputised).

SHEFFIELD: YORKSHIRE 207 for 5 dec (S. A. Kellett 41, C. White 74*); LEICESTERSHIRE 132 for 6 (P. W. Jarvis 4 for 32). DRAWN (Yorks 0, Leics 0).
No play 1st & 2nd days; 1–inns match played (12pts to winner, no bonus pts). Leics target 208 in 47 overs; were 68 for 6 (Jarvis 4 for 7 in 1st 9 overs), then V. J. Wells (29*)/P. A. Nixon (31*) 64* for 7th wkt to ensure draw.

July 14, 15, 16
SOUTHEND: GLOUCESTERSHIRE 356 for 8 dec (118.5 overs) (G. D. Hodgson 147, A. J. Wright 69, R. J. Scott 44, M. C. Ilott 5 for 79) and 230 for 4 dec (G. D. Hodgson 46, C. W. J. Athey 94); ESSEX 252 (73.1 overs) (M. E. Waugh 74, C. A. Walsh 4 for 46) and 335 for 6 (G. A. Gooch 55, P. J. Prichard 47, M. E. Waugh 125*, N. A. Foster 40). ESSEX WON BY 4 WICKETS (Essex 20:3/1, Gloucs 8:4/4).
Hodgson (HS) 368 mins, 19x4. Wright 11x4. S. G. Hinks (Gloucs) ret hurt (10*) with inj knee. Essex target 335 in 61 overs; reached with 13 balls to spare; Waugh (110 balls)/Foster 116 for 6th wkt in 16 overs.

PORTSMOUTH: HAMPSHIRE 158 (64.1 overs) (D. I. Gower 54) and 182 (D. I. Gower 48, M. C. J. Nicholas 41, I. R. Bishop 7 for 34); DERBYSHIRE 475 for 4 dec (129 overs) (P. D. Bowler 241*, T. J. G. O'Gorman 95, D. G. Cork 65*). DERBYSHIRE WON BY AN INNINGS AND 135 RUNS (Derbys 24:4/4, Hants 2:1/1).
1st inns Hants were 143 for 4; lost last 6 wkts for 15. M. D. Marshall took 1000th wkt in all cricket for Hants (J. E. Morris). HS Bowler; 387 balls, 26x4; HS of season to date; 102* between tea & close 2nd day; 259 for 3rd wkt with O'Gorman (Derbys record any wkt v Hants), 110* for 5th with Cork; HS for Derbys v Hants (prev 225, D. Smith, Chesterfield, 1935); HS in Derbys-Hants matches (prev 227, C. P. Mead, Ilkeston, 1933). BB Bishop. Hants 3rd defeat in 4 BAC matches; Derbys 1st Ch'ship win in Hants since 1958 (Bournemouth); 1st at Portsmouth since 1951; 1st inns victory over Hants since 1935 (Chesterfield).

SOUTHPORT: LEICESTERSHIRE 257 (67 overs) (T. J. Boon 76, V. J. Wells 51, D. K. Morrison 4 for 70, M. Watkinson 6 for 82) and 181 (N. E. Briers 46); LANCASHIRE 280 (96 overs) (G. Fowler 62, N. H. Fairbrother 51, D. J. Millns 4 for 65, G. J. Parsons 4 for 34) and 150 (C. J. Hawkes 4 for 18, G. J. Parsons 4 for 25). LEICESTERSHIRE WON BY 8 RUNS (Leics 23:3/4, Lancs 7:3/4).
Boon 11x4, 1x6. Wells (HS for Leics) 2x6 off Watkinson onto nearby railway line, losing both balls. 15 wkts 2nd day. Lancs target 159; were 100 for 2, 131 for 4, then lost last 6 wkts for 19. Hawkes BB in 2nd fc match (no wkts in prev match, in 1990).

UXBRIDGE: NORTHAMPTONSHIRE 369 (100.1 overs) (N. A. Felton 52, A. J. Lamb 65, K. M. Curran 82) and 163 for 5 dec (N. A. Felton 57, K. M. Curran 47*); MIDDLESEX 220 for 5 dec (58.2 overs) (D. L. Haynes 127*, M. R. Ramprakash 54) and 253 for 7 (D. L. Haynes 61, J. D. Carr 72, J. E. Emburey 50*). DRAWN (Middx 6:2/4, Northants 6:4/2).
Lamb 14x4. Haynes 232 mins, 187 balls, 17x4, 1x5, 1x6. Middx target 313 in 65 overs; K. R. Brown c&b A. R. Roberts 39 after deflection off silly point R. J. Bailey's ankle.

TRENT BRIDGE: NOTTINGHAMSHIRE 400 for 8 dec (121.4 overs) (M. A. Crawley 115, P. Johnson 58, D. W. Randall 51, C. L. Cairns 62, K. P. Evans 55*) and 176 for 2 dec (R. T. Robinson 64*, P. Johnson 51*); WORCESTERSHIRE 318 for 6 dec (92.1 overs) (G. A. Hick 213*) and 262 for 5 (W. P. C. Weston 43, D. A. Leatherdale 112, N. V. Radford 73*). WORCESTERSHIRE WON BY 5 WICKETS (Worcs 22:4/2, Notts 6:4/2).
Crawley 14x4. Johnson 10x4. Hick 318 mins, 24x4, 4x6; 67% of inns total; 148 for 6th wkt with S. J. Rhodes (36). Worcs target 259 in 64 overs; were 1 for 3 after 9 balls (T. S. Curtis, Hick, T. M. Moody all out for 0); Weston/Leatherdale (189 mins, 12x4) 116 for 4th wkt, Leatherdale/Radford (HS for Worcs; 60 balls, 6x4, 2x6) 110 for 5th wkt; Worcs won with 13 balls to spare.

GUILDFORD: SURREY 301 for 8 dec (96.1 overs) (D. J. Bicknell 44, G. P. Thorpe 52, M. A. Lynch 48, J. E. Benjamin 42) and 76; KENT 117 (42.2 overs) (M. P. Bicknell 4 for 47, J. E. Benjamin 5 for 29) and 332 (T. R. Ward 103, C. L. Hooper 131, M. P. Bicknell 4 for 62). KENT WON BY 72 RUNS (Kent 19:0/3, Surrey 8:4/4).
50th Ch'ship match at Woodbridge Road (Surrey have won 27, lost 8). D. M. Ward (Surrey) ret hurt (12*) with broken thumb; batted No. 7 2nd inns (out 2–3 weeks). Benjamin HS and eq BB. T. R. Ward 123 mins, 112 balls, 10x4, 4x6; 102 out of 116 for 1st wkt with M. R. Benson (14). Hooper (HS for Kent) 145 mins, 110 balls, 10x4, 3x6. Surrey target 149 in 43 overs; were 53 for 1, lost last 9 wkts for 23 in 21 overs; all out 40 balls left. Surrey's lowest total at Guildford (prev 77, v Derbys, 1939).

SHEFFIELD: YORKSHIRE 301 for 6 dec (125.5 overs) (S. A. Kellett 59, D. Byas 52, C. White 54*) and 62 for 0 dec; WARWICKSHIRE 88 for 0 dec (39 overs)

and 276 for 7 (R. G. Twose 66, D. A. Reeve 74). WARWICKSHIRE WON BY 3 WICKETS (Warwicks 18:0/2, Yorks 2:2/0).
White 3rd consec 50, 5th in 5 matches. 54.5 overs 2nd day. Warwicks target 276 in 91 overs; reached with 3 balls left. Reeve 3rd consec 50. P. Carrick took 1000th wkt for Yorks (Twose) on 40th birthday.

July 17, 18, 20
SOUTHEND: SUSSEX 429 for 9 dec (128.3 overs) (D. M. Smith 213, P. Moores 109, J. H. Childs 4 for 101) and 104 (P. M. Such 6 for 17); ESSEX 303 for 1 dec (66 overs) (G. A. Gooch 102, J. P. Stephenson 123*, P. J. Prichard 68*) and 231 for 2 (G. A. Gooch 108*, M. E. Waugh 85*). ESSEX WON BY 8 WICKETS (Essex 22:4/2, Sussex 4:4/0).
Smith (maiden 200; 426 mins, 362 balls, 33x4)Moores (230 mins, 187 balls, 15x4) 251 for 5th wkt. Gooch (100 in 93 balls, 20x4)Stephenson 179 for 1st wkt, Stephenson Prichard 124 for 2nd. Smith run out in both inns. 2nd inns Sussex were 76 for 2, lost last 7 wkts for 28 (Moores dnb septic toe). Essex target 231; reached before tea. BB Such (16–7–16–6). Gooch (2x100 in match for 3rd time; 15x4)Waugh (11x4, 1x6) 159* for 3rd wkt.*

CHELTENHAM: YORKSHIRE 364 (119.4 overs) (M. D. Moxon 183, S. A. Kellett 50, S. R. Tendulkar 45) and 30 for 2; GLOUCESTERSHIRE 257 (83.1 overs) (J. T. C. Vaughan 80, C. A. Walsh 44, P. J. Hartley 5 for 66). DRAWN (Gloucs 6:3/3, Yorks 8:4/4).
Moxon 414 mins, 366 balls, 23x4, 2x6; 103 for 1st wkt with Kellett, 124 for 3rd with Tendulkar. Gloucs were 45 for 5, 103 for 8; then Vaughan (HS for Gloucs)Walsh 64 for 9th wkt, VaughanM. Davies (32; HS) 90 for 10th. R. J. Blakey (Yorks wkpr) ct 5, st 1. No play 3rd day.*

PORTSMOUTH: HAMPSHIRE 338 for 9 dec (100.5 overs) (R. A. Smith 79, M. D. Marshall 70, S. L. Watkin 6 for 97) and 167 for 9 dec (R. A. Smith 56); GLAMORGAN 28 (79.1 overs) (M. P. Maynard 73, K. J. Shine 4 for 36) and 284 for 6 (S. P. James 73, H. Morris 48, D. L. Hemp 84*, S. D. Udal 4 for 89). DRAWN (Hants 8:4/4, Glam 5:2/3).
Smith 13x4, 2x6. Marshall 10x4. Maynard 9x4, 2x6. Glam target 298 in 72 overs; needed 14 more in 4.5 overs when violent thunderstorm ended play. HS Hemp.

LEICESTER: SOMERSET 327 (94.3 overs) (C. J. Tavaré 69, G. T. J. Townsend 49, G. D. Rose 59, R. P. Snell 81, D. J. Millns 5 for 64) and 108 for 6 (R. J. Harden 47 ret hurt); LEICESTERSHIRE 270 (105.4 overs) (V. J. Wells 42, P. A. Nixon 68, W. K. M. Benjamin 53). DRAWN (Leics 6:2/4, Som 7:4/3).
HS Snell (50 inc 10x4, 1x6). Leics were 89 for 6, then WellsNixon 89 for 7th wkt, BenjaminC. J. Hawkes (18) 66 for 9th wkt. 50 mins 3rd day.

UXBRIDGE: MIDDLESEX 202 (60.4 overs) (M. A. Roseberry 43, J. D. Carr 64, N. F. Williams 46*, P. J. Newport 4 for 59) and 321 (M. A. Roseberry 118, M. W. Gatting 66, K. R. Brown 50, N. V. Radford 5 for 68); WORCESTERSHIRE 346 (111.3 overs) (T. S. Curtis 40, G. A. Hick 168) and 118 for 8 (T. S. Curtis 60, P. C. R. Tufnell 4 for 24). DRAWN (Middx 6:2/4, Worcs 7:3/4).
Middx were 78 for 6, then Carr/Williams 97 for 7th wkt. Hick 362 mins, 304 balls, 15x4, 5x6; 83 for 10th wkt with R. D. Stemp (16). Roseberry 190 mins, 175 balls, 15x4. Worcs target 178 in 38 overs; were 104 for 2, 116 for 8; 9th-wkt pair S. R. Lampitt (2*)/Newport (2*) survived last 32 balls to draw.*

NORTHAMPTON: NORTHAMPTONSHIRE 345 for 8 dec (98.5 overs) (A. Fordham 122, N. A. Felton 66, D. J. Capel 59, A. A. Barnett 5 for 82) and 223 for 2 dec (A. Fordham 81, R. J. Bailey 76*); LANCASHIRE 298 (95 overs) (N. J. Speak 49, W. K. Hegg 76*) and 23 for 2. DRAWN (Northants 8:4/4, Lancs 6:3/3).

Fordham (285 mins, 13x4)/Felton 155 for 1st wkt. Hegg 5x4, 2x6. D. Ripley (Northants wkpr) absent 2nd day (influenza): Fordham deputised & ct S. P. Titchard. Lancs target 271 in 71 overs; rain stopped play after 10.1, no resumption.

TRENT BRIDGE: NOTTINGHAMSHIRE 431 for 6 dec (110 overs) (R. T. Robinson 164*, C. C. Lewis 107, C. L. Cairns 42); DURHAM 147 (59.5 overs) (M. P. Briers 53, C. L. Cairns 4 for 41) and 265 for 3 (W. Larkins 57, D. M. Jones 154*). DRAWN (Notts 8:4/4, Durham 2:0/2).
Robinson (330 mins)Lewis (15x4, 1x6) 185 for 5th wkt, Robinson/Cairns 102 for 6th. Larkins/Jones (100 in 99 balls; finger broken by Cairns delivery during inns) 169 for 2nd wkt. 23 overs 3rd day.

GUILDFORD: WARWICKSHIRE 372 for 6 dec (94 overs) (R. G. Twose 55, D. P. Ostler 192, T. L. Penney 70*) and 198 for 9 dec (J. E. Benjamin 4 for 81); SURREY 341 for 6 dec (103.3 overs) (A. J. Stewart 67, G. P. Thorpe 86, M. A. Lynch 63, A. D. Brown 56) and 131 for 7 (M. A. Feltham 50, A. A. Donald 6 for 49). DRAWN (Surrey 6:4/2, Warwicks 6:4/2).
Ostler (HS; 243 balls, 32x4, 1x6; 2nd-highest Ch'ship inns at Guildford, after C. G. Greenidge's 200* for Hants in 1977)Penney (HSBAC) 214 for 5th wkt in 45 overs. Brown maiden fc 50. 2nd inns Warwicks were 151 for 9, then T. A. Munton (7*) Donald (32*) 47* for 10th wkt. Surrey target 230 in 53 overs; were 45 for 6 (all wkts to Donald); rain stopped play with 41 balls left. N. F. Sargeant (Surrey) ret hurt (18*) after hit on jaw by Donald delivery.

July 21, 22, 23
DERBY: DERBYSHIRE 334 for 3 dec (100 overs) (J. E. Morris 82, T. J. G. O'Gorman 68*, C. J. Adams 112*) and 66 for 2 (P. D. Bowler 46); MIDDLESEX 216 for 2 dec (63 overs) (D. L. Haynes 70, M. A. Roseberry 100*). DRAWN (Derbys 4:4/0, Middx 3:2/1).
62 overs 1st day. A. M. Brown (36)/Morris (12x4) 124 for 2nd wkt. O'Gorman/ Adams (103* before lunch 2nd day) 192* for 4th wkt; both players awarded Derbys caps after inns. Haynes/Roseberry (7th fc 100 of 1992; 184 balls, 8x4) 147 for 1st wkt. 34 overs 3rd day.

CARDIFF: YORKSHIRE 348 for 8 dec (130 overs) (M. D.Moxon 103, R. J. Blakey 125*, P. W. Jarvis 45) and 102 for 2 dec (D. Byas 68*); GLAMORGAN 200 for 6 dec (90 overs) (S. P. James 80) and 219 for 9 (A. Dale 59*). DRAWN (Glam 4:2/2, Yorks 4:2/2).
Moxon 219 mins, 202 balls, 8x4, 1x6. Blakey 100 in 301 mins inc 8x4. In Glam 1st inns H. Morris ret hurt after hand badly bruised by Jarvis lifter; resumed later but out for 5. Glam target 251 in 53 overs; last pair Dale/M. Frost (0*) survived last 4 overs to draw.

CHELTENHAM: HAMPSHIRE 167 (63.3 overs) (T. C. Middleton 64, M. C. J. Nicholas 42, C. A. Walsh 6 for 33) and 274 for 8 dec (T. C. Middleton 47, R. S. M. Morris 64, J. R. Ayling 48); GLOUCESTERSHIRE 339 for 8 dec (122 overs) (G. D. Hodgson 56, R. J. Scott 41, M. W. Alleyne 86, R. C. Russell 75) and 95 for 7 (R. J. Scott 42, S. D. Udal 4 for 36). DRAWN (Gloucs 7:3/4, Hants 2:1/1).
1st inns Hants were 108 for 2, then Walsh 6 for 24 in 14 overs; Udal ret hurt (4*) after hit on forearm by Walsh delivery; resumed later but out for 4. Hodgson 211 mins. Alleyne/Russell 158 for 6th wkt. HS Morris. 2nd inns Walsh 3 for 57, match figs of 49–18–90–9. Gloucs target 103 in 9 overs; Scott 5x6; R. J. Maru 2–0–38–1.

CANTERBURY: KENT 275 (86 overs) (M. V. Fleming 47, M. A. Ealham 50, A. R. Caddick 4 for 105) and 160 for 8 dec (C. L. Hooper 48, G. R. Cowdrey 44, A. R. Caddick 6 for 52); SOMERSET 133 (50.4 overs) (N. D. Burns 42, M. J. McCague 5 for 23) and 220 (M. N. Lathwell 72, R. P. Davis 6 for 75). KENT WON BY 82 RUNS (Kent 23:3/4, Som 4:0/4).

68 overs 1st day. Fleming 37 balls, 7x4, 2x6. McCague 5 for 1 in 17 balls. 19 wkts 2nd day. Caddick BB & 1st 10w/m. Som target 303 in 90 overs; all out in 71.2; Lathwell 12x4, inc 4 consec 4s off McCague. Umpires reported pitch as unfit for fc cricket, but TCCB inspectors decided not to impose 25-pt penalty on Kent in view of preparation problems (water shortage has led to hosepipe/sprinkler ban in area for some time).

LEICESTER: DURHAM 145 (48.1 overs) (D. J. Millns 5 for 41, A. D. Mullally 4 for 39) and 116 (D. J. Millns 5 for 46, W. K. M. Benjamin 4 for 34); LEICESTERSHIRE 256 (85.2 overs) (N. E. Briers 93, J. J. Whitaker 40) and 6 for 0. LEICESTERSHIRE WON BY 10 WICKETS (Leics 23:3/4, Durham 4:0/4).
Durham without I. T. Botham (receiving OBE at Buckingham Palace 2nd day) & D. M. Jones (broken finger). Briers won toss for 9th consec time. 41 overs 1st day; Durham were 39 for 4 (Millns 4 wkts in 19 balls), 82 for 4, 86 for 7. Benjamin no-balled twice & warned after 3 consec bouncers to P. W. G. Parker, Briers 263 mins. 2nd inns Durham were 27 for 5. BB Mullally; Millns 2nd 10w/m. Leics' win took them to 2nd place in BAC table.

NORTHAMPTON: NORTHAMPTONSHIRE 344 for 9 dec (98.2 overs) (A. J. Lamb 209) and 218 for 4 dec (A. Fordham 75, A. J. Lamb 107); WARWICKSHIRE 316 for 7 dec (98.4 overs) (R. G. Twose 49, D. A . Reeve 48, T. L. Penney 100*, N. M. K. Smith 41) and 206 for 5 (A. J. Moles 66, R. G. Twose 78). DRAWN (Northants 7:4/3, Warwicks 8:4/4).
Northants were 4 for 2 after 7 balls; Lamb (337 mins, 297 balls, 20x4, 1x6; HS for Northants v Warwicks – prev 176 by R. M. Prideaux in 1972) 93 for 6th wkt with D. Ripley (18), 106 for 7th with A. R. Roberts (39). Penney 1st BAC 100 in 222 mins, 199 balls, 11x4. Lamb's 2nd 100 of match in 88 mins, 107 balls, 16x4, 2x6. Warwicks target 237 in 47 overs; Moles/Twose (4 consec 4s off R. M. Pearson) 141 for 1st wkt.

THE OVAL: SURREY 333 for 4 dec (89 overs) (D. J. Bicknell 60, P. D. Atkins 99, M. A. Lynch 97*) and 219 for 7 dec (A. D. Brown 111, M. G. Field-Buss 4 for 71); NOTTINGHAMSHIRE 201 for 2 dec (56.1 overs) (R. T. Robinson 73*, P. Johnson 107*) and 352 for 7 (P. R. Pollard 74, M. A. Crawley 95, P. Johnson 78, M. A. Feltham 4 for 118). NOTTINGHAMSHIRE WON BY 3 WICKETS (Notts 19:2/1, Surrey 4:4/0).
52 overs 1st day. Atkins eq HS BAC (also out for 99 v Lancs, Southport, 1988). Lynch 78 balls, 13x4, 1x6. Notts were 16 for 2, then Robinson/Johnson (12x4, 2x6) 185 for 3rd wkt. Brown maiden fc 100 in 79 balls; in all 119 mins, 91 balls, 11x4, 1x6. Notts target 352 in 68 overs; Pollard/Crawley 159 for 1st wkt; Johnson 63 balls; needed 25 from last 11 balls when G. W. Mike came in; he hit 3x6 in 4 balls from Feltham, then out off last ball of over; 6 needed from R. E. Bryson's last over of match; C. L. Cairns (16*) single off last ball to win.*

July 21, 22, 23
HOVE: SUSSEX 342 for 5 dec (90.1 overs) (D. M. Smith 105, J. W. Hall 140*, J. D. Fitton 4 for 81) and 302 for 3 dec (J. W. Hall 71, M. P. Speight 119*); LANCASHIRE 349 for 8 dec (90.2 overs) (J. P. Crawley 49, S. P. Titchard 54, N. J. Speak 59, G. D. Lloyd 96, J. D. Fitton 45) and 238 for 9 (J. P. Crawley 65, N. J. Speak 62, P. J. Martin 52*, E. S. H. Giddins 5 for 54). DRAWN (Sussex 7:4/3, Lancs 6:4/2).
Fc debut G. Chapple (Lancs; RHB, RFM). W. K. Hegg capt Lancs for 1st time. Smith (201 mins, 179 balls, 15x4)/Hall (HS; 100 in 280 mins inc 8x4) 172 for 1st wkt. Lloyd 13x4. 3rd morning Sussex added 238 in 110 mins agst 'friendly' bowling (Crawley 10–0–90–0); Speight fastest 100 of season to date in 56 mins, 62 balls, 12x4, 5x6; in all 71 mins, 82 balls 15x4, 5x6; 149 for 4th wkt with K. Greenfield (33*). Lancs target 296 in 71 overs. Giddins (BB) took wkt with last ball of over started by A. N. Jones, who left field after 5 balls (leg injury).*

KIDDERMINSTER: WORCESTERSHIRE 448 for 6 dec (121 overs) (T. M. Moody 178, D. B. D'Oliveira 100, G. R. Haynes 40*) and 186 for 5 dec (S. R. Lampitt 63, S. J. Rhodes 62*); ESSEX 300 for 5 dec (82.1 overs) (M. E. Waugh 138*, N. Hussain 78) and 0 for 0. DRAWN (Worcs 6:4/2, Essex 5:4/1).
Moody (25x4)/D. A. Leatherdale (36) 113 for 3rd wkt, Moody/D'Oliveira (out 1 ball after completing 1st BAC 100 for 2 yrs) 153 for 4th wkt in 39 overs. Waugh (14x4, 1x6)/Hussain (15x4) 153 for 3rd wkt in 39 overs. Essex target 335 in 54 overs; intermittent rain prevented any start, although players came onto field 3 times.

July 24, 25, 27
ABERGAVENNY: GLAMORGAN 276 (104 overs) (H. Morris 71, A. Dale 67, G. D. Rose 4 for 59) and 308 for 5 dec (H. Morris 117, M. P. Maynard 57, A. Dale 45*); SOMERSET 250 for 5 dec (90.2 overs) (A. N. Hayhurst 70, G. T. J. Townsend 46) and 293 for 8 (R. J. Harden 48, N. D. Burns 71*, G. D. Rose 50). DRAWN (Glam 5:3/2, Som 7:3/4).
R. J. Turner (CU Blue 1988–91, capt 1991; brother of former Som wkpr S. J.) BAC debut for Som. Townsend 7x4. 2nd inns Morris 196 mins, 183 balls, 21x4, 1x6. Som target 335 in 67 overs; 9th-wkt pair Burns/H. R. J. Trump (8) survived last 28 balls to draw.*

CHELTENHAM: SUSSEX 324 (88.2 overs) (D. M. Smith 61, N. J. Lenham 83, A. P. Wells 63, P. Moores 48, C. C. Remy 42, C. A. Walsh 4 for 39) and 242 for 9 dec (N. J. Lenham 52, M. C. J. Ball 5 for 101); GLOUCESTERSHIRE 221 (91.2 overs) (G. D. Hodgson 82, R. C. Russell 41, B. T. P. Donelan 6 for 77) and 346 for 6 (C. W. Athey 181, M. W. Alleyne 46, R. C. Russell 57). GLOUCESTERSHIRE WON BY 4 WICKETS (Gloucs 22:2/4, Sussex 8:4/4).
Lenham 14x4. HS Remy. Hodgson 12x4. BB Ball. Gloucs target 346 in 92 overs; Hodgson ret hurt (0) in 1st over after hit on hand by A. C. S. Pigott delivery; Athey (HS for Gloucs; 292 mins, 282 balls, 25x4)Russell 180 for 4th wkt; Alleyne 5x4, 3x6; reached target when Ball (6*) hit 4 off 1st ball of E. S. H. Giddins last over of match.*

LEICESTER: LEICESTERSHIRE 193 (70.1 overs) (T. J. Boon 58, N. A. Foster 4 for 47; M. C. Ilott 4 for 73) and 230 (T. J. Boon 52, N. E. Briers 61, J. J. Whitaker 40, S. J. W. Andrew 4 for 54); ESSEX 75 (23.4 overs) and 280 (P. J. Prichard 106, J. P. Stephenson 42, D. J. Millns 5 for 67). LEICESTERSHIRE WON BY 68 RUNS (Leics 21:1/4, Essex 4:0/4).
Briers won toss for 10th consec time in BAC. 1st inns Leics were 19 for 5, Essex 38 for 6; 20 wkts 1st day; 'wrong' balls with old-style higher seam used mistakenly in both 1st inns. Whitaker 8x4. Essex target 349 in 8 hours; Prichard/Stephenson 135 for 1st wkt. N. V. Knight broke finger fielding, batted No. 8 2nd inns (11). P. A. Nixon (Leics wkpr) ct 4 1st inns, 5 2nd.*

LORD'S: MIDDLESEX 366 (114 overs) (M. A. Roseberry 173, M. W. Gatting 90, P. J. Berry 7 for 113) and 159 for 3 dec (M. A. Roseberry 81); DURHAM 232 (104.2 overs) (P. J. Berry 76, J. E. Emburey 4 for 94, P. C. R. Tufnell 5 for 83) and 118 (P. W. G. Parker 42, J. E. Emburey 5 for 43). MIDDLESEX WON BY 175 RUNS (Middx 23:4/3, Durham 3:2/1).
Durham's 1st fc match at Lord's. D. A. Graveney capt Durham despite 2 fingers of inj bowling hand strapped together; did not bowl, batted No. 11 with runner 1st inns. Roseberry (HS; 3rd consec BAC 100, 8th of season; 16x4, 1x6)Gatting (13x4) 167 for 2nd wkt. BB Berry (took 3 for 78 2nd inns for 1st 10w/m). 1st inns Durham were 101 for 7, then Berry (maiden fc 50)S. P. Hughes (33) 89 for 8th wkt. Durham target 294 in 69 overs; all out in 42.3.

EDGBASTON: NOTTINGHAMSHIRE 415 for 7 dec (124 overs) (R. T. Robinson 189, M. Saxelby 66, G. W. Mike 61*) and 197 for 3 dec (R. T. Robinson 84, P. Johnson 107*); WARWICKSHIRE 266 for 8 dec (102.2 overs) T. A. Lloyd 47, T. L. Penney 40) and 229 (K. J. Piper 62*, A. A. Donald 41, D. B. Pennett 4

for 58). NOTTINGHAMSHIRE WON BY 117 RUNS (Notts 23:4/3, Warwicks 5:3/2).
Fc debuts R. J. Chapman (Notts; RFM), M. A. V. Bell (Warwicks; LFM). Robinson Saxelby (HSBAC) 152 for 5th wkt, Robinson/Mike (HS) 134 for 7th. B. N. French (Notts wkpr) ct 6 1st inns, 3 2nd. Johnson 100 in 66 balls; in all 53 mins, 68 balls, 15x4, 3x6; wkpr Piper removed pads & bowled (4.4–0–57–1, inc 1st fc wkt Robinson). Warwicks target 347 in 56 overs; were 77 for 7, Piper/Donald (HS for Warwicks) 87 for 9th wkt; all out with 7 balls left; BB Pennett.

WORCESTER: DERBYSHIRE 246 (91.1 overs) (P. D. Bowler 50, J. E. Morris 67, S. R. Lampitt 4 for 57, R. K. Illingworth 4 for 56) and 285 for 2 dec (P. D. Bowler 100*, C. J. Adams 140*); WORCESTERSHIRE 266 for 9 dec (101.1 overs) (T. S. Curtis 86) and 162 for 3 (T. S. Curtis 96, W. P. C. Weston 50*). DRAWN (Worcs 7:3/4, Derbys 5:3/2).
Bowler 6th BAC 100 of season in 201 mins, 213 balls, 10x4. Adams (HS; 20x4, 6x6) fastest-ever 100 for Derbys in 57 mins (65 balls), beating T. S. Worthington's 60 mins v Notts, Ilkeston, 1933. Bowler/Adams 186 for 3rd wkt agst declaration bowling (Curtis 16.4–2–72–2, T. M. Moody 2–0–35–0). Worcs target 266 in 51 overs; Curtis (passed career total of 15,000 fc runs during inns)Weston 156 for 1st wkt.*

July 31, August 1, 2
TAUNTON: SOMERSET 356 (95.2 overs) (A. N. Hayhurst 86, M. N. Lathwell 55, R. J. Harden 52, C. J. Tavaré 99, I. D. K. Salisbury 5 for 61) and 232 for 7 dec (M. N. Lathwell 45, C. J. Tavaré 55); SUSSEX 310 for 7 dec (85 overs) (A. P. Wells 103, M. P. Speight 122) and 159 for 4 (J. W. Hall 73*). DRAWN (Som 7:4/3, Sussex 8:4/4).
Salisbury 5 for 8 in 34 balls. 1st inns Lathwell 59 balls, 11x4. Wells (169 mins, 140 balls 12x4, 1x6)/Speight (182 mins 164 balls, 17x4, 2x6; from 88–100 with 2 consec 6s off H. R. J. Trump) 161 for 4th wkt in 38 overs. Sussex target 279 in 52 overs. Wells (24) run out when bowler Hayhurst deflected Hall straight-drive into stumps.

July 31, August 1, 3
DURHAM UNIVERSITY: DURHAM 189 (46.3 overs) (W. K. M. Benjamin 6 for 30) and 357 (S. Hutton 42, I. Smith 74, I. T. Botham 48, S. J. E. Brown 47*, M. P. Bicknell 5 for 120); SURREY 431 (104.2 overs) (P. D. Atkins 60, A. J. Stewart 42, A. D. Brown 175, R. E. Bryson 48) and 116 for 3 (D. J. Bicknell 49, G. P. Thorpe 60*). SURREY WON BY 7 WICKETS (Sy 24:4/4, Durham 4:1/3).
Benjamin (BB) 6 for 7 in 56 balls. Bryson 11–0–80–2. Brown (HS) 2nd consec 100 in 71 balls; in all 179 mins, 164 balls 25x4, 1x6. HS Bryson. Smith HS for Durham. 2nd inns Durham were 242 for 8 (scores level), then C. W. Scott (35)D. A. Graveney (36 in 44 overs) 45 for 9th wkt, Graveney/Brown (HS) 70 for 10th. Surrey target 116 in 39 overs; reached in 30.1.

SWANSEA: GLAMORGAN 354 for 7 dec (123.2 overs) (S. P. James 91, R. D. B. Croft 60*) and 255 for 4 dec (M. P. Maynard 113*, P. A. Cottey 65*); KENT 300 for 6 dec (56.1 overs) (T. R. Ward 85, N. R. Taylor 42, C. L. Hooper 100) and 273 (T. R. Ward 118, R. M. Ellison 41, R. D. B. Croft 6 for 112). GLAMORGAN WON BY 36 RUNS (Glam 21:3/2, Kent 6:4/2).
James 299 mins. 1st inns Ward 17x4 (50 in 50 balls inc 11x4), 2nd inns 14x4, 4x6. Hooper 100 in 75 balls; 13x4, 3x6, inc 2 consec 6s off D. J. Foster. Glam ended 2nd inns with 112 in 5 overs (S. A. Marsh 3–0–73–0, G. R. Cowdrey 2–0–39–0); Maynard 77 from 19 balls, inc 34 (5x6, 1x4) from Marsh over. Kent target 310 in 64 overs; were 180 for 8, then Ellison/R. P. Davis (34) 61 for 9th wkt; all out with 6.1 overs remaining.*

EDGBASTON: WARWICKSHIRE 433 for 7 dec (120 overs) (A. J. Moles 91, R. G. Twose 233, T. L. Penney 50*, A. D. Mullally 5 for 119); LEICESTERSHIRE

169 (71.1 overs) (L. Potter 56, T. A. Munton 5 for 46) and 140 (T. A. Munton 7 for 64). WARWICKSHIRE WON BY AN INNINGS AND 124 RUNS (Warwicks 24:4/4, Leics 1:1/0).
Twose HS: 29x4, 2x6; 1st 100 for Warwicks, maiden 200 out of 306; 1st Warwicks player to extend 1st 100 for county to 200 since R. B. Kanhai in 1968; 285 for 1st wkt with Moles (4th-highest opening stand for Warwicks). BB Mullally. In Leics 1st inns W. K. M. Benjamin ret ill (11*) with stomach upet. Munton BB in match.

HEADINGLEY: LANCASHIRE 399 for 8 dec (110 overs) (N. J. Speak 59, G. D. Lloyd 56, N. H. Fairbrother 166*, P. Carrick 4 for 129) and 182 for 3 dec (P. J. Martin 46, M. A. Atherton 53*); YORKSHIRE 300 for 3 dec (92.5 overs) (M. D. Moxon 90, S. A. Kellett 91, S. R. Tendulkar 56*) and 283 for 6 (S. A. Kellett 89, S. R. Tendulkar 48, R. J. Blakey 63). YORKSHIRE WON BY 4 WICKETS (Yorks 23:4/3, Lancs 5:4/1).
Fairbrother 219 balls, 18x4, 5x6; 20 off Carrick over; 5th 100 in Roses matches (one short of C. H. Lloyd's Lancs record 6). Moxon (14x4)Kellett 169 for 1st wkt. Yorks target 282 in 59 overs; Kellett/Blakey 121 for 4th wkt in 21 overs; reached with 8 balls remaining.

August 4, 5, 6
ILKESTON: DERBYSHIRE 268 (95.3 overs) (K. J. Barnett 47, J. E. Morris 50, F. A. Griffith 48, D. G. Cork 56, W. K. M. Benjamin 4 for 55, R. P. Gofton 4 for 81); LEICESTERSHIRE 160 (59.1 overs) (N. E. Briers 73*, F. A. Griffith 4 for 33) and 223 (T. J. Boon 45, J. D. R. Benson 42). DERBYSHIRE WON BY 139 RUNS (Derbys 23:3/4, Leics 5:1/4).
Griffith HS & BB. BB Gofton. 1st day play held up when sightscreen collapsed. Briers carried bat. Barnett/Morris (15x4, 4x6); 2nd 50 in 21 balls; to 100 with 2 consec 6s off A. D. Mullally) 180 for 2nd wkt. Leics target 363 in 91 overs; all out in 79.3.

DURHAM UNIVERSITY: DURHAM 214 (78.1 overs) (W. Larkins 67, M. A. Robinson 6 for 57) and 155 (C. W. Scott 54, P. W. Jarvis 4 for 43, M. A. Robinson 4 for 44); YORKSHIRE 108 (41.4 overs) (I. T. Botham 4 for 72, S. P. Hughes 5 for 25) and 263 for 5 (M. D. Moxon 44, P. Carrick 46, S. R. Tendulkar 100). YORKSHIRE WON BY 5 WICKETS (Yorks 20:0/4, Durham 6:2/4).
1st contest for 4-ft high Durham Light Infantry Cup, presented by regt for matches between Yorks & Durham. Robinson BB in inns and 1st 10w/m. 20 wkts 2nd day. Yorks were 86 for 2, lost last 8 wkts for 22 (Botham 4 for 7 in 22 balls; Hughes BB for Durham). 2nd inns Durham were 68 for 8, then Scott (7x4)D. A. Graveney (32*) 86 for 9th wkt. Yorks target 262. Tendulkar (16x4) 1st fc 100 for Yorks in 96 balls; from 89–100 with 11 in Botham over.

CHELMSFORD: NORTHAMPTONSHIRE 444 for 9 dec (128 overs) (A. Fordham 65, N. A. Felton 51, A. J. Lamb 83, D. J. Capel 61, C. E. L. Ambrose 49*); ESSEX 273 (101.4 overs) (P. J. Prichard 46, J. P. Stephenson 64, N. Hussain 52, N. V. Knight 69) and 158 (N. G. B. Cook 7 for 34). NORTHAMPTONSHIRE WON BY AN INNINGS AND 13 RUNS (Northants 23:4/3, Essex 5:3/2).
Northants capt Lamb rejected suggestion to play on same pitch as used for Essex v Pakistanis. Lamb (3 consec 4s off P. M. Such) 676 runs in 8 inns since dropped by England. 2nd inns Essex were 148 for 3, lost last 7 wkts for 10; Cook (BB) 6 for 2 in 41 balls.

CANTERBURY: KENT 369 (99 overs) (T. R. Ward 150, C. L. Hooper 65, G. R. Cowdrey 76*) and 242 for 7 dec (M. R. Benson 45, G. R. Cowdrey 60, S. A. Marsh 52*); MIDDLESEX 331 for 9 dec (113.3 overs) (J. D. Carr 42, J. C. Pooley 69, P. N. Weekes 46, J. E. Emburey 41) and 229 for 6 (D. L. Haynes 68, M. W. Gatting 102*). DRAWN (Kent 7:4/3, Middx 8:4/4).
Ward (249 mins, 196 balls, 28x4, 1x6)Hooper 160 for 3rd wkt; both passed 1000 runs

for season during stand. Middx target 281 in 49 overs; Gatting 6th 100 of season in 92 balls. Carr run out by M. V. Fleming in both inns.

LYTHAM: LANCASHIRE 376 for 3 dec (110 overs) (J. P. Crawley 172, N. J. Speak 95, N. H. Fairbrother 66*) and 167 for 5 dec (G. D. Lloyd 59, N. M. Kendrick 4 for 46); SURREY 253 for 2 dec (81 overs) D. J. Bicknell 120*, G. P. Thorpe 66) and 204 (A. D. Brown 62, M. P. Bicknell 58*, M. Watkinson 4 for 60). LANCASHIRE WON BY 86 RUNS (Lancs 20:4/0, Surrey 3:3/0).
Crawley (HS; 345 balls, 18x4)Speak 161 for 2nd wkt, Crawley/Fairbrother 152 for 3rd. D. J. Bicknell 100 in 226 balls, 10x4, 1x6. In Surrey 1st inns P. D. Atkins (33) ct after fierce cut off A. A. Barnett delivery lodged between close fielder Crawley's legs as he leapt to avoid being hit by ball. Surrey target 291 in 66 overs; were 83 for 5, then Brown/M. P. Bicknell 89 for 6th wkt. Lancs 1st BAC victory since May 16 (Leics).

WORKSOP: GLOUCESTERSHIRE 335 (136.3 overs) (C. W. J. Athey 133, R. J. Scott 65, J. T. C. Vaughan 50, R. C. Williams 44, E. E. Hemmings 4 for 78) and 112 (E. E. Hemmings 4 for 30); NOTTINGHAMSHIRE 302 for 8 dec (75.1 overs) (B. C. Broad 41, P. Johnson 98, C. L. Cairns 107*) and 135 (M. A. Crawley 44, C. A. Walsh 5 for 33). GLOUCESTERSHIRE WON BY 10 RUNS (Gloucs 21:2/3, Notts 6:4/2).
Athey (2nd consec 100; 17x4)Scott (225 mins; 78 balls on 54) 167 for 4th wkt in 62 overs. HS Williams. Johnson/Cairns (HS for Notts; 17x4, 3x6; to 100 with 6; another 6 over canal outside ground) 141 for 6th wkt in 27 overs. 20 wkts 2nd day. K. P. Evans 12–4–13–3 in Gloucs 2nd inns. Notts target 146 in 65 overs; were 8 for 3; all out in 50.5 overs.*

TAUNTON: SOMERSET 278 (85.4 overs) (M. N. Lathwell 45, C. J. Tavaré 44, K. H. MacLeay 74) and 264 (M. N. Lathwell 71, N. D. Burns 68, P. A. Booth 4 for 29); WARWICKSHIRE 276 (94 overs) (T. A. Lloyd 50, T. L. Penney 80, P. A. Smith 40) and 260 for 9 (R. G. Twose 45, P. A. Smith 45). DRAWN (Som 7:3/4, Warwicks 6:3/3).
In Som 1st inns A. N. Hayhurst ret hurt (0) in 1st over after finger disloc by A. A. Donald delivery (batted No. 10 2nd inns); R. J. Harden ret hurt (29*) after knuckle fractured by Donald delivery (dnb 2nd inns; out 2–3 weeks); Warwicks received only 3 bowling pts as only 8 wkts taken. Donald no-balled twice & warned after 3 bouncers in over to Lathwell (94 balls, 12x4), 2nd of which (1st no-ball) saw him tread on wkt in evading ball. MacLeay HS for Som. 2nd inns Booth 4 for 5 in 21 balls. Warwicks target 267 in 60 overs; needed 11 off A. R. Caddick's last over of match; Donald out 2nd ball; last pair Booth (22*)/M. A. V. Bell (2*) survived last 4 balls to draw.*

EASTBOURNE: SUSSEX 360 (96.2 overs) (M. P. Speight 179, P. Moores 43, F. D. Stephenson 80, S. L. Watkin 4 for 92) and 192 for 8 dec (A. P. Wells 74*); GLAMORGAN 281 for 8 dec (102.4 overs) (S. P. James 42, M. P. Maynard 49, R. D. B. Croft 49, I. D. K. Salisbury 4 for 75) and 199 for 5 (H. Morris 104*, P. A. Cottey 45). DRAWN (Sussex 7:4/3, Glam 7:3/4).
Speight (HS; 257 mins, 242 balls, 25x4) Moores 137 for 5th wkt, Speight/Stephenson 137 for 6th. Umpire J. H. Harris knocked out by Maynard throw-in; taken to hospital for check-up, replaced by Sussex asst secretary Mike Charman, later by R. Palmer. Glam target 272 in 54 overs; were 75 for 4, then Morris/Cottey 104 for 5th wkt.

WORCESTER: WORCESTERSHIRE 335 for 9 dec (127 overs) (T. S. Curtis 49, W. P. C. Weston 47, S. R. Lampitt 42, P. J. Newport 60, I. J. Turner 4 for 103) and 179 for 3 dec (W. P. C. Weston 57*, G. A. Hick 63); HAMPSHIRE 261 for 8 dec (82.3 overs) (R. S. M. Morris 49, M. D. Marshall 58, J. R. Ayling 48) and 251 for 6 (V. P. Terry 113, M. C. J. Nicholas 71). DRAWN (Worcs 6:3/3, Hants 6:3/3).
Turner 1st BAC match 1992 – 4 for 81 in 41 overs 1st day. A. N. Aymes (Hants

wkpr) ct 4, st 1 1st inns. Hants were 140 for 5, then Marshall (73 balls, 8x4, 2x6) Ayling 84 for 6th wkt. HS Weston. Hants target 254 in 61 overs; Terry/Nicholas (7x4, 2x6) 126 for 5th wkt.

August 7, 8, 10
CANTERBURY: HAMPSHIRE 288 (109 overs) (T. C. Middleton 52, J. R. Wood 44, M. C. J. Nicholas 59) and 70 (M. J. McCague 8 for 26); KENT 252 for 6 dec (68.1 overs) (M. R. Benson 44, M. V. Fleming 100*) and 109 for 1 (T. R. Ward 63, M. R. Benson 40*). KENT WON BY 9 WICKETS (Kent 22:3/3, Hants 5:3/2).
M. A. Ealham, C. L. Hooper, M. J. McCague awarded Kent caps before match. Middleton 194 mins, 3x4. Nicholas 7x4. Fleming 127 balls. McCague BB, inc 3–wkt maiden; BB of season to date; Hants total lowest of season to date. Ward 71 balls, 10x4.

OLD TRAFFORD: LANCASHIRE 349 for 5 dec (111.2 overs) (N. J. Speak 71, G. D. Lloyd 101, N. H. Fairbrother 70*) and forfeited second innings; WORCESTERSHIRE forfeited first innings and 197 for 8 (D. A. Leatherdale 40). DRAWN (Lancs 4:4/0, Worcs 2:0/2).
*Speak/Lloyd (4th 100 of season) 135 for 3rd wkt. No play 2nd day. Worcs target 350 in 83 overs; 9th-wkt pair R. K. Illingworth (16 *)/C. M. Tolley (4*) survived last 8 overs to draw.*

LORD'S: GLOUCESTERSHIRE 322 for 9 dec (122 overs) (G. D. Hodgson 64, C. W. J. Athey 41, R. J. Scott 44, N. F. Williams 4 for 64) and 141 (R. C. Russell 43*, N. F. Williams 8 for 75); MIDDLESEX 251 for 8 dec (77.3 overs) (M. W. Gatting 86) and 213 for 5 (J. D. Carr 66, J. C. Pooley 56*). MIDDLESEX WON BY 5 WICKETS (Middx 21:3/2, Gloucs 6:3/3).
Gatting 4x4 in C. A. Walsh over. 2nd inns Gloucs (39 for 4 at 2nd-day close) were 94 for 9, then Russell/Walsh (22) 47 for 10th wkt. BB Williams. Middx target 213 in 68 overs; reached in 62.

NORTHAMPTON: NORTHAMPTONSHIRE 224 (79.3 overs) (N. A. Felton 103, C. S. Pickles 4 for 40) and 174 for 7 dec (A. Fordham 40); YORKSHIRE 158 (58.5 overs) (D. J. Capel 4 for 61) and 174 for 5 (S. A. Kellett 41, C. White 40). DRAWN (Northants 6:2/4, Yorks 5:1/4).
Felton 1st BAC 100 since 1990. BB Pickles. In Yorks 1st inns C. E. L. Ambrose inj knee after 2.3 overs, did not bowl again in inns. 47 overs 2nd day. Yorks were 67 for 6. Yorks target 241 in 65 overs (7 overs later lost to bad light/rain); D. Byas ret hurt (37), nose broken by Ambrose delivery.*

TRENT BRIDGE: GLAMORGAN 334 for 8 dec (106.3 overs) (S. P. James 45, D. L. Hemp 51, A. Dale 150*) and 12 for 0 dec; NOTTINGHAMSHIRE 17 for 0 dec (5 overs) and 322 (P. R. Pollard 75, M. A. Crawley 88, D. W. Randall 43, B. N. French 59, S. R. Barwick 4 for 67). GLAMORGAN WON BY 7 RUNS (Glam 20:4/0, Notts 3:0/3).
HS Dale; 233 balls, 21x4, inc 3 consec 4s off J. A. Afford; 57 for 8th wkt with S. L. Watkin (2), 63 for 9th with D. J. Foster (17*). No play 2nd day. Notts target 330 in 100 overs; French 39 balls, 9x4; needed 8 from last 3 balls of Barwicks final over of match when last man P. Johnson came in, batting one-handed after breaking left hand in SL match on Aug 9; he was lbw 1st ball.*

EDGBASTON: DURHAM 136 (54.1 overs) (I. T. Botham 44, A. A. Donald 7 for 37) and 238 for 4 (W. Larkins 77, P. Bainbridge 71*); WARWICKSHIRE 316 for 4 dec (71 overs) (A. J. Moles 51, R. G. Twose 65, T. A. Lloyd 60, D. P. Ostler 45, D. A. Reeve 44*). DRAWN (Warwicks 8:4/4, Durham 1:0/1).
Durham were 28 for 4 (1st inns). Donald BB for Warwicks. 41 overs 2nd day. Larkins 13x4 as Durham avoided 5th consec BAC defeat.

EASTBOURNE; DERBYSHIRE 248 (90.5 overs) (J. E. Morris 68) and 142 (E. S. H. Giddins 5 for 32); SUSSEX 230 (95.2 overs) (C. C. Remy 47, M. P. Speight 42) and 161 for 6 (K. Greenfield 43, F. D. Stephenson 44*). SUSSEX WON BY 4 WICKETS (Sussex 22:2/4, Derbys 6:2/4).
Morris 13th 50 of season. Remy (HS) 165 balls, 1x4. Giddins (BB) 4 for 0 in 10 balls. Sussex target 161 in 54 overs; reached with 21 balls to spare. Sussex's 1st BAC victory at Eastbourne since 1986; their 1st win in 15 matches in all competitions 1992.

August 14, 15, 17
CHESTERFIELD: DERBYSHIRE 207 (55.2 overs) (K. J. Barnett 42) and 334 for 4 (K. J. Barnett 160, J. E. Morris 55, T. J. G. O'Gorman 62*); KENT 265 (90.4 overs) (T. R. Ward 87, N. R. Taylor 71, I. R. Bishop 5 for 60). DRAWN (Derbys 6:2/4, Kent 7:3/4).
M. J. McCague (Kent) 3 wkts & 3 slip catches in Derbys 1st inns. Ward 12x4, 1x6. Barnett (22x4)/Morris 135 for 2nd wkt. 3rd day disrupted by rain (50 overs lost).

HARTLEPOOL: GLAMORGAN 396 for 6 dec (103.1 overs) (H. Morris 126, A. Dale 68, P. A. Cottey 91); DURHAM 201 (60.4 overs) (I. T. Botham 54, D. J. Foster 5 for 87) and 313 for 7 (W. Larkins 140, P. Bainbridge 56, M. P. Briers 52). DRAWN (Durham 4:2/2, Glam 8:4/4).
Morris (6th BAC 100 of season) 4x4 in Botham over. Glam's HS of season to date. J. D. Glendenen (Durham) 'pair'; 4 ducks in last 5 BAC inns. Botham 69 balls, 7x4, 2x6. Larkins (19x4, 5x6, inc 2 consec 6s off S. R. Barwick)/Bainbridge 165 for 2nd wkt.

COLCHESTER: NOTTINGHAMSHIRE 249 (97 overs) (C. L. Cairns 82*, J. P. Stephenson 6 for 54) and 130 (P. M. Such 6 for 39, J. H. Childs 4 for 59); ESSEX 416 for 6 dec (130.5 overs) (J. P. Stephenson 74, P. J. Prichard 136, J. J. B. Lewis 53*, D. R. Pringle 48). ESSEX WON BY AN INNINGS AND 37 RUNS (Essex 24:4/4, Notts 3:2/1).
A. D. Brown (Essex wkpr) 1st match since 1988 (M. A. Garnham eye injury, 2nd XI wkpr. R. J. Rollins playing for Young England); ct 3, st 1 1st inns. BB Stephenson. Stephenson (8x4, 1x6)/Prichard (4th BAC 100 of season in 192 balls) 130 for 2nd wkt. Essex won with 8.1 overs to spare, Childs taking 2 wkts in last over; Such 30–15–39–6.

BOURNEMOUTH: HAMPSHIRE 260 (107.3 overs) (K. D. James 74, R. A. Smith 62, K. M. Curran 6 for 45) and 100 (J. P. Taylor 7 for 23); NORTHAMPTONSHIRE 338 for 8 dec (98 overs) (A. J. Lamb 160, D. Ripley 57, M. D. Marshall 4 for 49) and 23 for 0. NORTHAMPTONSHIRE WON BY 10 WICKETS (Northants 24:4/2, Hants 5:2/3).
James 251 mins. 1st inns Hants were 254 for 5, lost last 5 wkts for 6; all 10 wkts fell to catches although Northants also dropped 5 chances. Curran (1st spell 8–8–0–1) BB for Northants. Lamb 211 balls, 25x4, 1x6; 160 out of 232 while at crease. 2nd inns Hants were 79 for 3, 80 for 9; lost 6 wkts for 1 (5 in 7 balls); Taylor (BB) 4 wkts in over. At end of inns C. E. L. Ambrose bowled 13-ball over inc 7 no-balls; warned for bouncers to No. 11 K. J. Shine (12), who was out twice to no-balls during over. Ripley (Northants wkpr) ct 7 in match.*

UXBRIDGE: YORKSHIRE 286 (103 overs) (S. R. Tendulkar 82, R. J. Blakey 46, P. C. R. Tufnell 4 for 92) and 194 for 4 dec (S. R. Tendulkar 77*, R. J. Blakey 43*); MIDDLESEX 250 for 6 dec (98.3 overs) (D. L. Haynes 83, P. N. Weekes 64*) and 234 for 4 (M. W. Gatting 48, M. R. Ramprakash 94, P. N. Weekes 48*). MIDDLESEX WON BY 6 WICKETS (Middx 23:3/4, Yorks 5:3/2).
Tendulkar 196 mins, 9x4, 1x6 (1st inns), 3x6 (2nd). Ramprakash 16 in 108 balls 1st inns. Middx target 231 in 46 overs; reached with 5 balls to spare.

THE OVAL: LEICESTERSHIRE 216 (91.5 overs) (T. J. Boon 48, J. J. Whitaker 46, V. J. Wells 56, N. M. Kendrick 6 for 61) and 267 for 5 dec (J. J. Whitaker 48, V. J. Wells 44, R. P. Gofton 75, L. Potter 46*); SURREY 218 (73.3 overs) (M. A. Lynch 106, A. D. Mullally 4 for 56, G. J. Parsons 6 for 70) and 193 (G. P. Thorpe 44, M. A. Lynch 58, L. Potter 4 for 73). LEICESTERSHIRE WON BY 72 RUNS (Leics 22:2/4, Surrey 6:2/4).

Play suspended after 8 balls while groundstaff put coconut matting over nearby Test pitch, where new seed was attracting large numbers of pigeons. Wells (50 inc 9x4) HS for Leics. Kendrick (BB) last 4 wkts for 4 in 19 balls. Lynch (16x4, 2x6) to 100 with 6 off Parsons (BBBAC). HS Gofton. Surrey target 266 in 51 overs; all out with 3 balls remaining; Lynch (12x4) 50 in 39 balls; Potter BB for Leics; T. J. Boon (9 wkts in prev 13 seasons) 3–3–0–2. Ashes of former Surrey president W. D. Wickson were scattered over ground before 2nd days play.

August 18, 19, 20
CHESTERFIELD: GLAMORGAN 170 (76.2 overs) (P. A. Cottey 62, D. E. Malcolm 5 for 45) and 366 (H. Morris 52, A. Dale 82, M. P. Maynard 176); DERBYSHIRE 334 for 8 dec (124.2 overs) (P. D. Bowler 67, T. J. G. O'Gorman 42, F. A. Griffith 81, I. R. Bishop 90, S. D. Thomas 5 for 80) and 22 for 2. DRAWN (Derbys 6:2/4, Glam 3:1/2).

Fc debut S. D. Thomas (Glam; RFM; aged 17). Griffith (HS)Bishop 142 for 6th wkt. Maynard 195 balls, 28x4, 1x6; batted on despite 'steel band playing in my head' after hit on helmet by Bishop delivery early in inns; HS for Glam v Derbys (prev 170, N. V. H. Riches, Swansea, 1924); 132 for 3rd wkt with Dale. Derbys target 203 in min 20 overs; lost 2 wkts in S. L. Watkin's 1st over of inns.

COLCHESTER: SURREY 292 (92.1 overs) (D. J. Bicknell 53, M. A. Lynch 102, D. R. Pringle 4 for 63, P. M. Such 4 for 22) and 10 for 0; ESSEX 229 (107 overs) (J. J. B. Lewis 66, M. A. Garnham 59, M. P. Bicknell 4 for 53) DRAWN (Essex 6:2/4, Surrey 7:3/4).

D. J. Bicknell 9x4. Lynch 18x4. Lewis (257 balls, 281 mins)Garnham (189 balls) 118 for 5th wkt in 61 overs. No play 3rd day.

BRISTOL: GLOUCESTERSHIRE 346 (109 overs) (R. J. Scott 41, T. H. C. Hancock 82, J. T. C. Vaughan 99, D. J. Capel 4 for 65) and 176 for 8 dec (C. W. J. Athey 42, M. W. Alleyne 48); NORTHAMPTONSHIRE 251 for 6 dec (81.4 overs) (N. A. Felton 43, R. J. Bailey 91) and 232 (R. J. Bailey 92). GLOUCESTERSHIRE WON BY 39 RUNS (Gloucs 22:4/2, Northants 7:3/4).

Fc debut R. J. Warren (Northants; RHB). 1st inns Gloucs were 78 for 1, 78 for 4; 113 for 6, then Hancock (11x4)Vaughan (HS for Gloucs; 176 balls, 13x4) 141 for 7th wkt. Bailey 10x4 (1st inns). Northants target 272 in 54 overs; all out with 9 balls remaining.

BOURNEMOUTH: HAMPSHIRE 386 for 9 dec (117.2 overs) (M. C. J. Nicholas 95, J. R. Ayling 57, A. N. Aymes 53, J. E. Emburey 5 for 105); MIDDLESEX 115 (51.4 overs) (J. R. Ayling 5 for 12) and 346 for 9 (D. L. Haynes 44, M. A. Roseberry 52, M. W. Gatting 93, J. D. Carr 77*, S. D. Udal 4 for 101). DRAWN (Hants 8:4/4, Middx 2:0/2).

Last fc match at Dean Park for foreseeable future. M. R. Ramprakash omitted by Middx (disciplinary measure). Nicholas 11x4, 1x6. Ayling/Aymes 111 for 7th wkt. 1st inns Middx were 91 for 4, 98 for 9; Ayling (1st 5wi) 3 for 0 in 9 balls. Gatting 11th fc score of 85+ in 1992 (6x100). Carr 284 mins, 224 balls.

LEICESTER: KENT 502 for 4 dec (120 overs) (M. R. Benson 139, T. R. Ward 41, N. R. Taylor 144, C. L. Hooper 62*, M. V. Fleming 58); LEICESTERSHIRE 181 (59 overs) (M. J. McCague 7 for 52) and 183 (T. J. Boon 72, A. P. Igglesden 5 for 41). KENT WON BY AN INNINGS AND 138 RUNS (Kent 24:4/4, Leics 1:1/0).

Leics fc debut P. E. Robinson (Yorks). Benson (369 mins, 16x4)/Taylor (23x4) 235 for 2nd wkt. Fleming 50 in 37 balls, inc 6x4, 1x6. 2nd inns Leics were 171 for 4, lost last 6 wkts for 12, last 5 for 4 in 8 balls (Igglesden 3 wkts in over, R. P. Davis 2 wkts with consec balls).

WESTON-SUPER-MARE: SOMERSET 328 (123.2 overs) (G. D. Rose 51, R. P. Snell 75, A. R. Caddick 54*, R. D. Stemp 5 for 112) and 175 for 4 dec (N. A. Folland 82*); WORCESTERSHIRE 250 for 5 dec (96 overs) (D. B. D'Oliveira 65, G. R. Haynes 64) and 130 for 2 (W. P. C. Weston 66*). DRAWN (Som 5:3/2, Worcs 7:3/4).
Folland 1st fc match for Som; 106 balls, 12x4; prev HS 82 in only other fc match (Minor Cos v Indians, Trowbridge, 1990). Snell 83 balls, 8x4, 1x6. Caddick (maiden fc 50) H. R. J. Trump (28) 80 for 10th wkt. Worcs target 254 in min 62 overs. HS Weston.

EDGBASTON: WARWICKSHIRE 203 (79.1 overs) (A. J. Moles 86, R. G. Twose 53, M. Watkinson 4 for 41) and 187 (D. P. Ostler 56, T. L. Penney 40, M. Watkinson 6 for 62); LANCASHIRE 415 for 8 dec (128.2 overs) (M. A. Atherton 130, N. J. Speak 52, J. P. Crawley 74, J. D. Fitton 48*). LANCASHIRE WON BY AN INNINGS AND 25 RUNS (Lancs 24:4/4, Warwicks 3:2/1).
Moles (250 mins)/Twose 111 for 1st wkt, then Warwicks lost all 9 wkts for 92 (P. A. Smith did not bat – stomach upset). Watkinson (1st 10w/m) 1st hat-trick (Twose/Ostler/Penney, 1st inns). Atherton 21x4. 2nd inns Warwicks capt T. A. Lloyd batted 74 mins, 73 balls for 1.

SCARBOROUGH: NOTTINGHAMSHIRE 152 (56.1 overs) (C. L. Cairns 69) and 353 for 8 (B. C. Broad 120, R. T. Robinson 63, C. L. Cairns 61); YORKSHIRE 404 for 9 dec (117.2 overs) (R. J. Blakey 112*, P. W. Jarvis 55, P. J. Hartley 69). DRAWN (Yorks 8:4/4, Notts 4:1/3).
S. R. Tendulkar's last match for Yorks (returned to India to play in Duleep Trophy). 15 wkts 1st day; Notts were 34 for 4, then G. F. Archer (27 on BAC debut)/Cairns (8x4, 3x6) 103 for 5th wkt, then last 6 wkts went down for 15; M. D. Moxon (Yorks capt) ct 4. Yorks were 125 for 5, then Blakey (272 mins, 15x4)Jarvis 88 for 6th wkt, Blakey/Hartley 135 for 8th. Broad 343 mins, 15x4, 1x6. Cairns cleared 1st-inns arrears with 6 onto pavilion roof which dislodged several tiles.

August 21, 22, 24
SWANSEA: GLOUCESTERSHIRE 272 for 8 dec (113 overs) (R. J. Scott 45, C. W. J. Athey 49, R. C. Russell 66*) and 31 for 0 dec; GLAMORGAN 3 for 0 dec (2 overs) and 32 for 0. DRAWN (Glam 2:0/2, Gloucs 2:2/0).
G. D. Hodgson (Gloucs) 33 in 52 overs 1st day. 2 overs 2nd day. Glam target 301 in min 90 overs; rain stopped play after 8.

LEICESTER: NOTTINGHAMSHIRE 168 (61.2 overs) (W. K. M. Benjamin 4 for 66, G. J. Parsons 4 for 50) and 261 for 4 dec (B. C. Broad 122, G. F. Archer 52*); LEICESTERSHIRE 252 (100 overs) (N. E. Briers 70) and 134 for 6 (N. E. Briers 66*, J. A. Afford 4 for 35). DRAWN (Leics 7:3/4, Notts 5:1/4).
P. A. Nixon (Leics wkpr) ct 5 1st inns. Broad 272 mins, 284 balls, 8x4. HS Archer. Leics target 178 in 28 overs.

NORTHAMPTON: KENT 196 (97 overs) (S. A. Marsh 65) and 141 for 1 dec (T. R. Ward 95*, N. R. Taylor 44*); NORTHAMPTONSHIRE 85 for 2 dec (32 overs) (N. A. Felton 40) and 108 for 1 (N. A. Felton 50*). DRAWN (Northants 4:0/4, Kent 1:1/0).
Marsh 193 balls, 10x4. N. G. B. Cook (Northants) 16–9–18–2 1st inns. 22 overs 2nd day. Ward 89 balls, 11x4, 1x6. Northants target 253 in 69 overs; rain stopped play after 41 overs.

WESTON-SUPER-MARE: SOMERSET 370 for 8 dec (100 overs) (A. N. Hayhurst 82, M. N. Lathwell 73, C. J. Tavaré 115, R. J. Turner 41*) and forfeited second innings; HAMPSHIRE 47 for 1 dec (18.4 overs) and 62 for 1 (D. I. Gower 42*). DRAWN (Som 4:4/0, Hants 2:0/2).
Hayhurst/Lathwell 116 for 1st wkt, Hayhurst/Tavaré (119 balls, 20x4; century between lunch & tea 1st day) 122 for 2nd wkt. Turner HS for Som. 8.3 overs 2nd day. Hants target 324 in 97 overs; rain stopped play after 19.

HOVE: MIDDLESEX 445 for 7 dec (123 overs) (D. L. Haynes 177, M. W. Gatting 73, J. D. Carr 51) 63 for 0 dec; SUSSEX 187 for 3 dec (70.4 overs) (J. W. Hall 81) and 79 for 1 (J. W. Hall 41*). DRAWN (Sussex 2:1/1, Middx 5:4/1).
Haynes (50th fc 100, 14th for Middx; 330 mins, 282 balls, 21x4)Gatting (13x4) 178 for 2nd wkt. Carr 9x4, 1x6. 1st inns Hall 210 mins, 10x4; awarded county cap after inns. Sussex target 322 in 80 overs; rain stopped play after 30.

WORCESTER: DURHAM 199 (66.3 overs) (W. Larkins 40, I. Smith 44, N. V. Radford 5 for 60) and 199 for 2 (P. W. G. Parker 94, P. Bainbridge 65*); WORCESTERSHIRE 294 for 6 dec (96.2 overs) (T. S. Curtis 50, D. B. D'Oliveira 81, G. R. Haynes 41). DRAWN (Worcs 7:3/4, Durham 3:1/2).
D'Oliveira 13x4. D. A. Graveney (Durham capt) 30–16–49–2, inc 1st spell of 15–12–5–2. Parker (20x4, inc 4x4 in R. D. Stemp over)/Bainbridge 178 for 2nd wkt.

BRADFORD: YORKSHIRE 341 (102 overs) (M. D. Moxon 44, S. A. Kellett 78, D. Byas 70, A. P. Grayson 40, N. M. Kendrick 5 for 60) and forfeited second innings; SURREY 39 for 1 dec (18 overs) and 306 for 9 (G. P. Thorpe 79, M. A. Lynch 43, M. A. Feltham 41). SURREY WON BY 1 WICKET (Surrey 19:0/3, Yorks 4:4/0).
1st fc match at Park Avenue since 1985. Byas 74 balls, 10x4. 10 overs 2nd day. Surrey target 303 in 93 overs; Thorpe 12th 50 of season (no 100s yet); were 282 for 9, needing 21 from last 40 balls; Kendrick (18)/J. Boiling (10*) 24* for last wkt to win with 2 balls remaining. Surrey were the only victors in the last-ever scheduled round of 3–day Ch'ship matches.*

August 26, 27, 28
NORTHAMPTON: MIDDLESEX 95 (48.4 overs) (J. P. Taylor 5 for 24) and 105 (J. P. Taylor 5 for 30); NORTHAMPTONSHIRE 203 (74.1 overs) (A. Fordham 91, N. F. Williams 5 for 49). NORTHAMPTONSHIRE WON BY AN INNINGS AND 3 RUNS (Northants 22:2/4, Middx 4:0/4).
63.4 overs 1st day; 11 wkts fell; M. W. Gatting out 1st ball (b Taylor). No play 2nd day. Northants were 176 for 3, lost last 7 wkts for 27 (Williams 5 for 8 in 29 balls). 2nd inns Middx were 36 for 7; HS of inns was A. R. C. Fraser's 30 from No. 10; C. E. L. Ambrose 11–6–12–1, R. J. Bailey 0.1–0–0–1. Taylor 1st 10w/m. Northants won with over a day to spare.

August 26, 27, 28, 29
DERBY: DERBYSHIRE 320 for 9 dec (72.2 overs) (K. J. Barnett 68, P. D. Bowler 66, K. M. Krikken 57*, A. R. Caddick 5 for 77) and forfeited second innings; SOMERSET forfeited first innings and 199 (R. J. Turner 55 ret hurt, K. H. MacLeay 73, D. G. Cork 4 for 61). DERBYSHIRE WON BY 121 RUNS (Derbys 20:4/0, Som 4:0/4).
No play 1st & 2nd days, 70 overs 3rd day. Barnett 4x4 in Caddick's 1st over of match; Caddick later 3 wkts in 4 balls. Barnett passed 1000 fc runs for season during inns, for 10th consec year (eq A. Hamer's county record). Som target 321 in min 96 overs; all out in 59; were 59 for 5, then Turner (HS for Som)MacLeay 120 for 6th wkt before Turner ret hurt.*

DARLINGTON: HAMPSHIRE 303 for 6 dec (97.3 overs) (T. C. Middleton

127*, J. R. Ayling 90) and 229 for 5 dec (K. D. James 57, M. C. J. Nicholas 95*); DURHAM 250 for 4 dec (79.2 overs) (P. W. G. Parker 68, P. Bainbridge 84*, I. Smith 68*) and 194 for 8 (P. Bainbridge 83, K. J. Shine 6 for 68). DRAWN (Durham 5:3/2, Hants 5:4/1).
35 overs 1st day. Middleton (100 in 272 balls)Ayling (HSBAC) 195 for 5th wkt. Durham target 283 in 59 overs; Hants capt Nicholas upset when umpires took players off in light rain inside last hour.

CANTERBURY: KENT 189 (67.3 overs) (T. R. Ward 42, C. L. Hooper 41, C. A. Walsh 5 for 50) and 383 (T. R. Ward 41, N. R. Taylor 96, C. L. Hooper 65, M. V. Fleming 67, S. A. Marsh 70, C. A. Walsh 4 for 69); GLOUCESTERSHIRE 175 (74.5 overs) (M. J. McCague 5 for 42) and 164 (R. J. Scott 41, R. C. Russell 44*, M. J. McCague 5 for 44, R. P. Davis 5 for 61). KENT WON BY 233 RUNS (Kent 21:1/4, Gloucs 5:1/4).
1st inns Kent were 150 for 3, lost last 7 wkts for 39 (Walsh 4 for 7 in 33 balls). 2nd inns Ward/Taylor (140 mins, 13x4) 120 for 2nd wkt. A. J. Wright (Gloucs capt) inj hand fielding; batted No. 8 1st inns (scored 4). Gloucs target 398 in more than a day; McCague 5 for 7 in 23 balls for 1st 10w/m.

OLD TRAFFORD: LANCASHIRE 384 for 6 dec (96 overs) (M. A. Atherton 119, N. J. Speak 42, N. H. Fairbrother 67, G. D. Lloyd 77*, P. A. J. DeFreitas 44) and forfeited second innings; YORKSHIRE forfeited first innings and 121 for 3. DRAWN (Lancs 4:4/0, Yorks 2:0/2).
No play 1st or 2nd days, 65 overs 3rd. Atherton 4th 100 in consec Roses matches at Old Trafford (1st instance). DeFreitas 2x4, 5x6 off J. D. Batty. Yorks target 385 in min 71 overs; rain stopped play.

HOVE: SUSSEX 204 (69 overs) (P. Moores 73, M. C. Ilott 5 for 60) and 279 (M. P. Speight 126, F. D. Stephenson 49, D. R. Pringle 4 for 47); ESSEX 405 for 8 dec (132 overs) (G. A. Gooch 77, J. J. B. Lewis 133, D. R. Pringle 112*) and 80 for 1 (G. A. Gooch 46*). ESSEX WON BY 9 WICKETS (Essex 24:4/4, Sussex 3:2/1).
70 overs 1st day. Sussex 1st inns contained 8 lbws (eq English fc record, taken by Warwicks v Oxford Univ, The Parks, 1980). N. Hussain (Essex) broke finger attempting slip catch; dnb (out rest of season). Gooch/Lewis (HS) 131 for 2nd wkt, Lewis Pringle (10th fc 100; 10x4, 2x6) 105 for 5th. 2nd inns Sussex were 113 for 7 (still 88 behind), then Speight/Stephenson 136 for 8th wkt.

EDGBASTON: GLAMORGAN 316 (95 overs) (S. P. James 64, A. Dale 127, P. A. Cottey 67*, P. A. Smith 5 for 73) and forfeited second innings; WARWICKSHIRE forfeited first innings and 256 for 4 (R. G. Twose 51, T. A. Lloyd 53, D. P. Ostler 60, D. A. Reeve 40*). DRAWN (Warwicks 4:0/4, Glam 4:4/0).
22 overs 1st day, no play 2nd, 52 overs 3rd. Glam were 0 for 1 (H. Morris out for 0), then James/Dale (18x4, 1x6) 163 for 2nd wkt. Smith ended Glam inns with 3 wkts in over. Warwicks target 317 in 57 overs; rain stopped play with 9.2 to go. Twose 50 in 41 balls (11x4), Ostler 50 in 36 balls (8x4).

WORCESTER: WORCESTERSHIRE 162 (76.3 overs) (G. A. Hick 41, C. C. Lewis 4 for 64, C. L. Cairns 4 for 50) and 32 for 1; NOTTINGHAMSHIRE 321 for 9 dec (99 overs) (P. R. Pollard 41, D. W. Randall 66, C. L. Cairns 58, C. C. Lewis 70*, R. K. Illingworth 4 for 111). DRAWN (Worcs 5:1/4, Notts 8:4/4).
Uncapped M. A. Crawley capt Notts for 1st time (R. T. Robinson inj). 60 overs 1st day. Worcs were 72 for 1, 76 for 4 (Lewis 3 wkts in 9 balls). Hick 8x4. No play 2nd day. Rain cost 60 overs 4th day; total of 240 overs lost in match.

August 31, September 1, 2, 3
CHELMSFORD: HAMPSHIRE 233 (109.3 overs) (S. D. Udal 44, P. M. Such 4

for 23) and 229 (A. N. Aymes 65); ESSEX 298 (100.2 overs) (J. J. B. Lewis 43, P. J. Prichard 82, J. H. Childs 43, I. J. Turner 5 for 81) and 165 for 2 (J. P. Stephenson 83*, P. J. Prichard 55*). ESSEX WON BY 8 WICKETS (Essex 22:2/4, Hants 6:2/4).
HS Udal. Such 20–9–23–4. Essex were 219 for 9, then Such (35; HS)/Childs (HS; 5x4, 1x6) 79 for 10th wkt in 17 overs. BB Turner. 2nd inns Hants were 63 for 6 (still 2 behind), then Aymes (211 balls) 56 for 7th wkt with J. R. Ayling (31), 53 for 8th with Udal (32), 45 for 9th with Turner (16; 47 balls on 0*). Essex target 165; were 32 for 2, then Stephenson/Prichard 133* for 3rd wkt, to win match & BAC (£46,000) at 3.35 on Sept 3. Essex's 6th Ch'ship (1979–83–84–86–91).*

CARDIFF: GLAMORGAN 268 (101.1 overs) (H. Morris 80, P. A. Cottey 58, I. D. K. Salisbury 4 for 79); SUSSEX 146 for 7 (50 overs). DRAWN (Glam 6:3/3, Sussex 3:0/3).
R. D. B. Croft awarded Glam cap before match. D. M. Smith omitted by Sussex after dressing-room incident in SL match on Aug 30. C. M. Wells (Sussex) 24–12–26–3. 67.4 overs 1st day, 3 overs 2nd, no play 4th.

BRISTOL: GLOUCESTERSHIRE 302 for 7 dec (96.1 overs) (G. D. Hodgson 81, T. H. C. Hancock 74, J. T. C. Vaughan 51, R. C. Russell 40) and forfeited second innings; LEICESTERSHIRE forfeited first innings and 24 for 0. DRAWN (Gloucs 4:4/0, Leics 3:0/3).
No play 1st day, 18 overs 2nd, 34 overs 3rd. Leics target 303 in approx 60 overs; rain stopped play after 8.1.

TRENT BRIDGE: NOTTINGHAMSHIRE 166 (84.2 overs) (P. R. Pollard 44, M. Saxelby 57, D. G. Cork 5 for 36) and 385 (G. F. Archer 117, C. C. Lewis 82); DERBYSHIRE 330 (126.4 overs) (K. J. Barnett 156*) and 222 for 8 (P. D. Bowler 61, J. E. Morris 43, J. A. Afford 4 for 91). DERBYSHIRE WON BY 2 WICKETS (Derbys 23:3/4, Notts 4:1/3).
Pollard/Saxelby 107 for 1st wkt, then Notts lost all 10 wkts for 59, only capt M. A. Crawley (14) reaching double figs; Cork 5 for 10 in 63 balls; I. R. Bishop (3 for 24) ended inns with 2 wkts with consec balls. Barnett (439 mins, 384 balls, 21x4) carried bat for 1st time. 2nd inns Notts were 144 for 6 (still 20 behind), then Archer (maiden 100 in 5th fc match; 276 balls, 11x4, 3x6)/Lewis (11x4, 1x6) 168 for 7th wkt. Derbys target 222 in 62 overs; reached with 17 balls to spare. Bowler 1st to 2000 fc runs in 1992 when 30; 3rd Derbys player to score 2000 in season, after D. B. Carr (1959) & and M. Azharuddin (1991).*

THE OVAL: SURREY 557 (146.4 overs) (D. J. Bicknell 45, G. P. Thorpe 216, A. J. Stewart 76, A. D. Brown 129, A. P. van Troost 6 for 104); SOMERSET 352 (153.1 overs) (M. N. Lathwell 44, R. J. Turner 45, G. D. Rose 132, M. A. Feltham 4 for 75) and 124 for 3 (M. N. Lathwell 49, C. J. Tavaré 43*). DRAWN (Surrey 6:4/2, Som 3:2/1).
Thorpe maiden 200; 1st 100 of season after 12x50; 450 mins, 16x4; 146 for 3rd wkt with Stewart, 211 for 5th in 34 overs with Brown (100 in 78 balls; in all 102 balls, 14x4, 3x6). Surrey were 538 for 4, lost last 6 wkts for 19 (van Troost 4 for 1 in 15 balls). During 1st inns Lathwell passed 1000 fc runs in 1st full season (played 1 match in 1991). Rose (HS) 415 mins, 307 balls, 12x4; 128 for 6th wkt in 63 overs with Turner. TCCB conducted trials with in-stump TV camera during match.

WORCESTER: WORCESTERSHIRE 409 for 7 dec (142 overs) (G. A. Hick 146, S. J. Rhodes 116*); WARWICKSHIRE 210 for 6 (94 overs) (A. J. Moles 85*). DRAWN (Worcs 5:3/2, Warwicks 4:2/2).
35 overs 1st day, no play 4th. Hick (67th fc 100; 22x4)Rhodes (HS; 335 mins, 11x4) 116 for 5th wkt. Moles 236 balls. D. A. Reeve (Warwicks, 38) 6, 6, 4 from consec balls from Hick.

SCARBOROUGH: YORKSHIRE 508 (158.5 overs) (M. D. Moxon 77, S. A. Kellett 96, C. White 43, D. Byas 100, P. W. Jarvis 80) and 171 for 3 dec (M. D. Moxon 101*); NORTHAMPTONSHIRE 359 for 8 dec (145.2 overs) (R. J. Bailey 85, D. J. Capel 89, K. M. Curran 50, D. Ripley 49, M. A. Robinson 6 for 62) and 298 for 8 (A. Fordham 93, N. A. Felton 49, R. J. Bailey 58, D. J. Capel 66, J. D. Batty 4 for 95). DRAWN (Yorks 5:4/1, Northants 3:2/1).
Northants without capt A. J. Lamb (suspended), C. E. L. Ambrose (inj knee). Kellett HS of season; 5th score over 86. Moxon passed career aggregate of 15,000 fc runs during 1st inns. Byas (11x4; 3rd in consec fc matches at Scarborough, his home ground)/Jarvis (HS; 105 balls, 12x4, 1x6) 133 for 7th wkt (eq Yorks 7th-wkt record v Northants). P. J. Hartley (Yorks; 34) 3 consec 6s off N. G. B. Cook. 1st inns Bailey 8x4, 1x6; Capel 341 mins. Yorks faced 1 over 4th day, from wkpr Ripley (1–0–14–0) while A. R. Roberts kept wkt. Northants target 321 in 60 overs; were 242 for 2, but lost 6 wkts in last 11 overs. Capel 42 balls, 4x6 off Batty.

September 7, 8, 9
OLD TRAFFORD: SUSSEX 563 (161.5 overs) (N. J. Lenham 136, A. P. Wells 143, B. T. P. Donelan 68, P. Moores 74, A. A. Barnett 4 for 148); LANCASHIRE 174 (49.5 overs) (J. P. Crawley 43, G. D. Lloyd 56, I. D. K. Salisbury 6 for 29) and 207 (J. P. Crawley 93, I. D. K. Salisbury 5 for 54). SUSSEX WON BY AN INNINGS AND 182 RUNS (Sussex 24:4/4, Lancs 2:1/1).
Lenham (282 mins, 241 balls, 18x4)/Wells (5th 100 of season; 316 mins, 226 balls, 19x4) 263 for 3rd wkt. Salisbury BB in inns & match; 5 for 10 in 32 balls 1st inns. Lloyd 4x4 in F. D. Stephenson over. Sussex won with more than 4 sessions to spare.

TAUNTON: SOMERSET 534 (135.1 overs) (A. N. Hayhurst 102, M. N. Lathwell 50, R. J. Harden 126, C. J. Tavaré 124, N. D. Burns 54, S. P. Hughes 4 for 112) and 25 for 2; DURHAM 219 (44.4 overs) (I. Smith 110, N. A. Mallender 5 for 65, A. R. Caddick 4 for 62) and 339 (W. Larkins 117, J. A. Daley 88, I. T. Botham 74, A. R. Caddick 4 for 53). SOMERSET WON BY 8 WICKETS (Som 24:4/4, Durham 3:2/1).
Fc debut J. A. Daley (Durham; RHB). Hayhurst (285 mins, 229 balls, 11x4)/Harden (203 mins, 187 balls, 19x4, 1x6) 189 for 2nd wkt. Tavaré 208 mins, 160 balls, 16x4, 1x6. 1st inns Durham were 69 for 6, then Smith (1st 100 for Durham in 97 balls; in all 149 mins, 109 balls, 19x4)/D. A. Graveney (29) 106 for 6th wkt. C. W. Scott (Durham wkpr) ret hurt with fractured finger; resumed later (10); dnb 2nd inns. Larkins/Daley 201 for 4th wkt. P. Bainbridge (Durham) pair. Botham 71 balls, 14x4; 1st 8 scoring shots were 4s off R. P. Snell. Som won with over a day to spare.*

September 7, 8, 9, 10
DERBY: DERBYSHIRE 226 (68 overs) (T. J. G. O'Gorman 64, C. J. Adams 60, D. R. Pringle 5 for 36) and 309 (J. E. Morris 55, C. J. Adams 135, M. C. Ilott 6 for 87); ESSEX 96 (35.4 overs) (G. A. Gooch 53, I. R. Bishop 6 for 18) and 442 for 6 (J. P. Stephenson 97, N. Shahid 51, G. A. Gooch 123*, M. A. Garnham 66). ESSEX WON BY 4 WICKETS (Essex 20:0/4, Derbys 6:2/4).
P. J. Prichard capt Essex, even though Gooch played (& batted No. 6 in both inns). 20 wkts 1st day (Essex were 28 for 5, 59 for 8). BB Ilott. 2nd inns Derbys were 38 for 3, then Morris/Adams (181 mins, 156 balls, 20x4, 2x6) 163 for 4th wkt in 41 overs. Essex target 440 in over 2 days (231 overs). Stephenson 323 balls, 12x4. Gooch (98th fc 100; 373 mins, 298 balls, 12x4)/Garnham 129 for 6th wkt, Gooch/Pringle (28) 84* for 7th wkt to win. Essex's highest 4th-inns total to win; highest 4th-inns total agst Derbys; 3rd-highest winning 4th-inns total in Ch'ship (highest is Middx's 502 for 6 v Notts, Trent Bridge, 1925).*

CANTERBURY: GLAMORGAN 158 (49.2 overs) (A. Dale 48, A. P. Igglesden 5 for 45) and 389 (A. Dale 50, I. V. A. Richards 76, P. A. Cottey 141, M. V. Fleming 4 for 63); KENT 219 (98.1 overs) (N. R. Taylor 74, S. A. Marsh 60) and 242 (T. R. Ward 53, M. R. Benson 41, S. D. Thomas 5 for 79). GLAMOR-

GAN WON BY 86 RUNS (Glam 21:1/4, Kent 6:2/4).
15 wkts 1st day. Kent were 55 for 5 (C. L. Hooper/G. R. Cowdrey/M. V Fleming all ducks), then Taylor/Marsh 113 for 6th wkt in 53 overs. Richards/Cottey (HSBAC) 142 for 6th wkt in 46 overs. BB Fleming. Marsh (Kent wkpr) ct 5 1st inns. Kent target 329 in more than a day (min 135 overs). BB Thomas.

TRENT BRIDGE: SURREY 207 (70.2 overs) (R. E. Bryson 76, C. C. Lewis 4 for 65) and 411 (D. J. Bicknell 77, G. P. Thorpe 100, A. J. Stewart 85, M. A. Lynch 70, A. D. Brown 50*, C. C. Lewis 6 for 90); NOTTINGHAMSHIRE 357 (129 overs) M. Saxelby 43, C. C. Lewis 52, K. P. Evans 104, M. P. Bicknell 5 for 89) and 262 for 5 (R. T. Robinson 129*, G. F. Archer 66). NOTTINGHAMSHIRE WON BY 5 WICKETS (Notts 23:3/4, Surrey 5:2/3).
Surrey were 123 for 9, then Bryson (HS for Surrey; 90 balls, 10x4)/J. Boiling (14) 84 for 10th wkt. Notts were 159 for 6, last 4 wkts added 198. Evans (255 mins, 219 balls, 9x4)S. Bramhall (37*) 124 for 9th wkt. D. J. Bicknell (10x4)/Thorpe (10x4) 174 for 2nd wkt. Stewart (10x4)Lynch (10x4) 138 for 4th wkt. Surrey were 337 for 3, lost last 7 wkts for 74. Lewis BB for Notts. Notts target 262 in 84 overs; reached with 15 balls to spare; were 39 for 3, then Robinson/Archer 132 for 4th wkt.*

September 8, 9, 10, 11
LORD'S: WARWICKSHIRE 476 (141.2 overs) (R. G. Twose 84, T. A. Lloyd 40, T. L. Penney 151, K. J. Piper 72) and 57 for 2; MIDDLESEX 201 (72.2 overs) (D. L. Haynes 40, N. M. K. Smith 5 for 61) and 328 (M. W. Gatting 71, K. R. Brown 106, A. A. Donald 5 for 36). WARWICKSHIRE WON BY 8 WICKETS (Warwicks 24:4/4, Middx 5:3/2).
Twose awarded Warwicks cap after inns. Penney (HS; 15x4, 1x5, 1x6)Piper (10x4 192 for 8th wkt in 45 overs. Middx had no sub available when N. F. Williams injured; O. Henry (Scotland & South Africa; practising on ground in morning) took field. BB N. M. K. Smith. Lloyd 7.2–1–7–3 (1st inns). 2nd inns Haynes ret hurt (13) with ricked neck; resumed later (out for 28). Gatting 160 mins, 12x4. Brown (1st 100 of season) 12x4, 1x6. Twose (36*; 5x4, 2x6) ended match with 2x6 in J. E. Emburey over.*

September 12, 13, 14, 15
GATESHEAD FELL: DURHAM 312 (102.1 overs) (W. Larkins 53, P. W. G. Parker 70, J. D. Glendenen 76, S. P. Hughes 42, M. Watkinson 5 for 63) and 271 (P. W. G. Parker 52, J. A. Daley 80*, J. D. Glendenen 43, P. A. J. DeFreitas 6 for 94); LANCASHIRE 562 (161.1 overs) (G. D. Mendis 45, M. A. Atherton 199, M. Watkinson 46, P. J. Martin 133, I. D. Austin 58, P. Bainbridge 5 for 100) and 24 for 0. LANCASHIRE WON BY 10 WICKETS (Lancs 24:4/4, Durham 6:4/2).
72 overs 1st day. Glendenen (9x4) HSBAC, Hughes HS for Durham. Atherton (HS; 500 mins, 25x4)Martin (maiden fc 100; 14x4, 1x5, 1x6) 243 for 7th wkt (2 short of county rec). Highest fc total agst Durham. Bainbridge BB for Durham.

CARDIFF: GLAMORGAN 307 (84.1 overs) (S. P. James 52, M. P. Maynard 57, I. V. A. Richards 85, R. W. Sladdin 4 for 102) and forfeited second innings; DERBYSHIRE forfeited first innings and 244 (J. E. Morris 46, T. J. G. O'Gorman 41, R. D. B. Croft 6 for 49). GLAMORGAN WON BY 63 RUNS (Glam 20:4/0, Derbys 4:0/4).
Fc debuts (both Derbys) A. W. Richardson (RHB, RFM; son of G. W. – Derbys 1959–65 – & grandson of A. W. – Derbys 1928–36, capt 1931–36); T. A. Tweats (RHB, RM). No play 1st & 2nd days. Maynard (50 in 43 balls)/Richards (77 balls, 5x6) 107 for 4th wkt in 16 overs. Derbys target 308 in min 102 overs; rain cost 52 overs; Croft 7.3–0–49–6 as Derbys all out with 7.3 overs left. P. A. Cottey/A. Dale/ S. P. James awarded Glamorgan caps 4th day.

BRISTOL: ESSEX 128 (47.3 overs) (C. A. Walsh 7 for 38) and 382 (N. V. Knight

46, J. P. Stephenson 93, J. J. B. Lewis 53, G. A. Gooch 101); GLOUCESTER-
SHIRE 326 (130.2 overs) (M. W. Alleyne 93, M. G. N. Windows 71, S. J.
W. Andrew 4 for 58) and 187 for 3 (R. J. Scott 73, M. W. Alleyne 73*).
GLOUCESTERSHIRE WON BY 7 WICKETS (Gloucs 23:3/4, Essex 2:0/2).
*Fc debut M. G. N. Windows (RHB; son of former Gloucs allrounder A. R.). P. J.
Prichard capt Essex side inc Gooch (who batted No. 6) for 2nd match running. Essex
were 20 for 4, 94 for 8. Alleyne 13x4. 1st inns Gooch 20–8–27–1. N. Shahid (Essex)
'pair'. Gooch 99th fc 100* in 245 mins, 5x4. M. Davies (Gloucs; SLA) 37–21–30–2
(2nd inns). Gloucs target 185 in 46 overs; reached with 6.4 to spare; Scott (6x4, 3x6)/
Alleyne (8x4, 1x6) 103 for 2nd wkt.*

SOUTHAMPTON: HAMPSHIRE 231 (82.3 overs) (R. A. Smith 87) and 261
for 5 dec (T. C. Middleton 50, R. S. M. Morris 74, M. C. J. Nicholas 88*);
WORCESTERSHIRE 228 for 8 dec (98 overs) (R. K. Illingworth 43, D. B.
D'Oliveira 43, S. J. Rhodes 45) and 254 for 7 (S. J. Rhodes 107, S. R. Lampitt
69). DRAWN (Hants 5:2/3, Worcs 6:2/4).
*S. D. Udal awarded Hants cap during match. M. D. Marshall (Hants) ret hurt 1st
inns (27*) after hit on arm by P. J. Newport delivery. 36 overs 2nd day. Marshall (3
for 33, 1st inns) 3 for 0 in 10 balls. HS Morris. Worcs target 265 in 67 overs; were
70 for 4, then Rhodes (133 balls, 13x4, 1x6)Lampitt 166 for 5th wkt.*

LEICESTER: LEICESTERSHIRE 352 (120.2 overs) (T. J. Boon 81, B. F. Smith
86, W. K. M. Benjamin 71) and 240 for 5 dec (T. J. Boon 97, L. Potter 46);
NORTHAMPTONSHIRE 303 for 7 dec (96 overs) (R. J. Bailey 167*, K. M.
Curran 47) and 290 for 4 (M. B. Loye 40, A. J Lamb 122*, K. M. Curran 52).
NORTHAMPTONSHIRE WON BY 6 WICKETS (Northants 23:4/3, Leics 5:3/
2).
*Fc debut J. N. Snape (Northants; RHB, OS). 1st inns Northants dropped 9 catches;
Boon 10x4. 40 overs 2nd day. Bailey 20x4. Northants target 290 in 73 overs; reached
with 19 balls to spare; Lamb (2nd 50 in 40 mins, 36 balls)Curran 135 for 4th wkt in
24 overs. Northants clinched 3rd place in BAC (£13,250).*

TAUNTON: NOTTINGHAMSHIRE 265 (92.5 overs) (R. T. Robinson 74, G. F.
Archer 83*) and 188 (P. R. Pollard 42, M. Saxelby 64, H. R. J. Trump 4 for
53); SOMERSET 616 for 7 dec (162 overs) (R. J. Harden 187, C. J. Tavaré 125,
R. J. Turner 101*, G. D. Rose 40, K. P. Evans 4 for 96). SOMERSET WON BY
AN INNINGS AND 163 RUNS (Som 24:4/4, Notts 3:2/1).
*A. R. Caddick/M. N. Lathwell awarded Som caps 1st day. Archer 5th 50 in 12th fc
inns. Harden (HS; 390 mins)/Tavaré (200 balls, 21x4, 1x6) 265 for 3rd wkt in 71
overs. Turner maiden fc 100 in 225 balls. Soms HS at Taunton (prev 592 v Yorks,
1892), HS in Ch'ship since 1924. Match ended after 26 overs 4th day.*

THE OVAL: MIDDLESEX 441 (164.1 overs) (M. A. Roseberry 120, J. D. Carr
114, M. R. Ramprakash 117, R. E. Bryson 5 for 117, J. Boiling 4 for 126) and
32 for 0 dec; SURREY 141 for 3 dec (50 overs) (G. P. Thorpe 45, A. J. Stewart
51*) and 325 for 9 (D. J. Bicknell 87, A. J. Stewart 52, M. A. Butcher 47, P. C.
R. Tufnell 5 for 130). DRAWN (Surrey 0:0/0, Middx 4:3/1).
*Fc debuts I. J. Ward (Surrey), Aftab Habib (Middx; RHB), R. L. Johnson (Middx;
RHB, RFM). Roseberry (9th 100 of season in 258 balls, 10x4, 1x6; 2000 fc runs when
76*)/Carr (100 in 198 balls) 209 for 1st wkt. Boiling 49 consec overs 1st day. 12.1
overs 2nd day, during which M. W. Gatting out 25 short of 2000 fc runs in season;
scored 25* before declaring in 2nd inns. Surrey target 333 in 92 overs; needed 15 from
Tufnell's last over of match, but lost 2 wkts; Boiling (0*) survived last 2 balls of match
to draw. K. R. Brown (Middx wkpr) st 4. HS Butcher.*

HOVE: YORKSHIRE 232 (74 overs) (S. A. Kellett 53, A. A. Metcalfe 43, C.
White 71*, I. D. K. Salisbury 7 for 54) and 259 (M. D. Moxon 50, E. S. H.
Giddins 4 for 65, I. D. K. Salisbury 5 for 84); SUSSEX 432 (151.2 overs) (J. W.

Hall 90, N. J. Lenham 135, P. J. Hartley 8 for 111) and 61 for 4. SUSSEX WON BY 6 WICKETS (Sussex 23:3/4, Yorks 2:2/0).
Salisbury 4 for 0 in 13 balls 1st inns; BB in inns & match for 2nd consec game. Hall (259 balls, 9x4)Lenham (258 balls, 19x4) 224 for 1st wkt. BB Hartley. C. M. Wells (11*) ended match with 6 into pavilion off J. D. Batty.

EDGBASTON: KENT 603 for 8 dec (143.2 overs) (T. R. Ward 153, M. R. Benson 122, C. L. Hooper 102, N. R. Taylor 78, G. R. Cowdrey 88, N. M. K. Smith 4 for 160); WARWICKSHIRE 289 (94.2 overs) (D. P. Ostler 40, D. A. Reeve 51, T. A. Munton 47, T. A. Lloyd 76, A. P. Igglesden 5 for 91) and 171 (R. G. Twose 52, C. L. Hooper 4 for 57, R. P. Davis 5 for 41). KENT WON BY AN INNINGS AND 143 RUNS (Kent 24:4/4, Warwicks 4:3/1).
Ward (184 balls, 27x4, 1x6)Benson (15x4, 1x6) 290 for 1st wkt (record for any Kent wkt agst Warwicks). Hooper/Taylor 141 for 3rd wkt in 32 overs. Kent 468 for 3 after 100 overs. K. J . Piper inj finger, unable to keep wkt 2nd day (Ostler deputised & ct Hooper); Piper ct 2 at deep third man. Kent's HS since 1934, HS conceded by Warwicks since 1928, HS by any visiting county at Edgbaston since 1896. 1st inns Warwicks were 5 for 3, then Ostler/Reeve 96 for 4th wkt. HS Munton. Lloyd (batted No. 8 with runner after inj leg) 12x4, 1x6 in last match as capt. Hooper BB for Kent. Match over after 55 mins (20 overs) 4th day; Kent clinched 2nd place in BAC (£23,000).

BRITANNIC ASSURANCE CHAMPIONSHIP FIXTURES 1993

For details of venues, consult full first-class fixture list, page 206. For further information, check under relevant county in Grounds section.

ROUND 1

April 29–May 2 (all games in round include Sunday play):

Glam v Sussex
Gloucs v Middx
Hants v Somerset
Leics v Surrey
Notts v Worcs
Warwicks v Northants

BACFLASH – FIVE YEARS AGO
A tentative birth as four-day cricket, long part of the furniture in Australia and India, comes to England in the shape of six Championship games per county. The early matches, as expected, find the number-crunchers in seventh heaven, centuries from Maynard, Shastri and Holmes allowing Glamorgan to declare at 543 for 8 in a rain-stained draw against Somerset, the county's biggest score for 37 years and the highest total ever made at Sophia Gardens: not since 1949 had three Glamorgan batsmen made centuries in the same innings . . . the weather meddles nearly everywhere, although, since the quality of pitches leaves something to be desired, three days prove more than enough at Leicester (Agnew 11–122 to send Northants to an innings defeat), Headingley (Newman's career-best 8–29 seaming Derbyshire to a five-wicket win in a match with three fifties and a highest total of 192) and Worcester (Dilley's 9–117 ushering defending champions Notts to a six-wicket tanning) . . . runs just as hard to come by at Lord's, where Middlesex trounce Essex by 172 runs, Emburey's unbeaten 76 the highest score of a match decided by Williams' pace . . . a Light Blue leg-spinner dismisses Stewart during Surrey's game at Fenner's, then follows up with an undefeated century, adding the name Atherton to the list of young guns to follow.

ROUND 2

May 6–10:

Essex v Yorkshire
Lancs v Durham
Leics v Notts
Middx v Kent
Northants v Gloucs
Sussex v Surrey
Warwicks v Derbys

BACFLASH – 10 YEARS AGO
With the World Cup a month away, Richards gives due warning that he is in the mood to drive the West Indies to their third successive Prudential Trophy. A rousing 83 ensures Somerset begin their defence of the Benson & Hedges Cup in convincing fashion against Sussex, the John Player League champions, who get an encore a couple of days later as Richards delivers a majestic Sunday sermon with 96 not out . . . Gower flowers with 67 in Leicestershire's Benson & Hedges Cup 117–run romp against Worcestershire but the England vice-captain's hopes of a strong run-in to the World Cup are dashed by the weather gods, who appear to be in the vilest of moods: Leicestershire's first three Sunday fixtures are all abandoned, as are two of their four B&H zone matches . . . Headingley endures a similarly heartless start to the season as only 2¼ hours' play are possible in the Championship game against England captain Willis and his 1982 wooden spoonists, Warwickshire . . . champions Middlesex are marginally more fortunate against Lancashire, losing only 10 hours to the weather and none of the second day – Lord's first full day's play of 1983 after seven washouts.

ROUND 3

May 13–17:

Derbys v Glam
Durham v Hants
Kent v Warwicks
Middx v Notts
Somerset v Lancs
Surrey v Essex
Yorkshire v Worcs

BACFLASH – 15 YEARS AGO
In an astonishing gesture of conciliation to the rebels, the Sydney Cricket Ground Trust announces that it has invited Kerry Packer and his circus act to play in its stadium next winter, a decision greeted with scorn in England, where the establishment remain firmly opposed to coloured clothing, night games and bouncers at tailenders. In fact, for each Test this summer, the captains will exchange their lists of non-recognised batsmen and agree not to bowl anything short-pitched at them . . . led by their brilliant wicketkeeper Wasim Bari but deprived of their quintet of Packer stars, Pakistan underline their inexperience and lack of match practice by being trundled out for 80 by Essex. The remainder of the match is washed out, which means the hapless tourists have been able to play on just six of the 18 days scheduled so far . . . joint champions Middlesex slide to defeat at Chelmsford, an aggressive 76 from Fletcher and nine wickets from left-arm spinner East the crucial elements; Brearley makes 7 and 2, prompting calls for the selectors to emulate their Ryder Cup counterparts by appointing a non-playing captain.

ROUND 4

May 20–24:

Essex v Derbys
Glam v Northants
Gloucs v Durham
Hants v Yorkshire
Notts v Kent
Sussex v Leics
Worcs v Somerset

BACFLASH – 20 YEARS AGO
Requiring a further 191 runs to become the first player since Edrich 35 years ago to reach 1,000 runs by the end of May, Turner, the New Zealand opener, is dismissed for 2 by the emerging Derbyshire seamer, Hendrick, then makes 66 not out in the second innings to keep the target within sight . . . champions Warwickshire pick up their first win of the summer in a one-innings affair against Leicestershire, former England captain Smith (M J K) hitting an unbeaten 73 after seamer McVicker routs the visitors, led by current England captain Illingworth, for 188 . . . an unbroken ninth-wicket stand of 61 between Herman and Stephenson sets up a thrilling finish at Bristol, where Hampshire, 183 for 8 shortly before tea, still 61 behind, hold on to avert an innings defeat . . . at Trent Bridge, Sobers defies the Middlesex spinners, Titmus and Marriott, but has his thunder stolen by a mature knock of 65 from Randall, a skinny, livewire fielder and spirited batsman embarking on his first full season for Notts . . . Carrick, Yorkshire's 20-year-old slow left-armer, takes 5-24 to whisk Glamorgan out for 97 at Cardiff, yet, with only 164 wanted for their first win of the season, the visiting county descend, inexplicably, to 98 all out, losing their last eight wickets for 40 in under an hour.

ROUND 5

May 27–31:

Derbys v Hants
Durham v Kent
Gloucs v Worcs
Lancs v Warwicks
Middx v Sussex
Somerset v Glam

BACFLASH – 25 YEARS AGO
Mystery bowler Gleeson torments Somerset with his unique brand of leg-spin as the tourists, hailed as the latest 'worst Australian party ever to visit England', head for the first Test in ominous form despite the foul weather. Opener Redpath, renowned for his patience and defensive reliability, rattles up the fastest century of the season – 84 minutes – in the same match . . . in the Roses game, champions Yorkshire, fielding 10 past, present and future England caps, romp home by an innings against Lancashire under the captaincy of Trueman, who takes eight wickets . . . while Yorkshire stick with homegrown talent, other counties have taken advantage of the decision to drop import restrictions, two of whom, Notts and Warwickshire, serve up a rollercoaster contest at Trent Bridge. Put in, the visitors spiral to 93 all out, whereupon Sobers and fellow West Indian Murray earn Notts a lead of 189; the West Indies captain then dismisses Barber for a duck as Warwickshire slip to 6 for 3, only for another Caribbean star, Kanhai, to effect a dramatic transformation with a magnificent 253 as he and the Pakistani all-rounder, Ibadulla, forge an all-wicket county record of 402 in 6¾ hours to secure a draw . . . Hampshire's dashing new South African opener, Richards, strokes a century in each innings against Northants.

ROUND 6

June 3–7:

Essex v Somerset
Kent v Gloucs
Leics v Durham
Middx v Derbys
Northants v Worcs
Notts v Hants
Surrey v Lancs
Warwicks v Sussex
Yorkshire v Glam

BACFLASH – FIVE YEARS AGO:
Hallelujah! After 10 successive defeats, England at last come out of a Test against the West Indies unbowed, Gooch's match double of 73 and 146 at Trent Bridge supplemented by a velveteen 88 not out from Gower, holding Marshall, Ambrose, Walsh and Patterson at bay . . . a right old hoo-ha at Northampton ensues as the hosts elect to play on the same pitch used for the previous match against Leicestershire: Carrick, the Yorkshire captain, reports it as unfit after 15 wickets fall on the first day . . . another case for the pitch inspector at New Road as 19 wickets tumble on the second day of Worcestershire's draw with Lancashire, provoking calls for a points penalty to be levied on counties producing poor surfaces . . . even odder goings-on at Cardiff, where, by kind permission of the TCCB, Glamorgan are permitted to shave the pitch in the hope of encouraging spin, an experiment the enterprising Kent captain, Chris Cowdrey, is only too happy to accommodate: the less than hirsute surface that emerges is so devoid of pace that Glamorgan meander to 197 for 6 off 100 overs on the first day . . . Gladstone Small thinks big at Edgbaston, taking a career-best 7–15 to help Warwickshire dismiss Notts for 44, the lowest score of the 1988 season.

ROUND 7

June 10–14:

Derbys v Yorkshire
Durham v Middx
Hants v Kent
Lancs v Essex
Surrey v Glam
Sussex v Northants
Worcs v Leics

BACFLASH – 10 YEARS AGO
India, the 66–1 outsiders, create the biggest upset in World Cup history at Old Trafford, inflicting a 34–run defeat on the West Indies, the holders' first defeat in the competition after winning both previous tournaments in 1975 and 1979 . . . at Trent Bridge, Zimbabwe cause almost as much spluttering by beating Australia by 13 runs, captain Fletcher's 69 not out and 4–42 inspiring a famous day for African sport . . . Gower unusually savage at Taunton, lofting five sixes in a speedy 130 as England win a heavy scoring duel with Sri Lanka . . . Barnett, at 22 the youngest captain in Derbyshire history, learns the size of his task against Leicestershire: the visitors struggle to 178 for 8 before their No 10, Taylor, hits 47, a 100% improvement on his career-best, whereupon Derby collapse for 79 and 168 to lose by an innings . . . Edmonds and Emburey, neither required by England, share 26 victims to spin Middlesex to heavy victories over Surrey and the early Championship leaders, Hampshire . . . Lloyd, the promising young Warwickshire opener, reaches 50 off 38 balls, a season's fastest in the Sunday League, only to be overshadowed by Larkins, whose unbeaten 172 for Northants breaks the 40–over record.

ROUND 8

June 17–21:

Glam v Durham
Kent v Derbys
Lancs v Sussex
Northants v Hants
Notts v Essex
Somerset v Middx
Warwicks v Surrey
Yorkshire v Gloucs

BACFLASH – 15 YEARS AGO
A star is born. Even Father Time is alleged to have clapped his scythe in admiration after the Somerset all-rounder, Botham, becomes the first player in Test history to score a hundred and take eight wickets in an innings in the same game. In his first Test at Lord's, the muscular 22–year-old enters midway through the opening afternoon at 120 for 4 yet surges to his maiden Test century in England by the close, then bowls Pakistan out on the last morning with figures of 8 for 34, the best for his country since Laker's 10–53 at Old Trafford 22 summers ago. Most remarkable of all is the ball that ejects Haroon, who somehow contrives to surrender off and leg stumps while middle stays put. Maybe this young pup fancies himself as a magician . . . Kent see off Surrey and Middlesex – the side with whom they shared the 1977 Championship – in successive matches; unavailable for England owing to his Packer connections, Underwood accounts for 15 of the wickets as Surrey subside for 105 and 98, Middlesex for 278 and 163 . . . Derbyshire opener Borrington (77) and Tavaré of Kent (56) are the Gold Award winners as their counties dispose of Warwickshire and Somerset in the semi-finals of the Benson & Hedges Cup.

ROUND 9

June 24–28:

Derbys v Lancs
Durham v Worcs
Essex v Warwicks
Glam v Notts
Leics v Gloucs
Middx v Surrey
Northants v Somerset
Yorkshire v Kent

BACFLASH – 20 YEARS AGO
After 43 Tests without success against England, New Zealand come closer than ever to breaking the barrier at Lord's. The man responsible for thwarting Congdon's talented side is Fletcher, who finally justifies the selectors' patience with 178 in 6¼ hours, his first Test century in England. Trailing by 298 after the tourists' captain had forged a crisp, assured 175 – one run less than the Test-best he had racked up at Nottingham in the first Test – England were a fragile 70 runs on with two hours and two wickets left when Arnold edged his third ball to Wadsworth, only for the keeper to floor the chance. The Surrey swing bowler proceeded to keep Fletcher company until the Essex 'Gnome' was caught on the boundary with five minutes to go, by which time the match was saved . . . the semi-finals of the second Benson & Hedges Cup are both low-scoring, high-tension contests: a fine catch on the run and a stout 48, the highest individual innings of the two games, earns Ealham the Gold Award and Kent a 46-run win over Essex; drama to the last at Old Trafford, where Worcestershire, having dismissed Lancashire for 159 and requiring nine from the final over with two wickets standing, tie the scores off the sixth ball and win by virtue of having lost one fewer wicket.

ROUND 10

July 1–5:

Glam v Middx
Gloucs v Hants
Kent v Essex
Leics v Lancs
Northants v Notts
Somerset v Sussex
Surrey v Durham
Warwicks v Yorkshire
Worcs v Derbys

BACFLASH – 25 YEARS AGO
Yorkshire display all their mettle and steel at Sheffield, defeating Bill Lawry's tourists by an innings and 69 runs to record the county's first win over Australia since 1902. Although one up in the Test series, Australia were bowled out for 78 at Lord's and their batting woes continue in the heat and humidity of Bramall Lane, where, after Boycott's 86 allows Close the luxury of declaring at 355 for 9, Illingworth (4–44 and 4–23) and Trueman (3–32 and 3–51) cut the guests down for 148 and 138 . . . Kanhai enjoys a prosperous week, an aggressive 152 against Lancashire making him the first batsman to 1,000 runs (Prideaux, the Northants opener, gets there 2¼ hours later) followed by the Man of the Match award in the Gillette Cup third round tie against Hampshire . . . Procter, Gloucestershire's brilliant young South African all-rounder, destroys Derbyshire's first innings with 6–43 only for his side to collapse twice on a tricky Chesterfield pitch to go down by nine wickets . . . a fearsome proposition in helpful conditions, Underwood weaves his spell on an even more hazardous surface at Swansea, the unconventional England slow left-armer giving Kent an innings win over Glamorgan with match figures of 11–62.

ROUND 11

July 15–19:

Essex v Leics
Hants v Worcs
Lancs v Glam
Notts v Somerset
Surrey v Gloucs
Sussex v Kent
Warwicks v Middx
Yorkshire v Northants

BACFLASH – FIVE YEARS AGO
Coming in after West Indian keeper Dujon's cultured 141 has given the St Helens crowd something to warm to after a blank opening day, Richards gives his future employers a taste of butchery to come with four boundaries in an over off Thomas, Glamorgan's – and England's – fastest bowler; Hooper dispatches North, the home slow left-armer, for two sixes in one over, at which mid-off asks bowler how far he should drop back – 'Ilfracombe', replies North . . . a drying pitch rewards Barnett for a seemingly generous declaration against Northants at Derby, forfeitures leaving the visitors to make 309 in 90 overs only for the grunting Dane, Mortensen, to take 5–28 . . . a closer tussle at Southend, Lancashire chasing 289 in 82 overs and squeezing home with five balls and four wickets in hand thanks to Fairbrother's 111 and seven wickets from 47–year-old off-spinner 'Flat Jack' Simmons . . . Hampshire manage just one point on a awkward track at Edgbaston, Andy Lloyd's unbeaten 160 complemented by 10 wickets for the hostile Merrick as Warwickshire enhance their Championship credentials with an emphatic innings victory in barely two days' play.

ROUND 12

July 22-26:

Derbys v Sussex
Essex v Durham
Lancs v Notts
Leics v Warwicks
Middx v Hants
Northants v Surrey
Somerset v Kent
Worcs v Glam

BACFLASH – 10 YEARS AGO
Having limped away from The Oval one down in the Test series, Howarth's New Zealanders resume rude health in every sense with a 100-run win over Worcestershire on a pitch described by their matchwinner, Hadlee, as 'not fit for first-class or club cricket' . . . Chairman May and the rest of the England selectors make one change for next week's second Test at Leeds, dropping Somerset off-spinner Marks and recalling Kent pace bowler Dilley after an absence of nearly 18 months . . . at 8.50pm, in front of a rapt crowd of 22,000, Cowans scatters Foster's stumps and Essex's chances with the first ball of the final over to seal a four-run win for Middlesex, who thus land the Benson & Hedges Cup for the first time, an immediate success for their new captain, Gatting . . . Yorkshire's somewhat more venerable skipper, Illingworth, just turned 51, teases out two of the Sussex top five as the Sunday League champions go down to their likeliest successors at Hove . . . Larkins continues his purple patch with 31 fours and two sixes in a career-best 236 against Derbyshire, but home captain Barnett engineers a draw with knocks of 103 and 53 not out.

ROUND 13

July 29–August 2:

Durham v Sussex
Essex v Worcs
Gloucs v Derbys
Hants v Warwicks
Kent v Leics
Somerset v Yorkshire
Surrey v Notts

BACFLASH – 15 YEARS AGO
You're The One That I Want is still No 1 in the hit parade, but the most melodic sounds of the week come from the bat of Gower, whose 111 in the first Test against New Zealand at The Oval is the Leicestershire lad's maiden Test century. For the tourists, Congdon makes his record 59th appearance, Bracewell, 18, his first, the latter quickly ejecting Brearley and Gooch, only for Willis, Botham and Edmonds to bowl England along to a seven-wicket win . . . the Sussex fast bowler, Pigott, dismisses Intikhab, Jackman and Pocock of Surrey to record the only hat-trick of the Championship season: what makes the feat even more remarkable is that the 20-year-old Old Harrovian had never previously taken a wicket in first-class cricket . . . Essex beat Northamptonshire by 46 runs at Northampton when East takes the final wicket with the third ball of the 24th over to be delivered in the last hour; the highest score of the match comes courtesy of the burly new South African, Lamb, who collects his first hundred for Northants . . . Sunday League champions Leicestershire are washed out for the second successive weekend then lose their Gillette Cup quarter-final to Essex by three runs after rain reduces the contest to a 10–over slog; ditto at Leeds, where Imran Khan guides Sussex home.

ROUND 14

August 5–9:

Durham v Derbys
Glam v Warwicks
Gloucs v Lancs
Kent v Surrey
Middx v Leics
Northants v Essex
Notts v Yorkshire
Sussex v Worcs

BACFLASH - 20 YEARS AGO
Unprecedented and unpleasant scenes during the otherwise dull second Test between England and Kanhai's West Indians at Edgbaston. For the first time in a Test, every member of a touring side is attached to an English county. Of considerably greater significance is the threat by umpire Fagg to withdraw his labour, a less desirable first. Fagg's action is provoked by an explicit show of annoyance by Kanhai in the wake of the umpire's rejection of an early appeal against Boycott. The umpire requests an apology, and when this is not forthcoming he refuses to take his place on the field the next morning; only after talks between the chairman of selectors, Bedser, and the tourists' manager, Kentish, is the situation resolved to everyone's satisfaction. The West Indies' overrate – 26 before lunch on the Saturday with 20,000 people waiting to be entertained – brings a warning from the umpires during the interval . . . Championship leaders Hampshire maintain their unbeaten record by sinking Derbyshire at Portsmouth, where Gilliat leads from the front with a bright century and spinners O'Sullivan and Sainsbury set up a 10–wicket victory . . . Hendrick, the Derbyshire seamer, has a poor build-up to his one-day international debut, failing to take a wicket against the bottom club, Notts, whose out-of-form captain Sobers tunes up for his farewell Test in England with a fluent unbeaten century.

ROUND 15

August 12–16:

Derbys v Somerset
Hants v Lancs
Leics v Glam
Northants v Durham
Sussex v Notts
Warwicks v Gloucs
Worcs v Surrey
Yorkshire v Middx

BACFLASH – 25 YEARS AGO
Foul weather, such a factor in the Australian escapes at Lord's and, to a lesser extent, Edgbaston, comes to the tourists' aid yet again after some of England's finest young players threaten to embarrass them. Brimful of promising batsmen such as Fletcher, Denness and Amiss, as well as the 6ft 7in South African all-rounder, Greig, the President of MCC's XI reduce the Australians to 140 for 8 in their second innings, 167 on, when rain has the final say, off-spinner Birkenshaw pressing his claims for international recognition with a match return of 8–94 . . . having ruined both the Bass Charrington Single-Wicket competition and the touring Americans' game against Surrey, rain also ravages the Gillette Cup semi-finals: two-time winners Sussex take three days to prevail over Gloucestershire while Warwickshire, the 1966 winners, finally squeeze past Middlesex at the fourth attempt – so much for this thing they call one-day cricket . . . Kent gain ground in their pursuit of Championship leaders Yorkshire by dint of a remarkable victory at Wellingborough: needing 125 with all second-innings wickets standing and a day at their disposal, Northants slide to 63 for 5, recover to 102 for 6, get as far as 117 for 7, then lose their last three men for two runs as nerves fray in the face of Underwood's mastery.

ROUND 16

August 19–23:

Derbys v Surrey
Durham v Warwicks
Glam v Hants
Gioucs v Essex
Lancs v Yorks
Middx v Northants
Somerset v Leics
Worcs v Kent

BACFLASH – 5 YEARS AGO
After a much-publicised incident involving DeFreitas, Agnew, a salt cellar and a kitbag, Leicestershire bring an end to some unseemly in-fighting by agreeing to release their young England all-rounder, whereupon DeFreitas makes a point or three by contributing five wickets to the seven-wicket thrashing meted out to Somerset . . . surprise Championship leaders Kent are frustrated by the weather at Bristol as the elements ruin any prospects of victory over Gloucestershire, who finish on 161 for 7, 66 short of an unlikely triumph themselves, when Cowdrey recalls Igglesden and the umpires promptly decree the light to be too poor . . . contrasting fortunes for the NatWest finalists: Middlesex beat Warwickshire by seven wickets at Lord's while double-chasing Worcestershire go down by 77 runs to Essex in the big game at New Road, Foster bowling Pridgeon with 22 balls remaining to cut the gap between Kent's closest rivals to five points . . . Notts, so mighty at Trent Bridge for so long, kiss goodbye to their title in a nine-wicket loss to Surrey, for whom Richards, fresh from keeping wicket for England against the West Indies at The Oval, makes the highest score of the match.

ROUND 17

August 26–30:

Essex v Middx
Glam v Gloucs
Hants v Sussex
Lancs v Kent
Northants v Leics
Notts v Derbys
Surrey v Somerset
Warwicks v Worcs
Yorkshire v Durham

BACFLASH – 10 YEARS AGO
Shaken by New Zealand's first Test win on English soil a month earlier, Willis and his team stir themselves to clinch the series at Trent Bridge, where a stand of 186 in 32 overs between Botham (103) and Randall (83) on the first evening ignites a 165-run victory wrapped up by the new slow left-armer, Cook of Leicestershire, with nine wickets in his second Test . . . Essex take another sizeable stride towards the Championship at Colchester, drubbing Worcestershire by an innings as McEwan's 189 not out brings up his 2,000 for the summer, the first Chelmsford batsman to achieve the feat since 1955 . . . Middlesex stay on the scent at Lord's by completing the double over neighbours Surrey, Emburey (5–38) dismissing Curtis with 20 minutes left to decide matters . . . Larkins begins a prosperous week against Glamorgan with 145 out of Northamptonshire's 284 at Wantage Road, then makes a similarly substantial donation to his county's 529 for 8 declared with 252 in the return at Cardiff . . . in the same match, Jones the Bat reaches 1,000 in a season for the 23rd time and passes 36,000 runs; the Glamorgan opener's solitary England cap came during a marvellous series against the Rest of the World that has since been expunged from the official records.

ROUND 18

August 31–September 4:

Durham v Notts
Kent v Northants
Leics v Yorkshire
Somerset v Gloucs
Surrey v Hants
Sussex v Essex
Worcs v Lancs

BACFLASH – 15 YEARS AGO
Botham appears primed to cap a memorable season when his controlled effort of 80 steers Somerset to a useful 207 for 7 in the Gillette Cup final against Sussex. At 110 for 4, the first winners of the 60-over competition are wobbling, but Garner and Botham are mysteriously removed from the attack, enabling Parker, 21, to compile a stylish 62 not out and so generate a five-wicket win: a happy ending for the county whose captain, Greig, one of Packer's right-hand men, had resigned amid bitter scenes earlier in the summer . . . crowned champions already, Kent relax against the spin of Waller and suffer a 45-run reverse at Hove, only their third defeat of the season compared with 13 victories . . . Greenidge strides out to open the Hampshire first innings against Glamorgan with ambitions of becoming the first player from the county to register four successive centuries – and makes a duck . . . Ormrod of Worcestershire is caught behind at New Road, the irrepressible Botham's 100th first-class victim of the season . . . rounding off the worst campaign in the club's long and illustrious history, Surrey slip to 16th in the Championship following a 10-wicket loss to Middlesex, Brearley and Featherstone polishing things off on the second evening by racing to 69 off 11 overs.

ROUND 19

September 9–13:

Derbys v Northants
Glam v Essex
Gloucs v Notts
Hants v Leics
Middx v Lancs
Warwicks v Somerset
Yorkshire v Sussex

BACFLASH – 20 YEARS AGO
South Africa's Richards and his West Indian partner, Greenidge, share an opening-stand 241 against Kent as Hampshire, the newly-crowned champions, conclude the season by preserving their unbeaten record. Greenidge, 22, came from Barbados to Berkshire as a boy and has apparently been asked by Illingworth, the England captain, to make himself available for his adopted country. Five Championship centuries, and the verve with which he has made more than 1,600 runs, suggest Illingworth should be persistent . . . Turner, the first batsman since 1938 to make 1,000 first-class runs by the end of May, tops the first-class batting averages with 2,416 runs at 67.11, 1,036 for Worcestershire and 1,380 for New Zealand – including nine centuries . . . at 38, Cartwright, the veteran Somerset and former England medium-pacer, heads the bowling averages with 89 wickets at 15.84 runs apiece, nearly two runs per wicket cheaper than the runner-up, Sainsbury, 39 . . . 'G A Gooch showed fine all-round ability' is the *Wisden* verdict on the leading bowler in Essex's march to the 2nd XI Championship . . . others awaiting the call include the fast bowler, Roberts (Hampshire), openers Fowler (Lancashire), Briers (Leicestershire) and Mendis (Sussex), off-spinner Emburey (Middlesex) and middle-order colleague Gatting.

ROUND 20

September 16–20:

Durham v Somerset
Essex v Hants
Kent v Glam
Lancs v Northants
Leics v Derbys
Notts v Warwicks
Surrey v Yorkshire
Sussex v Gloucs
Worcs v Middx

BACFLASH – 25 YEARS AGO
It's that time again. All the prizes have been distributed: Yorkshire have retained the Championship and Australia the Ashes, Warwickshire extracting revenge for their 1964 defeat by beating one-day experts Sussex in the Gillette Cup final. Now to the averages. Kept out of the last two Tests by an injured back, Boycott heads the batting charts with 1,487 runs at 64.65, nearly 17 ahead of his closest rival, Richards of Hampshire, the heaviest scorer with 2,395 . . . with 84 wickets at 23.38 and 2,009 runs at 44.64, Sobers is far and away the pre-eminent all-rounder, although his most memorable contribution to a miserable summer enlivened almost exclusively by overseas players, was undoubtedly those historic six sixes in one over off the unfortunate Nash at Swansea . . . Cottam, the Hampshire pace bowler, leads the wicket-takers with 130, Wheatley, the Glamorgan seamer, heading the averages with 92 victims at 12.95 . . . Hemmings, the young Warwickshire medium-pacer, props up the batting table with 121 runs at 10.08 during a season in which only Boycott averaged 50 or more . . . often unplayable on the damp, uncovered pitches, 105 bowlers pay less than 30 runs per wicket [Editor's note: a quarter of a century later, that number was down to 44, while 26 batsmen averaged over 50] . . . Eton hail M J J Faber as their finest batsman since the war, while P H Edmonds, a Zambian, tops both batting and bowling averages at Cranbrook School.

WHERE ARE THEY NOW?

Jack Richards, Surrey and England keeper in 1988, was released by his county that winter, moved to the Netherlands and has not been seen on a first-class square since . . . Chris Cowdrey, who captained England during the 1988 season, retired last summer, as did Graham Dilley, who opened the England attack that year . . . Jon Agnew, who threw Phil DeFreitas' bag over the balcony at Leicester in 1988, is now the BBC's cricket correspondent . . . Richard Hadlee, New Zealand's leading bowler in 1983, retired with a Test record haul of 431 wickets and is now Sir Richard Hadlee . . . Mike Brearley, England captain in 1978, is now a psychologist and sometime journalist . . . David Gower, who scored his first Test century in 1978, is now hoping he has not scored his last . . . Ian Botham, that 1978 analysis against Pakistan still the best for England since 1956, is now in his final season (so he says) and is hoping he has not taken his last Test wicket . . . Gordon Greenidge, who was asked to make himself available for England in 1973, won 108 caps for his native West Indies and now works for the Barbadian Tourist Board . . . Mike Hendrick, who made his England one-day debut in 1973, is now the Nottinghamshire manager . . . Mike (M J K) Smith, a pillar of the Warwickshire middle-order in 1973, is now club chairman . . . Ossie Wheatley, who topped the 1968 bowling averages, is now the chairman of the TCCB cricket committee . . . Bob Cottam, highest wicket-taker in 1968, now coaches Warwickshire . . . Phil Edmonds, Cranbrook's leading player in 1968 and winner of 51 England caps, is now a businessman who made a successful if brief comeback for Middlesex last summer at the age of 41 . . . Mark Faber, Eton starlet from the Class of '68, played little first-class cricket and died in 1991 . . . Eddie Hemmings, who finished bottom of the 1968 batting averages, turned into an England spinner and is still going strong at 44. *Plus ça change.* . . .

WHAT, WHERE & HOW

Guide to English first-class grounds and county membership

WHAT are the benefits and costs of becoming a member of a county cricket club? Where can you watch first-class cricket in England and Wales? How do you get to these venues? Apart from excluding the homes of Cambridge and Oxford University on the grounds that the fare available there is invariably second-class (Oxford, with fitting humility, admit the public for free), what follows is a comprehensive guide to the what, where and how of county cricket.

Key:

All venues listed will stage at least one Britannic Assurance Championship or other major first-class match during the 1993 season. All BAC games (plus the Tetley Bitter Shield match between England A and the champion county) are of four days' duration, the dates shown indicating the first and last days. Tourist matches are all of three days' duration. A full 1993 fixture list, including other first-class as well as one-day and international matches, can be found on page ??.

Fixtures:

Owing to the ramifications of the four-day Championship each county now plays the other once, the first time such a format has been followed, giving a total of 17 games apiece. It was therefore decided that exactly half the 18 participants would have one more home BAC match in 1993 (nine) than the other half. This was done by adopting the plan employed for the 1992 Sunday League fixtures, the first competition to accommodate 18 counties playing each other once. The counties thus having the extra home date in 1993 are Durham, Essex, Lancashire, Leicestershire, Middlesex, Northamptonshire, Surrey, Sussex, Warwickshire. The situation will reverse in 1994, leading to a similar rota over subsequent seasons. (The revamped Benson & Hedges Cup, incidentally, was more problematic, since seven counties were needed to fill the preliminary round places alongside Scotland, the Minor Counties and the Combined Universities. Logically enough – although some argued that it might have been fairer to take into account each county's record in the competition – the nominees for 1993 were the first seven counties according to alphabetical order: Derbyshire, Durham, Essex, Glamorgan, Gloucestershire, Hampshire and Kent. In 1994, the next seven – Lancashire, Leicestershire, Middlesex, Northamptonshire, Nottinghamshire, Somerset and Surrey – will take their stead. Sussex, Warwickshire, Worcestershire and Yorkshire thus have a decided advantage: a free pass into the first round until 1995.)

Admission:

Daily prices vary from county to county for BAC games (£3 to £6) and the AXA Equity & Law League (£6 to £7.50) while those for NatWest Trophy and Benson & Hedges Cup ties are standardised by the Test and County Cricket Board. Reductions, of course, are available for the young, the ageing and the unemployed. At less than £1 an hour this represents pretty good value for money considering the increasingly extortionate cost of venturing into cinemas, theatres, concerts and Premier League football grounds. Even if the weather is foul, you can put the world to rights with the bloke three rows away, grab a week's worth of 40 winks, read the newspaper from cover to cover, have a rummage in the bookshop and perhaps even browse round a museum (at Old Trafford, Lord's, Trent Bridge and Taunton). Happily, seating room is rarely in short supply, queues are unusual and advance booking is needed only for major Cup ties. A call to the ground before leaving home is always a wise precaution; to its credit, the TCCB has introduced a 'Raincheck' refund scheme in the event of the weather restricting play during international games, but, as yet, there is no equivalent at county level. Being the most susceptible of all spectator sports to the whims of the weather gods, cricket can be grateful for having such hardy and tolerant followers.

International & Knockout Cup Prices 1993:
(Advance booking through county or in person strongly advised. New raincheck system in operation during Test matches whereby refunds – or parts thereof – are made in the event of severe weather interruption. Unfortunately, county cricket has yet to adopt such a revolutionary measure, so have a long hard look at the clouds before you pay):
Test matches (per day): £12, £16, £20, £25, £30. There may be some latitude at certain venues such as Old Trafford, where reduced admission has been introduced for children on the first day and families on the Sunday.
Texaco Trophy (55 overs): £10 (restricted view), £20, £28, £37, £40.
Benson & Hedges Cup: Preliminary round: £6, members £3; first round: £10/£5; quarter-finals: £12; semi-finals: £14; final: as per Texaco.
NatWest Trophy: first round: £8; second round: £10; quarter-finals: £12; semi-finals: £14; final: as per Texaco.

Hours of Play:
Ostensibly, BAC matches start at 11am and finish at 6.30pm, but the requirement that a certain number of overs be bowled each day (110 on the first three, 102 on the fourth) means that play rarely signs off on time unless the spinners are on all day. On average, 6.45 is a fair bet, although 7.30 is far from uncommon. Strangely enough, Benson & Hedges Cup games begin at the same time and encompass the same number of overs, yet the competition is littered with instances of games trundling on well past eight. Although much is made of slovenly over-rates it has never been clear quite how objectionable they are to those outside the fourth estate. Granted, the participants in a one-day match are cheating when they prevent the contest from being concluded within the time advertised. Time-wasting, moreover, is indefensible. On the other hand, no other sport requires a team to be on duty for an eight-hour day, six days a week. Cricket, particularly the first-class game, is slow, sedate, contemplative, a form of physical chess. Brighter, certainly, than it was before the hatching of the limited-over golden goose, and definitely more enterprising (for all F. S. Trueman's claims to the contrary) but, like the Sri Lankan seam attack, short on real pace. Still, far better this more modest, lighthearted andante than the grumpy, ill-focused allegro of soccer and rugby.

Playing Hours for Major County Fixtures:
BAC: The majority of matches begin on Thursdays, carry on through Friday and Saturday, pause for 24 hours then conclude on a Monday. Only the first round of matches in 1993, beginning Thursday April 29, include Sunday play. Day 1 to 3 – 11am to 6.30pm or when 110 overs have been bowled in the day, whichever is the later. Lunch 1.15–1.55; Tea 4.10–4.30. Day 4 – 11am to 5.30 6pm, or when 102 overs have been bowled, including 20 from 5pm unless the respective captains accept that there is no prospect of a conclusive result and agree to draw stumps at 5.30. If one side declares at 5.20 and there is still another innings to come, the compulsory 10–minute gap between innings means that play can terminate then. Lunch 1.00–1.40; Tea 3.40–4.00. In September, it should be noted, all these times go back half an hour owing to the shortening daylight hours. Bad weather, the biggest cross the English game has to bear, may necessitate changes to interval times in order to permit the maximum playing time. Furthermore, if one team is nine wickets down at the appointed time, the tea break will be delayed.

Tourist match: Day 1 and 2 – 11am to 6.30pm. Lunch 1.00–1.40; Tea 4.00–4.20. Day 3 – 11am–5.30/6pm (same rules apply as above). No minimum over requirement.

AXA Equity & Law League (one-day, 50 overs per side): Sunday 12 noon to completion of match. Tea break between innings (approx 3.15–3.35pm).

Benson & Hedges Cup (one-day, 55 overs per side): 11am to 7.30pm. Lunch 1.15–1.55; Tea after 25 overs of second innings, although this may vary according to the state of the game/weather. All games on Tuesday except final, which takes place at Lord's on a Saturday.

NatWest Trophy (one-day, 60 overs per side): 10.30am to 8pm. Lunch 12.45–1.25; Tea after 25 overs of second innings. All games on Tuesday except final, which takes place at Lord's on a Saturday. NB: Playing hours in one-day cup competitions can be extended at the discretion of teams and umpires so long as the light is not deemed inadequate or dangerous.

Membership:

Essentially, joining a club means cut-rate admission. After all, to pay to watch all 44 days' cricket scheduled at, say, New Road and Kidderminster in 1993 would cost £237, whereas Worcestershire charge full members £62 (members aged 63 and upwards pay £41 while juniors pay £26 and students £39). Strangely enough, now that English cricket has finally embraced marketing departments and coloured jammies, no one seems to have hit upon the idea of a discounted County Championship match ticket (four days for the price of two, say). Only Lancashire and Leicestershire require applicants to be proposed and seconded: if you do not know any existing members prepared to do so, the membership departments at Grace Road and Old Trafford will arrange a personal interview with committee members, who will act as proposer and seconder. The process, however, is essentially no more than a formality. To apply for membership, contact the headquarters of your preferred county – or call there in person – and request a form.

The benefits are largely uniform: free admission to all your county's home BAC and first-class fixtures, at all venues, as well as their home AXA Equity & Law League and 2nd XI fixtures (admission to Benson & Hedges/NatWest ties must be paid); admission to the members' enclosure/pavilion (at the discretion of the management this privilege extends to away venues, upon payment of the ground admission charge); one or two guests permitted to accompany you into the pavilion (upon payment of their admission); priority booking for one-day Cup games (check with club when tickets come on sale); entitlement to wear club tie and/or scarf; free yearbook (enlarging – Essex's had 301 pages in 1992 – and improving every year); regular newsletters and info about club dinners and functions. There are also schemes designed to encourage you to introduce a new member, the reward being a reduction or partial refund on your own subscription (a full rebate if you bring along three new full members to Middlesex).

Membership also enables you to be put forward as a candidate to sit on one of the multifarious committees that help make various commercial and cricketing decisions at your club. These decisions ultimately find a voice on the Test and County Cricket Board, the body that really runs the game in England (hanging stubbornly on to the notion that their club still has some clout, some misguided if seemingly well-intentioned MCC members sought to demonstrate otherwise when they protested at David Gower's non-selection for India last winter). The board, which convenes four times a year, comprises a representative from each first-class county – the club chairman – alongside counterparts from the MCC (why?) and the Minor Counties Association.

Although subscriptions for all save life members are made on an annual basis (direct debits encouraged), there are alternatives. Durham, to take one example, offer a Silver Membership covering four years (1993 to 1996) for the price of three to anyone signing on before December 31 of the preceding year.

Rates vary according to age, and incentives like Durham's (Worcestershire promised a Club Diary for those paying before January 1, 1993) are widely offered for early payment. In some cases, substantial reductions are also available for the disabled, while most counties operate a discounted family membership scheme. All have reduced rates for juniors (under 18) and seniors (60 and over) and all bar one permit women to enter the hallowed portals of the main pavilion. In Middlesex's defence, they are the one county to have no say in the running of their headquarter ground.

The four main categories of membership are as follows:

1. FULL: Open to people aged, generally, between 18 and 60 and residing within a radius of about 20 miles of the club offices. Every county secretary's office has a map outlining the exclusion zone. As the title implies, this entitles the member to full benefits, so too those paying the senior and country rates.

2. LIFE: Same benefits as a full member – for life. Looks a lot on paper – Essex charge £2300 – but a snip for the committed.

3. EXECUTIVE: An upmarket innovation ushered in by the growth of the corporate entertainment biz, this category is for those who want to mix business with pleasure. Middlesex now have an Executive Club, 'strictly limited' to 200 members, each of whom pay £175 per year for all the usual benefits of full membership, plus use of the club's executive box in the Tavern Stand for themselves and up to eight guests. Lunch, coffee and biccies included but not pints and shorts.

4. COUNTRY: Clubs differ in their methods of calculating who is eligible for 'Country' status, a reduced-rate category aimed at potential supporters residing outside the immediate vicinity. To qualify you must live a certain number of miles outside the county HQ, but, as with the criteria for full members, the precise amount may vary. Lancashire, for instance, offer Country membership 'to those persons who permanently reside more than 50 miles in a straight line from Lancashire County Cricket Club and do not have business interests in the Manchester area'. At Hampshire, 'Country Membership applies to members living in the Isle of Wight or outside a 20–mile radius from Southampton or Portsmouth'; they also have a category for 'Hampshire Exiles'. As from 1993 Lancashire have added 'Country Membership 30–50 Miles', a new category targeting those living a short train ride away.

Directions:

Speaking of the iron horse, one of the delights of county-hopping is the opportunity it affords to drink in Britain by rail before privatisation destroys the romance and puts the boot into a batch of unprofitable lines. The 'How to Get There' section therefore encompasses rail as well as bus and road. For those coming by car, there are AA (and sometimes RAC) 'County Cricket' signs leading to nearly every venue from the nearest motorway exit, and always within a couple of miles of the ground.

Refreshments/Amenities:

Perhaps the main advantage of joining a county is that access to the pavilion usually means access to the best tuck, not to mention the best ale (public bars are more prevalent in outground marquees than headquarter grounds). Compared with our more commercially-minded friends in the US of A, to whom fast food is something to be celebrated rather than sneered at, the most charitable thing one can say about the food at the common or garden British sporting venue is that it is a monument to mediocrity. Bouncing burgers, dodgy doughnuts, tepid tea – the tradition is a proud one. Having said that, things are beginning to improve in county cricket, particularly for those with fatter wallets. Most headquarters have in-house restaurants and catered executive boxes, while outgrounds are thickly populated by catered marquees for sponsors. There has even been the odd imaginative venture such as the scrumptious al fresco seafood bar at Canterbury.

For those who plonk down their fivers and click through the turnstiles, the fare is at least becoming more cosmopolitan, what with pizza slices, Chicken Kiev and chicken tikka now rubbing aromas with the staple steak' n' kidney pie/chips/cheese roll/hot dog/fruit bun selection. Rain or shine, ice cream vans are always close at hand at outgrounds, kiosks plentiful at headquarters. Prices, sensibly, are not excessive. All the same, for the non-member, it is a toss-up at most venues as to whether filling a flask, wrapping a few sarnies in clingfilm and plucking an apple from the garden constitutes a safer bet. Whether you can say the same of those pongy portaloos at some of the outgrounds is another matter. On the whole, though, conveniences are reasonably hygienic and thick on the ground, as are the club shops. These tend to vary in size, some taking in videos, magazines, books and confectionery, all purveying an assortment of club-related paraphernalia. As a rule of thumb, headquarter grounds, unsurprisingly, are better equipped all round than the irregularly-used outgrounds, where so much is temporary and therefore basic.

Views/Seating:
Sitting behind the bowler's arm, ideally above ground level, is generally accepted as the best vantage point. This allows the game to be seen head-on, which makes it easier to appreciate how the ball is behaving, whether a slip fielder has taken a catch cleanly, whether the batsman really did get that edge or whether the ball that struck his pads would have hit the wicket. Although this generally means sitting in the pavilion and therefore being a member, the opposite end of the ground is just as good where seating permits, such as the T. N. Pearce Stand at Chelmsford. Whatever you do, *don't* sit in front of the sightscreen, unless, that is, you actively enjoy people shouting at you. Sitting square of the wicket has its rewards too: not only do distances seem clearer, but watching a bowler side-on can be even more aesthetically pleasing. It is not, however, the perfect spot from which to accuse the umpire of fluffing an lbw decision. Being at an angle to the wicket, though imperfect, often permits a better slant on catches, and offers an equally fine perspective on strokes. Wherever you are, binoculars are heartily recommended.

Seating is either wood or plastic (deckchairs are available at Hove and other seaside venues) and not terribly comfortable. Cushions (up for hire at some grounds) are imperative for long stints on a bench. Standing at the bar can be just as comfy. One comforting thought: there will never be a shortage of spaces at a Championship game.

Notes:
Admission – prices are quoted only for county HQ: all outgrounds charge the same. Parking – with the exception of senior international matches, Cup games and the odd Sunday slog, this presents few problems for members, for whom passes are generally available at moderate cost. Non-members, on the other hand, may be directed to an adjoining area at the Test venues. Disabled facilities – improving all the time in terms of toilets, lifts and access, and there is always someone around to lend a hand.

DERBYSHIRE
Chief executive: Bob Lark
DERBY (HQ): Address: County Cricket Ground, Nottingham Road, Derby
DE2 6DA
Phone: 0332 383211

How to Get There:
Rail: Derby Midland BR; 1¼ miles away.
Bus: 29, 42–47 from BR station to bus station (0332 754433). From there, almost any bus to the ground.
Road: From north: Exit M2 junction 28. Follow signs to Derby via A38 or A6 to Pentagon Island. The ground is on the north side of the roundabout.

From south: Exit M2 junction 24. Follow signs to Derby via A6 then A52 to Spondon then A61 to Pentagon Island.
From east: Exit M2 junction 25. Follow signs to Derby via A52 and A61 to Pentagon Island.
From west: A52, A38 and A5111, then A61 to Pentagon Island.

Membership: Full Member: £60; Senior: £30; Junior: £15; Student (under 25 and in full-time education): £33; Full Country: £35; Senior Country: £22; Junior Country: £9; Student Country: £28; Executive (E1): £160 – includes car park pass; Executive (E2): £265 – includes guest ticket and two car park passes; Executive: £500+ VAT – includes three guest tickets, all transferable, plus four car park passes; Patron £105 – includes one guest ticket, one car park pass and access to own seating area; Patron Country: £68; Club/Firm: £175 – includes four transferable tickets; Car park pass: £30. Contact county for details of life membership and 'Friends of Derbyshire' associate membership.
Admission: BAC: Adult £5, Junior/Senior £2.
AXA League: Adult £7, Junior/Senior £3.
Disabled facilities: Access to Grandstand difficult. Parking for up to 8 cars next to South Stand boundary and also outside perimeter.
BAC fixtures 1993: v Glamorgan (13–17 May); v Hampshire (27–31 May); v Lancashire (24–28 June); v Sussex (22–26 July); v Somerset (12–16 Aug); v Northamptonshire (9–13 Sept). Tourist match: v Australia (13–15 July).
Capacity: 9,500 approx.

Extras: Occupies part of the old Nottingham Road racecourse: what was the jockeys' quarters is now part changing-room and part administrative centre. The present grandstand is the very same one the Victorians stood in to place their bets. At one juncture the wicket ran from east to west instead of the customary north–south, leading to stoppages for *good* light as batsmen were dazzled by the sinking sun. It was here that Derbyshire made their highest first-class score, 645, against Hampshire in 1898. Alan Ward, their great white pace hope of the early Seventies produced the most spectacular over in 40-over cricket here in 1970, taking four Sussex wickets with successive balls. Wickets tend to favour seamers.

CHESTERFIELD: Address: Chesterfield Cricket Club, Queen's Park,
Boythorpe Avenue, Chesterfield, Derbyshire
Phone: 0246 273090

How to Get There:
Rail: Chesterfield BR; ¾ mile away.
Bus: 1 from BR station to ¼ mile from ground. Many services to bus station (200m from ground; 0246 76666).
Road: From north: Exit M12 junction 30. Follow signs to Chesterfield then Buxton via A619, then A632 to Queen's Park.
From east: Follow A632 or A617 to Chesterfield, then on to Queen's Park.
From south: Exit M1 junction 29. Follow signs to Chesterfield via either A617 or A61. Then on to Queen's Park.
From west: Take either A619 or A632 to Chesterfield, then Queen's Park.

Disabled facilities: Space for up to 8 cars next to boundary at pavilion end and on former cycle track surrounding perimeter.
BAC fixtures 1993: v Yorkshire (10–14 June).
Capacity: 7,500 approx.

Extras: Bandstand and park setting, not forgetting the marvellous All Saints' Church spire in all its twisted, glistered glory, make this the most attractive venue in the Midlands by a mile or two. A place, noted *Barclay's World of Cricket*, where 'miner and mechanic have a "meadow game" at hand in an appropriate setting'. In 1904, a prototype Essex Man named Percy Perrin went potty here, breaching the boundary 68 times – still the world record – in his unbeaten 343. Pitches tend to encourage pace and strokeplay.

ILKESTON: Address: Ilkeston Rutland Cricket Club, Recreation Ground, Oakwell Drive, Ilkeston, Derbyshire
Phone: 0602 303036/440440 x 353

How to Get There:
Rail: Langley Mill BR (4 miles); Nottingham Midland BR (9 miles).
Bus: Barton 4, 18 or 51 from Nottingham, Broad Marsh, close to Nottingham BR station (0602 254881).
Road: From north: Exit M1 junction 26. Follow signs to Ilkeston via A610 and A6096. Ground situated in town centre off A6007.
From east: Take the A609 to Ilkeston.
From south: Exit M1 junction 25. Follow signs to Stapleford via A52, then A609.
From west: Take A609 or A6096.

Disabled facilities: Good access with exception of main pavilion terrace; no reserved area.
BAC fixture 1993: v Surrey (19–22 Aug).
Capacity: 7,000 approx.

Extras: Club home to two esteemed Derbyshire miners of the seam, Cliff Gladwin (who won the first Test against South Africa in 1948–49 by scampering a leg-bye off the last ball of the match) and Les Jackson, this bowl-shaped venue forms a part of what was once the estate of the Duke of Rutland. Locals dubbed it the 'Queen of the Erewash Valley'. The highest innings made here by a Derbyshire batsman is the 217 forged against Surrey in 1976 by Eddie Barlow. Porthos to Mike Procter's Aramis and Barry Richards's D'Artagnan, it was this pugnacious South African musketeer who instilled spirit and dash in the modern Peakites. Side attractions include facilities for tennis, bowls and putting.

DURHAM
Executive director: Geoff Cook

CHESTER-LE-STREET (HQ): Address: Durham County Cricket Club, County Ground, Riverside, Chester-le-Street, Co. Durham DH3 3QR
Phone: 091 387 1717
Fax: 091 387 1616
Ground address: Chester-le-Street Cricket Club, The Pavilion, Ropery Lane, Chester-le-Street, Co. Durham
Phone: 091 388 3684

How to Get There:
Rail: Chester-le-Street BR; ¼ mile away.
Bus: X1, X2, X46, X69, 722–724 and 737 (091 386 4411 x 2337).
Road: From north: A1(M) to Chester-le-Street junction; follow A167 to Durham via Shields Road, Park Road North and Central; right at Ropery Lane roundabout for ground and car parks.
From south: A167 from Durham or A1(M) to Chester-le-Street junction, then as north.
From east: as north.
From west: A693 or A167 to Chester-le-Street; take Ropery Lane for ground from town centre.

Membership: Full Member; £70; Full Member & Spouse; £110; Senior: £42; Senior & Spouse: £70; Disabled: £42; Student; £35, Overseas: £28; Family: £125; Junior: £10. Country Membership (living outside a 50-mile radius): Full: £42; & Spouse: £70; Senior: £42; Junior: £7.50. Gold (Life) Membership: Full (under

40): £1500; Full & Spouse (under 40): £2250; Full (under 50): £1000; Full & Spouse (under 50): £1500; Senior: £500; Senior & Spouse: £750.
Admission: BAC: Adults £6, Junior/Senior £3. AXA League: Adults £7, Junior/Senior £3.50.
Disabled facilities: Ask for assistance; ring in advance for parking.
BAC fixture 1993: v Nottinghamshire (31 Aug–4 Sept).
Capacity: 5,000.

Extras: The Ropery Lane ground lies roughly half a mile to the north of the proposed new county HQ and ground, Riverside Stadium, scheduled for completion by 1995 but already home to the administrative offices. Ropery Lane itself staged Durham's first minor county fixture, against Northumberland in 1903. Club professionals who strutted their stuff here before the county gained first-class status in 1992 included Test luminaries such as the dashing Pakistani all rounder Wasim Raja. The greatest entertainer to frequent these parts, though, was the late lamented Colin Milburn, a Durham native whose huge grin, equally expansive girth and even more massive blows jollied up world cricket during the slumbering Sixties and snoozy early Seventies.

DARLINGTON: Address: Darlington Cricket and Athletic Club, Feethams Cricket Ground, South Terrace, Darlington, Co. Durham DL1 5JD.
Phone: 0325 466415.
How to Get There:
Rail: Darlington BR; ¼ mile from ground.
Bus: 2 runs between station and ground; 1, 1A, 3A, 3B, 4, 4A, 5, 6, 6A, 7, 11A, X13, X14, X35, X50, X51, X70, 68, 68A, 722 and 723 run between bus station (¼ mile from ground) and surrounds.
Road: From north: A1(M); A167 to Darlington and town centre; follow signs to Northallerton along Victoria Road; left after roundabout into South Terrace.
From south: A1(M) to A66(M); follow signs to Darlington and town centre, then as per north directions.
From west: A167 to Darlington and town centre; third exit off roundabout into Victoria Road, then as per north directions.
From east: A167 to Darlington and town centre then as per north directions.

Disabled facilities: Reserved area to the left of the pavilion.
BAC fixtures 1993: v Kent (27–31 May); v Warwickshire (19–23 Aug).
Capacity: 5,000.

Extras: Only the football stand at the Feethams End divides the playing area from that of Darlington FC, an unhappy reminder that muddied oafs once shared this expansive ground. It was certainly big enough to stage the rather grandiloquently-titled (and sadly extinct) Darlington Olympian Games. W. G. Grace turned out here for a North Yorkshire and South Durham League XI in 1907, a visitation commemorated in the pavilion by a copy of the scorecard.

DURHAM UNIVERSITY: Address: Durham University Cricket Club, Estates and Building Dept, Hollow Drift, Green Lane, Durham DH1 3LA
Phone: 091 374 3064
How to Get There:
Rail: Durham BR; 1¼ miles away.
Bus: 20, 41, 57 to ¼ mile from ground (091 386 4511 x 2337).
Road: From north: A1(M) to Durham City junction (north); follow A690 for Durham and city centre then over New Elvet Bridge; take left into Old Elvet for Green Lane and ground.
From south: A1(M) to Durham City junction (south); A177 for Durham and city centre; then as north.
From east: A690 for Durham and city centre then as north, or A1(M) to Durham

City junction (south); A177 for Durham and city centre then as north.
From west: A167 to Durham and city centre; Leazes Bridge and New Elvet Bridge; as north.

Disabled facilities: Position available near pavilion by prior request; parking area.
BAC fixtures 1993: v Sussex (29 July–2 Aug); v Derbyshire (5–9 Aug).
Tour match: v Australia (17–19 July).
Capacity: 5,000.

Extras: Home to the students who make the Blues blush. Durham University have monopolised the University Athletic Union title for the past decade or more, supplying the likes of Graeme Fowler, Paul Allott, Tim Curtis and John Stephenson to the Test team. When, in 1989, Durham players were first permitted to infiltrate the ranks of the 'Combined Universities' XI (the combination had hitherto been wholly Oxbridge), the quintet selected – Martin Speight, James Boiling, Tim O'Gorman, Jon Longley and Nasser Hussain – helped their side beat Surrey and Worcestershire and ultimately reach the quarter-finals of the Benson & Hedges Cup for the first and, so far, only time. A proper Combined Universities XI would certainly be more worthy of first-class status than the recent batch of undergrads.
NB: Parking for up to 250 cars available in adjacent football field but not inside ground.

GATESHEAD FELL: Address: Gateshead Fell Cricket Club, Eastwood Gardens, Gateshead NE9 5UB
Phone: 091 487 5746

How To Get There:
Rail: Newcastle-upon-Tyne (Central) BR; 5 miles to Gateshead by Interchange to bus service providing link to ground.
Bus: G2, G3, 27, 35 and 93 from Interchange Metro to Low Fell, via Dryden Road to ground (091 222 0404).
Road: From north: A167 from Newcastle-upon-Tyne to Gateshead along Durham Road; take Dryden Road for ground in Eastwood Gardens, following signs.
From south: A1(M); A167 to Gateshead (south) before reaching Gateshead College; right into Valley Drive then at first junction right into Dryden Road; first left for Eastwood Gardens.
From east: A184 to Gateshead and Felling; follow signs for county cricket to Dryden Road and Eastwood Gardens.
From west: A692, A6528, A69 or A694 to Gateshead; as east.

Disabled facilities: Reserved area at Rugby Ground End close to the sight-screen; arrange parking in advance.
BAC fixtures 1993: v Middlesex (10–14 June).
Capacity: 4,500 approx.

Extras: Should Damien Martyn find himself hailed as Australia's latest New Bradman during the Ashes tour Gateshead Fell CC will undoubtedly come under the spotlight: the West Australian batsman played here for a spell a couple of years ago. So, too, a little earlier, did Richie Richardson. According to the local humorists, if you are unable to make out the spire of St John's Church from the pavilion then it must be raining – and if you can, it soon will be. Durham lost their 1991 Holt Cup match here against Northumberland after a bowl-out against a set of unguarded stumps, a form of expediency that encapsulated the game's need to outlaw stalemate and deal only in winners and losers. The Gateshead Metrocentre, Europe's largest, is worth investigating at lunchtime.

HARTLEPOOL: Address: Hartlepool Cricket Club, 38 Tunstall Avenue, Hartlepool, Cleveland TS26 8NE
Phone: 0429 260875

How to Get There:
Rail: Hartlepool BR; 1½ miles away.
Bus: From Hartlepool bus station – 15 stops nearby; also 22, 241, 242 and 244 (091 386 4411 x 2337).
Road: From north: A19 to Elwick Road (signposted county cricket); down Park Drive to ground, which lies west of the town centre close to Ward Jackson Park.
From south: A19 then as north.
From west: as north.

Disabled facilities: Reserved area at Egerton Road End; arrange parking in advance.
BAC fixture 1993: v Somerset (16–20 Sept).
Capacity: 3,000 approx.

Extras: What with West Hartlepool in Courage Division One and Hartlepool United spending much of the 1992-93 Football League season flirting with promotion to the First Division, this sporting backwater is clearly making strides towards the big pond. Pleasant park setting for this unassuming club ground. Its regular tenants are currently celebrating their 138th anniversary.

STOCKTON-ON-TEES: Address: Stockton Cricket Club, The Grangefield Ground, Oxbridge Avenue, Stockton-on-Tees, Cleveland TS18 4JF
Phone: 0642 672835

How to Get There:
Rail: Stockton BR via connection from Darlington InterCity; 1 mile away.
Bus: 55A, 61, 163, 235 – get off at Grangefield Road and Grays Road (091 386 4411 x 2337).
Road: From north: A19 (or A689 to A19); take Billingham/Norton turn-off; follow Stockton ring road A1027 to Oxbridge Road for Grangefield Road.
From south: A19 to Stockton then ring road for Grangefield Road or A66 Darlington to Middlesbrough; take Eaglescliffe junction and approach via Darlington Road, Hartburn Avenue, then on to ring road and Oxbridge Avenue.
From east: A178 to Stockton; ring road and follow signs to Grangefield Road and ground or as north.
From west: A66, A67 or A177 to Stockton; follow signs to Grangefield Road and ground or as south.

Disabled facilities: Vantage points open to request; arrange parking in advance.
BAC fixtures 1993: v Hampshire (13–17 May); v Worcestershire (24–28 June).
Capacity: 5,000.

Extras: Founded in 1816, Stockton CC were of sufficient standing in the mid-19th century to entertain the All-England XI seven times between 1847 and 1860. The ground itself, first purchased in 1891, was also the venue for Durham's final Minor Counties Championship fixture. The pavilion dates back to the 1890s, when its basement was used as a stable for the horses used to roll and cut the pitch. The club room is named the Chris Old Room, a tribute to a considerable, if fitful, all-round talent who graced the Yorkshire and England teams with no little panache during the late 1970s. Unfortunately, 'Chilly' Old is most frequently remembered as the leading hypochondriac of his era.

ESSEX
Secretary/General manager: Peter Edwards

CHELMSFORD (HQ): Address: County Cricket Ground, New Writtle Street, Chelmsford CM2 0PG
Phone: 0245 252420
Prospects of Play: 0245 287921

How to Get There:
Rail: Chelmsford BR; ½ mile away.
Bus: Any bus to Chelmsford bus station, ½ mile from ground.
Road: From north: Exit M1 junction 8. Follow signs to Chelmsford via A120 and A130. Ground near town centre, on southern bank of River Cam off Parkway (A130).
From south: Exit M25 junction 28. Take A12 to Chelmsford, then A130.
From east: Take A414 or A12 to A130.
From west: Take A414, then A130.

Membership: Full: £58, Husband & Wife: £102; Senior: £35; Husband & Wife: £61; Student: £25; Junior: £17; Corporate Patron: £265; Club: £70; Life: Aged 20 or over: £2300; 30+: £1620; 40+: £1150; 50+: £810; 60+: £580.
Admission: BAC Adult £5, Senior Junior £2.50; Sunday League: £7/£3.50; Tourist match: £8£4; v England A £5£2.50.
Disabled facilities: Request position in advance – few restrictions.
BAC fixtures 1993: v Yorkshire (6–10 June); v Derbyshire (20–24 May); v Somerset (3–7 June); v Durham (22–26 July); v Worcs (29 July–2 July); v Hampshire (16–20 Sept). Tourist match: v Australia (14–16 Aug). Tetley Bitter Shield: v England A (22–26 April).
Capacity: 9,500.

Extras: A spanking new fast food outlet and revamped restaurant reflect the rise and rise of a club that, barely 20 years ago, was regarded in cricket circles with the same mixture of affection and sympathy Chelsea FC generated in the Thirties; a music-hall turn, good for a laugh but never likely to take the thing seriously enough to win anything. These days, despite secretary Peter Edwards' insistence that the prospect of four-day cricket is driving members away, sheer demand means that this remains one of the hardest clubs to join outside that posh joint in St John's Wood. Be warned: for the past couple of seasons, there has been no point in applying after April. Fortunately, they still don't take it *that* seriously and the aura of chumminess persists. The newly unveiled statue of Graham Gooch almost says it all: a similar tribute to the world's humblest Svengali, Keith Fletcher, cannot be far away.

COLCHESTER: Address: Colchester and East Essex Cricket Club, Castle Park (Lower), Sportsway off Cathpool Road, Colchester, Essex
Phone: 0206 769071

How to Get There:
Rail: Colchester BR; ¾ mile away.
Bus: Any Eastern National and Colchester Corporation bus to bus station. Ground ¾ mile away.
Road: From north: A12 or A134 to Colchester, then to Castle Park via A12.
From south: A12 to Colchester or B1025B1026, then A12.
From east: A120, A137 or A133 to Colchester.
From west: A120 or A604 to Colchester.

Disabled facilities: As Chelmsford, but beware, the high water table can lead to flooding and the perimeter may prove hazardous for wheelchairs.
BAC fixtures 1993: v Middlesex (26–30 Aug).
Capacity: 6,000 approx.

Extras: It was here in 1938 that Arthur Fagg, later to become the first umpire to go on strike in the middle of a Test, achieved the greatest individual batting 'double' in first-class history by collecting a double century in each innings for Kent, a unique feat. The vast distance from pavilion to middle, incidentally, means that batsmen are in greater danger of being 'timed out' here than at any other outground in the land, which doubtless had a bearing on the decision to extend the time allowed from two minutes to three. The walk into town, in fact, is only slightly longer. The bookie's caravan opposite the pavilion is a popular diversion, offering bets on anything from how many wickets the bowling side can manage before tea to which batsman scores the most runs in the match: a nod to cricket's one-time function as a gambler's plaything. The wind can be powerful, never more so than in 1992, when it gusted the press tent over. One of the falling poles almost decapitated somebody. Graham Gooch's grin was cruel.

ILFORD: Address: Ilford Cricket Club, Valentine's Park, Cranbrook Road,
Ilford, Essex
Phone: 081 518 2990/554 8381

How to Get There:
Rail: Ilford BR and Gants Hill (Central Line, London Underground) are both ¾ mile away.
Bus: 123, 129, 144, 150, 167, 179, 247 and 296 all pass Ilford and Gants Hill stations.
Road: From north: Exit M25 junction 27; take M11 and A12 to Gants Hill; at roundabout, take Cranbrook Road.
From south: Take A13, then A117 and A124 to Ilford.
From east: Exit M25 either 28 or 29; A12 or A126 to Ilford.
From west: Take A13, than A117 and A124 to Ilford.

Disabled facilities: No restrictions.
BAC fixture 1993: v Warwickshire (24–28 June).
Capacity: 12,000 approx.

Extras: As recent double hundreds from Mark Waugh, Salim Malik and Desmond Haynes indicate, not forgetting Essex's hell-for-leather chase against Middlesex in 1992, the strip here is usually bountiful for batting buffs. After all, this is the ground where Alfred and Rose Gooch's lad learned his trade. The honour of being the most attractive first-class venue in Essex may not amount to much, but Valentine's Park really does arouse affection. Vying with Victoria Park as one of the prettiest parks in East London, and among the most expansive in the capital period, its late Victorian landlord, Mrs Ingleby, sold Ilford CC the lease before adding two conditions: that the sightscreens be lowered so that she could not see them from her bedroom window, and that the pavilion be erected under the trees. A place for the kids.

SOUTHEND-ON-SEA: Address: Southend-on-Sea Cricket Club,
Southchurch Park, Northumberland Crescent, Southend-on-Sea, Essex
Phone: 0702 6151967876

How to Get There:
Rail: Southend East BR; ½ mile away.
Bus: 7, 8, 67 and 68. Eastern National 20 (Shoeburyness to Hullbridge) passes Southend Central and Victoria BR stations.
Road: From north and west: M25 junction 29; A127 or A130; follow signs to Southend; A13 to Southchurch and ground, 1½ miles east of town centre.

Disabled facilities: No restrictions, though request may be needed at boating lake end.

BAC fixtures 1993: v Leicestershire (15–19 July).
Capacity: 8,000.

Extras: For 40 years, Southchurch Park was famed for a piece of plunder by the 1948 Australians, one of the two greatest touring sides ever to spellbind these shores. Essex dismissed them, sure, but only at the extortionate exchange rate of 721 runs, the most ever amassed in a day. In 1989, however, infamy arrived when Essex were docked 25 Championship points for preparing a poor pitch against Yorkshire, the first time such a punishment had been levied and one that ultimately cost the hosts the title. The smell of cockles and whelks may be too much to resist at lunchtime; the more health-conscious might fancy a set at the adjoining tennis courts before play starts. Parking spaces across road in field.

GLAMORGAN
Secretary: Gwyn Stone
CARDIFF (HQ): Address: Cardiff Athletic Club, Sophia Gardens, Cathedral Road, Cardiff CF1 9XR
Phone: 0222 343478
Fax: 0222 377044

How to Get There:
Rail: Ground lies one mile from Cardiff Central BR (0222 396521).
Bus: 36, 62 from BR station. Also 21, 25 or 33.
Road: From north: A470 to Cardiff; at junction with Cardiff bypass take A48 to Port Talbot; Cathedral Road is off A48.
From east: Exit M4 junction 29 on to A48, then as north.
From west: A4160 to Cardiff; exit at A48, then as north.

Membership: A reciprocal arrangement with Gloucestershire, Somerset and Worcestershire allows Glamorgan members to use the facilities of their grounds as well. Better still, the reduction in home fixtures has prompted Glamorgan to cut prices by 66% for this year and next.
Full Membership: £15; Junior Membership: £10 (plus 10% discount in club shop and specially organised coaching clinics); Vice-President: £50; Executive Member: £117.50; Gold Member: £30; Gold Vice-President: £65.
Disabled facilities: Request suitable position; arrange parking space in advance.
Admission: BAC: Adults £5; Junior/Senior £2; AXA League: Adults £7; Junior Senior £3.
BAC fixtures 1993: v Sussex (29 April–2 May); v Middlesex (1–5 July); v Warwickshire (5–9 Aug); v Essex (9–13 Sept).
Capacity: 10,000.

Extras: Named after the second wife of the second Marquis of Bute, Sophia Gardens became the Glamorgan CC headquarters in the mid-1960s after the club left nearby Cardiff Arms Park, though not the shadow of rugby that will forever shroud Welsh cricket. There is an electronic scoreboard, and the Welsh National Sports Centre lurks behind the pavilion, but the overall feel is more modest, if no less pleasant for that. In fact, that immortal soul of the Welsh greensward, Wilf Wooller, once went so far as to describe it as rural. There was nothing rustic, mind, about the unbeaten 313 fashioned here in 1990 by Jimmy Cook, the elegant Transvaalian schoolteacher who gave so many masterclasses for Somerset not so long ago.

ABERGAVENNY: Address: Abergavenny Cricket Club, The Pavilion, Pen-y-Pound Cricket Ground, Avenue Road, Abergavenny, Gwent
Phone: 0873 852350

How to Get There:
Rail: Abergavenny BR; 2 miles away.
Bus: Take National Welsh 20 (Newport-Hereford) or National Welsh 21 (Newport-Brecon) to bus station (0222 371331).
Road: From north: A465 or A40 to Abergavenny. Ground in Avenue Road off A40 (Brecon Road).
From south: Exit M4 junction 26; A4042 to Abergavenny.
From east: A40 or A465; then as north.

Disabled facilities: No reserved area so request suitable position; parking available at Avenue Road End by prior arrangement.
BAC fixture 1993: v Gloucestershire (26–30 Aug).
Capacity: 5,000 approx.

Extras: Cute, postage stamp of a ground lying at the foot of Sugar Loaf Mountain and close to the hilly splendours of the Brecon Beacons National Park. The pavilion is new, having been rebuilt in 1977 following a fire. Known as Pen-y-Pound by the locals, its short boundaries have been pounded with particular relish by Graeme Hick in recent years. A knock of 159 here in 1988 settled the BAC race in Worcestershire's favour, while an unconquered 252 two years later swelled his ground average to 205.50. Fortunately for Watkin, Croft and co, Glamorgan bribed the TCCB fixture computer: Gloucestershire are in town this season.

COLWYN BAY: Address: Colwyn Bay Cricket Club, The Pavilion, 77 Penrhyn Avenue, Rhos-on-Sea, Colwyn Bay, Clwyd, North Wales LL28 4LR
Phone: 0492 44103

How to Get There:
Rail: Colwyn Bay BR; 1½ miles away.
Bus: M16 from BR station.
Road: From north: A470 or A546 to Rhos-on-Sea or as east.
From south: A470 or B5106 or B5113 to Colwyn Bay; A55 to Rhos-on-Sea; ground in Penrhyn Avenue.
From east: A55 or A547 to Colwyn Bay; A55 to junction signposted Rhos-on-Sea; take exit and then Llandudno Road for Church Road – Colwyn Bay CC and car park.
From west: A5 then A55 to Colwyn Bay; take Rhos-on-Sea turn-off; then as east.

Disabled facilities: Reserved area on path between scoreboard and pavilion at Penrhyn Avenue end of the ground, near pedestrian entrance.
BAC fixture 1993: v Durham (17–21 June).
Capacity: 5,000 approx.

Extras: S. F. Barnes, by common consent the finest bowler of them all, turned his arm over here to productive effect while residing near the beachfront. That hale and hearty fellow Wilf Wooller hails from Rhos-on-Sea – it was his grandfather who built the original pavilion – and he it was who did most to bring first-class cricket to North Wales. Among the club's donations was £15,000 to the Prisoners of War Fund and the Liverpool Air Raid Disaster Fund and a benefit match for Cyril Washbrook in 1948. That was the year the much-loved Lancashire and England opener raised a record sum for a beneficiary, one that lasted for over 30 years – £14,000. An elevated pew beneath the banks of municipal housing on the Embankment side affords terrific views over the sea.

NEATH: Address: Neath Cricket Club, The Pavilion, The Gnoll Cricket Ground, Dyfed Road, Gnoll, Neath, West Glamorgan
Phone: 0639 643719

How to Get There:
Rail: Neath BR; ½ mile away.
Bus: South Wales Transport facilities from locale to bus station, ¼ mile from ground.
Road: From north: A465 or A474 to Neath. The ground is north-west of the town centre between the River Neath and B4434.
From east or south: Exit M4 junction 41; follow A48 and A474 to Neath; as north.
From west: Exit M4 junction 44; A48 and A465 to Neath.

Disabled facilities: No reserved area so request position.
Tour match 1993: v Australia (31 July–2 Aug).
Capacity: 6,000.

Extras: The shadow of the oval ball looms largest over The Gnoll – the All Blacks of Neath RFC play next door. The refurbished indoor school was opened in 1984 by the late Cyril Walters, an amateur dasher who played for the club during the 1930s and whose record of making more than 40 in over 70% of his Test innings is unmatched to this day for anyone visiting the crease on at least 10 occasions. The pavilion has a somewhat sadistic concept of history, housing the bat with which another esteemed old boy, W.G. himself, once sustained a duck here, as well as a plaque commemorating the good Doctor's pair in 1868. Somerset's batsmen went to the opposite extreme in 1990, running up the record 40–over total of 360 for 4 as Graham Rose rushed to the fastest century in the competition's history.

SWANSEA: Address: Swansea Cricket and Football Club, The Pavilion, St Helen's Cricket Ground, Bryn Road, Swansea, West Glamorgan
Phone: 0792 466321

How to Get There:
Rail: Swansea BR (1½ miles away) or Swansea High Street station (½ mile away).
Bus: 1, 2, 3 and 14 from bus station (0792 475511) or South Wales Transport to Mumbles, Sketty, Oystermouth and Brynmill.
Road: From north: A465, A4067 or A48 to city centre; ground is off Mumbles Road (A4067).
From east: Exit M4 junction 44; follow signs to Swansea A4217 and A4067 to Mumbles Road.
From west: Exit M4 junction 47; A483 and A4216 to Mumbles Road.

Disabled facilities: No reserved area, so request position, ideally at Sea End near sightscreen. Pavilion enclosure risky due to steep steps.
BAC fixtures 1993: v Northamptonshire (20–24 May); v Nottinghamshire (24–28 June); v Hampshire (19–23 Aug).
Capacity: 25,000.

Extras: Another seaside venue, another ground more readily associated with the 15-a-side game, St Helen's was originally the property of an order of Augustinian nuns. In 1976, Clive Lloyd hammered the then joint fastest double century in first-class history here (in two hours flat), but immortality is reserved for another Caribbean crusader, Sir Garfield Sobers, who, in 1968, drove, pulled and hooked Malcolm Nash for six sixes in an over, the first time such a deed had been seen at this level. Steep terraces overlook the beach and offer an excellent panoramic view. Unfortunately, in the view of many West Walians, not one that is witnessed enough. In the tradition of the regional squabble, the fact that Cardiff is hosting four BAC games to the three scheduled here rankles further still.

GLOUCESTERSHIRE
Secretary: Philip August

BRISTOL (HQ): Address: Phoenix County Cricket Ground, Nevil Road, Bishopston, Bristol, Avon BS7 9EJ
Phone: 0272 245216
Fax: 0272 241193
ScoreLine: 0891 567505

How to Get There:
Rail: Three BR stations in striking range: Montpelier (¾ mile away); Bristol Temple Meads (2½ miles); Bristol Parkway (5 miles).
Bus: 78 (City Line) from Temple Meads BR; 72/73 from Parkway BR; 71–78 from city centre.
Road: From north: Exit M5 junction 17; A38 to Bristol city centre; follow signs to ground.
From south: Take A37 or A4 to city centre.
From east: Exit M4 junction 19; M32 to junction 2; A38.
From west: A370, A369 or A38 to city centre.

Membership: Full: Single £53; Husband & Wife £74; Senior £27; Senior Husband & Wife £38; Junior £18; Student £26; Spouse of Life Member £26; Country (20 miles outside radius of Bristol) £27. Life: Single under-40 £557; Single 40–55 £462; Single 55–65 £378; Single over 65 £257; Husband & Wife under 40 £840; Husband & Wife 40–55 £698; Husband & Wife 55–65 £378. Business Patrons (five guest tickets) £117.50; (10 tickets) £194. Car park season tickets (subject to availability of space): All home grounds £15; Outgrounds £10. NB: Reductions of around 10% are available for Country members in all categories, and of about 5% for all applicants paying by the end of the January preceding the season.
Admission: BAC Adults £5; Under-16s/Seniors £2.50.
Disabled facilities: Ring in advance for assistance since no specific areas allotted. Reserved parking spaces overlooking pitch. Lift in the pavilion.
BAC fixtures 1993: v Middlesex (29 April–2 May); v Durham (20–24 May); v Hampshire (1–5 July); v Essex (19–23 Aug); v Nottinghamshire (9–13 Sept).
Tour match: v Australia (12–14 June).
Capacity: 8,000.

Extras: Home to cricket's other Grace Gates, the Phoenix Ground was laid out according to W. G.'s own specification. The landlords since 1976 have been the Phoenix Assurance Company, a reminder of the similarly cash-strapped days of 1916, when it became Fry's Ground after the chocolate company bailed the club out of debt. Compared with most HQs it may seem rather spartan, but the place positively reeks of great ghosts besides Grace: disdainful Wally Hammond and galloping Gilbert Jessop of long ago, silken Zaheer Abbas and the mighty Mike Procter of fresher vintage. A humble setting for immortality but never a drab one. Best vantage point (other than top floor of pavilion) is the roof of the Hammond Room, now furnished with new seating for approximately 500.

CHELTENHAM: Address: Cheltenham College, College Sports Ground, Thirlestaine Road, Cheltenham, Gloucestershire
Phone: 0242 522000

How to Get There:
Rail: Cheltenham Spa BR; 1 mile away.
Bus: Cheltenham and District L from city centre.

Road: From north: Exit M5 junction 10; A4019 to Cheltenham and city centre, or A435 to city centre.
From south: Exit M4 junction 15; A419, A417 then B4070 and A435 to Cheltenham and city centre.
From east: A436 or A40 to Charlton Kings and Cheltenham to city centre.
From west: Exit M5 junction 11; A40 to centre.

Disabled facilities: No special area – ring in advance for assistance. Can be treacherous underfoot in the wet.
BAC fixtures 1993: v Derbyshire (29 July–1 Aug), v Lancashire (5–9 Aug).
Capacity: 8,000.

Extras: Flanked by the elegance of Cheltenham College, this remains one of the most atmospheric, refined and distinctive grounds on the circuit. The pavilion can be found in the college gym, imposing trees ring the outfield and a mood of relaxed, timeless academia abounds at the only school ground still in regular first-class employ. The remarkable Procter outdid himself here in 1979, pinning Richard Lumb, Bill Athey and John Hampshire leg-before with successive deliveries to match his own historic hat-trick against Essex seven years earlier, then thrashing the fastest century of the summer later that same Festival Week. Hammond operated his own cartel a few decades previously, pouching 10 slip catches and scoring two hundreds against Surrey, then picking up 15 Worcestershire wickets in the very next match. The most renowned feat accomplished here, however, was the 10 for 66 claimed in 1921 by the Australian leg-spinner and wit, Arthur Mailey, an accomplishment that gave birth to one of the better (not to mention more wittily-titled) cricketing autobiographies, *10 for 66 And All That*. Best of all, the hot dog I had here in 1990 contained what was without doubt the leanest, tastiest sausage in the known universe.

GLOUCESTER: Address: Winget Sports Cricket Club, Winget Sports Ground, Tuffley Avenue, Gloucester GL1 5NS
Phone: 0452 423011

How to Get There:
Rail: Gloucester Central BR; 1 mile.
Bus: 8, 20a or 50 from city centre.
Road: From north: Exit M5 junction 11; A40 and A38 to Gloucester and Tuffley; ground in Tuffley Avenue (off A38).
STOP PRESS: Venue for Glos/Worcs game moved to King's School, Gloucester.

Disabled facilities: Ring in advance for assistance; parking spaces at Scoreboard End.
BAC fixture 1993: v Worcestershire (27–31 May).
Capacity: 6,000 approx. Spectators advised to bring their own seats for major matches.

Extras: Saved from being turned into a housing estate when Gloucester Council acquired the remaining 13 acres of the original 33–acre plot. The new owners hoped the county club might transfer its HQ there. It didn't happen. Known as The Gloucestershire Railway Carriage and Wagon Company Ground from 1923 to 1962, this venue still offers clues to its steamy past. The pavilion on the bowling green near to the main pavilion, for instance, is in fact a carriage built for the Central Argentine Railway in 1914. Dispatched by sea to Argentina the following year, it survived a torpedo attack (which was more than the ship did) and was duly transported back to Gloucester. Scene of the third greatest bowling performance in English first-class history: Charlie Parker's 17 for 56 against Essex in 1925.

HAMPSHIRE
Chief executive: Tony Baker
SOUTHAMPTON (HQ): Address: County Cricket Ground, Northlands Road, Southampton SO9 2TY
Phone: 0703 333788333789
Fax: 0703 330121

How to Get There:
Rail: Southampton Central BR; 1 mile away.
Bus: 47 (Hampshire Bus); 147 Southampton-Winchester bus; 48 Southampton-Eastleigh (Solent Blue Line) all pass within ¼ mile of ground.
Road: From north: Exit M3 junction 10; take The Avenue (A33) to Southampton and city centre OR take A3037 and A35 to city centre. The ground lies west of Southampton Common.
From east: Exit M27 junction 5; follow city centre signs; then A33 as above.
From west: Exit M27 junction 3; take M271, A35 or A3024 to city centre.

Membership: Full: Ordinary £67; Senior £43; 18–21 and Students £33; Junior £18. Country: Ordinary £55; Senior £36; 18–21 and Students £29. Company: £400 (10 guest tickets). Life: Under-40 £1500; 40–59 £1100; 60 and over £500. Car park season ticket: £40.

Admission:

	Full	Senior	Junior
BAC	£5.50	£4	£2.50
AXA Equity & Law	£6.50	£4	£2.50
Tour match	£8	£5	£2.50

Disabled facilities: No reserved area so request position. Parking space limited within ground.
BAC fixtures 1993: v Somerset (29 April–2 May); v Yorkshire (20–24 May); v Warwickshire (29 July–1 Aug); v Lancashire (12–16 Aug); v Leicestershire (9–13 Sept). Tour match: v Australia (26–28 June).
Capacity: 7,000.

Extras: There are those who feel that Hampshire should be based on Broadhalfpenny Down, and ideally rename themselves Hambledon. With its fitness centre, squash club and seven hospitality boxes, however, Northlands Road casts forward rather than back. Not far forward enough, as it happens, since the club is scheduled to up sticks within a couple of years and put down roots at a new greenfield site east of the city centre. Going with them, no doubt, will be the admirable Vic Isaacs, scorer, statistician and probably the most reliable and cheerful public address announcer around. And to think his mum wanted him to be a doctor. On the stairs leading from the secretary's present office to the cramped press quarters is an array of marvellous monochrome snapshots. The most stirring is the one snapped at Bournemouth in 1961 when Colin Ingleby-Mackenzie led the county to their first Championship; Dean Park, unhappily, was a casualty of the four-day rearrangements.

BASINGSTOKE: Address: Basingstoke And North Hants Cricket Club, May's Bounty, Bounty Road, Basingstoke, Hampshire
Phone: 0256 473646

How to Get There:
Rail: Basingstoke BR; ¾ mile away.
Bus: 322, 323, 324 (Hampshire Bus) from Basingstoke BR station to near ground.

Road: From north: Exit M4 junction 11; A33 and follow signs to Basingstoke or exit M4 junction 12, take A4 and A340 and follow signs to Basingstoke; ground is ½ mile from town centre south-west off the Winchester Road (A30).
From south: Take A339 or A32 to A30.
From east: Exit M3 junction 6; follow signs to Basingstoke via A30.
From west: Exit M3 junction 7; follow signs to Basingstoke.

Disabled facilities: No reserved area so request position.
BAC fixtures 1993: v Kent (10–14 June).
Capacity: 5,000 approx.

Extras: In 1991 an exchange of views here summed up the humour of county cricket rather neatly. After making a dogged 57 for Lancashire on a damp pitch, Graeme Fowler complained to the press that the surface had been 'constructed like shredded wheat'; the next morning the groundsman offered him a bowl of the self-same cereal. A safe, pretty, tranquil haven amid the redbrick sprawl of AA buildings and endless loops of ring roads, May's Bounty is quite the most gorgeous name ever to adorn a cricket ground. A fine place to stroll around to boot. Basingstoke Total Abstinence CC have played here in the past, although one may safely assume that that great wine connoisseur, John Arlott, the Basingstoke Boy himself, never featured in their lineup. The Voice of Cricket saw his first match here.

PORTSMOUTH: Address: United Services Portsmouth, United Services Officers Ground, Burnaby Road, Portsmouth, Hampshire
Phone: 0705 22351

How to Get There:
Rail: Portsmouth and Southsea BR (500m away); Portsmouth Harbour BR (½ mile).
Bus: Local services to The Hard Interchange, ½ mile from ground.
Road: From north: A3 or A3(M); follow signs to Portsmouth and Isle of Wight Ferry Terminal. Ground is in Old Portsmouth off London Road (A3), close to Guildhall and United Services' Sports Club.
From east: A27; A2030 signposted to Portsmouth and Ferry Terminal.
From west: Exit M27 junction 12; M275 signs to harbour and Ferry Terminal.

Disabled facilities: No reserved area so request position.
BAC fixtures 1993: v Worcestershire (15–19 July); v Sussex (26–30 Aug).
Capacity: 10,000 approx. Temporary seating for only 2,500 so spectators are advised to bring own seating for major matches.

Extras: County cricket's one and only military venue forms part of the United Services Officers sports complex. 1993 brings the centenary of the Australians' game here against Cambridge and Oxford Past and Present, a somewhat one-sided affair wherein the tourists mustered 843, the most ever chalked up by an Australian side in England. The scorecard, appropriately enough, is on display in the pavilion. If the pitches have a tendency to be flat, this may have something to do with the roller, the heaviest in the business at 5.5 tons.

KENT
Secretary: Stuart Anderson
CANTERBURY (HQ): Address: St Lawrence Cricket Ground, Old Dover Road, Canterbury, Kent CT1 3NZ
Phone: 0227 456886
Fax: 0227 762168
Prospects Of Play: 0227 457323

How to Get There:
Rail: Canterbury East BR station (1 mile), Canterbury West BR (1½ miles).

Bus: 15, 16, 17 from Canterbury bus station going to Folkestone; 339 from centre.
Road: From north: A290, A291 and A28; to follow signs to Canterbury and city centre; ground is situated ½ mile south of city centre and signposted.
From south: A2, A28 and B2068; follow signs to Canterbury.
From east: A257 to Canterbury.
From west: Exit M2 junction 7; A2 to Bridge turn-off to Canterbury bypass; A290 to city centre.

Membership: Life: under 21 £1,600; under 40 £1,200; under 60 £1,000; over 60 £850. Harris Room Ordinary: £350; Single: £200; Member, Friend & Car: £106; Member & Friend: 78; Full: £47; Junior: £16; Student: £30; concessionary rates for country members unconfirmed at time of writing.
Admission: BAC: Adults £5.50; Juniors/Seniors £3; car parking £6.50 (you can drive to the boundary edge and sit there all day); Stands £2.50. AXA Equity & Law League: Adults £6.50; Juniors/Seniors £3.50; car parking £6.50; Stands £3.50.
Disabled facilities: In Frank Woolley Stand next to pavilion; arrange alternatives in advance.
BAC fixtures 1993: v Warwickshire (13–17 May); v Derbyshire (17–21 June); v Leicestershire (29 July–1 Aug); v Surrey (5–9 Aug); v Northamptonshire (31 Aug–4 Sept); v Glamorgan (16–20 Sept). Tour match: v Australia (11–13 Aug).
Capacity: 14,000

Extras: Less regal than one might suppose from the club's traditionally haughty image and lengthy history here (Kent will have trod the turf for 150 years come 1997), this remains one of the more unremarkable county HQs. At the same time, it is the only one to host a Festival Week, the prototype at that since Canterbury Week began life in 1841. In 1992 Carl Hooper equalled a feat only achieved hitherto by another West Indian, Learie Constantine, dispatching a ball with such impeccable timing that he cleared the hulking lime tree in the outfield; in the normal course of play, if a shot strikes the trunk or gets caught in the branches, four runs are awarded automatically. The aforementioned seafood bar is not the only culinary treat: the doughnuts are simply superb. Affiliated to the club is the Ames-Levett Sports Centre (0227 456889) where you'll find cricket nets as well as the usual badminton and aerobics etc.

MAIDSTONE: Address: The Mote Cricket Club, Mote Park, Willow Way,
Maidstone, Kent ME15 7RN
Phone: 0622 54159/54545

How to Get There:
Rail: Maidstone East BR (1 mile); Maidstone West BR (1¼ miles).
Bus: 85 from High Street (¼ mile from both BR stations); 5 and 12.
Road: From north: Exit M20 junction 6; A229 or junction 7 then A249, both to town centre. Take Ashford Road (A20) through Square Hill Park to Mote Park.
From south: Take A26, A229 or A274 to town centre.
From east: Exit M20 junction 8, then A20 to town centre.
From west: Exit M20 junction 5, follow signs to Maidstone and town centre.

Disabled facilities: No reserved areas so request position. Car spaces at south end of the ground.
BAC fixtures 1993: v Essex (1–5 July).
Capacity: 8,000 approx.

Extras: Set in 558 acres of parkland dating back to the 13th century, the playing area at the Mote lies at the foot of an embankment, allowing spectators the rare luxury of sprawling on the grass. The smaller of the two pavilions (the larger one, unusually for an irregular venue, is arranged on two levels) is referred to as the Tabernacle: it was originally used by Lord Bearstead, the last private landlord of the now council-owned Mote Estate, as a private pavilion. Picturesque setting and a place for the whole family thanks to adjacent attractions such as a lake and a golf course.

TUNBRIDGE WELLS: Address: Tunbridge Wells Cricket Club, Nevill Cricket Ground, Nevill Gate, Warwick Park, Tunbridge Wells, Kent TN2 5ES
Phone: 0892 20846

How to Get There:
Rail: Tunbridge Wells BR; ¾ mile away.
Bus: 280, 283, 254, 256, 252, 791 to Frant Road End; 285 to Hawkenbury End.
Road: From north: A21, A26 or A227 to Tunbridge Wells; ground is ½ mile south of city centre off Hastings Road (A267) then Rodean Road and Warwick Park.
From south: A267 to Tunbridge Wells.
From east or west: A264 to Tunbridge Wells.

Disabled facilities: Close to main pavilion or request alternative position.
BAC fixtures 1993: v Gloucestershire (3–7 June).
Capacity: 5,500 approx with seating for 2,500.

Extras: From the candy-striped marquees to the swarms of rhododendrons, the Nevill Ground is one of the two most visually alluring venues on the circuit. Fitting, perhaps, that its greatest calamity should have been sustained at the hands of the fairer sex: fire damage followed a suffragette demo in 1913, forcing the pavilion to be rebuilt. Tunbridge Wells CC was founded in 1762, and the whole place drips with history. During the first world war, the cavalry used it as a picketing area, leaving their steeds on the square. Little wonder Tich Freeman's leg-spin was able to cause such havoc there in subsequent years. In 1932 there was so much turn that he and Northamptonshire's Vallance Jupp took 28 of the 30 wickets to fall between them.

LANCASHIRE
Secretary: Rose Fitzgibbon
OLD TRAFFORD (HQ): Address: Old Trafford Cricket Ground, Talbot Road, Manchester M16 6PX
Phone: 061 872 0261

How to Get There:
Rail: Adjoining Old Trafford Station, a new Metrolink tram service station connected to Manchester Piccadilly BR.
Bus: 112, 115, 113 and 720 from Piccadilly bus station.
Road: From north: M61, then M63; exit junction 4 and follow signs Manchester A5081 then into Warwick Road, right into Talbot Road and on to Old Trafford. Ground is 2½ miles south-west of the city centre on the east side of the A56, the main road in the Old Trafford district.
From south: Exit M6 junction 19, then follow signs to Stockport on A556, then to Altrincham on the A56; at Altrincham follow signs to Manchester; ground signposted on right off Talbot Road.
From east: Exit M62 junction 17, then A56 and follow signposts to ground. Altrincham A56 and follow signs.
From west: M62, then M63 and exit at junction 4. Then as north.

Membership: Full: £76 (includes £20 entrance fee) 22+; £30 (inc £7.50 entrance) 65+; £25 18–21; £22.50 Unemployed/Disabled. Country (over 50 miles away): £48 (inc £20 entrance) 18+; £22.50 (inc £7.50 entrance) 65+; £15 Unemployed/Disabled. Life member: £815 (inc £100 entrance). Overseas, company and affiliated memberships also available, along with special rates for Country

members living between 30 and 50 miles away, a new category. Car park pass (unreserved): £33. Car parking generally limited to members, though there may be some space on the adjoining practice ground. For major matches, extra space available nearby at the other Old Trafford, home of Manchester United, and the Stretford Sports Centre.
Admission: BAC: Adults £6 (pavilion transfers, enabling admission to pavilion area, £4); Juniors/Seniors £2.50 (pavilion transfers for seniors £2). AXA League: £7; Juniors/Seniors £3.50.
Disabled facilities: E Stand enclosure for wheelchairs, and for members in reserved area next to pavilion.
BAC fixtures 1993: v Durham (6–10 May); v Essex (10–14 June); v Sussex (17–21 June); v Glamorgan (15–19 July); v Nottinghamshire (22–26 July); v Yorkshire (19–23 Aug); v Northamptonshire (16–20 Sept). Tour match: v Australia (28–30 July) contingent on county losing in NWT first round.
Capacity: 21,500.

Extras: Legendary for rain, Jim Laker's n-n-n-n-nineteen Australian wickets in 1956 and perhaps the greatest of all Ian Botham's batting extravaganzas, the erstwhile premises of Sir Thomas de Trafford are now among the most modern around, a far cry from the days when the pavilion was used as a hospital during the Great War and later bombed in the Blitz. The club even went as far as to allow women into the pavilion in 1990, leaving Lord's alone in its shameful chauvinism. Scene of the first great one-day match, the Gillette Cup semi-final of 1971, wherein David Hughes, now Lancashire manager, saw off Gloucestershire at 8.55pm, his 24 runs in the 56th over coming amid light more suitable to the local Odeon. Scene, also, of the dullest Test ever 'played' in England, the 1964 Ashes yawnathon wherein Bobby Simpson, now Australia's coach, converted his maiden Test century into 311, still a ground record and the highest score by an Australian captain. For the only time in Test history, both teams topped 600 in their first innings, which left time for the princely sum of two more overs. Even Ted Dexter was slow-handclapped. The museum is not only a sight more stimulating, it is also free of charge. The F Stand, newly opened this season, is a smart two-tiered replacement for the old Wilson Stand, while two other stands, E2 and E3, are designated as alcohol-free areas. Smokers coming here need never feel they are being singled out for victimisation.

LIVERPOOL: Address: Liverpool Cricket Club, Aigburth Road, Grassendale, Liverpool L19 3QF
Phone: 051 427 2930
How to Get There:
Rail: Aigburth BR; ½ mile away.
Bus: 82 (Mersey Bus); Crosville X5 or H25 from Lime Street.
Road: From north: Exit M6 junction 28; follow signs to Liverpool on A48 then A562 to Aigburth; ground situated south-east of the city centre in the Aigburth and Grassendale area.
From east: Exit M6 at junction 21A and on to M62; take junction 4 and follow signs to Aigburth or B5180 and A561 to ground.
From west: Take Mersey Tunnel into Liverpool then follow A562.

Disabled facilities: Small reserved area on Riversdale Road side; otherwise request preferred position.
BAC fixtures 1993: v Warwickshire (27–31 May).
Capacity: 9,000 approx, with around 7,000 seats.

Extras: Lancashire's oldest home venue outside Old Trafford, the headquarters of Liverpool CC looks the part with its smart, spacious pavilion and extensive dressing-rooms, which are among the largest in the game. Gordon Greenidge certainly had an affinity for Aigburth, racking up three centuries in four days here for Hampshire in 1983, then returning the following summer to pile on another 186 on behalf of the West Indies. Parking within the ground is for players and officials only, but there is space for members (only) on the lower ground adjacent to the Merseyrail line off Riversdale Road; street parking for anyone else. For Lancastrians, the fact that this year's visitors are Warwickshire will stir fond memories of the meeting between the protagonists at Southport in 1982, when Dennis Amiss and his troops amassed 523 yet still contrived to lose by 10 wickets.

LYTHAM: Address: Lytham Cricket Club, Church Road, Lytham, Lancashire
Phone: 0253 734137

How to Get There:
Rail: Lytham BR; ½ mile away.
Bus: 11A to Lytham from town centre; 167 (St Anne's-Preston) and 193 St Anne's-Kirkham) also pass the ground.
Road: From north: Exit M6 junction 32, then M55 to junction 3; A585 to Kirkham and B5259 to Lytham. The ground is situated ¼ mile west of the town centre and the seafront.
From east: Take A583 and A584 to Lytham.

Disabled facilities: No reserved area so request position.
BAC fixtures 1993: v Kent (26–30 Aug).
Capacity: 6,000 approx.

Extras: Considering the head office of the Football League and an Open Championship links course both lurk dangerously close, it is unsurprising that cricket should have taken a back seat in Lytham until Lancashire held their inaugural Championship venture here in 1985. That introduction was certainly memorable for David Makinson, an unassuming No. 10 in the home order, who swatted seven sixes off the Northamptonshire off-spinner, Richard Williams.

LEICESTERSHIRE
Chief executive: Mike Turner
LEICESTER (HQ): Address: County Cricket Ground, Grace Road, Leicester
LE2 8AD
Phone: 0533 832128
Prospects of Play: 0533 836236

How to Get There:
Rail: Leicester Midland BR station (2 miles); South Wigston BR (2½ miles).
Bus: 68, 73 from Belvoir Street (¼ mile from station); 23 from city centre.
Road: From north: Exit M1 junction 22, or A46A607 to city centre and follow signs to Rugby into Almond Road, then Aylestone Road and signs to ground.
From south: Exit M69 to M1, then A50 to city centre.
From east: Take A47 to city centre.
From west: Exit M1 junction 21, or M69 exit at A46, then A426 on to Park Hill Drive and follow signs to ground.

Membership: Full: £47.50; Age Concessions: £31.50; Family: £66; Age Concessions: £44. Junior: £21; Car park pass: £17. Life (under 40): £656; Life (over 40): £493.50; Life (Concessions): £331. 25% commission if you introduce a new member.
Admission: BAC: Adults £3; Junior/Senior £1.50. AXA League: Adults £7; JuniorSenior £3.50.
Disabled facilities: No reserved area so request position. Limited space for cars at Hawkesbury Road end.
BAC fixtures 1993: v Surrey (29 April–2 May); v Nottinghamshire (6–10 May);

v Durham (3–7 June); v Gloucestershire (24–28 June); v Lancashire (1–5 July); v Warwickshire (22–26 July); v Glamorgan (12–16 Aug); v Yorkshire (31 Aug–4 Sept); v Derbyshire (16–20 Sept). Tour match: v Australia (29–31 May).
Capacity: 12,000

Extras: Along with Middlesex, Nottinghamshire and Warwickshire, Leicestershire are one of four clubs to have dispensed with outgrounds for the abbreviated Championship programme, so the plainest of the county venues will host all of Leicestershire's BAC games this season. The two finest innings ever played here were entirely worthy of the ground's graceful if illusory name: Keith Miller dashed off an unbeaten 281 for the 1956 Australians; 23 years later David Gower sculpted the highest score of his career, 228, against Glamorgan, more than any Leicestershire player has ever made on home turf. An indoor cricket complex is under construction, bringing Grace Road closer to the model envisaged a decade or so ago when the ground was considered the likeliest next member of the exclusive Test club. Recommendations: 1) Bring along a blanket to drape over the windscreen if you come by car on a sunny day: the reflection can distract the batsmen; 2) Get your lunch order in early if you want to enjoy it at the adjoining pub: the recession has caused a cutback on bar staff and the queues can be horrendous.

MIDDLESEX
Secretary: Joe Hardstaff
LORD'S (HQ): Address: Middlesex County Cricket Club, Lord's Cricket Ground, London NW8 8QN
Phone: 071 289 1300286 1310
Fax: 071 289 9100
Credit Card Bookings: 071 289 5005
Recorded Information: 071 266 2022

How to Get There:
Rail: St John's Wood (London Underground Jubilee Line); turn left, ground ¼ mile.
Bus: 6, 8, 13, 16, 16A, 46, 74, 82, 113, 159; 719, 757, 768 and 797 coaches.
Road: From north: M1 to termination at Brent CrossStaples Corner; take North Circular Road and follow signs to Swiss Cottage then follow Finchley Road to St John's Wood and signs to Lord's. Ground is opposite St John's Wood Church and bounded by Wellington Road, Wellington Place, St John's Wood Road and Grove End Road.
From south: From Hyde Park Corner, follow ring road signs to north into Park Lane (A4202); then on to Portman Street (A41) and follow signs to Aylesbury and the north. At St John's Wood roundabout turn left into St John's Wood Road.
From east: Follow signs to West End (A503). At Camden Town, follow Regent's Park (A4201) past London Mosque then turn right into Hanover Gate and follow Park Road (A41) for St John's Wood.
From west: A40(M)/M41; follow signs to Central London and Paddington; Edgware Road (A5); turn right into St John's Wood Road.

Membership: Gentleman Members: Full £60; Senior £33; Country £30; MCC members £18. Lady Members: Full £43; Senior & Country £25; Junior (11–17) £17; Abroad List £20; Executive £175; Student: £20. Life membership available, cost dependent on age. Reductions for introducing new members. Members of the Executive Club (limited to 200) enjoy all the normal members benefits plus use of the executive box in the Tavern Stand, reduced membership of the Middlesex Squash Centre and invitations to special functions.
Admission: BAC: Adults £6; Junior/Senior £3.
Disabled facilities: Reserved sections between pavilion and Sir George Allen Stand, and in front of Warner Stand.

BAC fixtures 1993: v Kent (6–10 May); v Nottinghamshire (13–17 May); v Sussex (27–31 May); v Derbyshire (3–7 June); v Surrey (24–28 June); v Hampshire (22–26 July); v Leicestershire (5–9 Aug); v Northamptonshire (19–23 Aug); v Lancashire (9–13 Sept). Tour match: v Australia (3–5 May).
Capacity: 28,000

Extras: Melbourne's cavernous concrete bowl and Sydney's greater intimacy and pantiled roofs may run it close, but Thomas Lord's plot remains the mother and father of all cricket grounds. Lord's, however, has two faces. One is the jam-packed model seen at Tests and Cup finals, dressed up to the nines, buzzing and preening, stuffiness diluted by a raucous human touch. The other is the scantily-clad, inanimate arena Middlesex play in. Yet in many ways an empty Lord's is more rewarding. No queues for one thing, more seating options for another (all right, so half the place is out of bounds to non-MCC folk, but basking in the sun on the Grandstand balcony ranks among life's greatest pleasures). There is also more scope for a leisurely roam, a dip into one of the two bookshops, a tour of the museum, a jar in the Tavern and maybe even a snooze in the Lord Harris Memorial Garden. Above all, there is an aura of affable ordinariness, of approachability, making time stand still. It doesn't, of course. Tucked away in the Gubby Allen Stand is the Middlesex Room, a belated concession to the second-class members on the premises, some of whom have the audacity to wear skirts. Filled pitta bread sandwiches a house speciality.

NORTHAMPTONSHIRE
Chief executive: Steve Coverdale
NORTHAMPTON (HQ): Address: County Cricket Ground, Wantage Road, Northampton NN1 4NJ
Phone: 0604 32917
Fax: 0604 232855
CricketLine: 0891 567511
Prospects of Play: 0604 37040

How to Get There:
Rail: Northampton BR station; 2 miles.
Bus: 1 from BR station to near ground.
Road: From north: Exit M1 junction 16 (signposted from junction 15 too); A45 and follow signs to Northampton and city centre; A43 to Kettering and follow signs to ground via Abingdon Road.
From south: Exit M1 junction 15, then A508 and A43 to Wellingborough Road and Wantage Road. Follow signposts.
From east: A45, A4500 or A428 to Northampton and follow signs to ground.
From west: A45 or A43 to city centre.

Membership: Vice-President: £115; Country Vice-President: £100; Full: £51; Country: £45; Senior: £33; Student: £22; Family: £110; Executive Club: (Individual) £220 + VAT; (Individual & Guest) £275 + VAT. Life Member: Under 40 £1,530; 40–49 £1,200; 50–59 £900; 60–64 £675; 65 and over £500.
Admission: BAC: Adults £6; Junior/Senior £3. AXA League: Adults £7; Junior/Senior £3.50.
Disabled facilities: No reserved area so request position. Special toilets just installed in the Spencer Pavilion.
BAC fixtures 1993: v Gloucestershire (6–10 May); v Worcestershire (3–7 June); v Hampshire (17–21 June); v Nottinghamshire (1–5 July); v Surrey (22–26 July); v Essex (5–9 Aug); v Durham (12–16 Aug); v Leicestershire (26–30 Aug). Tetley Bitter Challenge: v Australia (16 May, 1–day); v Australia (28–30 July) If Northamptonshire are otherwise engaged in the NatWest Trophy quarter-finals, Lancashire will entertain the tourists at Old Trafford).
Capacity: 5,500

Extras: With the home turf of Northampton Town AFC a half-hit slog away, Wantage Road suffers from being the only playing arena in the country in which two professional sports clubs share digs 12 months a year. Indeed, only the comparatively new players' pavilion here keeps Grace Road at the bottom of the HQ Charisma Table. It is hard to credit that 21,000 turned up to see Lindwall, Miller and the rest of the 1953 Australians. Still, a substantial effort has been made to spruce things up and cater for the executive set, while the hoi polloi are well served by the Abingdon hostelry 200 yards from the main entrance. More importantly, there remains an earthy, unprepossessing feel to the place that manages to invoke the spirit of Colin Milburn even better than Chester-le-Street. Various blazers and caps belonging to the great man can be found in the newly refurbished pavilion, in the recently-opened Colin Milburn Room. It was here that another thunderous bat, that of Percy Fender, gave birth to the most dissected of all innings. Even now, 73 years on, the number-crunchers still cannot agree on how many balls he received, but the Surrey man sped to his century in 35 minutes, a world record that stood, proud and seemingly unassailable, for seven decades. Until, that is, Tom Moody contrived to steal it, with a little bit of help from his friends, the Glamorgan declaration bowlers. Now that the four-day Championship is with us, thank goodness, the hammiest actors on the circuit should find employment harder to come by.

LUTON: Address: Luton Town Cricket Club, Wardown Park, Old Bedford Road, Luton, Bedfordshire
Phone: 0582 27855

How to Get There:
Rail: Luton (BR) Midland and Thameslink; 1 mile.
Bus: 26 from Mill Street (200m from BR station; 0582 404074); 6 from town centre – both to ground.
Road: From north: M1 junction 11; A505 and follow signs to Luton then Dunstable Road for town centre; take A6 to New Bedford Road for Wardown Park.
From south: M12 junction 1010A; follow signs to Luton and town centre; signs to A6 and New Bedford Road; as north.
From east: A505 to Luton; take New Bedford Road from town centre; as north.
NB: Enter at New Bedford Road and park on grass.

Disabled facilities: In members' enclosure and by sightscreen at Pavilion End.
BAC fixtures 1993: v Somerset (24–28 June).
Capacity: 2,500.

Extras: A breezy, comparatively idyllic counterpoint to Northampton, it is surprising to note that Wardown Park was first used as a Championship venue as recently as 1986. To some, the sparse use of Tring is criminal, but in spite of all the Lorraine Chase/Campari connotations this really is a splendid place to watch cricket, from the coiffeured lawns of Wardown House to the museum devoted to all things Luton (a feast for hat fans). Tom Graveney's decision to play here one Sunday brought a premature end to the international career of the most sublime English strokeplayer of the postwar era, Gower notwithstanding. At the time, in 1969, Test matches had rituals known as rest days and they meant precisely that, rest. But when Tom trotted off to attend one of his benefit matches – having been warned not to – the selectors took exception and never picked him again. Whoever built the prototype Englishman gave him a distinct distaste for genius.

NOTTINGHAMSHIRE
Secretary: Brian Robson

TRENT BRIDGE (HQ): Address: County Cricket Ground, Trent Bridge, Bridgford Road, Nottingham NG2 6AG
Phone: 0602 821525
Prospects of Play: 0602 822753

How to Get There:
Rail: 1 mile from Nottingham Midland BR station.
Bus: 12, 69, 85, 90–97 link BR station with ground.
Road: From north: Exit M1 junction 26, follow A610 signs to Nottingham and on to Melton Mowbray. The Trent Bridge (A606) crosses river and leaves you facing the ground.
From south: Exit M1 junction 24; follow signs for Nottingham (south) and then into Bridgford Road.
From east: Take A52 signposted for Nottingham into West Bridgford and follow Bridgford Road to ground.
From west: A52; follow signs to Nottingham, Melton Mowbray and Trent Bridge.

Membership: Full: £55; Senior: £35; Junior: £31; Student/Under-16: £17; Husband & Wife: £83; Senior Husband & Wife: £56. Country Full: £49; Country Husband & Wife: £72. Company (includes minimum five guest tickets): £220. Patron (Test and one-day admission included provided you sit in patron's enclosure): £133; Patron Senior: £99; Patron Junior: £70; Patron Student/Under-16: £56; Patron Husband & Wife: £239; Patron Senior Husband & Wife: £184; Patron Country: £127; Patron Country Husband & Wife: £228; Patron Company: £610. Executive: £290 + VAT; Executive + 1 guest: £470 (further permutations available; includes admission to swanky executive suite); Executive Husband & Wife: £550.
Admission: BAC: Adults £3, Junior/Senior £1.50. AXA League: Adults £6, Junior/Senior £3.
Disabled facilities: Plenty of space on boundary edge – request position. Parking off Fox Road.
BAC fixtures 1993: v Worcestershire (29 April–1 May); v Kent (20–24 May); v Hampshire (3–7 June); v Esssex (17–21 June); v Somerset (15–19 July); v Yorkshire (5–9 Aug); v Derbyshire (26–30 Aug); v Warwickshire (16–20 Sept). Tourist match: v Australians (9–11 June) (If county are otherwise engaged in the Benson & Hedges Cup semi-finals, Warwickshire or Somerset will entertain the tourists.)
Capacity: 15,000

Extras: Proving that it is possible to embrace the new while still holding hands with the past, Trent Bridge offers the best of both. A look at the ground record-holders reveals the touch of class: Compton, O'Reilly, Bedser and Macartney. The pavilion museum is a must, Peter Wynne-Thomas's nearby sports bookshop is similarly crammed with gems and the scoreboard packs more information than any of the competition. The William Clarke Stand (in memory of the bricklayer who laid the ground out in his back garden) is merely one of the latest developments, but somehow one feels forever young in the kingdom of Derek William Randall. Never the greatest judge of a single, Boycott, in his first Test for three years, ran out 'Arkle' here in 1977: if 'Sir Geoffrey' hadn't gone on to make a century the odds on him reaching the dressing-room without being lynched would not have been all that good. Perhaps it was symbolic that this ground's most durable and treasured feature, Parr's Tree, having survived so many of George Parr's lofted drives, should have fallen prey to a gale in 1976. That was the year England first picked the hyperactive Retford lad; a few months later, Randall was casting his quirky spell at the Centenary Test in Melbourne in what remains the finest innings in living memory played against the old enemy by an Englishman not named Botham. Catch him before he vanishes into retirement: we will never know another quite like him. The rare honour of a second benefit has scarcely been bestowed upon a worthier cause.

SOMERSET
Chief executive: Peter Anderson

TAUNTON (HQ): Address: The County Ground, St James's Street, Taunton
TA1 1JT
Phone: 0823 272946/253666/254287
Cricketcall: 0898 121424

How to Get There:
Rail: Taunton BR; ½ mile.
Bus: Many buses from surrounding areas to town bus station – ground is 500m from there. There is also a shuttle from the town centre.
Road: From north: Exit M5 junction 25, then follow A358 from Creech Castle roundabout to town centre; next roundabout take exit signposted to ground.
From south: A358 or B3170; as north.
From east: as north.
From west: Exit M5 junction 26; A38 to Taunton and town centre; follow signs to ground.

Membership: Full: £58; 2nd Full Member (member of same family, living in same home): £42; Senior: £39; Junior: £16; Young Persons (18–21): £23; Vice-President: £66; 2nd Vice-President (member of family and occupying same household) £52; Vice-President Family: £118 (£5 extra per child after first); Family Member: £100 (£5 extra per child after first); Country: £39; Executive Business Club: £420 + VAT; Company Patron: (£120).
Admission: BAC: Adults £5; Junior/Senior £3. AXA League: Adults £7.50; JuniorSenior £4. Tour match: Adults £6; Junior/Senior £3.
Disabled facilities: Special enclosure in front of the old pavilion.
BAC fixtures 1993: v Lancashire (13–17 May); v Glamorgan (27–31 May); v Sussex (1–5 July); v Kent (22–26 July); v Yorkshire (29 July–2 Aug); v Gloucestershire (31 Aug to 4 Sept). Tour match: v Australians (8–10 May).
Capacity: 8,000

Extras: Having come down to earth since the end of the Botham-Richards-Garner wonder years, the westernmost ground on the circuit is once again wearing its customary cloak of wistfulness, even allowing for the prim new redbrick Colin Atkinson Pavilion. The ambience is bright and chirpy, evocative of more innocent times. W. G. and Hobbs both notched their 100th hundreds here, Archie MacLaren his 424; as Hick's 405 in 1988 amplified, the pitches seldom need taming these days either. Nestling in a beautifully restored listed building, the museum behind the club shop is the most unusual and fascinating of its ilk, exhibits ranging from Joel Garner's size 13 boot to a mock-up of the pavilion as it was a century ago, complete with original features. If you cannot make out the Quantock Hills on the horizon, so they say, it's time to put that brolly up.

BATH: Address: Recreation Ground, William Street off Great Pultney Street,
Bath, Avon
Phone: 0225 25180

How to Get There:
Rail: Bath Spa BR; ½ mile.
Bus: 4, 18 link BR station with the ground. Entrance from William Streetvia rugby field from Spring Gardens Road.
Road: From north: Exit M4 at junction 18 then take A46 signposted to Bath;

ground is off Great Pultney Street (A36) east of the city centre by the River Avon and next to the rugby club.
From south: Take A367 or A36 to Bath.
From east: Exit M4 at junction 18; as north or exit M4 at junction 17 and take A429 and A4.
From west: Take A4, A431 or A36 to Bath.

Disabled facilities: Reserved area in front of members' enclosure; parking in rugby field.
BAC fixtures 1993: v Middlesex (17–21 June).
Capacity: 8,000

Extras: The architectural majesty of Bath Abbey and Queen's Crescent present reason enough to venture to this spa town, even if the best rugger club in England is usually the main focus of attention at the Rec. Mike Gatting, who might have made a useful prop forward himself, mauled Somerset good and proper here, coming in at 15 for 2 to belt a career-best 258 in 1985, then picking up from where he left off with another 196 the following summer. As it happens, four-day games are probably the only way to obtain a result, so soporific are the pitches, not unlike the town itself. Being in the bowels of a bowl has its disadvantages: it can be steamy in the heat, a quagmire in the wet. Oh, and don't be fooled: the Bath CC ground on the other side of North Parade Road is not the one you want.

WESTON-SUPER-MARE: Address: Clarence Park East, Walliscote Road, Weston-Super-Mare, Somerset
Phone: 0934 642345

How to Get There:
Rail: Weston-Super-Mare BR; ½ mile.
Bus: 5 links BR station with ground.
Road: From north: Exit M5 junction 21; take A370 signposted to town centre and seafront; signs to ground, which is at Clarence Park East in Walliscote Road.
From south: Exit M5 at junction 22; A370 to Weston-Super-Mare.
From east: A370 or A368 signposted to Weston-Super-Mare.

Disabled facilities: Reserved area on concrete in south-west corner of ground.
BAC fixtures 1993: v Leicestershire (19–23 Aug).
Capacity: 6,000.

Extras: Altogether charming, and thankfully spared the chop, but beware the portaloos when the tide comes in. Mixed blessings extend to the middle: while Botham once hit 10 sixes in an innings here, Viv Richards was once driven to vault the perimeter hoardings to sort out a visiting racist in the crowd. Pitches tend to be conducive to spin and have always favoured bowlers in the main, never more so than during the first county venture here in 1914. Drake and Booth were the only Yorkshire bowlers used in the entire contest, the former claiming all 10 Somerset second-innings wickets in the space of nine overs.

SURREY
Chief executive: Glyn Woodman
THE OVAL: Address: The Fosters Oval, Kennington, London SE11 5SS
Phone: 071 582 6660
Credit Card Bookings: 071 582 7764
Fax: 071 735 7769
Prospects of Play: 071 582 6660
Ken Barrington Centre: 071 582 9495

How to Get There:
Rail: 200m from Oval station (London Underground, Northern Line); 600m from Vauxhall BR and London Underground (Victoria Line).
Bus: 3, 36, 36A, 36B, 59, 95, 109, 133, 155–159, 185 and 196.
Road: From north: From Edgware Road (A5) follow signs to Marble Arch; go down Park Lane (A202) and follow signs to Vauxhall Bridge; right on Harleyford Road for Kennington and The Oval.
From east: Follow A202 to Kennington and Harleyford Road.
From south: Exit M25 at junction 6, 7, 8 or 9 for, respectively, A22, A23, A24 or A243; follow signs to Central London; as north.
From west: M3, M4, A23 or A24; follow signs to Central London; as north.

Membership: Full: £78; Senior Citizen: £45; Youth (18–23): £31; Junior Season Ticket (up to 17): £15; Country & Overseas (50 miles or more 'as the crow flies' from The Oval): £45; Country & Overseas Senior Citizen: £33; Full Inclusive (additional benefits: free admission to Test, international and Cup matches at ground, priority booking in November and December); £140. Full members can introduce 12 guests per season (up to a maximum of four per day) into the Members' Pavilion during selected matches – not international games or Cup quarter-/semi-finals. Members 'generally' permitted to use members' or Cup quarter-semi-finals. Members 'generally' permitted to use members' facilities at other counties when Surrey play there, upon payment of ground charge of course.
Admission: BAC: Adults £7; Senior/Under-16/UB40 £3; AXA League: Adults £7; Senior/Under-16/UB40 £3.
BAC fixtures 1993: v Essex (13–17 May); v Lancashire (3–7 June); v Glamorgan (10–14 June); v Durham (1–5 July); v Nottinghamshire (29 July–2 Aug); v Somerset (26–30 Aug); v Hampshire (31 Aug to 4 Sept); v Yorkshire (16–20 Sept). Tour match: v Australians (25–27 May). (If county otherwise engaged in the Benson & Hedges Cup quarter-finals, Yorkshire, Northamptonshire or Nottinghamshire will entertain the tourists.)
Capacity: 16,000

Extras: Potentially cricket's answer to the Lloyds Building, The Oval is on course to overtake Edgbaston as the English ground of the future. Not content with their time-honoured tradition for hiring only the speediest scoreboard operators, Prince Charles's tenants have brought in conference facilities, Chef-in-a-Box lunches and Aussie Rules. Then there's the newly-completed Ken Barrington Centre. Commemorating a batsman who had St George tattooed on his heart, it offers a multitude of courts, pitches and fitness apparatus in addition to physiotherapy, yoga and a sports injuries clinic. Even the plastic bucket seats seem more agreeable on the botty. A flourish is supplied by the restored art deco tube trains that sometimes drop you on the doorstep, a sentimental nod to the Fifties fun days of Laker and Lock, May and Surridge. In actual fact, despite all these concessions to commercialism, The Oval somehow clings to the cheeky, fish 'n' chippiness it had back then. So long as the gasworks and The Cricketers' pub remain intact, it probably always will.

GUILDFORD: Address: Guildford Cricket Club, Woodbridge Road,
Guildford, Surrey
Phone: 0483 572181
How to Get There:
Rail: Guildford BR station and London Road BR station both ¾ mile away.
Bus: Green Line buses to bus station, ½ mile from ground.
Road: From north: Take A320 and follow signs to Guildford and town centre; ground is north of the town but watch directions on ring road with care.
From east: Exit M25 junction 10; A3 or A25 signposted to Guildford.

From south: Take either A281 or A3100 and follow signs to Guildford; pick up A320; as north.
From west: Take either A3 or A31 and follow signs to town centre.

Disabled facilities: No reserved area so request position.
BAC fixture 1993: v Gloucestershire (15–19 July).
Capacity: 7,500, seating for half.

Extras: Like Tunbridge Wells, Horsham and Hove, this can be a treasure trove for secondhand bookhunters provided the weather stays fair. Small wonder the dealers pitch their trestle tables here. Links between Guildford and cricket, after all, can be traced back to 1598, the earliest known reference to the game being played in Surrey coming in the form of a document mentioning John Derrick, a student at the Free School of Guildford who, along with some classmates, 'did run and play there at cricket'. An endearing, cosy venue with a temptingly short boundary on the Woodbridge Road side, the ground retains a strong scent of the village green in spite of its bustling market town environment. Parking beyond the railings, needless to add, is not advised for those who like their windows unshattered and their doors undented. Surrey will certainly be looking to emerge unscathed following their accident here in 1992, when their last nine wickets crashed for 23 against Kent.

SUSSEX
Secretary: Nigel Bett
HOVE (HQ): Address: County Cricket Ground, Eaton Road, Hove, East Sussex BN3 3AN
Phone: 0273 732161
Prospects of Play: 0273 772766

How to Get There:
Rail: Hove BR (½ mile); Brighton Thameslink (1 mile).
Bus: 7 (to Brighton and Hove) between the two BR stations passes the ground. Also 1, 2, 3, 5 5B, 6, 19, 26, 33, 37, 43, 43A, 46, 49 and 59.
Road: From north: Exit M25 junction 7; follow M23 and A23 to Brighton; follow to signs to Pyecombe and Hove then to ground.
From east: A27 to Brighton and town centre or cross A277 into Wilbury Road; ground right.
From west: A27 to Hove or A259 (seafront).

Membership: Full (member + one transferable ticket): £77/£61/£47; Ordinary: £54/£38/£31; Student(18–21): £23; Junior (up to 18): £14; Cricket Clubs (club may purchase up to four transferable tickets): £23; Business House (four transferable tickets): £125; Family (2 adults and 2 children under 12): £84/£68/£61. Alternative prices according to the following order for applicants residing in a) Brighton, Hove, Lewes or Shoreham; b) the rest of Sussex; c) outside Sussex. All members have free parking facility subject to space (very limited).
Admission: BAC: Adult £3, Junior/Senior £1. AXA League: Adult £6, Junior/Senior £3.50.
Disabled facilities: Reserved area plus parking spaces opposite pavilion; enter from Palmeira Road.
BAC fixtures 1993: v Surrey (6–10 May); v Northamptonshire (10–14 June); v Worcestershire (5–9 Aug); v Essex (31 Aug–4 Sept); v Gloucestershire (16–20 Sept). Tour match: v Australians (13–15 May).
Capacity: 6,000.

Extras: Closer in feel to a retirement home than a stage for cricketing excellence, Hove is a wonderfully musty relic worthy of a preservation order. Preservation is indeed a club speciality: when Sussex relocated here from the neighbouring Royal Brunswick ground in 1872, they removed the turf, rolled it up and relaid it on their brand new barley field. Some tentative steps have been taken and a major facelift remains on the agenda (economic climate permitting), but for now, savour the seaside aroma (the beach is a few hundred yards away), the peeling walls, the beer garden and the rock cakes. No matter how the developers transform Eaton Road, however, off-drives from the Cromwell Road End will carry on taunting fielders as the ball hurries down the slope towards the Gilligan Stand. The arm responsible for the best bowling here for Sussex belonged to one J. E. B. B. P. Q. C. Dwyer, whose seven forenames almost matched his 16 Derbyshire wickets in 1906. That evergreen fast bowler, Tony Pigott, the solitary Old Harrovian in the first-class game, runs the squash club.

ARUNDEL: Address: Friends of Arundel Castle Cricket Club, The Pavilion, Arundel Park, Arundel, West Sussex BN18 9LH
Phone: 0903 882462

How to Get There:
Rail: Arundel BR; 1 mile.
Bus: Southdown 212, 230 (Worthing to Arundel Castle) (0903 37661).
Road: From north: A29 and A284 to Arundel; entrance to Arundel Park via Arundel bypass on London Road, north of town centre; enter park through stables and parkland; follow signs.
From south: A284 to Arundel and town centre; follow signs to Arundel Park and London Road for ground.
From east: A27 to Arundel and town centre then as south.
From west: A27 to Arundel town centre then as south.

Disabled facilities: No reserved area so request position on path near pavilion.
BAC fixture 1993: v Kent (15–19 July).
Capacity: 10,000 approx. Bring your own seating for tourist matches.

Extras: If Hove smells of old socks, Arundel Castle has the whiff of battle. On busy days, such as those limited-over bunfights between the tourists and Duchess Lavinia's hand-picked XI, anyone intending to brave the front row of the deckchairs at this seductive venue is advised to bring along a tin hat or two. An Allan Border drive scored a direct hit on some luckless soul in 1989, so be warned. In 1975, Lavinia, Duchess of Norfolk, whose late husband Bernard served both as MCC president and England manager in Australia, vowed to do everything she could to ensure that cricket would continue at Arundel Park. Her aim was to preserve the ground's inimitable aura of genteel playfulness and to assist in 'the promotion, encouragement and maintenance of the playing of cricket'. This paved the way for the formation of Friends of Arundel Castle CC, and, more recently, the Friends of Arundel Castle CC Foundation. Championship cricket, as a result, is now a regular visitor. The pavilion, appropriately, extends precisely 22 yards from end to end.

EASTBOURNE: Address: Eastbourne Cricket Club, Eastbourne Saffrons Sports Club, The Saffrons, Compton Place Road, Eastbourne, East Sussex
Phone: 0323 24328

How to Get There:
Rail: Eastbourne BR; ½ mile.
Bus: 8B passes ground.
Road: From north: Take A22 and follow signs to Eastbourne and town centre; A259 to Grove Road and Saffrons Road; first right into Meads Road for ground.
From east: Take A259 and follow signs to town centre.
From west: A259 again.

Disabled facilities: Reserved area on football stand side.

BAC fixtures 1993: v Nottinghamshire (12–16 Aug).
Capacity: 8,000; 3,000 seats.

Extras: A bountiful source of saffron during its days as a perfick part of Larkin's Field, The Saffrons runs May's Bounty a close second as the English MECCA – Most Exquisitely Christened County Arena. Pat Pocock and his off-breaks acquired seven wickets in 11 balls here in 1972, the most devastating short bowling spell in Championship history, but perhaps the most memorable performance was the tragic Harold Gimblett's *tour de force* in 1948: 310 in 7¾ hours with 37 fours and two sixes, which survived as Somerset's highest individual innings until Viv Richards outstripped it in 1985. The Saffrons is a recreation ground for football and bowls as well. It was among these same blue-remembered hills that Warwick Armstrong's 1921 Australian invincibles were so improbably vanquished in what remains one of the game's greatest upsets.

HORSHAM: Address: Horsham Cricket Club, Cricket Field Road, Worthing Road, Horsham, West Sussex
Phone: 0403 54628

How to Get There:
Rail: Horsham BR; 1 mile.
Bus: H1, H2, H5 link BR station with ground.
Road: From north: Exit M25 junction 9; A24 to Horsham and town centre then follow signs.
From south: A24 or A281 and follow signs to Horsham and town centre.
From east: A264 and follow signs to town centre then cricket.
From west: A281 or A264 and follow signs to centre.

Disabled facilities: No reserved area, request position.
BAC fixture 1993: v Leicestershire (20–24 May).
Capacity: 5,500 approx; around 1,000 seats so BYO.

Extras: Horsham CC, the owners, celebrated their bicentenary in 1971, and have resided here since 1851. The boundaries may be short on the scoreboard side, but the carry to the north is a lengthy one: Viv Richards has tried his luck and Franklyn Stephenson and Alan Wells launched some massive blows to defeat Durham in a frantic finish last summer, but only one batsman, Sussex's 'Jacko' Watson, has ever propelled a delivery into the River Arun. The willow trees fuse with the twisted spire of St Mary's Church to create an elegiac atmosphere and make one wonder why Horsham has enjoyed such an intermittent presence on the first-class scene. Then again, Sussex are spoiled for choice.

WARWICKSHIRE
Secretary: David Heath
EDGBASTON (HQ): Address: County Ground, Edgbaston Road, Edgbaston, Birmingham B5 7QU
Phone: 021 446 4422
Fax: 021 446 4544
Prospects of Play: 021 440 3624
Rapid Cricketline: 0891 567516
Text Match Cricketline: 0891 567567/567555

How to Get There:
Rail: Birmingham New Street BR; 1¾ miles.
Bus: 45, 46, 47 (West Midlands Travel) link New Street with ground.
Road: From north: Exit M6 junction 6; follow A38 to and through city centre; left into Priory Road; entrance on left in Edgbaston Road.
From south: A441, A435, A34, A41 or A45 to city centre.

From east: A45, A41 or A34 and follow signs to city centre and to ground.
From west: Exit M5 junction 4, follow A38 to city centre; go through Selly Oak and then follow signs to ground.

Membership: Full: £54; Senior: £27.50; Student: £24; Junior Season Ticket: £16 (free membership of Junior Bears Club for 8–16s); Country: £42; Senior/Distant Country: £23; Husband & Wife: £71; Senior Husband & Wife: £42; Country Husband & Wife: £56; Patron: £110; Senior Patron £65; Country Patron: £85. Joining fee: £15 (Seniors £10). Car park pass: £19; Cycle pass: £3.50.
Admission: BAC: Adult £5; Junior/Senior £2.50. AXA League: Adults £6, Junior/Senior £3 Family (2 adults, 2 juniors) £12.
Disabled facilities: Beneath the Thwaite Scoreboard and Sydney Barnes Stand, by prior arrangement in other areas; parking spaces galore.
BAC fixtures 1993: v Northamptonshire (29 April–2 May); v Derbyhire (6–10 May); v Sussex (3–7 June); v Surrey (17–21 June); v Yorkshire (1–5 July); v Middlesex (15–19 July); v Gloucestershire (12–16 Aug); v Worcestershire (26–30 Aug); v Somerset (9–13 Sept).
Tour match: v Australians (9–11 June). (If county are otherwise engaged in the Benson & Hedges Cup semi-finals, Nottinghamshire or Somerset will entertain the tourists.)
Capacity: 17,500.

Extras: Leased by Warwickshire in 1884 when no more than 'a meadow of rough grazing land', Edgbaston was the first English ground really to put spectators first. Extensive redevelopment began after the second world war and the upshot is that this expertly-run, capacious stadium (complete with vast car park) is now a concrete monument to modernity. It was also the first venue to employ the 'Brumbrella', a motorised pitch cover that resembles a beached whale and has the wherewithal to make conditions playable far sooner than conventional covers permit. Mind you, Warwickshire have been trying to leave the past behind ever since 1896, when they conceded the little matter of 887 here against Yorkshire, the loftiest Championship total of all. The fast food in the William Austell Stand is excellent and once you've finished there, take an amble down to the secondhand book and magazine stalls just inside the main gate. There must be something in the air: England have a better record here than at any other Test ground.

WORCESTERSHIRE
Secretary: Reverend Mike Vockins
WORCESTER (HQ): Address: County Cricket Ground, New Road,
Worcester WR2 4QQ
Phone: 0905 748474
Fax: 0905 748005
Prospects of Play: 0905 422011
Rapid Cricketline: 0891 567517567555

How to Get There:
Rail: Worcester Foregate Street BR (½ mile); Worcester Shrub Street BR (1 mile).
Bus: 23, 24, 25, 26 run between Angel Place (200m from Foregate Street BR) to ground.
Road: From north: Exit M5 junction 5; A38 to Worcester and city centre. Then A44 for New Road or take A443 or A449 to city centre; ground lies south of the centre and south of the River Severn, close to Bridge Street off a one-way ring road.
From south: Exit M5 junction 7, follow A44 to city centre.
From east: A422 or A44 and follow signs to city centre.
From west: Take A44, A4103 or A419 to city centre.

Membership:

		Country
Full	£62	£52
Senior	£41	£36
Junior	£26	£23
Student	£39	£34
Family (2+2)	£150	£124
Life	£350–750	
Car Park	£36	£27

Executive:	Plus one guest	£340
	two guests	£420
	three guests	£500

Admission: BAC: Adult £5; Junior/Senior £3. AXA League: Adult £7; Junior/Senior £4.
Disabled facilities: Two reserved areas but most buildings are six feet or so above ground owing to flooding risks and can only be entered via a flight of steps.
BAC fixtures 1993: v Somerset (20–24 May); v Leicestershire (10–14 June); v Glamorgan (22–26 July); v Surrey (12–16 Aug); v Kent (19–23 Aug); v Lancashire (31 Aug–4 Sept); v Middlesex (16–20 Sept).
Tour match: v Australians (5–7 May).
Capacity: 8,500.

Extras: On the morning of Worcestershire's first game here after moving from Boughton Park in 1899, the groundstaff were still painting the sightscreen. Apart from the floods that drowned the playing area a couple of winters ago, New Road has been dressed for the occasion ever since. From the Tudoresque scoreboard and those scrummy cream teas in the Ladies' Stand to the lunchtime walks along the Severn and those childhood memories of Graveney and D'Oliveira, all rounded off by a handsome 14th century cathedral, this is the editor's nomination as Most Bewitching County Venue. An appeal, deservedly, has been launched to raise funds for a cricket centre that will bear Basil D'Oliveira's name. Cyclists, meanwhile, will be pleased to learn that racks have been installed near the Members' gates at the rear of the pavilion, with more planned for the turnstiles. Bradman put Fred Root and the rest of the Worcestershire attack on the rack here in 1930, making 236 in his first innings on English soil: when he reached 200, related one contemporary report, 'the cathedral bells, appropriately, were chiming *Last Rose of Summer*'. Another batsman to bloom was Middlesex's Jack Robertson, who made 331 in a day in 1949 only to find one of his tyres punctured when he walked back to the car park. He was genuinely surprised when none of the home bowlers volunteered to help change it.

KIDDERMINSTER: Address: Kidderminster Cricket Club, Chester Road Sports Club, Offmore Lane, Chester Road, Kidderminster, Worcestershire DY10 1TH.
Phone: 0562 4175

How to Get There:
Rail: Kidderminster BR; ½ mile.
Bus: Midland Red from surrounding areas to bus station – ground ¾ mile from there; 7 passes ground.
Road: From north: Exit M5 junction 3; A456 to Kidderminster then take A449 bypass for Offmore Lane and ground or A449 then A442 to Kidderminster.
From south: M5 junction 6; A449 to Kidderminster; as north.
From east: A456 or A448 to Kidderminster; as north.
From west: A456 or 451 to Kidderminster; as north.

Disabled facilities: No reserved area so request position.
BAC fixture 1993: v Derbyshire (1–5 July).
Capacity: 5,500 approx; around 2,000 seats.

Extras: Chester Road has one thing in common with Lord's: its own Long Room, a tea and recreation room with a substantial bar open to members. Such uppitiness doubtless stems from the ground's blueblooded roots: the landlord from whom Kidderminster CC secured the lease in 1896 was the Earl of Dudley. Duncan Fearnley, Worcestershire chairman and batmaker to the stars, enjoyed his finest hour here (5½ of them, actually), scoring his only first-class century against Derbyshire in 1966 in a match finished off in the grandest of manners with a six by Tom Graveney. Their captain that day, Don Kenyon, owns the ground record with 259 against Yorkshire, the highest innings by an Englishman in the 1956 season. The pavilion, built in 1925, cost the princely sum of £886.

YORKSHIRE
Secretary: Chris Hassell
LEEDS: BASS HEADINGLEY (HQ): Address: The Pavilion, Headingley Cricket Ground, St Michael's Lane, Leeds LS6 3BR
Phone: 0532 787395
Prospects of Play: 0532 787394

How to Get There:
Rail: Headingley BR (½ mile); Leeds City BR (2½ miles).
Bus: 7, 74, 75, 76, 77 (Yorkshire Rider) from Leeds City BR to ground; 1, 4, 56, 93 and 96 from city centre; 38, 39, 93 and 96 from the suburbs.
Road: From north: A660, A61 or A58 and follow signs to Leeds and city centre; follow signs for Kirkstall and Headingley; ground is off the A660, about 1½ miles north-west of the city centre.
From east: A64, A63 or M62 and M1 and follow signs to Leeds city centre; A660 to Headingley.
From south: Exit M1 at junction 43 and then go on to Leeds city centre or A653 or A61 to city centre.
From west: A58, A62, A647, M62 or M621 and follow signs to Leeds city centre.

Membership: Full £60; Retired £40; Country (150 miles+ from York) £40; Lady £50; Retired Lady £28; Country Lady £28; Student £35; Junior £21; Affiliated Club £60; Corporate £75; Additional Corporate £40; Life £1200; Life (Retired) £800.
Admission: BAC and tourist match: Adult £6.50; Junior/Senior £3.50. AXA: Adult £7.50; Junior/Senior £3.50.
Disabled facilities: Reserved areas available, or by prior arrangement.
BAC fixtures 1993: v Kent (24–28 June); v Durham (26–30 Aug).
Tour match: v Australians (25–27 May) (If Yorkshire are otherwise engaged in the Benson & Hedges Cup quarter-finals Surrey, Northamptonshire or Nottinghamshire will entertain the tourists.)
Capacity: 20,000.

Extras: With so many parts of the county to satisfy, Yorkshire, predictably, are the one county to play more home matches at outgrounds than headquarters, considerably more in fact. Now owned by a brewery – understandably, even fewer people refer to it as Bass Headingley than call the Oval the Fosters Oval – Headingley itself has undergone some highly effective nipping and tucking over the past couple of seasons, the product of a £2.5m investment being a Test venue eminently worthy of the status. Somewhat surprisingly, there is no museum as yet, although one is planned. There will be much ground to cover: Lord Hawke's moustache; Bradman's 300 in a day in 1930; Trueman's delivery stride; Boycott's 100th 100; the supporters of the less-than-innocent

George Davis who dug up the pitch and caused the 1975 Ashes Test to be abandoned; the Botham-Willis miracle of 1981; the leaking pipe that stopped play in 1988, and, most recently, Gooch's heroic 154 that downed the West Indies in 1991. Tributes to Lancastrians are not anticipated. Parking is limited inside the ground but available in adjoining streets.

BRADFORD: Address: The Yorkshire Academy of Cricket; Bradford Park Avenue Cricket Ground; Canterbury Avenue, Bradford, West Yorkshire
Phone: 0274 391564

How to Get There:
Rail: Bradford BR; 1¼ miles.
Bus: Yorkshire Rider (various numbers) from surrounding area to Bradford bus station (0532 457676); ¾ mile walk from there.
Road: From north: A650, A6038 or A658 to Bradford and city centre; follow signs to Halifax; ground south-west of centre off Great Horton Road on A647 to Halifax.
From south: M1 junction 42; M62 to junction 26; M606 then follow signs to Bradford city centre; as north; or A650, A641 or A6306 to city centre; as north.

Disabled facilities: No reserved area but request position, ideally at City End near scoreboard.
BAC fixture 1993: v Worcestershire (13–17 May).
Capacity: 8,000.

Extras: Described in *Barclays World of Cricket* a dozen years ago as 'a Yorkshire citadel', Park Avenue has lost much (if not its slope) in the transition to cricket academy. Gone is the Victorian pavilion, usurped by a car park; gone are the days when 20,000 (over 30,000 for Gloucestershire's visit in 1947) could be accommodated; even the neighbours, Bradford Park Avenue FC, have vamoosed, their home demolished. A bank of industrial units dominates the City End now. Small wonder a few disgruntled diehards have disowned the place. Not that the trade-off has been negligible for Yorkshire: two of their most promising players, Jeremy Batty and Paul Grayson, are both graduates.

HARROGATE: Address: Harrogate Cticket Club, The Pavilion, St George's Cricket Ground, St George's Road, Harrogate, North Yorkshire
Phone: 0423 561301

How to Get There:
Rail: Harrogate BR; 1¼ miles.
Bus: 36, 653 from Harrogate BR (destination LeedsBradford) pass end of St George's Road.
Road: From north: A1 and A6055 to Harrogate or A61 to town centre; ground is off A61 to Leeds, about ½ mile south of town centre. Signpost in middle of a roundabout.
From south: A1 and A661 to Harrogate or A61; as north.
From east: A59 to Harrogate and town centre; A61 then as north.
From west: A59 or B6162 to Harrogate and town centre; as east.

Disabled facilities: No reserved area so request position, ideally on walkway at northern end.
BAC fixture 1993: v Northamptonshire (15–19 July).
Capacity: 8,000; seating for 5,000.

Extras: For nearly two decades the exclusive home of one of the lesser-spotted county competitions, the Tilcon Trophy, Harrogate's stint in the spotlight has been cut short this season by the sponsor's reluctant withdrawal. St George's may not quite match the pristine prettiness of the town but its three permanent terraces do mean that it boasts more copious seating than most outgrounds.

So much so that no fewer than 15,000, a ground record, were on hand in 1986 to see India play Pakistan in a charity match for Help The Aged. One set of gates is named after Maurice Leyland, an indomitable middle-order rock for England between the wars who frequently turned out for his home town club here. Ray Illingworth sealed Yorkshire's last-but-one Championship title here in 1967 with a career-best haul of 14 for 64 against Gloucestershire.

MIDDLESBROUGH: Address: Middlesbrough Cricket Club, Acklam Park, Green Lane, Acklam, Middlesbrough, Cleveland
Phone: 0642 818567

How to Get There:
Rail: Middlesbrough BR; 1½ miles.
Bus: 14, 15, 16 (Cleveland Transit) or 24 link from bus station 400m from ground.
Road: From north: A1(M) to A177 exit; follow to Middlesbrough, or A19 or A178 to town centre; ground is south of the centre in Green Lane.
From south: A1 then A168 or A19 and follow signs to Green Lane or A172 then as west.
From west: A66 and follow signs to Middlesbrough, than A19 to Acklam turn-off using A174 or A1130.

Disabled facilities: Area railed off at Rugby Ground End next to sightscreen.
BAC fixture 1993: v Glamorgan (3–7 June).
Capacity: 10,000.

Extras: The induction of Durham last spring deprived Acklam Park of its unique place on the cricketing map as the most northerly first-class venue. The continued absence of Hull from the BAC calendar nevertheless means that this remains the only Yorkshire outground outside the county boundaries to stage Championship matches. There were probably a few second thoughts rumbling round Headingley in 1965, however, Hampshire routing Yorkshire for 23, their record low. This rather undermined the local groundsman's assertion just a few years earlier that his pitch was as good as any on the Yorkshire circuit. This year's guests, Glamorgan, might not want to dwell too much on the fact that it was off their bowling 10 years ago that Yorkshire made their highest score here, 408 for 4 declared. Expect Viv Richards to lead a march on the all-comers' mark of 436 set by Sussex in 1991 courtesy of Alan Wells' ground record 253 not out.

SCARBOROUGH: Address: The Pavilion, North Marine Road, Scarborough, North Yorkshire YO12 7TJ
Phone: 0723 365625

How to Get There:
Rail: Scarborough Central BR; ¾ mile.
Bus: United Automobile Services from Whitby and Middlesbrough; East Yorkshire Motor Services from Bridlington and Hull; West Yorkshire Road Car Company from Malton, York and Leeds.
Road: From north: A171 or A165 and follow signs to Scarborough and seafront; ground north of the town centre off North Marine Road (B1364) by Trafalgar Square.
From south: A64 or A165 to Scarborough and seafront.
From west: Take A170 to Scarborough, then B1364.

Disabled facilities: Reserved area in Trafalgar Square enclosure.
BAC fixtures 1993: v Middlesex (12–16 Aug); v Sussex (9–13 Sept).
Capacity: 15,000.

Extras: The North Marine Ground is the best-known outground in the country and arguably cricket's finest seaside outpost. Scarborough CC have been in occupation since 1863 and set the most famous Festival Week in motion 13 years later. Over the past century and more, virtually everyone who is anyone has caught the festive mood at some stage, from Bradman and Benaud to I Zingari and Michael Parkinson's XI, and most of them have demonstrated their good humour by scoring a sackful of runs. A ground where bowlers serve and batsmen dine, New Zealand's Ken Rutherford made 317 in a day here in 1986, and Hobbs 266, the highest individual score in Gentleman v Players history, in 1925. Richie himself tucked in, walloping 11 sixes against T. N. Pearce's XI in 1953. A little more low-key nowadays, the Joshua Tetley Trophy Festival runs from 6–8 September this summer.

SHEFFIELD: Address: Sheffield Amateur Sports Club, Abbeydale Park, Abbeydale Park Road South, Dore, Sheffield, South Yorkshire S17 3LJ
Phone: 0742 362040367011

How to Get There:
Rail: Dore, a link line station from Sheffield Midland BR; 100 metres.
Bus: 17, 24 from Sheffield Station BR, both stop 700m from ground.
Road: From north: Exit M1 junction 34, follow signs to Sheffield and city centre; A621 to Bakewell and Baslow; ground is at Dore (near Totley) off Abbeydale Park Road South. Alternatively, follow either A6102, A61, A6135 or A618 to Sheffield city centre, then A621.
From south: Exit M1 junction 29, follow A617 to Chesterfield, bypass Dronfield, take A61 and exit at Greenhill roundabout; B6054 to Dore and Totley or A16, A621 then as north.
From east: Exit M1 junction 33 and follow A630 to Sheffield city centre; or A57 then as north.
From west: A625 or A621; follow signs to Dore and Totley.

Disabled facilities: No reserved area so request position; toilet in pavilion.
BAC fixture 1993: v Gloucestershire (17–21 June).
Capacity: 8,000; 3,500 seats.

Extras: Lying close to the upmarket suburbs of Dore and Totley, Abbeydale Park has had the disinct misfortune to succeed the fondly remembered Bramall Lane, Yorkshire's original HQ and site of a solitary Test in 1902. If England had not lost to Australia that long-ago July, who knows whether there might have been more. As it was, willow and leather were eventually booted out by studs and shinpads. Yet while nostalgia for Bramall Lane remains, Abbeydale Park has diluted it. A handful of Yorkshire batsmen were whisked off to hospital after Wayne Daniel had started operating on one particularly vicious track here, but the predominant mood at this comely, tree-lined ground is one of serenity. An apt note on which to end a guide to the stages of English cricket.

WHO'S WHO GUIDE TO 1993 COUNTY SQUADS

Note: Championship Ratings refer to a county's strength in batting and bowling, up to a maximum of five bats and five balls. All previews by the Editor unless stated.

*Championship Points
For the first time since 1974, a new method of awarding first-innings bonus points in Championship fixtures has been introduced for the 1993 season. The major change sees batting points awarded for 200 runs or more instead of 150 and upwards, and 120 overs, rather than 100, being available for the accumulation of said bonus points. Up to four points for batting and four for bowling may be earned. The maximum number of points a county can take from a match is 24.

Bonus Points
Batting: 200–249 – 1 point; 250–299 – 2 points; 300–349 – 3 points; 350+ – 4 points.
Bowling: 3–4 wickets – 1 point; 5–6 wickets – 2 points; 7–8 wickets – 3 points; 9–10 wickets – 4 points.

Points are also awarded for the following: Win – 16 + bonus points; Tie – 8 to each side + bonus points; Draw (with scores level) – 8 to side batting fourth + bonus points. If less than eight hours' playing time remains when the first ball is bowled and the captains agree to a one-innings game, no bonus points will be available and the winning side scores 12 points. Any county adjudged to have prepared an unsuitable pitch (i.e. one considered by the inspector of pitches to be unfit for first-class cricket) may incur a penalty of 25 points, to be deducted from their total at that point in the season.

Note: * denotes player capped by current county; † denotes captain; *i* denotes overseas import.

All career figures relate to first-class (fc) cricket (individual bests are for Championship unless otherwise stated) and are correct to the end of the 1992 English season (for winter update consult *The Cricketer Quarterly*). Championship records date from 1864. Date of club formation relates to founding of present club.
Acknowledgements: Association of Cricket Statisticians and TCCB/Bull Computer Statistics/Richard Lockwood.

Abbreviations: BAC = Britannic Assurance Championship; NWT GC = NatWest Trophy Gillette Cup; B&H = Benson & Hedges Cup; SL = Sunday League; b = birthplace; RHB = right-hand batsman; LHB = left-hand batsman; RF = right-arm fast bowler; LF = left-arm fast; RFM = right arm/fast-medium; LFM = left-arm fast-medium; RM = right-arm medium; RAS = right-arm seamer; LAS = left-arm seamer; OS = off-spinner; SLA = slow left-armer; LS = leg-spinner; WK = wicketkeeper; HS = highest score; BB = best bowling; Ct = caught; St = stumped (for regular wicketkeepers only); 100s = centuries; 1000r = 1000 runs in a season; 100w = 100 wickets in a season; 50w = 50 wickets in a season; 5w/i = five wickets in an innings; 10w/m = ten wickets in a match.
(Details given only if feat has been accomplished, so no BB if player has failed to take a wicket).

DERBYSHIRE

BAC positions last five seasons: 5th (1992); 3rd; 12th; 6th; 14th.
Club formed: 1870.
Honours: Champions 1 (1936); NWTGC 1 (1981); B&H 0 (finalists 1978, 1988); SL 1 (1990).

It is more than 30 years since Derbyshire finished among the top five in successive seasons. There is no reason to think that, after coming third and fifth, they are feeling vertiginous. Under a settled captain in Kim Barnett, with a group of cricketers on the cusp of achievement, and enviable strength in quick bowling, they could go on to better things.

There is an important caveat. The pace of Derby pitches has long been something to carp about, and although a slow surface at Chelmsford has not stopped Essex winning Championships, Derbyshire lack the turning pitches Essex have encouraged on their outgrounds – and the men to exploit them. Chesterfield, by comparison, is anything but slow.

The outstanding performance last season was Peter Bowler's. In a top five adorned by shotmakers like Barnett and John Morris (whose decision to resign, after much deliberation, was a relief) he provides the necessary adhesion. It would be wrong, though, to imply he is a blocker pure and simple. To make 2,044 runs at an average of 65, as he did, you have to play a few shots.

Barnett enters his 11th season as captain in the knowledge that Derbyshire can meet all-comers as equals. If he can get the best out of his quick bowlers, and often, they will be rather more than equals. Ian Bishop and Devon Malcolm are genuinely fast and Dominic Cork, one of English cricket's brightest hopes, is another year older. Cork's 74 wickets in 1992 proved a good enough performance to earn a place in England's one-day side at the end of the season. Making comparisons is a mug's game at the best of times so no one should invoke the spirit of other all-rounders. But it would be a pity if this young man, not yet 22, did not go on to justify all his good notices.

Chris Adams and Tim O'Gorman are the young batsmen with miles to go before they sleep. The batting, entertaining as it can be, still has the sort of soft centre which a bit more of Bowler's application could cure. In Karl Krikken they have a good 'un, the kind of wicketkeeper who is better than first appearances suggest. (Michael Henderson)

CHAMPIONSHIP RATING: Three bats, 3½ balls.
PREDICTED POSITION: 6th.

Overseas player: IAN BISHOP

Two years ago it appeared that Ian Bishop's career was ending before it had properly begun. The Trinidadian fast bowler, who made such a lively impression on his first tour of England in 1988 and had risen to become one of the most feared practitioners of his craft, was suffering from a back injury which threatened his livelihood.

He missed the 1991 Wisden Trophy series in England and the whole of the following winter, refining a supple action upon recovery, but Derbyshire needed evidence of his return to full fitness last spring before they re-engaged him and chief executive Bob Lark flew to Port-of-Spain to see for himself. Bishop convinced him and accordingly returned to England, where he took 64 Championship wickets at 17.46 to justify the club's decision.

Now 25, and restored to the West Indies side as Curtly Ambrose's new ball partner, Bishop enjoyed a successful return to Test cricket in Australia. He, it was, in fact, who took the first wicket of the series by having Mark Taylor caught behind, and who also emerged as one of the few redeeming features of the West Indies' defeat in Melbourne, where Border, Steve Waugh and Taylor were all dispatched in the second innings to produce a match collection of 6–129, the best by any seam bowler on either side.

A born-again Christian, Bishop should be at the height of his powers this summer. Coming straight from an arduous series against Pakistan could mean a little fatigue at first, but he will be assisted by Derbyshire's policy of rotating their team of quicker bowlers to keep their powder dry. (Michael Henderson)

PLAYING STAFF 1993:

*ADAMS Christopher John b Whitwell, 6/5/70; RHB RAS; HS 140 not out; BB 4–29; 100s 8; 1000r 1.

AGRAWALLA Amritash b Calcutta, India, 2/3/71; RHB LS. Yet to make fc debut.

*†BARNETT Kim John b Stoke-on-Trent, 17/7/60; RHB LS; HS 239 not out; BB 6–28; 100s 38; 1000r 10; 5w/i 2. Captain since 1983. Tests 4.

*BASE Simon John b Maidstone, 2/1/60; RHB RAS; HS 58; BB 7–60; 5w/i 12; 10w/m 1; 50w 1. Previous county: Glamorgan (1986–87).

i*BISHOP Ian Raphael b Port of Spain, Trinidad, 24/10/67; RHB RF; HS 103 not out; BB 7–34; 100s 1; 5w/i 19; 10w/m 1; 50w 2. Tests 11.

*BOWLER Peter Duncan b Plymouth, 30/7/63; RHB OS; HS 241 not out; BB 3–41; 100s 18; 1000r 5. Previous county: Leicestershire (1986), for whom he became the first player to score 100 on debut. First player to score 100 on debut for two counties.

CORK Dominic Gerald b Newcastle-under-Lyme, 7/8/71; RHB RAS; HS 72 not out; BB 8–53; 5w/i 3; 10w/m 1: 50w 1. England A cap.

GRIFFITH Frank Alexander b Leyton, London, 15/8/68; RHB RAS; HS 81; BB 4–33.

HARRIS Andrew b Ashton, 26/6/73; RHB RAS. Yet to make fc debut.

KRIKKEN Karl Matthew Giles b Bolton, 9/4/69; RHB WK; HS 77 not out; Ct 175; St 12.

LOVELL David b Adelaide, Australia, 16/2/69; RHB SLA. Yet to make fc debut.

*MAHER Bernard Joseph Michael b Hillingdon, Middx. 11/2/58; RHB WK; HS 126 (v New Zealand), 121 not out (BAC); BB 2–69; 100s 4; Ct 280; St 14.

*MALCOLM Devon Eugene b Kingston, Jamaica 22/2/63; RHB RF; HS 51, BB 7–74 (for England XI), 6–68 (BAC); 5w/i 10; 10w/m 1; 50w 2. Tests 21.

*MORRIS John Edward b Crewe, 1/4/64; RHB RAS; HS 191; BB 1–13; 100s 29; 1000r 7. Tests 3.

*MORTENSEN Ole Henrik b Vejle, Denmark, 29/1/58; RHB RAS; HS 74 not out; BB 6–27; 50w 2; 5w/i 15; 10w/m 1; hat-trick 1.

*O'GORMAN Timothy Joseph Gerard b Woking, 15/5/67; RHB OS; HS 148; BB 1–17; 100s 5; 1000r 2.

RICHARDSON Alastair William b Derby, 23/10/72; RHB RFM; HS 5.

ROLLINS Adrian Stewart b Barking, 8/2/72; RHB RAS. Set county 2nd XI record for run aggregate in 1992. Yet to make fc debut.

SLADDIN Richard William b Halifax, 8/1/69; RHB SLA; HS 39; BB 6-58; 5w/i 2.

STEER Gary b Birmingham, 17/8/70; RHB RAS WK. Yet to make fc debut.

TWEATS Timothy Andrew b Stoke-on-Trent, 18/4/74; RHB RAS; HS 24.

*WARNER Allan Esmond b Birmingham, 12/5/59; RHB RAS; HS 91; BB 5-27; 5w/i 2.

WHITAKER Paul Robert b Keighley, 28/6/73; LHB OS. Yet to make fc debut.

In: A. Agrawalla, A. Harris, D. Lovell, A. Rollins, G. Steer.
Out: A. M. Brown, S. C. Goldsmith, M. Jean-Jacques (Hants).

Player of the Year 1992: P. D. Bowler.
Colt to follow: D. G. Cork.

DERBYSHIRE BAC AVERAGES 1992

BATTING	M	I	NO	Runs	HS	Av	100	50
P. D. Bowler	22	35	7	1862	241*	66.50	6	9
K. J. Barnett	18	29	5	1270	160	52.92	4	4
J. E. Morris	21	30	0	1236	120	41.20	3	11
S. C. Goldsmith	9	10	3	270	100*	38.57	1	1
C. J. Adams	21	29	4	924	140*	36.96	4	2
F. A. Griffith	6	8	1	242	81	34.57	0	1
T. J. G. O'Gorman	22	33	6	880	95	32.59	0	7
D. G. Cork	17	19	2	504	72*	29.65	0	3
O. H. Mortensen	13	12	10	47	13*	23.50	0	0
I. R. Bishop	20	21	2	388	90	20.42	0	1
D. E. Malcolm	14	13	4	144	26	16.00	0	0
K. M. Krikken	21	24	3	323	57*	15.38	0	1
A. E. Warner	15	13	2	151	29	13.73	0	0
A. M. Brown	6	6	0	74	36	12.33	0	0
R. W. Sladdin	11	13	2	126	39	11.45	0	0

Also batted: S. J. Base (2 matches) 3, 0*; M. Jean-Jacques (2) 0,6; A. W. Richardson (1) 5; T. A. Tweats (1) 24.

BOWLING	O	M	R	W	Av	BB	5i	10m
S. J. Base	35	8	100	7	14.29	5-35	1	0
I. R. Bishop	483	116	1118	64	17.47	7-34	4	0
F. A. Griffith	102	25	350	14	25.00	4-33	0	0
M. Jean-Jacques	35.4	5	135	5	27.00	4-46	0	0
D. G. Cork	406.2	67	1237	44	28.11	5-36	2	0
A. E. Warner	335.5	79	817	27	30.26	4-52	0	0
O. H. Mortensen	307	76	736	19	38.74	2-22	0	0
D. E. Malcolm	318.2	48	1130	29	38.97	5-45	1	0
R. W. Sladdin	420.2	110	1212	30	40.40	4-102	0	0

Also bowled: C. J. Adams 56-3-229-2, K. J. Barnett 77.4-11-250-4, P. D. Bowler 17-3-69-0, A. M. Brown 3-0-9-0, S. C. Goldsmith 113-21-391-3, T. J. G. O'Gorman 27-0-141-1, A. W. Richardson 13-2-38-2.

HUNDREDS (18)
- 6 – P. D. Bowler: 122 v Worcs (Derby), 104* v Lancs (Blackpool), 155 v Notts (Derby), 147* v Somerset (Taunton), 241* v Hants (Portsmouth), 100* v Worcs (Worcester).
- 4 – C. J. Adams: 121 v Worcs (Derby), 112* v Middx (Derby), 140* v Worcs (Worcester), 135 v Essex (Derby). K. J. Barnett: 140* v Surrey (Oval), 117* v Leics (Ilkeston), 160 v Kent (Chesterfield), 156* v Notts (Trent Bridge).
- 3 – J. E. Morris: 120 v Notts (Derby), 109 v Somerset (Taunton), 107 v Leics (Ilkeston).
- 1 – S. C. Goldsmith: 100* v Worcs (Derby).

DURHAM
BAC positions last five seasons: 18th; – – – –
Club formed: 1882.
Honours: Champions 0 (best: 18th, 1992); NWTGC 0 (best: quarter-finals, 1992); B&H 0 (best: zone stages, 1992); SL 0 (best: 6th, 1992). Awarded first-class status 1992.
Note: Durham do not award county caps in the conventional sense.

Predicting that the freshmen of Durham would run away with last season's wooden spoon was hardly the most inspired piece of crystal-ball gazing of 1992. That, after all, was the fate that befell Glamorgan, the last county to enter the Championship ranks 71 years earlier.

Yet, in contrast to the Welshmen, who relied predominantly on amateur turns, Durham could at least boast a goodly number of seasoned pros: Dean Jones, Paul Parker, Wayne Larkins, Phil Bainbridge, Simon Hughes, David Graveney and, of course, the Beloved Entertainer, Ian Botham. Until mid-June, moreover, with Simon Brown's sprightly left-arm seam causing unsuspected havoc, the formula worked. The batting, touted as the newcomers' strong suit, collapsed against Derbyshire and a place in the Benson & Hedges Cup quarter-finals went a-begging, but the veterans soon recovered their poise, Larkins, Parker and Jones doing most of the spadework as Glamorgan (a symbolic maiden Championship victory) and Somerset were beaten in quick succession. At this juncture, Chester-le-Street's answer to Dad's Army lay fourth, and Brown, previously surplus to requirements at Northampton, was the leading wicket-taker in the country. However, his decline further diluted an already weak attack, and for all Hughes' endeavour, the lack of penetration triggered a swift descent. One particularly disappointing element was the inability of another seamer, Steve McEwan, to capitalise on the abundant promise he had shown in spurring Worcestershire to the 1989 BAC title. The slight shoulders of Anderson Cummins will bear a heavy load.

On the other hand, only Leicestershire gathered fewer batting points than the county Lilliputians, while those traditional Gullivers, Lancashire, Surrey and Yorkshire, all achieved fewer bowling points. This illusory statistic scarcely flattered the spinners, among whom the captain, Graveney, claimed more victims – 28 – than his accomplices, Mark Briers and Phil Berry, managed between them. Berry took 10 wickets against Middlesex and five in his remaining half-dozen appearances.

The future looks brighter. Geoff Cook has brought through some likely lads, notably Jimmy Daley, a graduate from the MCC Young Cricketers who made two mature half-centuries in his four innings; Stewart Hutton, a cussed opener, and John Wood, a burly fast bowler. Once Paul Henderson has filled out, he, too, will be a more than useful manipulator of the seam. Their progress – a process which the arrival of another wise owl, Graeme Fowler, may well hasten – will do more to dictate the course of Durham's sophomore term than a few turns from the Beloved Entertainer fresh from shoulder surgery. Patience, though, remains essential.

CHAMPIONSHIP RATING: two bats, two balls.
PREDICTED POSITION: 17th.

Overseas player: ANDERSON CUMMINS
While Linden Joseph, arguably the best of the young Caribbean speedsters, has failed to attract any county suitors since his unhappy spell at Hampshire in 1990, two contemporaries have been snapped up. Of the pair, Andy Cummins, a wiry package from the prolific Bajan conveyor belt, may take longer to impose himself.

Although he made his debut as recently as January, he has probably had his fill of Test cricket already. After emerging as his side's most successful seamer in the World Cup and the one-day curtain-raiser, he was controversially excluded from the West Indies squad for last year's first-ever meeting with South Africa in his native Bridgetown. It was a costly omission, literally. Angered by Richie Richardson's elevation to the captaincy over the head of Desmond Haynes, and further agitated by Malcolm Marshall's acrimonious exit, Cummins' compatriots had had enough. Casting the youngster in the unwitting and unwanted role of *agent provocateur*, they expressed their disquiet by staging a boycott, one that contributed greatly to the crippling losses sustained by the West Indies board.

Doubtless steeled by the experience, Cummins will also have learned much from pounding his beat on the bone-hard pitches of Australia. Making up in accuracy and stamina for what he lacks in raw pace, he may not be the wrecking ball the members would have preferred, but then there are precious few of those around. What Durham do have is a scalpel, and a deft one at that. An instrument to be handled with care.

PLAYING STAFF 1993:

BAINBRIDGE Philip b Sneyd Green, Stoke-on-Trent, 16/4/58; RHB RAS; HS 169 (for Gloucs), 92 not out (for Dur); BB 8–53 (for Gloucs), 5–100 (for Dur); 100s 22; 1000r 8; 5w/i 8. Previous county: Gloucestershire (1977–90).

BERRY Philip John b Saltburn, Yorkshire 28/12/66; RHB OS; HS 76; BB 7–113; 5w/i 1. Previous county: Yorkshire (1986–90).

BOTHAM Ian Terence b Heswall, Cheshire, 24/11/55; RHB RAS; HS 228 (for Som), 105 (for Dur); BB 8–34 (for England), 7–54 (for Worcs), 4–72 (for Dur); 100s 37; 1000r 4; 5w/i 59; 10w/m 8; 100w 1 (for Som) 50w 7; hat-trick 1 (for MCC). Tests 102 (12 as captain). Previous counties: Somerset (1974–86, captain 1984–85), Worcestershire (1987–91).

BRIERS Mark Paul b Kegworth, 21/4/68; RHB LS; HS 62 not out; BB 3–109.

BROWN Simon John Emmerson b Cleadon, 29/6/69; RHB LAS; HS 47 not out*; BB 7–105; 50w 1; 5w/i 3. Previous county: Northamptonshire (1987–90).

COX David b Southall, Middx, 2/3/72; LHB SLA. Yet to make fc debut.

*i*CUMMINS Anderson Cleophas b Packer's Valley, Barbados, 7/5/66; RHB RFM; HS 45 not out (for Barbados); BB 4–26 (for Barbados). Yet to make BAC debut.

DALEY James Arthur b Sunderland, 24/9/73; RHB RAS; HS 88.

FOTHERGILL Andrew Robert b Newcastle-upon-Tyne, 10/2/62; RHB WK; HS 23; Ct 10; St 1.

FOWLER Graeme b Accrington, Lancs 20/4/57; LHB RAS; HS 226 (for Lancs); BB 2–34 (for Lancs); 100s 35; 1000r 8. Tests 21. Previous county: Lancashire (1979–92).

GLENDENEN John David b Middlesbrough, 20/6/65; RHB RAS; HS 117; 100s 1.

†*GRAVENEY David Anthony b Bristol 2/1/53; RHB SLA; HS 119 (for Gloucs), 36 (for Dur); BB 8–85 (for Gloucs), 3–22 (for Dur); 100s 2; 50w 6; 5w/i 38; 10/m 7; hat-trick 1 (for Gloucs). Previous counties: Gloucestershire (1972–90, captain 1981–88), Somerset (1991).

HENDERSON Paul William b Stockton-on-Tees, 22/10/74; RHB RFM; HS 46; BB 3–59.

HUGHES Simon Peter b Kingston-upon-Thames, 20/12/59; RHB RAS; HS 53 (for Middx), 42 (for Dur); BB 7–35 (for Middx), 5–25 (for Dur); 50w 2; 5w/i 10. Previous county: Middlesex (1980–91).

HUTTON Stewart b Stockton-on-Tees, 30/11/69; LHB RAS. HS 78.

LARKINS Wayne b Roxton, Beds, 22/11/53; RHB RAS; HS 252 (for Northants), 143 (for Dur); BB 5–59 (for Northants), 0–4 (for Dur); 100s 53; 1000r 12; 5w/i 1. Tests 13. Previous county: Northamptonshire (1972–91).

McEWAN Steven Michael b Worcester, 5/5/62; RHB RAS; HS 54 (for Worcs), 22 (for Dur); BB 6–34 (for Worcs), 3–52 (for Dur); 50w 1; 5w/i 3; hat-trick 1. Previous county: Worcestershire (1985–90).

PARKER Paul William Giles b Bulawayo, Zimbabwe, 15/1/56; RHB RAS; HS 215 (for Cambridge U), 140 (BAC, for Suss), 124 (for Dur); BB 2–21 (for Suss), 0–31 (for Dur); 100s 44; 1000r 9. Tests 1. Previous county: Sussex (1976–91, captain 1988–91).

SCOTT Christopher Wilmot b Thorpe-on-the-Hill, Lincs, 23/1/64; RHB WK; HS 78 (Notts), 57 not out (for Dur); Ct 162; St 11. Previous county: Nottinghamshire (1981–91).

SEARLE Jason b Bremhill, Wilts, 16/5/76; RHB OS. Yet to make fc debut.

SMITH Ian b Chopwell, 11/3/67; RHB RAS; HS 116 (for Glam), 110 (for Dur); BB 3–48 (for Glam), 3–85 (for Dur); 100s 4. Previous county: Glamorgan (1985–91).

WOOD John b Wakefield, 22/7/70; RHB RFM; HS 28; BB 5–68; 5w/i 1.

In: A. C. Cummins, G. Fowler (Lancs).
Out: G. K. Brown, D. M. Jones.

Player of the Year 1992: P. W. G. Parker.
Colt to follow: J. A. Daley.

DURHAM BAC AVERAGES 1992

BATTING	M	I	NO	Runs	HS	Av	100	50
J. A. Daley	2	4	1	190	88	63.33	0	2
D. M. Jones	12	20	5	904	157	60.27	2	5
P. Bainbridge	16	29	8	899	92*	42.81	0	8
P. W. G. Parker	18	32	2	1218	124	40.60	2	8
W. Larkins	21	39	0	1417	143	36.33	3	8
I. T. Botham	14	23	2	705	105	33.57	1	4
I. Smith	11	16	1	435	110	29.00	1	2
S. Hutton	8	15	0	406	78	27.07	0	2
C. W. Scott	17	24	5	433	57*	22.79	0	2
G. K. Brown	3	6	0	136	48	22.67	0	0
M. P. Briers	15	26	4	447	62*	20.32	0	4
S. J. E. Brown	19	23	13	195	47	19.50	0	0
J. D. Glendenen	15	25	1	421	76	17.54	0	3
P. W. Henderson	5	7	0	119	46	17.00	0	0
P. J. Berry	7	13	2	184	76	16.73	0	1
D. A. Graveney	20	29	9	333	36	16.65	0	0
J. Wood	7	6	1	80	28	16.00	0	0
S. P. Hughes	19	24	4	227	42	11.35	0	0
A. R. Fothergill	5	7	1	58	23	9.67	0	0
S. M. McEwan	8	12	1	58	22	5.27	0	0

BOWLING	O	M	R	W	Av	BB	5i	10m
I. Smith	82	17	231	8	28.88	3–85	0	0
J. Wood	120.2	12	510	16	31.8	5–68	1	0
S. J. E. Brown	476.1	70	1847	56	32.98	7–105	3	0
P. J. Berry	141.3	20	527	15	35.13	7–113	1	1
P. W. Henderson	96	14	405	10	40.50	3–59	0	0
I. T. Botham	303	60	1010	24	42.08	4–72	0	0
P. Bainbridge	177.1	36	555	13	42.69	5–100	1	0
D. A. Graveney	376.4	86	1196	28	42.71	3–22	0	0
M. P. Briers	121.3	22	485	11	44.09	3–109	0	0
S. P. Hughes	519.3	94	1594	34	46.88	5–25	1	0
S. M. McEwan	180	30	657	12	54.75	3–107	0	0

Also bowled: G. K. Brown 90–1–64–0, S. Hutton 0.1–0–4–0, D. M. Jones 16.3–1–67–0, W. Larkins 2–1–4–0, P. W. G. Parker 3.2–0–31–0.

HUNDREDS (9)

3 – W. Larkins: 143 v Glam (Cardiff), 140 v Glam (Hartlepool), 117 v Somerset (Taunton).

2 – D. M. Jones: 157 v Northants (Stockton), 154* v Notts (Trent Bridge). P. W. G. Parker: 117 v Leics (Durham Univ), 124 v Glam (Cardiff).

1 – I. T. Botham: 105 v Leics (Durham Univ). I. Smith: 110 v Somerset (Taunton).

ESSEX

BAC positions last five seasons: Champions; Champions; 2nd; 2nd; 3rd.
Club formed: 1876.
Honours: Champions 6 (1979, 1983–84, 1986, 1991–92); NWTGC 1 (1985); B&H 1 (1979); SL 3 (1981, 1984–85).

What can they possibly do for an encore? Tempted though they may have been to develop a serious superiority complex over the past decade or so, even the staunchest Essex supporters must have been taken aback by last summer's remarkable Championship triumph. Neil Foster missed more than half the campaign; the attendance records of Derek Pringle and Graham Gooch were only marginally better; Mark Waugh, in the finest fettle of his short career, returned to Australia with seven games to go and the pack closing fast. For much of the time, the fourth-choice captain was in charge. There could therefore have been no finer tribute to the departing Keith Fletcher than the manner in which his pupils subsequently secured Chelmsford's sixth BAC pennant in 14 seasons. For Alan Butcher, the incoming coach, to be greeted in a similar style may, however, be too stern a request.

Then again, Essex are used to defying predictions. When Foster broke down last June a severe migraine loomed. Neither Don Topley nor Steve Andrew were in form, and Mark Ilott had only just recovered from back surgery. Yet Ilott's rising star shone brightly amid the ensuing sweat and toil, his 64 wickets richly if dearly earned. More crucially, Peter Such, hesitant and constrained for so long, strode to the fore in the second half of the season, bouncing back from a broken hand to glean a career-best 6 for 17 to spin out Sussex and winding up with a place on the A tour. John Childs wheeled away contentedly at the other end, a wily old fisherman reeling in batsmen by the shoal.

Vigorous batting was the key, however. Take the opening day against Lancashire at Ilford. In his one substantial innings of an otherwise dispiriting year, Nasser Hussain hustled to 173 not out off 193 balls, Waugh roared to an unbeaten 219 from 243 and the pair elbowed aside Gibb and Horsfall's 41-year-old record for the county's third wicket in an unbroken stand of 347, Essex ultimately passing 500 inside 100 overs. The scoring rate from gun to tape was rarely less than hectic, affording invaluable extra time for the undermanned attack to complete the job. The return of Salim Malik is unlikely to add an air of sobriety.

Paul Prichard, an imaginative and fitting choice as the Britannic Assurance Player of the Year, will again hope to combine his customary zestful strokeplay and bounce in the field with the calm, unflustered approach he brought to his duties as caretaker captain last summer. A worthy if fortunate deputy in 1992 (Foster and Pringle both began term ahead of him in the pecking order), Prichard has made a timely start on the inside and emerged as the favourite to succeed Gooch.

For now, though, a fresh challenge awaits. The presence of stylish strokeplayers such as Nick Knight, Nadeem Shahid and reserve wicketkeeper Robert Rollins alongside the more conscientious Jonathan Lewis, indicates the advent of a new breed. Fortunately for their rivals, however, Essex's prospects of becoming the first county to complete a hat-trick of Championships since Yorkshire pulled it off 25 years ago are undermined by nagging doubts over the strength and durability of the old one. Unless Foster, in his benefit year, can somehow drag one more 70-wicket haul out of his banger of a body, the encore may have to come on a larger stage. Lord's in mid-July or early September, perhaps.

CHAMPIONSHIP RATING: five bats, 3½ balls.
PREDICTED POSITION: 2nd.

Overseas player: SALIM MALIK

It may sound like a backhanded compliment, but this modest, whimsical banker from Lahore can consider himself the finest substitute in the business. The most accomplished batsman on view in last summer's Test series, Salim Malik returns for a second stint on the shores of the River Cam only by dint of the fact that Mark Waugh will be busy attending to his country's needs.

Not that Essex will be unduly bothered by the trade. Over the past two summers, the Pakistani's capacity for gliding, stroking and generally easing the ball to all corners of the field has yielded eight centuries, 16 fifties and 3,156 runs at an average in excess of 75. Indeed, he took such an immediate liking to the county treadmill that he surpassed his career-best no fewer than five times in 1991. As a sideline, he also dabbled in some of the flightiest leg-spin seen here for some time, profitably at that, inducing any number of cricked necks as the hypnotised batsmen waited for the ball to rebound from a passing cloud.

Quick to attune to the inimitable Chelmsford bonhomie and badinage, Salim's own good-humoured outlook soon endeared him to colleagues and opponents alike, and when a bout of homesickness coincided with a quiet week, the county graciously granted leave of absence to visit his family. He will be more battle-hardened this time, an ominous prospect for opposing bowlers who spent last summer seeing his name perched at the top of the first-class averages. Described ludicrously as a 'flat-track bully' by Imran Khan, with whom he does not see eye-to-eye, he was omitted, perversely from Pakistan's recent tour of the Caribbean. That sharpness of eye, sureness of touch and relish for the battle should make a point or three.

PLAYING STAFF 1993:

ANDREW Stephen Jon Walter b London, 27/1/66; RHB RFM; HS 35; BB 7–92 (for Hants), 5–55 (for Ess); 5w/i 5. Previous county: Hampshire (1984–89).

BODEN David Jonathan Peter b Eccleshall, Staffs, 26/11/70; RHB RAS; HS 5 (v Cambridge U); BB 4–11 (for Middx v Oxford U). Yet to make BAC debut. Previous county: Middlesex (1989).

*CHILDS John Henry b Plymouth, 15/8/51; HS 43; BB 9–56 (for Gloucs), 8–58 (for Ess); 50w 7; 5w/i 45; 10w/m 8. Previous county: Gloucestershire (1975–84). Tests 2.

COUSINS Darren Mark b Cambridge, 24/9/71; RHB RAS. Yet to make fc debut.

*FOSTER Neil Alan b Colchester, 6/5/62; RHB RFM; HS 107 not out; BB 8–99; 100s 1; 50w 9; 100w 2; 5w/i 49; 10w/m 8. Tests 28.

FRASER Alastair Gregory James b Edgware, Middx, 17/10/67; RHB RAS; HS 52 not out; BB 3–46 (for Middx), 1–58 (Ess). Brother of Angus (Middx) Previous county: Middlesex (1986–89).

*GARNHAM Michael Anthony b Johannesburg, South Africa, 20/8/60; RHB WK; HS 123; Ct 362; St 31. Previous counties: Gloucestershire (1979), Leicestershire (1980–85 and 1988).

†*GOOCH Graham Alan b Leytonstone, 23/7/53; RHB RAS; HS 333 (for England), 275 (for Ess); BB 7–14; 100s 99; 1000r 15 (plus 1 on tour); 5w/i 3. Captain 1986–87, 1989 to date. Tests 99 (captain 28).

*HUSSAIN Nasser b Madras, India, 28/3/68; RHB RAS; HS 197; 100s 10; 1000r 1. Tests 3.

ILOTT Mark Christopher b Watford, Herts; 27/8/70; LHB LFM; HS 42 not out; BB 6–87; 50w 1; 5w/i 5. England A cap.

KHAN Gul b Gujrat, Pakistan, 31/12/73; RHB. Yet to make fc debut.

KNIGHT Nicholas Verity b Watford, 28/11/69; LHB RAS; HS 109; 100s 3.

LEWIS Jonathan James Benjamin b Isleworth, Middx, 21/5/70; RHB RAS; HS 133; 100s 2.

*PRICHARD Paul John b Billericay, 7/1/65; RHB RAS; HS 245; BB 1–28; 100s 16; 1000r 5. BAC Cricketer of the Year 1992. England A cap.

*PRINGLE Derek Raymond b Nairobi, Kenya, 18/9/58; RHB RAS; HS 128; BB 7–18; 100s 9; 50w 6; 5w/i 25; 10w/i 3. Tests 30.

ROLLINS Robert John b Plaistow, 30/1/74; RHB WK. HS 13 (v Pakistan); Ct 2. Yet to make BAC debut.

*i*SALIM MALIK b Lahore, Pakistan, 16/4/63; RHB LS; HS 215; BB 5–19 (for Habib Bank), 3–26 (for Ess); 100s 30; 1000r 1 (plus 2 on tour). Tests 71.

SHAHID Nadeem b Karachi, Pakistan, 23/4/69; RHB LS; HS 132; BB 3–91; 100s 2; 1000r 1.

*STEPHENSON John Patrick b Stebbing, 14/3/65; RHB RAS; HS 202 not out; BB 6–54; 100s 15; 1000r 4; 5w/i 1. Tests 1.

*SUCH Peter Mark b Helensburgh, Dumbartonshire, 12/6/64; RHB OS; HS 35 not out; BB 6–17; 5w/i 9. Previous counties: Nottinghamshire (1982–86), Leicestershire (1987–89). England A cap.

TENNANT Lloyd b Walsall, 9/4/68; RHB RAS; BB 4–54 (for Leicestershire). Yet to make fc debut for Essex. Previous county: Leicestershire (1986–91).

*TOPLEY Thomas Donald b Canterbury, 25/2/64; RHB RAS; HS 66; BB 7–75; 50w 3; 5w/i 15; 10w/m 2.

Beneficiary '93: N. A. Foster.

In: Salim Malik (returning), A. R. Butcher (coach).
Out: K. A. Butler, W. G. Lovell, A. C. Richards, M. E. Waugh.

Player of the Year 1992: J. H. Childs/P. M. Such.
Colt to follow: N. Shahid.

ESSEX BAC AVERAGES 1992

BATTING	M	I	NO	Runs	HS	Av	100	50
G. A. Gooch	11	18	3	1246	160	83.07	6	4
M. E. Waugh	15	23	7	1253	219*	78.31	4	5
J. P. Stephenson	19	33	5	1309	159*	46.75	3	8
N. Hussain	17	21	3	833	172*	46.28	1	5
J. J. B. Lewis	11	16	4	555	133	46.25	1	4
D. R. Pringle	12	12	3	405	112*	45.00	1	2
P. J. Prichard	21	36	4	1399	136	43.72	4	8
N. V. Knight	18	27	5	603	109	27.41	1	2
N. Shahid	13	18	0	467	132	25.94	1	2
N. A. Foster	10	13	0	290	54	22.31	0	2
M. A. Garnham	21	24	3	445	66	21.19	0	3
P. M. Such	13	11	3	100	35*	12.50	0	0
J. H. Childs	19	15	6	105	43	11.67	0	0
T. D. Topley	10	11	2	99	29	11.00	0	0
M. C. Ilott	21	19	3	143	28	8.94	0	0
S. J. W. Andrew	9	10	4	29	14*	4.83	0	0

Also batted: A. G. J. Fraser (1 match) 2. A. D. Brown played in one match but did not bat.

BOWLING	O	M	R	W	Av	BB	5i	10m
N. Shahid	34	4	143	7	20.43	2-22	0	0
D. R. Pringle	324.5	83	870	39	22.31	5-63	1	0
P. M. Such	393.1	125	895	39	22.95	6-17	3	0
J. H. Childs	624.5	197	1598	64	24.97	6-82	3	0
N. A. Foster	226	56	634	23	27.57	4-47	0	0
M. E. Waugh	173.4	31	614	21	29.24	3-38	0	0
M. C. Ilott	625.3	137	2077	62	33.50	6-87	3	0
S. J. W. Andrew	247	43	779	21	37.10	4-54	0	0
T. D. Topley	223.4	47	753	18	41.83	4-67	0	0
J. P. Stephenson	226.4	45	773	18	42.94	6-54	1	0

Also bowled: A. G. J. Fraser 11-3-58-1, G. A. Gooch 69-21-149-3, N. Hussain 4-0-38-1, P. J. Prichard 8-0-100-0.

HUNDREDS (22)

6 – G. A. Gooch: 160 v Leics (Chelmsford), 113 v Durham (Hartlepool), 102 & 108* v Sussex (Southend), 123* v Derbys (Derby), 101 v Gloucs (Bristol).

4 – P. J. Prichard: 102 v Leics (Chelmsford), 133 v Kent (Tunbridge Wells), 106 v Leics (Leicester), 136 v Notts (Colchester). M. E. Waugh: 120 v Kent (Chelmsford), 219* v Lancs (Ilford), 125* v Gloucs (Southend), 138* v Worcs (Kidderminster).

3 – J. P. Stephenson: 113* & 159* v Somerset (Taunton), 123* v Sussex (Southend).

1 – N. Hussain: 172* v Lancs (Ilford). N. V. Knight: 109 v Middx (Ilford). J. J. B. Lewis: 133 v Sussex (Hove). D. R. Pringle: 112* v Sussex (Hove). N. Shahid: 132 v Kent (Chelmsford).

GLAMORGAN
BAC positions last five seasons: 14th; 12th; 8th; 17th; 17th.
Club formed: 1888.
Honours: Champions 2 (1948, 1969); NWTGC 0 (best: finalists 1977); B&H 0 (best: semi-finals, 1988); SL 0 (best: 5th, 1988).

After a long spell in which realistic Glamorgan supporters limited pre-season optimism to hoping they would not finish bottom in the Championship – or, failing that, would win a match – the last three seasons have awakened hope of better things. Not yet perhaps of a pennant – the attack remains too dependent upon Steve Watkin and Robert Croft – but at least of a place in the top half and a tilt at a one-day title.

While the England selectors persistently fail to appreciate Hugh Morris's talents for accumulation and leadership, Glamorgan showed greater discernment in restoring him to the captaincy. Whatever the technical doubts, there are none over his temperament. Being relieved of the vice-captaincy last summer followed a series of international rejections, yet prolific scoring throughout suggests any mental vulnerability when he resigned the leadership in 1989, citing poor form, has long gone.

Morris will hope that Matthew Maynard, passed over for the captaincy after leading for most of 1992, reacts as positively as he did. If Maynard and Viv Richards return to anything like their best Glamorgan will not be a side to declare against. Steve James, Tony Cottey and Adrian Dale, all in their mid-20s, enjoyed simultaneous rites of passage last season – 1,000 Championship runs for the first time and county caps. Alan Butcher's batting, therefore, was hardly missed. The former skipper's departure to coach Essex should ease the pressure on Morris after recent disagreements.

But if that run supply is ever to generate titles, the bowling must be strengthened. Watkin will doubtless continue to bowl his full, wicket-taking length and should top 50 without much difficulty, but could do with more support. Hence the aura of anticipation surrounding Darren Thomas, a 17-year-old from Llanelli, home of Jeff Jones, the county's best-ever paceman. Beating Wayne Larkins for pace and taking 18 wickets – including two 'five-fers' – in six Championship outings suggested real promise. He misses half the season to complete studies, reducing any attempt to hurry him.

Glamorgan's continued insistence on playing more games at Cardiff than Swansea, where they have a consistently better record, makes even less sense with the arrival of the four-day game. Two of last season's five wins, after all, came when Croft spun Warwickshire and Kent out at St Helens. So mature a performer that it is a shock to be reminded that he is only 22, he would be even more dangerous with Mark Davies, released last year to become Gloucestershire's leading spinner, at the other end. Glamorgan can only hope Somerset's decision to offload Roland Lefebvre, whose forthright batting and medium-pace could be particularly useful on Sundays, proves as misplaced. Whoever is bowling, they can be confident that Colin Metson will maintain his immaculate standards while waiting for the selectors to rediscover wicket-keeping as a specialist skill. (Huw Richards)

CHAMPIONSHIP RATING: three bats, three balls.
PREDICTED POSITION: 12th.

Overseas player: VIVIAN RICHARDS
If cricket had a baseball-style Hall of Fame, Vivian Richards would be certain of election as soon as he was eligible. He is third (at time of writing) in the all-time list of Test run scorers with 8,540 at 50.23 including 24 centuries, but unmatched in the last quarter-century for sheer presence at the crease.

Last season was his worst ever. Dogged by fitness problems, falling well short of 1,000 runs and barely averaging 30, he led some observers to conclude that his final summer, at the age of 41 and under the captaincy of the man whose catch ended his last Test innings, might be one too many. The presence is still there, as is the trademark punch through mid-wicket, and some blinding slip catches show there is little wrong with his hand-eye coordination, despite all that talk of waning eyesight. But have the concentration and the desire necessary for long innings survived? It is not as if he had anything left to prove.

But no modern player has a greater sense of occasion than the 'Master Blaster', and he will want his finale to be worthy of an extraordinary career. Pre-season preparation has been limited to a chat show tour of Britain in partnership with Ian Botham, followed by a refusal to go on Glamorgan's tour of South Africa, typical of a man with a consistent, principled record of opposition to contact with apartheid. The storybook finish would be a NatWest final appearance. If Glamorgan do make it, his past record in Lord's finals means that nobody would bet against a matchwinning century to end the county's unwanted distinction as the only county, Durham apart, without a one-day crown. (Huw Richards)

PLAYING STAFF 1993:

*BARWICK Stephen Royston b Neath, 6/9/60; RHB RAS; HS 30; BB 8–42; 50w 2; 5w/i 9; 10w/m 1.

BASTIEN Steven b Stepney, London, 13/3/63; RHB RAS; HS 36*; BB 6–75; 5w/i 5.

BUTCHER Gary Peter b Clapham, London, 11/3/75; RHB RM. Son of A. R. (Essex) and brother of M. A. (Surrey). Yet to make fc debut.

*COTTEY Phillip Anthony b Swansea, 2/6/66; RHB OS; HS 141; BB 2–42 (for E. Transvaal), 1–49 (for Glam); 100s 5; 1000r 2.

*CROFT Robert Damien Bale b Swansea, 25/5/70; RHB OS; HS 91 not out; BB 8–66; 50w 1; 5w/i 6; 10w/m 1. England A cap.

*DALE Adrian b Germiston, SA, 24/10/68; RHB RAS; HS 150 not out; BB 3–21: 100s 4; 1000r 1.

DALTON Alistair John b Bridgend, 27/4/73; RHB RM. Yet to make fc debut.

*FROST Mark b Barking, Essex, 21/10/62; RHB RFM; HS 12; BB 7–99; 50w 2: 5w/i 4; 10w/m 2. Previous county: Surrey (1988–89).

HEMP David Lloyd b Bermuda, 15/11/70; LHB RAS; HS 84 not out.

*JAMES Stephen Peter b Lydney, Gloucs, 7/9/67; RHB; HS 152 not out; 100s 10; 1000r 2.

JONES Robin Owen b Crewe, 4/10/73; RHB OS. Yet to make fc debut.

LEFEBVRE Roland Phillippe b Rotterdam, Netherlands 7/2/63; RHB RAS; HS 100; BB 6–53; 100s 1; 5w/i 2. Previous county: Somerset (1990–92). Yet to make fc debut for Glamorgan.

MAYNARD Matthew Peter b Oldham, 21/3/66; RHB RAS; HS 243; BB 3–21; 100s 25; 1000r 7. Scored century on fc debut. Tests 1.

*METSON Colin Peter b Cuffley, 2/7/63; RHB RAS WK; HS 96; Ct 386; St 30.

†*MORRIS Hugh b Cardiff, 5/10/63; LHB RAS; HS 160 not out; BB 1–6; 100s 30; 1000r 6. Captain 1986–89, reappointed for 1993. Tests 3.

PARKIN Owen Thomas b Coventry, 24/9/72; RHB RAS. Yet to make fc debut.

PURDIE Scott b Strathclyde, 18/4/74; RHB RFM. Yet to make fc debut.

*i*RICHARDS Isaac Vivian Alexander b St John's, Antigua, 7/3/52; RHB OB; HS 322 (for Som), 164 not out (for Glam); BB 5–88 (for West Indies), 2–27 (for Glam); 100s 112; 1000r 13 (plus three overseas); 5w/i 1. Tests 121 (for West Indies), 50 as captain. Previous county: Somerset (1974–86).

SHAW Adrian David b Neath, 17/2/72; RHB WK. Yet to make fc debut.

THOMAS Stuart Darren b Llanelli, 25/1/75; LHB RFM; HS 10; BB 5–79; 5w/i 2.

*WATKIN Steven Llewellyn b Maesteg, 15/9/64; RHB RAS; HS 41; BB 8–59; 50w 4; 5w/i 16; 10w/m 3. Tests 2.

In: R. P. Lefebvre (Somerset).
Out: A. R. Butcher (Essex coach). C. S. Cowdrey (retired), D. J. Foster, S. Kirnon.

Player of the Year 1992: H. Morris.
Colt to follow: S. D. Thomas.

GLAMORGAN BAC AVERAGES 1992

BATTING	M	I	NO	Runs	HS	Av	100	50
P. A. Cottey	18	25	5	1008	141	50.40	2	5
H. Morris	22	36	3	1546	146	46.85	6	5
A. R. Butcher	2	3	1	90	59*	45.00	0	1
A. Dale	20	30	4	1056	150*	40.62	2	6
M. P. Maynard	22	35	4	1191	176	38.42	2	7
I. V. A. Richards	14	23	0	722	127	31.39	1	4
R. D. B. Croft	22	32	9	592	60*	25.74	0	2
D. L. Hemp	10	15	2	276	84*	21.23	0	2
C. P. Metson	22	27	6	417	46*	19.86	0	0
D. J. Foster	7	4	1	40	17*	13.33	0	0
S. L. Watkin	21	23	4	147	41	7.74	0	0
S. D. Thomas	6	7	2	25	10	5.00	0	0
S. R. Barwick	17	14	4	31	9*	3.10	0	0
S. Bastien	10	10	3	21	9*	3.00	0	0
M. Frost	6	4	1	4	4	1.33	0	0

BOWLING	O	M	R	W	Av	BB	5i	10m
S. D. Thomas	113.2	18	404	18	22.44	5–79	2	0
R. D. B. Croft	610.4	114	2010	65	30.92	8–66	5	1
S. L. Watkin	665.3	146	2046	66	31.00	6–97	1	0
A. Dale	211	53	594	15	39.60	3–30	0	0
S. R. Barwick	578	152	1545	36	42.92	4–67	0	0
D. J. Foster	171.3	25	737	17	43.35	5–87	1	0
S. Bastien	305.3	73	954	19	50.21	5–95	1	0
M. Frost	155.1	24	664	9	73.78	3–100	0	0

Also bowled: P. A. Cottey 6–2–25–0, M. P. Maynard 7–0–72–1, C. P. Metson 1–1–0–0, H. Morris 4.5–0–57–0, I. V. A. Richards 12–2–34–0.

HUNDREDS (15)
6 – H. Morris: 146 v Middx (Lord's), 104 v Lancs (Colwyn Bay), 123 v Worcs (Worcester), 117 v Somerset (Abergavenny), 104* v Sussex (Eastbourne), 126 v Durham (Hartlepool).
2 – P. A. Cottey: 112* v Durham (Cardiff), 141 v Kent (Canterbury). A. Dale: 150* v Notts (Trent Bridge), 127 v Warwicks (Edgbaston). S. P. James: 152* v Lancs (Colwyn Bay), 105 v Surrey (Neath). M. P. Maynard: 113* v Kent (Swansea), 176 v Derbys (Chesterfield).
1 – I. V. A. Richards: 127 v Warwicks (Swansea).

GLOUCESTERSHIRE
BAC positions last five seasons: 10th; 13th; 13th; 9th; 10th.
Club formed: 1871.
Honours: Champions 3 (1874, 1876–77) plus 1 shared (1873); NWTGC 1 (1973); B&H 1 (1977); SL 0 (best: 2nd, 1988).

While the boundary that spirited David Gower past Geoff Boycott as England's greatest Test runmaker was the most uplifting moment of 1992, the most depressing was Syd Lawrence's breakdown in New Zealand. The photo that dominated the back pages next morning would have melted the hardest heart. Writhing on the turf, clutching a shattered kneecap, this gentlest of fast bowlers was howling, though more, one suspects, in disappointment than in pain. The international comeback he had fought so hard to achieve was over almost as soon as it had begun. He was his usual bubbly self at the Lilleshall Rehabilitation Centre during the winter, and looking in excellent, ever more muscular trim, only to fracture the same kneecap in training. Few county servants have deserved a bumper benefit year more than he.

Lawrence's absence makes one fear for Gloucestershire. With 'Syd' and Courtney Walsh in harness and form, the county can field a spearhead to match any on the circuit, one backed by the burgeoning left-arm spin of Mark Davies. Between extreme pace and stealth, however, there is little else to worry opposing batsmen. Justin Vaughan, an all-rounder on the rise, promised much with his swing and cut last term, so much so that he has since been capped by New Zealand and is now ineligible.

The parting of the ways with Bill Athey can only further weaken a less than solid batting order, from which only three other members reached three figures in the 1992 Championship. Tony Wright, a positive, affable captain, was one, although his bat had a hollow ring for the most part. Tall and assiduous, opener Dean Hodgson remains a good prospect, but Mark Alleyne's learning curve needs to resume an upward trend. Fruition should be near for the youngest player in Gloucestershire history to score both a century and a double-century.

Among those trying to force their way in, Matt Windows, son of the former Bristol stalwart, Tony, is a bruising young batsman whose belligerence was a feature of last summer's Bull Under-19 Tests against Sri Lanka; Ricardo Williams a gifted all-rounder and winner of the 1992 Rapid Cricketline Player of the Year award, his namesake a more than capable deputy behind the stumps for Jack Russell.

That said, Williams will almost certainly spend more time in the wings than he would like. Russell's days as an automatic Test selection, bafflingly, appear at an end, a state of affairs rendered all the more perplexing and unjust by his 985 runs at 42.82 in 1992, the inventive left-hander's best return yet. The dearth of bona fide all-rounders, a natural reaction to the twilight of the Botham-Imran-Hadlee-Kapil Dev era, has prompted a switch in emphasis.

The batsman-wicketkeeper is back in vogue, reducing Russell's craft to a humble trade. His main employers, thank goodness, know better. They may be supping their soup from pine cutlery come October, but at least we can rest assured that Bristol remains a fad-free zone.

CHAMPIONSHIP RATING: two bats, two balls.
PREDICTED POSITION: 18th.

Overseas player: COURTNEY WALSH

Thou shalt not play at one's best during one's benefit season, so they say, but this Jamaican giraffe disobeyed with a vengeance in 1992. Leading the first-class lists with 92 scalps at less than 16 runs apiece, however, was merely the latest stage in a period of self-affirmation for this cunning, underrated fast bowler.

The early comparisons with Michael Holding were inevitable, even if the two Jamaicans differ hugely. Walsh is now the senior member of the West Indies pace platoon, yet Curtly Ambrose and Ian Bishop are the big names. He deserves more. Essentially a stock bowler, he mixes in a clever slower ball and a brute of a bouncer, ingredients in a vat containing more than 1,000 victims.

Omitted from the West Indies World Cup squad after taking a record number of wickets in a Red Stripe Cup campaign – his fielding was deemed a liability – Walsh was recalled to face South Africa in Bridgetown, where a devastating spell of 4 for 8 on the final morning set the table for an astonishing victory after defeat had seemed certain. He carried on blooming over the subsequent months and the acclaim, at last, rang out when he was nominated for that most cherished of all county gongs, the Cricketers' Association Player of the Year.

Then, in January, came Adelaide and The Ball. Australia need two to win with their last man, Craig McDermott, on strike. Final ball of the over . . . Walsh pings one in short . . . batsman fails to remove gloves . . . Junior Murray engulfs the deflection . . . joy unbounded as Walsh leaps into the arms of Phil Simmons, arms outstretched, mouth agape. The West Indies have prevailed by the smallest margin in the 1,200 or so performances staged under the Test banner since 1877. Unsung, but never unappreciated.

PLAYING STAFF 1993:

*ALLEYNE Mark Wayne b Tottenham, London, 23/5/68; RHB RAS; HS 256; BB 4–48; 100s 5; 1000r 1.

BABINGTON Andrew Mark b London, 22/7/63; LHB RAS; HS 58; BB 8–107; 5w/i 3; hat-trick 1. Previous county: Sussex (1986–90).

BALL Martyn Charles John b Bristol, 26/4/70; RHB OS; HS 54; BB 5–101; 5w/i 2.

*BROAD Brian Christopher b Bristol, 29/9/57; LHB RAS; HS 227 not out (for Notts), 145 (for Gloucs); BB 2–14; 100s 47; 1000r 10. Tests 25. Previous counties: Gloucestershire (1979–83), Nottinghamshire (1984–1992).

COOPER Kevin Edwin b Hucknall 27/12/57. LHB, RAS; HS 46; BB 8–44; 100w 1; 50w 8: 5w/i 25; 10w/m 1. Previous county: Nottinghamshire (1976–92). Yet to make fc debut for Gloucestershire.

CUNLIFFE Robert John b Banbury, 8/11/73; RHB. Yet to make fc debut.

DAVIES Mark b Neath, 18/4/69; RHB SLA; HS 32*; BB 4–73; 50w 1. Previous county: Glamorgan (1990–91).

DAWSON Robert Ian b Exmouth, 29/3/70; RHB RAS; HS 29.

De la PENA Jason Michael b London, 16/9/72; RHB RAS; HS 1*; BB 2–69.

GERRARD Martin James b Southmead, Bristol, 19/5/67; RHB LAS; HS 42; BB 2–51.

HANCOCK Timothy Harold Coulter b Reading, 20/4/72; RHB RM; HS 102; BB 2–43; 100s 1.

HINKS Simon Graham b Northfleet, Kent, 12/10/60; LHB RAS; HS 234 (for Kent), 88 not out (for Gloucs); BB 2–18 (for Kent); 100s 11; 1000r 3. Previous county: Kent (1982–91).

*HODGSON Geoffrey Dean b Carlisle, 22/10/66; RHB; HS 147; 100s 3; 1000r 3.

HORRELL Ryan b Barnstaple, 7/4/73; LHB SLA. Yet to make fc debut.

*LAWRENCE David Valentine b Gloucester, 28/1/64; RHB RF; HS 66; BB 7–47; 50w 5; 5w/i 21; 10w/m 1; hat-trick 1. Tests 5.

*RUSSELL Robert Charles (Jack) b Stroud, 15/8/63; LHB WK; HS 128 not out; 100s 4; Ct 563; St 84. Tests 31.

SCOTT Richard James b Bournemouth, 2/11/63; LHB RAS; HS 127; BB 3–43; 100s 3. Previous county: Hampshire (1986–90).

SMITH Andrew Michael b Dewsbury, 1/10/67; RHB LAS; HS 51 not out; BB 4–41.

*i*WALSH Courtney Andrew b Kingston, Jamaica, 30/10/62; RHB RFM; HS 63 not out; BB 9–72; 50w 5; 100w 1; 5w/i 55; 10w/i 11; hat-trick 1 (for West Indies). Cricketers' Association Player of the Year 1992. Tests 51.

WIGHT Robert Marcus b London, 12/9/69; RHB OS; HS 62 not out (for Cambridge U); BB 3–65 (for Cambridge U). Yet to make BAC debut.

WILLIAMS Ricardo Cecil b Camberwell, London, 3/2/68; RHB RAS; HS 44; BB 3–44 (v Pakistan), 1–46 (BAC). Rapid Cricketline Player of 1992.

WILLIAMS Richard Charles James b Southmead, Bristol, 8/8/69; LHB WK; HS 18 not out; Ct 54; St 8.

WINDOWS Matthew Guy Newman b Bristol, 5/4/73; RHB; HS 71.

†*WRIGHT Anthony John b Stevenage, 27/6/62; RHB RAS; HS 161; BB 1–16; 100s 12; 1000r 4. Captain since 1990.

Beneficiary '93: D. V. Lawrence.

In: B. C. Broad (Notts), R. J. Cunliffe, P. W. Romaines (assistant coach), A. W. Stovold (coach), R. M. Wight.
Out: C. W. J. Athey (Sussex), A. J. Hunt, J. T. C. Vaughan.

Colt to follow: M. G. N. Windows.

GLOUCESTERSHIRE BAC AVERAGES 1992

BATTING	M	I	NO	Runs	HS	Av	100	50
R. C. Russell	16	28	9	904	75	47.58	0	5
J. T. C. Vaughan	10	16	4	450	99	37.50	0	4
G. D. Hodgson	20	34	1	1214	147	36.79	2	8
M. W. Alleyne	21	34	3	1030	93	33.23	0	7
C. W. J. Athey	20	32	0	1022	181	31.94	2	4
S. G. Hinks	10	16	3	402	88*	30.92	0	3
T. H. C. Hancock	9	15	1	396	102	28.29	1	2
A. J. Wright	18	31	3	754	128	26.93	1	3
R. J. Scott	19	31	3	751	73	26.82	0	4
A. M. Smith	11	12	5	165	51*	23.57	0	1
R. C. J. Williams	5	5	2	51	18*	17.00	0	0
M. C. J. Ball	12	21	6	201	54	13.40	0	2
R. C. Williams	6	9	1	100	44	12.50	0	0
C. A. Walsh	18	27	3	280	51	11.67	0	1
A. M. Babington	8	9	3	63	24	10.50	0	0
M. Davies	18	21	9	123	32*	10.25	0	0
R. I. Dawson	5	6	0	58	29	9.67	0	0
M. J. Gerrard	4	4	1	6	4	2.00	0	0

Also batted: M. G. N. Windows (1 match) 71.

BOWLING	O	M	R	W	Av	BB	5i	10m
C. A. Walsh	587.2	138	1469	92	15.97	7–27	8	2
M. Davies	529.5	138	1537	55	27.95	4–73	0	0
A. M. Smith	232.2	35	764	23	33.22	3–53	0	0
J. T. C. Vaughan	178.4	40	499	15	33.27	3–46	0	0
M. W. Alleyne	133.1	29	489	14	34.93	3–25	0	0
M. C. J. Ball	322	61	1072	28	38.29	5–101	1	0
M. J. Gerrard	93	20	297	7	42.43	2–51	0	0
A. M. Babington	162	17	642	14	45.86	8–107	1	0
R. J. Scott	267.4	39	959	20	47.95	2–9	0	0

Also bowled: C. W. J. Athey 58–7–184–2, T. H. C. Hancock 26.4–2–102–3, S. G. Hinks 2.5–1–14–0, G. D. Hodgson 4–0–65–0, R. C. Williams 48–5–209–2, A. J. Wright 2–0–27–0.

HUNDREDS (6)
2 — C. W. J. Athey: 181 v Sussex (Cheltenham) 133 v Notts (Worksop). G. D. Hodgson: 124 v Yorks (Headlingley), 147 v Essex (Southend).
1 — T. H. C. Hancock: 102 v Somerset (Taunton). A. J. Wright: 128 v Kent (Bristol).

HAMPSHIRE
BAC position last five seasons: 15th; 9th; 3rd; 6th; 15th.

Club formed: 1863.
Honours: Champions 2 (1961, 1973); NWT/GC 1 (1991); B&H 2 (1988, 1992); Sunday League 3 (1975, 1978, 1986).

Considering they lifted a knockout trophy for the second time in as many seasons and claimed the bronze in the Sunday League, it may seem churlish to suggest that Hampshire yet again failed to do themselves justice last summer. Leading the Championship table with nearly half the programme over, they nevertheless sank like a stone in the event they prized the most.

The portents are for more of the same. Mark Nicholas, the latest budding cricketer-journalist, enters his ninth year at the helm with talent to spare but consistency at a premium. Robin Smith tends to settle for third gear on the county circuit, Gower for second. As quick as any English pace bowler when the mood takes him, Kevin Shine intersperses days of barnstorming menace – viz those 13 Lancashire wickets at Old Trafford last May – with wild, innocuous interludes. Effective though he is, furthermore, Malcolm Marshall is not what he was.

In Jon Ayling and Shaun Udal, however, Hampshire have two prime young assets whose increasing maturity hints at substance to come. A willowy seam and swing merchant who sensibly declines to strain for too much speed, Ayling headed all England-qualified bowlers in last year's averages. He also registered a career-high of 90 with the bat, a weapon he must wield more purposefully if he is ever to try on Botham's 10–league boots. With all these green shoots of spin springing up Udal's omission from the A team was just about defensible. Nursed astutely by the protective Nicholas, he nonetheless enjoyed his first full Championship season enormously, and finished it as the club's top wicket-taker by some distance with 109 in all competitions. No other bowler in the country snared 50 victims in each format.

The seam attack will be bolstered by the recruitment of Jamie Byrne, born in Lancashire but discovered in South Africa by Marshall, who rates him as decidedly nippy, and Martin Jean-Jacques, a steady Dominican who should prove a useful foil to Shine and Marshall. The batting holds greater possibilities and more uncertainties. No, the middle order is not to be trusted, but provided Paul Terry stays healthy, the opening act will be as reliable as a favourite watch. Granted, watching Tony Middleton occupy the crease is not the most edifying experience for the purist, but his capacity for graft is invaluable.

Gower is too easily distracted, mostly by his pursuit of some higher plane, to follow suit. Then again, that is his principal attraction. A hero so cool he never sweats. If this national treasure is ever to decorate the international gallery again, as indeed he ought, maybe he would be better off boring us a little. That way, at least he would *look* the part, a mandatory qualification in the Age of the Work Ethic. All that can be certain is that he wants that place back. Happily, he has a knack of getting what he wants.

Nevertheless, it is hard to picture Gower acquiring his first Championship medal this term. Hampshire's spark is too fitful to ignite a season-long challenge for a pennant that last flew over the Northlands Road pavilion 20 long summers ago. Compensation, however, is well within reach over the shorter haul.

CHAMPIONSHIP RATING: three bats, three balls.
PREDICTED POSITION: 8th.

Overseas player: MALCOLM MARSHALL
Carlsberg might do well to sign up Hampshire's faithful hired gun for one of their ad campaigns. After all, he *is* probably the best fast bowler of his

generation. To those who feel Sir Richard Hadlee's market-leading brand of seam was delivered at a few mph below full throttle, there is no probably about it.

Marshall and Hadlee had much in common. Relentlessly accurate, unafraid of experimentation and, above all, driven by an inner demon that demands success and detests half-measures. Not that the Bajan's body language mirrors this intensity. More than any of his peers he has adopted the swagger and strut of Viv Richards, the ultra-cool dude who knows he is the quickest draw in town.

Marshall, of course, was precisely that, and more. There were 376 Test wickets all told, the most by a West Indian. Indeed, the 400 he craved would surely have been his had the selectors not been in such a rush to get rid of the old guard. All but ostracised by the tour committee during the last World Cup, one of the leading architects of the most powerful empire in cricket history bade an unhappy, hurt farewell.

Better to reflect on the peaks. That supple, scampering approach, the coil and snappy release; the irresistible force who blew away 35 less than immovable English objects here in 1988, many of them courtesy of fast-motion leg-breaks; the bandit who defied a broken thumb and doctor's orders to bat one-armed at Leeds four years earlier; the boyish, pleased-as-punch grin when Nicholas insisted he held the Benson & Hedges Cup aloft last July. Never mind that his batting has never been quite what he thought it could or even should have been. This is someone who can make a ball talk, past his prime or not. If a prosperous winter in South Africa is anything to go by, batsmen are advised not to relax just yet.

PLAYING STAFF 1993:

*AYLING Jonathan Richard b Portsmouth, 13/6/67; RHB RAS; HS 121; BB 5–12; 100s 1; 5w/i 1. Took wicket with first ball in fc cricket.

*AYMES Adrian Nigel b Southampton, 4/6/64; RHB WK; HS 65; Ct 120; St 9.

BOVILL James Noel Bruce b High Wycombe, 26/6/71; RHB RAS. Yet to make fc debut.

BYRNE James Robert b Manchester, 1/4/73; RHB RFM. Yet to make fc debut.

*CONNOR Cardigan Adolphus b The Valley, Anguilla, 24/3/61; RHB RAS; HS 51; BB 7–31; 50w 3; 5w/i 10; 10w/m 1.

COX Rupert Michael Fiennes b Guildford, 20/8/67; LHB OS; HS 104 not out; 100s 1.

FLINT Darren Peter John b Basingstoke, 14/6/70; RHB SLA. Yet to make fc debut.

GARAWAY Mark b Swindon, 20/7/73; RHB WK. Yet to make fc debut.

*GOWER David Ivon b Tunbridge Wells, 1/4/57; LHB OS; HS 228 (for Leics), 155 (for Hants); BB 3–47 (for Leics); 100s 49; 1000r 12. Tests 117 (captain 32). Previous county: Leicestershire (1975–89, captain 1984–86).

*JAMES Kevan David b Lambeth, London, 18/3/61; LHB LAS; HS 162; BB 6–22; 100s 8; 1000r 2; 5w/i 7. Previous county: Middlesex (1980–84).

JEAN-JACQUES Martin b Soufriere, Dominica, 2/8/60; RHB RAS; HS 73; BB

8–77; 5w/i 2; 10w/m 1. Previous county: Derbyshire (1986–92). Yet to make fc debut for Hampshire.

LANEY Jason Scott b Winchester, 27/4/73; RHB OS. Yet to make fc debut.

i*MARSHALL Malcolm Denzil b Barbados, 18/4/58; RHB RFM; HS 117; BB 8–71; 100s 6; 50w 8+4 overseas; 100w 2; 5w/i 83; 10w/m 13; hat-tricks 2. Tests 81.

*MARU Rajesh Jamandass b Nairobi, Kenya, 28/10/62; RHB SLA; HS 74; BB 8–41; 5w/i 15; 10w/m 1. Previous county: Middlesex (1980–83).

*MIDDLETON Tony Charles b Winchester, 1/2/64; RHB SLA; HS 221; BB 2–41; 100s 12; 1000r 2. England A cap.

MORRIS Robert Sean Millner b Gt Horwood, Bucks, 10/9/68; RHB OS; HS 74.

†*NICHOLAS Mark Charles Jefford b London, 29/9/57; HB RAS; HS 206 not out (v Oxford U), 158 (BAC); BB 6–37; 100s 29; 1000r 8; 5wi 2. Captain since 1985. England A cap.

SHINE Kevin James b Bracknell, Berks, 22/2/69; RHB RF; HS 26 not out; BB 8–47; 5w/i 5; 10w/m 1; hat-trick 1.

*SMITH Robin Arnold b Durban, South Africa, 13/9/63; RHB LS; HS 209 not out; BB 2–20; 100s 33; 1000r 6. Tests 36.

*TERRY Vivian Paul b Osnabruck, Germany, 14/1/59; RHB RAS; HS 190; 100s 27; 1000r 8. Tests 2.

THURSFIELD Martin John b South Shields, 14/12/71; RHB RAS; BB 1–11 (v Oxford U). Yet to make BAC debut. Previous county: Middlesex (1990).

*TREMLETT Timothy Maurice b Wellington, Somerset, 26/7/56; RHB RAS; HS 102 not out; BB 6–53; 100s 1; 50w 4; 5wi 11. Cricket and coaching administrator since 1990.

TURNER Ian John b Denmead, 18/7/68; RHB SLA; HS 39*; BB 5–81; 5w/i 1.

*UDAL Shaun David b Farnborough, 18/3/69; RHB OS; HS 44; BB 8–50; 50w 1; 5w/i 2.

WOOD Julian Ross b Winchester, 21/11/68; LHB RAS; HS 96; BB 1–5.

Beneficiary '93: T. M. Tremlett.

In: J. N. B. Bovill, J. Byrne, M. Garaway, M. Jean-Jacques, J. S. Laney.
Out: P-J Bakker, R. J. Parks.

Player of the Year 1992: T. C. Middleton.
Colt to follow: S. D. Udal.

HAMPSHIRE BAC AVERAGES 1992

BATTING	M	I	NO	Runs	HS	Av	100	50
V. P. Terry	11	17	2	766	141	51.07	3	3
T. C. Middleton	22	37	4	1628	221	49.33	5	7
D. I. Gower	16	26	5	1005	155	47.86	1	6
M. C. J. Nicholas	20	30	5	972	95*	38.88	0	6
R. A. Smith	11	18	2	599	107*	37.49	1	4
K. D. James	21	33	2	1006	116	32.45	1	7
J. R. Wood	8	9	1	244	57	30.50	0	1
M. D. Marshall	19	25	5	513	70	25.65	0	2
R. J. Parks	5	7	2	125	33	25.00	0	0
R. S. M. Morris	4	8	0	198	74	24.75	0	2
A. N. Aymes	17	21	4	336	65	19.76	0	2
J. R. Ayling	17	25	1	472	90	19.67	0	2
S. D. Udal	21	26	8	346	44	19.22	0	0
C. A. Connor	16	13	5	127	51	15.88	0	1
P. J. Bakker	5	5	1	63	22	15.75	0	0
K. J. Shine	14	10	6	59	22*	14.75	0	0
R. J. Maru	6	8	3	71	23*	14.20	0	0
R. M. F. Cox	3	3	0	26	13	8.67	0	0
I. J. Turner	6	7	1	31	16	5.17	0	0

BOWLING	O	M	R	W	Av	BB	5i	10m
J. R. Ayling	326.2	69	939	43	21.84	5–12	1	0
R. J. Maru	157.2	54	331	15	22.07	4–8	0	0
I. J. Turner	182.4	51	519	19	27.32	5–81	1	0
M. D. Marshall	529	134	1348	49	27.51	6–58	1	0
K. J. Shine	289.5	40	1161	38	30.55	8–47	3	1
P. J. Bakker	137	43	363	11	33.00	4–38	0	0
S. D. Udal	637.2	156	1867	50	37.34	8–50	1	0
C. A. Connor	417.2	69	1386	32	43.31	5–58	1	0
K. D. James	230.3	52	705	12	58.75	2–23	0	0

Also bowled: A. N. Aymes 7–0–75–1, T. C. Middleton 10–0–57–0, M. C. J. Nicholas 22.3–2–71–2, R. A. Smith 8.1–0–41–0.

HUNDREDS (11)
5 – T. C. Middleton: 153 v Sussex (Southampton), 221 v Surrey (Southampton), 138* v Lancs (Old Trafford), 124 v Warwicks (Edgbaston), 127* v Durham (Darlington).
3 – V. P. Terry: 141 v Sussex (Southampton), 131 v Surrey (Southampton), 113 v Worcs (Worcester).
1 – D. I. Gower: 155 v Yorks (Basingstoke). K. D. James: 116 v Yorks (Headlingley). R. A. Smith: 107* v Sussex (Southampton).

KENT
BAC position last five seasons: 2nd; 6th; 16th; 15th; 2nd.
Club formed: 1859.
Honours: Champions 6 (1906, 1909, 1910, 1913, 1970, 1978) plus 1 shared (1977); NWTGC 2 (1967, 1974); B&H 3 (1973, 1976, 1978); SL 3 (1972–73, 1976).

Counting the shared Championship of 1977, Kent landed no fewer than 10 major trophies during the Seventies, an act that took an inordinate amount of following. Fifteen long and often fretful years after the last honour claimed by this proud, expectant club, the side that Mark Benson and Daryl Foster have built is ready to step out.

First and foremost, Kent possess the only top six worthy of sharing a bandstand with Graham Gooch and his Chelmsford Syncopators. Benson himself, shabbily treated by the Peter May regime and the most unfortunate one-cap wonder in the game, recalls John Edrich more with each passing year. His opening ally, Trevor Ward, can shred an attack at 22 paces with his clean, disdainful strokeplay. Currently playing with as much assurance as at any time in his 14 years at Canterbury, Neil Taylor is a ballast at No. 3. Graham Cowdrey's response to being the sole family representative at Canterbury last season was to become a fluent batsman in his own right and had the time of his life. Matthew Fleming is more brazen, less trustworthy, yet liable to win a match singlehanded. Carl Hooper is . . . Carl Hooper, of whom more elsewhere. Supplementing this rhythmic sextet is Steve Marsh, wicketkeeper first, batsman second and certainly no disgrace to the traditions set by his eminent predecessors, Ames, Evans and Knott.

The bowling, it must be conceded, inspires less confidence. All the same, there should be no shortage of first-innings leads to play with, and the attack certainly has the capacity to bowl sides out twice. Having elected to throw his hat in with England, Martin McCague knows full well that if he can bristle from April to September with the same urgency, consistency and downright nastiness he summoned in the second half of last summer, Kentish gratitude may not be his only reward. Alan Igglesden, another one-cap wonder, is still capable of hurrying the best, Richard Ellison, the beneficiary, remains a sometime sultan of swing, Mark Ealham a younger but no less shrewd operator of the seam. Richard Davis's left-arm spin, meanwhile, goes from strength to strength, thrusting the spectre of Underwood ever further behind him.

One fresh face is that of Duncan Spencer, schooled, like McCague, in Western Australia and introduced to the Kent League by Ward. According to manager Foster, who spent much of the close season scrutinising him in Perth, Spencer has real pace. Luckily, and again like McCague, he also has British roots, having been born in Burnley. Of the other fringe players, Dean Headley was Middlesex's leading one-day bowler in 1992 while Nigel Llong has the makings of a more than presentable off-spinner. Davis's deputy is the slow left-armer from Bombay, Minal Patel, best remembered for destroying Leicestershire in 1990 and so helping bring an end, for the time being, to Dartford's tenure as a Championship venue. For Kent, conversely, 1993 is part of a new beginning. Win or fail, they should certainly go the distance.

CHAMPIONSHIP RATING: 4½ bats, 3½ balls.
PREDICTED POSITION: 3rd.

Overseas player: CARL HOOPER
Other batsmen have taken longer to justify their international standing than Carl Hooper. Mike Gatting, for instance, needed 53 visits to the crease before scoring his first Test century, Bobby Simpson, the Australian manager, 51. This slim, quiet Guyanan required just three, becoming, at 21 years and 12 days, the third youngest player ever to make a hundred for the West Indies.

More than five years on, however, he has the dubious distinction of being the game's greatest enigma.

Whether he is batting or bowling, one has only to watch Hooper for a few minutes to appreciate the gifts. With Jeff Dujon having vacated his share of the throne and David Gower afflicted with a dose of middle-aged angst, the Kent No. 4 is as elegant a purveyor of fine shots as there is in the game. Timing is all, yet at the same time he strikes the ball straighter and harder than the Hampshire master. Those fast-developing off-breaks offer a similar contrast: flight, drift and tweak are all coming on, delivered in easeful fashion and spiced by a vicious faster ball. In 1992 he took 35 wickets, swallowed 25 slip catches and ran up more than 1,300 runs in his maiden Championship season, and, for good measure, made several sparkling contributions to Kent's Benson & Hedges Cup run.

Mark Benson is of the opinion that Hooper has it in him to become one of the top five batsmen in the world. Why, then, does he struggle to sustain a Test average of 30? And why, after nearly 40 caps, are the mental lapses still so frequent and his Test place still so insecure? The West Indies selectors, to their immense credit, have tolerated the failures, offering the patience every player cries out for but lamentably few receive. The game would be the greatest sufferer should he prove unworthy of that faith. He isn't.

PLAYING STAFF 1993:

†*BENSON Mark Richard b Shoreham, Sussex, 6/7/58; LHB OS; HS 257; BB 2–55; 100s 42; 1000r 11. Captain since 1991. Tests 1.

BRIMSON Matthew Thomas b Plumstead, London, 1/12/70; RHB SLA. Yet to make fc debut.

*COWDREY Graham Robert b Farnborough, 27/6/64; RHB RAS; HS 147; B 1–5; 100s 11; 1000r 3.

*DAVIS Richard Peter b Margate, 18/3/66; RHB SLA; HS 67; BB 7–64; 50w 2; 5w/i 11; 10w/m 1.

EALHAM Mark Alan b Ashford, 27/8/69; RHB RAS; HS 67; BB 5–39; 5w/i 2.

*ELLISON Richard Mark b Ashford, 21/9/59; LHB RAS; HS 108 (v Oxford U), 98 (BAC); BB 7–33; 100s 1; 50w 4; 5w/i 18; 10w/m 2. Tests 11.

*FLEMING Matthew Valentine b Macclesfield, Cheshire, 12/12/64; RHB RAS; HS 116; BB 4–63; 100s 4.

FULTON David Paul b Lewisham, London, 15/11/71; RHB. HS 42 (v Cambridge U). Yet to make BAC debut.

HEADLEY Dean Warren b Stourbridge, 27/1/70; RHB RAS; HS 91 (for Middx); BB 5–46 (for Middx); 5w/i 2. Previous county: Middlesex (1991–92). Yet to make fc debut for Kent.

i*HOOPER Carl Llewellyn b Georgetown, Guyana, 15/12/66; RHB OS; HS 196 (for Guyana), 131 (for Kent); BB 5–33; 100s 13; 1000r 1 (plus 1 on tour); 5w/i 5. Tests 32.

*IGGLESDEN Alan Paul b Farnborough, 8/10/64; RHB RFM; HS 41; BB 6–34; 50w 3; 5w/i 14; 10w/m 2. Tests 1.

LLONG Nigel James b Ashford, 11/2/69; LHB OS; HS 92; BB 3–50 (v Cambridge U), 3–70 (BAC).

LONGLEY Jonathan Ian b New Jersey, USA, 12/4/69; RHB; HS 110 (v Cambridge U), 35 (BAC).

*McCAGUE Martin John b Larne, N. Ireland, 24/5/69; RHB RFM; HS 29; BB 8–26; 50w 1; 5w/i 7; 10w/m 1.

*MARSH Steven Andrew b Westminster, 27/1/61; RHB WK; HS 125; BB 2–20; 100s 6; Ct 367; St 31. Holds world record (joint) with eight catches in one innings; first player to hold eight catches in one inns and score a century in the same match.

PATEL Minal Mahesh b Bombay, India, 7/7/70; RHB SLA; HS 43; BB 6–57; 5w/i 2; 10w/m 1.

*PENN Christopher b Dover, 19/6/63; LHB RAS; HS 115; BB 7–70; 100s 1; 50w 2; 5w/i 12.

PRESTON Nicholas William b Dartford, 22/1/72; RHB RFM. Yet to make fc debut.

SPENCER Duncan b Burnley, 23/4/72; RHB RF. Yet to make fc debut.

*TAYLOR Neil Royston b Orpington, 21/7/59; RHB OS; HS 204; BB 2–20; 100s 38; 1000r 9.

WALKER Matthew Jonathan b Gravesend, 6/1/74; LHB OS. Yet to make fc debut. England Under-19 captain.

*WARD Trevor Robert b Farningham, 18/1/68; RHB OS; HS 235 not out; BB 2–48; 100s 13; 1000r 2.

WREN Timothy Neil b Folkestone, 26/3/70; RHB LAS; HS 16; BB 3–14 (v Oxford U), 2–78 (BAC).

Beneficiary '93: R. M. Ellison.

In: D. W. Headley (Middlesex); D. J. Spencer.

Player of the Year 1992: M. J. McCague.
Colt to follow: T. R. Ward.

KENT BAC AVERAGES 1992

BATTING	M	I	NO	Runs	HS	Av	100	50
N. R. Taylor	21	35	7	1508	144	53.86	1	11
G. R. Cowdrey	21	31	6	1291	147	51.64	3	7
T. R. Ward	21	37	3	1648	153	48.47	5	9
C. L. Hooper	21	32	4	1329	131	47.46	5	7
M. R. Benson	21	35	2	1482	139	44.91	4	6
S. A. Marsh	21	28	3	816	125	32.64	1	6
N. J. Llong	3	3	0	94	92	31.33	0	1
M. V. Fleming	21	32	2	797	100*	26.57	1	4
R. P. Davis	17	23	11	297	54*	24.75	0	1
M. A. Ealham	16	25	5	426	67*	21.30	0	4
R. M. Ellison	18	20	7	258	41	19.85	0	0
J. I. Longley	2	3	0	59	35	19.67	0	0
M. J. McCague	16	18	5	120	25*	9.23	0	0
A. P. Igglesden	16	13	5	67	16	8.38	0	0
C. Penn	6	4	1	12	9	4.00	0	0

G. J. Kersey played in one match but did not bat.

BOWLING	O	M	R	W	Av	BB	5i	10m
R. P. Davis	536	141	1469	67	21.93	7–64	5	0
M. J. McCague	457.2	86	1430	53	26.98	8–26	5	1
M. V. Fleming	245	46	696	24	29.00	4–63	0	0
A. P. Igglesden	480.4	95	1413	46	30.72	5–41	3	0
M. A. Ealham	392.3	69	1193	36	33.14	4–67	0	0
C. L. Hooper	500.5	114	1307	35	37.34	4–57	0	0
R. M. Ellison	401.5	80	1204	29	41.52	6–95	2	0
C. Penn	141	22	460	5	92.00	2–69	0	0

Also bowled: M. R. Benson 3–0–25–1, G. R. Cowdrey 48–9–213–2, N. J. Llong 28–4–109–3, S. A. Marsh 8–0–126–0, T. R. Ward 39.5–4–109–0.

HUNDREDS (20)

5 – C. L. Hooper: 115* v Durham (Canterbury), 121 v Sussex (Hove), 131 v Surrey (Guildford), 100 v Glam (Swansea), 102 v Warwicks (Edgbaston). T. R. Ward: 140* v Worcs (Tunbridge Wells), 103 v Surrey (Guildford), 118 v Glam (Swansea), 150 v Middx (Canterbury), 153 v Warwicks (Edgbaston).

4 – M. R. Benson: 117 v Sussex (Hove), 131 v Notts (Maidstone), 139 v Leics (Leicester), 122 v Warwicks (Edgbaston).

3 – G. R. Cowdrey: 127 v Yorks (Canterbury), 147 v Gloucs (Bristol), 115 v Durham (Gateshead Fell).

1 – M. V. Fleming: 100* v Hants (Canterbury). S. A. Marsh: 125 v Yorks (Canterbury). N. R. Taylor: 144 v Leics (Leicester).

LANCASHIRE

BAC position last five seasons: 12th; 8th; 6th; 4th; 9th.
Club formed: 1864.
Honours: Champions 8 (1881, 1897, 1904, 1926–28, 1930, 1934) plus 4 shared (1879, 1882, 1889, 1950); NWTGC 5 (1970–72, 1975, 1900); B&H 2 (1984, 1990); SL 3 (1969–70, 1989).

Lancashire's performance over the past two seasons has fallen so far short of their expectations that the scope for improvement is so vast they can hardly fail. They began 1992 with high hopes of challenging Essex for the Championship but their ambitions evaporated before the end of June when it became clear their bowling resources were painfully inadequate.

For much of the summer their cricket was overshadowed by agitation in the committee and dressing-rooms about an absent friend. Following the publication of a book about him, it was uncertain whether Wasim Akram, who was touring with the Pakistanis, would return to Old Trafford. Comments in the book about the all-rounder, which were attributed to Graeme Fowler and pulled at the last minute, preceded Fowler's departure at the end of the season along with his mucker Paul Allott.

Alan Ormrod, who had been the cricket manager for six years, in which time Lancashire won all three one-day competitions, was the real casualty. His dismissal in August cleared the way for David Hughes, nominally his chief-of-staff, to succeed him and for David Lloyd, a former county captain, to return as the club coach.

When their positions are reviewed at the end of this year Lancashire expect their judgement to have been vindicated, for a chorus of approval greeted Lloyd's appointment. He is widely regarded for his work with young players and although he insisted on retaining his extra-curricular jobs in television and radio, Old Trafford is united in believing his return is 'a good thing'.

There is no shortage of youthful talent for him to work with. John Crawley has already announced himself as a batsman of genuine class and Glenn Chapple, in his few opportunities so far, has shown he has the makings of a proper seam and swing bowler.

Given Lancashire's shortcomings in the spinning sphere the signing of Alex Barnett from Middlesex prompted hopes which were never likely to be fulfilled within his first season. One year on, with a new coach who was himself a slow left-armer, Barnett is better equipped to grow up.

As ever much depends on the form and fitness of Wasim. At his best no one can bowl better but in order to get the best out of him consistently Lancashire must be prudent and rest him from time to time. To be champions, though, they need plenty of wickets from other quarters. (Michael Henderson)

CHAMPIONSHIP RATING: three bats, three balls.
PREDICTED POSITION: 11th.

Overseas player: WASIM AKRAM
'They all laughed at Christopher Columbus . . .' Imran Khan also attracted scorn when he marked Wasim down in 1987 as his long-term heir. Lancashire listened and demonstrated a marked faith in this perceived potential by offering the young man the luxury of a six-year contract. Six years later few can dispute the Pakistan captain's right to be called the world's finest all-round cricketer, although Lancashire have not always seen the best of him.

His outstanding new ball partnership with Waqar Younis has enabled Pakistan to become the strongest team in world cricket. And although his batting could benefit from the sort of discipline which helped Pakistan win the Lord's Test last year, he remains a most natural striker of the ball.

Lancashire, no less than Wasim, must hope their relationship has not been impaired by the imbroglios of the past two summers. In 1991 he was fined

£1,000 for making insulting remarks to Roy Palmer, the umpire who had removed him from the attack. Last year the row about a book detailing his and Waqar's rise fanned the original dispute to flame once more. Undercurrents of this ilk should be at a premium now that he has assumed the leadership of his country.

Wasim eventually signed a four-year contract which will take him through to a benefit. If he fulfils even three-quarters of his potential by then Lancashire will also have benefited. (Michael Henderson)

PLAYING STAFF 1993:

*ATHERTON Michael Andrew b Manchester, 23/3/68; RHB LS; HS 199; BB 6–78; 100s 26; 1000r 5; 5w/i 3. Tests 21.

*AUSTIN Ian David b Haslingden, 30/5/66; LHB, RAS; HS 115 not out; BB 5–79; 100s 2; 5w/i 1.

*BARNETT Alexander Anthony b Malaga, Spain, 11/9/70; RHB SLA; HS 17; BB 5–78; 5w/i 2. Previous county: Middlesex (1991).

CHAPPLE Glen b Skipton, Yorkshire, 23/1/74; RHB RFM; HS 18; BB 3–40.

CORDINGLEY Gareth b Darwen, 23/1/73; RHB RAS. Yet to make fc debut.

CRAWLEY John Paul b Malden, Essex, 21/9/71; RHB RAS; HS 172; BB 1–90; 100s 3; 1000r 1. Brother of M. A. (Notts).

*DeFREITAS Phillip Anthony Jason b Scotts Head, Dominica, 18/2/66; RHB RFM; HS 113; BB 7–70; 100s 4; 50w 5; 5w/i 27; 10w/m 2. Tests 31.

DERBYSHIRE Nicholas Alexander b Ramsbottom, 11/9/70; RHB RAS. Yet to make fc debut.

†*FAIRBROTHER Neil Harvey b Warrington, Cheshire, 9/9/63; LHB LAS; HS 366; BB 2–91; 100s 26; 1000r 8. Captain since 1992. Tests 7.

FIELDING Jonathan b Bury, 13/3/73; RHB SLA. Yet to make fc debut.

FITTON John Dexter b Littleborough, 24/8/65; LHB OS; HS 60; BB 6–59; 5w/i 3.

FLETCHER Stuart David b Keighley 8/6/64; RHB RAS; HS 28 not out (for Yorks), 23 (for Lancs); BB 8–58 (for Yorks), 2–53 (for Lancs); 50w 1; 5w/i 5. Previous county: Yorkshire (1983–91).

GALLIAN Jason Edward Richie b New South Wales, Australia, 25/6/71; RHB RM; HS 112 (for Oxford U); BB 4–29 (for Oxford U); 100s 1. Yet to make BAC debut for Lancashire.

HARVEY Mark b Burnley, 26/6/74; RHB RM Yet to make fc debut.

*HEGG Warren Kevin b Radcliffe, 23/2/68; RHB WK; HS 130; 100s 2. Ct 284; St 35. Holds world record (joint) with 11 catches in a match. England A cap.

HENDERSON Jonathan b Rochdale, 16/1/75; RHB RM. Yet to make fc debut.

IRANI Ronald Charles b Leigh, 26/10/71; RHB RAS; HS 31 not out (v Oxford U), 22 (BAC); BB 2–21.

*LLOYD Graham David b Accrington, 1/7/69; RHB RAS; HS 132; BB 1–57; 100s 7; 1000r 1. England A cap.

MARTIN Peter James b Accrington, 15/11/68; RHB RFM; HS 133; BB 4–30.

*MENDIS Gehan Dixon b Colombo, Sri Lanka, 24/4/55; RHB RAS; HS 209 not out (for Suss), 203 not out (for Lancs); BB 1–65; 100s 40; 1000r 12. Previous county: Sussex (1974–85).

SHARP Marcus Anthony b Oxford, 1/6/70; LHB RAS. HS O (v Oxford U); BB 1–21 (v Oxford U). Yet to make BAC debut.

*SPEAK Nicholas Jason b Manchester, 21/10/66; RHB OS; HS 232; BB 1–0; 100s 6; 1000r 1.

*STANWORTH John b Oldham, 30/9/60; RHB WK; HS 50 not out; Ct 63; St 10.

TITCHARD Stephen Paul b Warrington, 17/12/67; RHB RAS; HS 135; 100s 1.

*i*WASIM AKRAM b Lahore, Pakistan, 3/6/66; LHB LF; HS 123 (for Pakistan), 122 (for Lancs); BB 7–42 (for World XI), 7–53 (for Lancs); 50w 2+2 on tour; 5w/i 35; 10w/m 7; hat-trick 1. Tests 44.

*WATKINSON Michael b Westhoughton, 1/8/61; RHB RAS; HS 138; BB 7–25; 100s 3; 50w 4; 5w/i 20; 10w/m 1; hat-trick 1.

WOOD Nathan b Yorkshire, 4/10/74; LHB. Yet to make fc debut.

YATES Gary b Ashton-under-Lyne, 20/9/67; RHB OS; HS 106; BB 4–94 (v Sri Lanka), 3–47 (BAC).

Beneficiary '93: G. D. Mendis.

In: Wasim Akram (returning), D. P. Hughes (manager), D. Lloyd (coach).
Out: P. J. W. Allott, G. Fowler (Durham), D. K. Morrison, J. A. Ormrod (manager).

Colt to follow: J. P. Crawley.

LANCASHIRE BAC AVERAGES 1992

BATTING	M	I	NO	Runs	HS	Av	100	50
N. H. Fairbrother	11	16	5	644	166*	58.55	1	5
N. J. Speak	22	36	3	1892	232	57.33	4	12
J. P. Crawley	7	10	0	558	172	55.80	1	3
M. A. Atherton	17	30	5	1351	199	54.04	5	4
G. D. Lloyd	22	35	9	1310	132	50.38	4	9
W. K. Hegg	18	24	7	618	80	36.35	0	4
S. P. Titchard	13	22	3	647	74	34.05	0	6
G. Fowler	10	18	2	502	66	31.38	0	4
P. A. J. DeFreitas	11	12	1	322	72	29.27	0	3
I. D. Austin	8	10	2	230	115*	28.75	1	1
P. J. Martin	21	24	6	492	133	27.33	1	2
J. D. Fitton	7	8	2	135	48*	22.50	0	0
G. D. Mendis	5	8	1	145	45	20.71	0	0
S. D. Fletcher	5	4	1	62	23	20.67	0	0
M. Watkinson	19	24	1	466	96	20.26	0	1
R. C. Irani	5	6	0	68	22	11.33	0	0
D. K. Morrison	14	12	1	113	30	10.27	0	0
A. A. Barnett	21	16	10	61	17	10.17	0	0

Also batted: G. Chapple (2 matches) 1*, 18; J. Stanworth (4) 21.

BOWLING	O	M	R	W	Av	BB	5i	10m
G. Chapple	48	17	128	5	25.60	3–40	0	0
D. K. Morrison	335.4	52	1209	36	33.58	6–48	1	0
P. A. J. DeFreitas	290.5	51	912	27	33.78	6–94	1	0
J. D. Fitton	166.1	37	453	13	34.85	4–81	0	0
M. Watkinson	629.2	128	2118	59	35.90	6–62	3	1
P. J. Martin	512.3	128	1476	36	41.00	4–45	0	0
I. D. Austin	164.5	41	522	12	43.50	3–44	0	0
A. A. Barnett	571.5	79	2092	43	48.65	5–78	2	0

Also bowled: M. A. Atherton 66.1–4–337–3, J. P. Crawley 10–0–90–1, S. D. Fletcher 83–16–363–4, G. Fowler 5–0–60–1, R. C. Irani 33–5–137–3, G. D. Lloyd 7–0–45–0, N. J. Speak 6–0–66–0.

HUNDREDS (17)
- 5 – M. A. Atherton: 140* v Derbys (Blackpool), 135 v Middx (Old Trafford), 130 v Warwicks (Edgbaston), 119 v Yorks (Old Trafford), 199 v Durham (Gateshead Fell).
- 4 – G. D. Lloyd: 132 v Kent (Old Trafford), 102* v Hants (Old Trafford), 103* v Middx (Old Trafford), 101 v Worcs (Old Trafford). N. J. Speak: 232 v Leics (Leicester), 102 v Somerset (Old Trafford), 144 v Gloucs (Old Trafford), 111 v Middx (Old Trafford).
- 1 – I. D. Austin: 115* v Derbys (Blackpool). J. P. Crawley: 172 v Surrey (Lytham). N. H. Fairbrother: 166* v Yorks (Headingley). P. J. Martin: 133 v Durham (Gateshead Fell).

LEICESTERSHIRE

BAC positions last five seasons: 8th; 16th; 7th; 13th; 8th.
Club formed: 1879.
Honours: Champions 1 (1975); NWTGC 0 (best: finalists, 1992); B&H 3 (1972, 1975, 1985); SL 2 (1974, 1977).

As tales of the unexpected go, Leicestershire won the county Booker Prize with something to spare last year. The calamities of Bobby Simpson's second season had led to a less than happy parting of the ways between club and manager. The attack looked more toothless than ruthless, the batting more stolid than solid. By mid-August, however, hats were being eaten. Nigel Briers and his side lay second in the Championship behind Essex, their impending visitors in the NatWest Trophy semi-finals.

A few days later, the first half of a most unlikely double crept nearer when Essex were seen off from the very last ball at Grace Road, but while the losers found consolation elsewhere Leicestershire had shot their bolt. Drifting steadily out of the Championship picture as injuries to David Millns and Vince Wells blunted the attack, they ultimately bowed meekly to Northants at Lord's.

No matter. In a happier side than of late, individuals had meshed together to create a whole greater than the totality of its parts, a team in the truest sense. Leicestershire had every reason to indulge in a bit of back-slapping. By the same token there was also a sense of a team playing above itself for a while before returning to normality. The shortcomings persist, making it difficult to envisage a prolonged involvement in the Championship race.

James Whitaker, a fitful, occasionally thrilling talent, may well mark his benefit year by rediscovering his consistency, and ex-Yorkie Phil Robinson, now freely available after his thumb-twiddling summer of 1992, has plenty of punch left. Young Ben Smith looks a county stalwart in the making, if not more. Overall, though, the batting still lacks urgency and authority. Justin Benson, a man worth a place on slip fielding alone in a strong order, will need to tune the other strings in his bow, while Wells's runs could be more useful than his wickets. All that said, Briers and his equally unflappable opening compadre, Tim Boon, may take to the extended opportunities for crease occupation like dogs to trees.

If Championships were won on seam bowling alone Leicestershire would be in with a shout. The pace, swing and variety of Millns, Winston Benjamin and left-armer Alan Mullally can be as effective as any. Wells, furthermore, is one of those nagging medium-pacers who is always bound to get wickets. But Championships are won on spin as much as anything, as Essex and Middlesex have proved. In that department, despite the presence of manager Jack Birkenshaw, formerly a sometime purveyor of off-breaks for England, the cupboard – with all due deference to Laurie Potter newcomer and Adrian Pierson – is not well stocked. Twenty-five BAC victims at 40.84 are not the sort of figures one expects of a county's premier twirly man, but then Potter is no specialist. Leicestershire are fortunate in having two of those vying for one spot behind the stumps, where Paul Nixon's bat could block Phil Whitticase's comeback from injury. They also play on a seamers' track at home. Without a proficient slow man, however, the four-day game may find them out.

CHAMPIONSHIP RATING: two bats, three balls.
PREDICTED POSITION: 16th.

Overseas player: WINSTON BENJAMIN
The splendidly-christened Winston Keithroy Matthew Benjamin is one of three pacy Benjamins treading the county boards this summer. The most gifted of the trio, he has also experienced the most turbulent career.

A clever, whippety bowler with an economical run, confident with a bat in his hands, Benjamin was still some weeks short of his 23rd birthday when he made his Test debut for the West Indies in Delhi six winters ago. Assuming instant novelty status when subsequently dropped in favour of a spinner, he took five wickets and hit a critical 40 to square the series against Pakistan the following spring, striking the winning boundary. It remains his highest score at this level. Along loped Curtly Ambrose, and although Benjamin worked his way back into the side for the last three Tests in England that summer and topped the bowling averages, 1993 began with him still in search of his ninth Test cap.

While this obviously had something to do with the abundance of pedigree fast bowlers at the West Indies' disposal, the main impediment was a persistent knee problem, one that persuaded him to announce his retirement from county cricket at the end of the 1990 season. There was also an unfortunate domestic accident around this time, but many pointed to a further factor, namely a strained relationship with Bobby Simpson, then the Leicestershire manager.

The events may not have been connected but the Antiguan revoked his decision once manager and club had parted company. Following hard on an exacting if encouraging World Cup – only Andy Cummins took more wickets for the West Indies – he showed glimpses of his class with bat and ball last summer, only Briers and Boon making more half-centuries and only Millns taking more wickets. Indeed, Millns is the first to attribute his success to the unselfishness of his opening partner. A modicum of luck could be all Benjamin needs to make up for lost time. A career-best-equalling 7 for 54 for the Leeward Islands against Jamaica during the winter, followed by a more than useful comeback against Pakistan, suggests he still has the wherewithal to make the most of it.

PLAYING STAFF 1993:

‡*BENJAMIN Winston Keithroy Matthew b St John's, Antigua, 31/12/63; RHB RFM; HS 101 not out; BB 7–54; 100s 1; 50w 1; 5w/i 17; 10w/m 2; hat-trick 1 (v Australia). Tests 8.

BENSON Justin David Ramsay b Dublin, 1/3/67; RHB RAS; HS 133 not out; BB 2–24; 100s 2.

*BOON Timothy James b Doncaster, 1/11/61; RHB RAS; HS 144; BB 3–40; 100s 12; 1000r 7.

†*BRIERS Nigel Edwin b Leicester, 15/1/55; RHB RAS; HS 201 not out; BB 4–29; 100s 24; 1000r 9. Captain since 1990.

HEPWORTH Peter Nash b Ackworth, W. Yorkshire, 4/5/67; RHB OS; HS 115; BB 3–51; 100s 2.

*MILLNS David James b Mansfield, 27/2/65; LHB RF; HS 44; BB 9–37; 50w 2; 5w/i 11; 10w/m 2. Previous county: Nottinghamshire (1988–89). England A cap.

MULLALLY Alan David b Southend, 12/7/69; RHB LFM; HS 34; BB 5–119; 5w/i 1. Previous county: Hampshire (1988).

NIXON Paul Andrew b Carlisle, 21/10/70; LHB WK; HS 107 not out; 100s 1; Ct 109; St 9.

*PARSONS Gordon James b Slough, 17/10/59; LHB RAS; HS 76 (for Boland), 69 (for Leics); BB 9–72 (for Boland), 6–11 (v Oxford U), 6–70 (BAC); 50w 2;

5w/i 18; 10w/m 1. Previous counties: Warwickshire (1986–88), Leicestershire (1978–85 and 1989 to date).

PIERSON Adrian Roger Kirshaw b Enfield, Middx, 21/7/63. RHB OS. HS 42 not out (Warwicks v Northants); BB 6–82 (Warwicks v Derbys); 5w/i 3. Previous county: Warwickshire 1985–91. Yet to make debut for Leicestershire.

PLENDER Ian Foster b Gateshead, 11/5/72; RHB RAS. Yet to make fc debut.

*POTTER Laurie b Bexleyheath, Kent, 7/11/62; RHB SLA; HS 165 not out (for Griqualand West), 121 not out (for Leics); BB 4–52 (for GW), 4–73 (for Leics); 100s 7; 1000r 3. Previous county: Kent (1981–85).

ROBINSON Phillip Edward b Keighley, 3/8/63; RHB LAS; HS 189 (for Yorks), 19 (for Leics); 100s 7; 1000r 3. Previous county: Yorkshire (1984–91).

SMITH Benjamin Francis b Corby, Northants, 3/4/72; RHB RAS; HS 100 not out; BB 1–5; 100s 1.

WELLS Vincent John b Dartford, Kent, 6/8/65; RHB RAS; HS 58 (for Kent), 56 (for Leics); BB 5–43 (for Kent), 4–26 (for Leics); 5w/i 1. Previous county: Kent (1987–91).

*WHITAKER John James b Skipton, Yorks, 5/5/62; RHB OS; HS 200 not out; BB 1–29; 100s 24; 1000r 8. Tests 1.

*WHITTICASE Philip b Wythall, Birmingham, 15/3/65; RHB WK; HS 114 not out; 100s 1; Ct 303; St 13.

Beneficiary '93: J. J. Whitaker.

In: A. R. K. Pierson, P. E. Robinson (Yorkshire).
Out: M. I. Gidley, R. P. Gofton, C. J. Hawkes, A. Roseberry.

Player of the Year 1992: D. J. Millns.
Colt to follow: B. F. Smith.

LEICESTERSHIRE BAC AVERAGES 1992

BATTING	M	I	NO	Runs	HS	Av	100	50
T. J. Boon	22	38	3	1383	139	39.51	2	9
N. E. Briers	22	39	6	1092	122*	33.09	1	9
V. J. Wells	16	23	6	526	56	30.94	0	3
L. Potter	21	33	3	797	96	26.57	0	4
P. A. Nixon	15	23	6	451	107*	26.53	1	1
B. F. Smith	14	20	3	441	100*	25.94	1	3
J. J. Whitaker	20	31	2	701	74	24.17	0	1
J. D. R. Benson	17	26	1	571	122	22.84	1	1
W. K. M. Benjamin	20	25	3	453	72	20.59	0	4
C. J. Hawkes	3	4	1	60	18	20.00	0	0
M. I. Gidley	5	10	2	143	39	17.88	0	0
D. J. Millns	17	17	9	143	33*	17.88	0	0
R. P. Gofton	4	6	0	100	75	16.67	0	1
G. J. Parsons	13	14	2	142	35	11.83	0	0
P. N. Hepworth	8	13	1	131	29	10.92	0	0
P. Whitticase	7	10	3	62	18*	8.86	0	0
A. D. Mullally	17	21	6	112	21	7.47	0	0

Also batted: P. E. Robinson (1 match) 0, 19.

BOWLING	O	M	R	W	Av	BB	5i	10m
D. J. Millns	434.3	103	1401	68	20.60	6–87	6	1
V. J. Wells	293	90	738	33	22.36	4–26	0	0
C. J. Hawkes	42	11	122	5	24.40	4–18	0	0
G. J. Parsons	335.2	88	943	36	26.19	6–70	2	0
W. K. M. Benjamin	489	102	1498	47	31.87	4–34	0	0
A. D. Mullally	476	115	1365	38	35.92	5–119	1	0
R. P. Gofton	46	10	203	5	40.60	4–81	0	0
L. Potter	344.1	78	1021	25	40.84	4–73	0	0

Also bowled: J. D. R. Benson 35–4–109–3, T. J. Boon 29–4–175–4, M. I. Gidley 80–20–248–2, P. N. Hepworth 68.4–9–301–3, J. J. Whitaker 8–0–86–1.

HUNDREDS (6)

2 – T. J. Boon: 110 v Durham (Durham Univ), 139 v Lancs (Leicester).
1 – J. D. R. Benson: 122 v Middx (Leicester). N. E. Briers: 122* v Worcs (Leicester). P. A. Nixon: 107* v Hants (Leicester). B. F. Smith: 100* v Durham (Durham Univ).

MIDDLESEX

BAC position last five seasons: 11th; 15th; Champions; 3rd; 7th.
Club formed: 1864.
Honours: Champions 10 (1866, 1903, 1920–21, 1947, 1976, 1980, 1982, 1985, 1990) plus 2 shared (1949, 1977); NWTGC 4 (1977, 1980, 1984, 1988); B&H 2 (1983, 1986); SL 1 (1992).

There was a time, notably during their run of five outright and one shared Championship between 1976 and 1990, when Middlesex would have looked forward to a full season of four-day cricket. The fourth day would have been required only if the weather stopped them winning in three. Now there are doubts.

Last season's prize came over 40 overs, admittedly, something of a breakthrough in itself but far from being the best barometer of a side's Championship prospects. A small corps of experience has been boosted by the arrival of Mark Feltham, a particularly handy man for tethering opposing batsmen in the one-dayers, but Test calls and injury could expose a rather soft underbelly.

The batting, as well as the side, will be led by the irrepressible Mike Gatting, for whom the season's new format should be met with a hearty smack of the lips. Able support will come from Desmond Haynes and the increasingly confident Mike Roseberry, arguably the finest of all Middlesex opening pairs. Should Gatting and John Emburey both be called to the national colours (it would be unwise to write the latter off just yet), Roseberry may well gain an early taste of the captaincy rumoured to be heading his way once the current incumbent retires. Not that that is likely to happen for some time yet.

If Mark Ramprakash can come to terms with his own ability and Keith Brown can make a better fist of combining two jobs Harry Sharp may have problems keeping score. The downside, however, is that Ramprakash could end up being pressed into Ashes service alongside Gatting, which would demand a great deal of Jason Pooley, Aftab Habib and Matthew Keech, three young batsmen with potential but precious little first-team experience. The gap could yawn.

If Richard Yeabsley shines at Oxford early in the season then he may be a useful reinforcement for the fast-medium attack, an area of some concern now that Ricardo Ellcock and Dean Headley have gone. Each of the three main strike bowlers, Angus Fraser, Neil Williams and Norman Cowans, has a history of injury, Fraser the most serious as well as the most recent. Whether the arthroscopic surgery he underwent on his troublesome hip clarifies the matter remains to be seen. A better strike bowler than a stock bowler, it is uncertain what he will be good for in 1993, and the same goes for the other two, particularly since Cowans will also have to cope with the distractions of his well-deserved benefit. Chas Taylor, a skilful left-armer, will aim to exorcise an inexplicably fallow second half of 1992, but experienced reinforcements are thin on the ground. It is hard to see any of this quartet producing hostile bursts or long spells of containment, which means that Emburey and Phil Tufnell, when available, may have their edge blunted by the need to perform a holding role. The progress of Paul Weekes, with bat and off-breaks, will be monitored closely.

All this points to a classic Middlesex season. Some champagne days when the game is made to look beautiful and simple, some flat beer ones when the batsmen appear strokeless and the bowlers cannot find line and length. The outlook is for the latter to outweigh the former. (Paul Filer)

CHAMPIONSHIP RATING: three bats, 2½ balls.
PREDICTED POSITION: 14th.

Overseas player: DESMOND HAYNES

When the co-founder of Test cricket's most profitable firm of openers first signed for Middlesex in 1989 his lot was an unenviable one. Having just won the International Cricketer of the Year award for his performances in Australia Desmond Haynes may well have been at his peak, but many suspected the 33-year-old had left it a little late to jump on the county merry-go-round. He also had to replace two players instead of the customary one owing to the premature death of opener Wilf Slack and the retirement of Wayne Daniel, the county's longtime and much-loved overseas pace spearhead as well as an old adversary from Haynes's Barbados schooldays.

That the last remaining player from the Clive Lloyd empire-building days should since have become every bit as popular as Daniel says as much for him as the runs he has stockpiled. He was voted Britannic Assurance Player of the Year for the eight centuries and 2,346 runs that propelled Middlesex's charge to the 1990 pennant, and his colleagues were even quicker to pay homage to the expertise and enthusiasm he brought to the dressing-room. None more so than Mike Roseberry, who evolved that season from a struggling greenhorn into a thinking batsman. The absence of his tutor, Roseberry readily admits, contributed to his hiccup the following summer. As if to underscore the point, the return of Haynes in 1992 found him enjoying his sunniest summer yet.

That expansive, almost permanent grin is an accurate reflection of the Haynes spirit, pricked when he was passed over as West Indies captain but still as resilient as any in spite of the advancing years. His 16 one-day international centuries are a world record, testimony to the game's most adaptable opener. The shadow of Gordon Greenidge looms no more.

PLAYING STAFF 1993:

BALLINGER Richard John b Wimbledon, 18/9/73. RHB RFM. Yet to make first team debut.

*BROWN Keith Robert b Edmonton, 18/3/63; RHB RAS WK; HS 200 not out; BB 2–7; 100s 10; 1000r 2; Ct 177; St 11.

*CARR John Donald b St John's Wood, 15/6/63; RHB RAS; HS 156; BB 6–61; 100s 12; 1000r 4; 5w/i 3.

*COWANS Norman George b Enfield St Mary, Jamaica, 17/4/61; RHB RAS; HS 66; BB 6–31; 50w 6; 5w/i 23; 10w/m 1. Tests 19.

DUTCH Keith Philip b Harrow, 21/3/73. RHB OS. Yet to make first team debut.

*EMBUREY John Ernest b Peckham, 20/8/52; RHB OS; HS 133; BB 7–27; 100s 5; 50w 14; 100w 1; 5w/i 63; 10w/m 9. Tests 60 (captain 2).

FARBRACE Paul b Ash, Kent, 7/7/67; RHB WK; HS 79 (v Cambridge U), 75 not out (for Kent, BAC), 50 (for Middx); Ct 81; St 12. Previous county: Kent (1987–90).

FELTHAM Mark Andrew b London, 26/6/63; RHB RM; HS 101 (for Surrey); BB 6–53; 50w 1; 5wi 6. Previous county: Surrey (1983–92). Yet to make fc debut for Middlesex.

*FRASER Angus Robert Charles b Billinge, Lancashire, 8/8/65; RHB RM; HS 92; BB 7–77; 50w 3; 5w/i 16; 10w/m 2. Tests 11.

†*GATTING Michael William b Kingsbury, 6/6/57; RHB RM; HS 258; BB 5–34; 100s 72; 1000r 14; 5w/i 2. Captain since 1983. Tests 68 (captain 23).

HABIB Aftab b Reading, 7/2/72; RHB RM; HS 12.

HARRISON Jason Christian b Amersham, Bucks, 15/1/72; RHB OS. Yet to make fc debut.

*¡*HAYNES Desmond Leo b Holders Hill, Barbados, 15/2/56; RHB RAS; HS 255 not out; BB 1–2 (for West Indies), 1–4 (for Middx); 100s 50; 1000r 3+4 overseas. Tests 103 (captain 4).

JOHNSON Richard Leonard b Chertsey, Surrey, 29/12/74; RHB RAS; HS 1; BB 1–25.

KEECH Matthew b Hampstead, 21/10/70; RHB RAS; HS 58 not out.

POOLEY Jason Calvin b Hammersmith, 8/8/69; LHB; HS 88.

RADFORD Toby Alexander b Caerphilly, Glamorgan, 3/12/71; RHB OS. Yet to make fc debut.

*RAMPRAKASH Mark Ravin b Bushey, Herts, 5/9/69; RHB OS; HS 233; BB 1–0; 100s 12; 1000r 4. Tests 9.

*ROSEBERRY Michael Anthony b Houghton-le-Spring, 28/11/66; RHB RAS; HS 173; BB 1–0; 100s 15; 1000r 3. England A cap.

SIMS Robin Jason b Hillingdon, 22/11/70; LHB WK. HS3 (v Pakistan). Yet to make BAC debut.

TAYLOR Charles William b Banbury, 12/8/66; LHB LAS; HS 21; BB 5–33; 5w/i 1.

*TUFNELL Philip Clive Roderick b Hadley Wood, Herts, 29/4/66; RHB SLA; HS 37; BB 7–47 (for England), 7–116 (for Middx); 50w 3; 5w/i 19; 10w/m 2. Tests 10.

WALKER David Anthony b Hampstead, 18/6/75. RHB LAS; Yet to make fc debut.

WEEKES Paul Nicholas b Hackney, 8/7/69; LHB OS; HS 89 not out; BB 3–57.

*WILLIAMS Neil FitzGerald b Hope Well, St Vincent, 2/7/62; RHB RFM; HS 77 not out; BB 8–75; 50w 3; 5w/i 16; 10w/m 2. Tests 1.

Beneficiary '93: N. G. Cowans.

In: M. A. Feltham (Surrey).
Out: R. M. Ellcock (retired), D. W. Headley (Kent), I. J. Hutchinson, S. A. Sylvester, R. Whittington.

Player of the Year 1992: M. A. Roseberry.
Colt to follow: P. N. Weekes.

MIDDLESEX BAC AVERAGES 1992

BATTING	M	I	NO	Runs	HS	Av	100	50
M. W. Gatting	22	35	6	1980	170	68.28	6	10
J. C. Pooley	2	4	1	149	69	49.67	0	2
M. A. Roseberry	22	38	3	1724	173	49.26	6	8
M. R. Ramprakash	14	24	2	1042	233	47.36	3	5
D. L. Haynes	20	35	2	1513	177	45.85	3	10
J. D. Carr	22	34	6	1068	114	38.14	2	7
P. N. Weekes	14	17	5	431	89*	35.92	0	2
D. W. Headley	14	12	3	268	91	29.78	0	1
J. E. Emburey	22	27	6	554	102	26.38	1	3
K. R. Brown	22	33	5	651	106	23.25	1	2
A. R. C. Fraser	16	18	7	188	33	17.09	0	0
N. F. Williams	17	17	3	186	46*	13.29	0	0
P. C. R. Tufnell	14	13	7	55	12	9.17	0	0
C. W. Taylor	16	13	6	64	14	9.14	0	0

Also batted: Aftab Habib (1 match) 12, 7*; R. L. Johnson (1) 1; S. A. Sylvester (2) 0*. P. H. Edmonds played in one match but did not bat.

BOWLING	O	M	R	W	Av	BB	5i	10m
J. E. Emburey	848.5	245	2064	80	25.80	5–23	3	0
N. F. Williams	437	86	1283	48	26.73	8–75	2	1
P. C. R. Tufnell	517.2	122	1366	41	33.32	5–83	2	0
D. W. Headley	304.3	62	968	26	37.23	3–31	0	0
C. W. Taylor	379.2	74	1337	32	41.78	4–50	0	0
P. N. Weekes	155	36	428	10	42.80	3–61	0	0
A. R. C. Fraser	366.2	69	1158	18	64.33	3–59	0	0

Also bowled: J. D. Carr 41–14–100–3, P. H. Edmonds 28–10–48–4, M. W. Gatting 6–0–38–0, D. L. Haynes 2.4–0–5–1, R. L. Johnson 14–2–71–1, M. R. Ramprakash 10–1–41–0, M. A. Roseberry 10–2–71–0, S. A. Sylvester 42–9–123–2.

HUNDREDS (22)
6 – M. W. Gatting: 170 v Glam (Lord's), 103 v Lancs (Lord's), 117 & 163* v Warwicks (Coventry), 126* v Lancs (Old Trafford), 102* v Kent (Canterbury). M. A. Roseberry: 148 v Notts (Trent Bridge), 102 v Leics (Lord's),

118 v Worcs (Uxbridge), 100* v Derbys (Derby), 173 v Durham (Lord's), 120 v Surrey (Oval).
3 – D. L. Haynes: 144 v Notts (Trent Bridge), 127* v Northants (Uxbridge), 177 v Sussex (Hove). M. R. Ramprakash: 108 v Lancs (Lord's), 233 v Surrey (Lord's), 117 v Surrey (Oval).
2 – J. D. Carr: 102 v Essex (Ilford), 114 v Surrey (Oval).
1 – K. R. Brown: 106 v Warwicks (Lord's). J. E. Emburey: 102 v Leics (Leicester).

NORTHAMPTONSHIRE
BAC position last five seasons: 3rd; 10th; 11th; 5th; 12th.
Club formed: 1878.
Honours: Champions 0 (best: 2nd, 1912, 1957, 1965, 1976); NWTGC 2 (1976, 1992); B&H 1 (1980); SL 0 (best: 3rd, 1991).

When Nick Cook cocked a mighty snook at his detractors by spinning Northants to victory at Chelmsford last August, a county held its breath, again. After 77 attempts, were the tenants of Wantage Road about to take possession of their first Championship? Predictably, the void was still intact six weeks later, the blow softened by triumph in the NatWest final but the sense of a missed opportunity acute.

To begin in such sober fashion may seem somewhat inappropriate, but the achievements of 1992 need a context if they are to be fully appreciated. Over the past 20 years Northants have received transfusions from a host of imported bluebloods. Try adding a wicketkeeper and a couple of openers to this luminous list: Allan Lamb, Mushtaq Mohammad, Kevin Curran, Roger Harper, Eldine Baptiste, Curtly Ambrose, Sarfraz Nawaz and Bishen Bedi. Yet, just as Somerset's vaunted overseas contingent has failed to break the famine at Taunton, so Northamptonshire's star parts have been unable to create a completely satisfying whole.

Last season's collection, however, was responsible for the county's most successful season ever bar 1976, when they won the Gillette Cup (as was), the first trophy in the club's history, then lost the pennant by 17 points. This time the margin of defeat was 52, third place a just reward for the labours of Lamb and his flock.

Relieved of his post by England, the captain addressed rejection in his usual bullish manner and will presumably continue to drop the selectors the unsubtlest of hints from his berth at the heart of a forceful order. Vice-captain Rob Bailey, the unluckiest four-cap wonder in the land, will be keen to maintain his increasingly assertive form in his benefit year; David Capel has been reborn since the miseries of 1991 and Alan Fordham, a lordly Man of the Match at Lord's, is shaping up as an international opener for the none-too distant future. Kevin Curran, meanwhile, can be expected to top up last year's meagre tank of runs.

Not quite the roaring success envisaged in the two years since his transfer from Gloucestershire, Curran should exert a greater influence with his lively seam and swing, Capel too. Most counties would be grateful for one multi-purpose player, but Northants have two capable of notching 2,000 runs and 100 wickets between them. As bowlers they will assist the new ball duo of Ambrose and left-armer Paul Taylor, whose rollercoaster ride from Derbyshire donkey to shop assistant to England tourist constitutes the most far-fetched and heartwarming fairytale in recent county folklore.

David Ripley's riposte to the threat of Wayne Noon was to have a career year with bat and gloves, making two crucial hundreds and topping the national dismissals table. In Mal Loye, Tim Walton, Jeremy Snape and the two Richards, Pearson and Montgomerie, moreover Northants possess a quintet of bright young things. They will be there or thereabouts again, but a lot will depend on how Cook is cooking and how much energy and desire Phil Neale, Mike Procter's replacement as manager, can coax out of Ambrose. Possibly too much.

CHAMPIONSHIP RATING: four bats, 2½ balls.
PREDICTED POSITION: 4th.

Overseas player: CURTLY AMBROSE
About a year ago, the word was that Curtly Ambrose had had his fill of bowling fast for a living. The flame, apparently, had been dimmed by the constant globetrotting and the demands of being the premier strike bowler for county, country and the entire Caribbean. Long Tall Curtly, it was said, had lost his demon.

At face value his 1992 return mirrored this apparent disenchantment. Fifty Championship wickets at 26.14, although more than acceptable by most standards, certainly looks well below par. Now ask Paul Taylor how many wickets his partner earned for him through the pressure he brought to bear from the opposite end. The Leeward Island stick insect may well not have been at full steam, but his is a presence whose importance can never be condensed into a random arrangement of numbers.

An extremely private, almost wordless assassin, he decided to let the numbers do the talking when he adjourned to Australia. Despite appalling luck at the start of the rubber, he ran amok at the end claiming 19 victims in the last two Tests and, with 33 wickets in the series, equalling the record for Australia–West Indies Tests. The enthusiasm, palpably, was back.

There are few clues to his menace in that coltish trot to the crease. Caution sets in when the right wrist begins to wag. This means the sap is rising. Arrowing deliveries into the target's ribs from only fractionally short of a length, disconcerting his upper torso with lift and bullying his feet with that malevolent yorker: the resulting cocktail has more than a touch of the Molotov about it. Nobody witnessing the spell that mesmerised England in Bridgetown four winters ago – or the one that shoved South Africa over the edge on the same ground last spring, or the one that paved the way for that impossibly narrow win in Adelaide in January, or the 7–1 spell that hypnotised Border and company in Perth – can question the skill or the temperament. He may even be mellowing. After walking off with the Player of the Series and International Cricketer of the Year awards he broke his silence with the press. 'My ambition,' he proclaimed, 'is to play Test cricket for a long time, because when you are on top it feels grand.' Whether the world's batsmen will feel as grand over the coming few years, is open to doubt.

PLAYING STAFF 1993:

*i*AMBROSE Curtly Elconn Lynwall b Swetes Village, Antigua, 21/9/63; LHB RF; HS 509 (for West Indies), 55 not out (for North); BB 8–45 (for WI), 7–89 (for North); 50w 3; 5w/i 19; 10w/m 3. Tests 34.

*BAILEY Robert John b Biddulph, Stoke-on-Trent, 28/10/63; RHB OS; HS 224 not out; BB 3–27; 100s 29; 1000r 9. Tests 4.

BOWEN Mark Nicholas b Redcar, 6/12/67; RHB RM; HS 5; BB 1–35.

*CAPEL David John b Northampton, 6/7/63; RHB RAS; HS 134 (for Eastern Province), 126 (for North); BB 7–46; 100s 12; 1000r 3; 50w 3; 5w/i 12. Tests 15.

*COOK Nicholas Grant Billson b Leicester, 17/6/56; RHB SLA; HS 75 (for

Leics), 64 (for North); BB 7–34: 50w 8; 5w/i 31 10w/m 4. Tests 15. Previous county: Leicestershire (1978–85).

*CURRAN Kevin Malcolm b Rusape, Zimbabwe, 7/9/59; RHB RAS; HS 144 not out (for Gloucs), 898 not out (for North); BB 7–47 (for Natal), 7–54 (for Gloucs), 6–45 (for North); 100s 18; 1000r 5; 50w 4; 5w/i 12; 10w/m 4. Previous county: Gloucestershire (1985–90).

*FELTON Nigel Alfred b Guildford, 24/10/60; LHB OS; HS 173 not out (for Som), 122 (for North); BB 1–48; 100s 13; 1000r 4. Previous county: Somerset (1982–88).

*FORDHAM Alan b Bedford, 9/11/64; RHB RAS; HS 206 not out; BB 1–25; 100s 14; 1000r 3.

HUGHES John Gareth b Wellingborough, 3/5/71; RHB RAS; HS 2; BB 2–57.

INNES Kevin b Northampton, 24/9/75. RHB RAS. Yet to make fc debut.

†*LAMB Allan Joseph b Langebaanweg, South Africa, 20/6/54; RHB RAS; HS 294 (for Orange Free State), 235 (for North); BB 2–29; 100s 79; 1000r 12. Captain since 1989. Tests 79 (captain 3).

LOYE Malachy Bernhard b Northampton, 27/9/72; RHB OS; HS 46.

MONTGOMERIE Richard Robert b Rugby, 3/7/71; RHB OS; HS 103 not out (for Oxford U), 7 (BAC).

NOON Wayne Michael b Grimsby, 5/2/71; RHB WK; HS 37 (v Australia), 36 (BAC). Ct 21, St 2.

PEARSON Richard Michael b Batley, Yorks, 27/1/72; RHB OS; HS 33 not out (for Cambridge U; yet to score in BAC), BB 5–108 (for Cambridge U), 2–90 (BAC).

PENBERTHY Anthony Leonard b Troon, Cornwall, 1/9/69; LHB RAS; HS 101 not out (v Cambridge U), 83 (BAC); BB 4–91. 100s 1. Took wicket with first ball in fc cricket.

RIKA Craig b Bradford, 18/1/74; RHB RFM. Yet to make fc debut.

*RIPLEY David b Leeds, 13/9/66; RHB WK; HS 134 not out; 100s 6; Ct 369; St 55.

ROBERTS Andrew Richard b Kettering, 16/4/71; RHB LS; HS 62; BB 6–72; 5w/i 1.

SNAPE Jeremy Nicholas b Stoke-on-Trent, 27/4/73; RHB OS; BB 1–20.

STANLEY Neil Alan b Bedford, 16/5/68; RHB OS; HS 132; 100s 1.

TAYLOR Jonathan Paul b Ashby-de-la-Zouch, 8/8/64; LHB LFM; HS 74 not out; BB 7–23; 50w 1; 5w/i 4; 10w/m 1. Previous county: Derbyshire (1984–86).

TOMLINSON Jamie b Isle of Man, 14/8/71; RHB RFM. Yet to make fc debut.

*WALKER Alan b Emley, Yorks, 7/7/62; LHB RAS; HS 41 not out; BB 6–50; 50w 1; 5w/i 2.

WALTON Timothy Charles b Low Lead, 8/11/72; RHB RM. Yet to make fc debut.

WARREN Russell John b Northampton, 10/9/71; RHB OS; HS 19.

Beneficiary '93: R. J. Bailey.

In: P. A. Neale (manager).
Out: S. J. Green, M. J. Procter (manager), R. G. Williams (retired).

Player of the Year 1992: A. J. Lamb.
Colt to follow: J. N. Snape.

NORTHAMPTONSHIRE BAC AVERAGES 1992

BATTING	M	I	NO	Runs	HS	Av	100	50
A. J. Lamb	15	23	4	1350	209	71.05	6	5
R. J. Bailey	22	37	7	1514	167*	50.47	2	7
A. R. Fordham	22	39	2	1693	192	45.76	4	7
D. Ripley	21	29	9	782	107*	39.10	2	3
N. A. Felton	21	35	3	1075	103	33.59	1	9
D. J. Capel	22	32	4	888	103	31.71	1	5
N. G. B. Cook	16	9	5	108	37	27.00	0	0
K. M. Curran	20	28	1	685	82	25.37	0	5
C. E. L. Ambrose	18	20	10	200	49*	20.00	0	0
J. P. Taylor	22	17	8	180	74*	20.00	0	1
A. R. Roberts	13	17	3	259	62	18.50	0	1
M. B. Loye	10	14	1	195	46	15.00	0	0
R. J. Warren	2	3	1	27	19	13.50	0	0
A. L. Penberthy	9	12	1	147	33	13.36	0	0
R. G. Williams	2	3	0	29	14	9.67	0	0

Also batted: M. N. Bowen (2 matches) 5; N. A. Stanley (1) 16, 7*; A. Walker (1) 39. W. M. Noon, R. M. Pearson and J. N. Snape all played in one match but did not bat.

BOWLING	O	M	R	W	Av	BB	5i	10m
N. G. B. Cook	285.1	79	831	34	24.44	7–34	1	1
D. J. Capel	440	91	1181	48	24.60	5–61	1	0
C. E. L. Ambrose	543.4	151	1307	50	26.14	4–53	0	0
K. M. Curran	436.4	95	1318	48	27.46	6–45	1	0
J. P. Taylor	630.2	117	1977	68	29.07	7–23	3	1
R. J. Bailey	120.1	31	291	9	32.33	1–0	0	0
A. R. Roberts	298.2	55	982	20	49.10	4–101	0	0
A. L. Penberthy	95	18	279	5	55.80	2–58	0	0

Also bowled: M. N. Bowen 43–6–159–1, N. A. Felton 14–2–93–0, A. Fordham 12.2–0–72–0, R. M. Pearson 35.4–2–130–2, D. Ripley 1–0–14–0, J. N. Snape 26–8–62–1, A. Walker 45–14–90–2, R. G. Williams 31–5–83–4.

HUNDREDS (16)
6 – A. J. Lamb: 101 v Worcs (Worcester), 109* v Glam (Luton), 209 & 107 v Warwicks (Northampton), 160 v Hants (Bournemouth), 122* v Leics (Leicester).
4 – A. Fordham: 192 v Surrey (Northampton), 119 v Notts (Trent Bridge), 137 v Glam (Luton), 122 v Lancs (Northampton).
2 – R. J. Bailey: 165 v Glam (Luton), 167* v Leics (Leicester). D. Ripley: 104 v Durham (Stockton), 107* v Somerset (Bath).
1 – D. J. Capel: 103 v Surrey (Oval). N. A. Felton: 103 v Yorks (Northampton).

NOTTINGHAMSHIRE

BAC position last five seasons: 4th; 4th; 13th; 11th; 5th.
Club formed: 1841.
Honours: Champions 14 (1865, 1868, 1871–72, 1875, 1880, 1883–1886, 1907, 1929, 1981, 1987) plus 5 shared (1869, 1873, 1879, 1882, 1889); NWTGC 1 (1987); B&H 1 (1989); SL 1 (1991).

Despite maintaining fourth position Nottinghamshire will view 1992 as a year largely wasted. There was enough talent within the club to make a serious challenge for the Championship ('they are 25 points ahead of the rest of us', a rival claimed last April) but their inability to show it led to a shake-up before the end of the summer.

Mike Hendrick, who was brought back to run the ship after the dismissal of John Birch, must be commended for his clarity of thought. It would have been easy for him to sail along with the crew he inherited. Instead, after taking a long look at the personnel, he chose to banish two experienced personalities from the dressing-room so that younger men would have a better chance.

Tim Robinson may be considered fortunate to retain the captaincy after five unconvincing seasons. In his defence it should be pointed out that Notts have won two one-day competitions in that time and begun to lay foundations for the 1990s after the departure of Clive Rice and Richard Hadlee.

Hendrick was recalled for a purpose, however, and responded by supporting the captain in the most public manner. After lengthy conversations with Chris Broad and Eddie Hemmings he felt it would be in the club's best interests if they were released. The feeling is that there is sufficient talent in the 2nd XI to justify the decision.

Broad's attitude may have been questionable but his departure leaves a mighty gap to fill. Yet again last season he opened the innings with distinction and, although he rejected the club's offer of a new contract the year before, it must have been a surprise to him as much as anyone when he was released after nine seasons at Trent Bridge with a benefit to come.

Hemmings was a different case. His bowling has come to resemble that of a civil servant, waiting for his watch and chain. The surprise is that Sussex were so eager to sign him; so a career which began when England's footballers won the World Cup enters its 27th year.

How seriously Notts challenge for the Championship this year depends on how Chris Lewis buckles down to the job and, no less important, what progress Chris Cairns makes. Lewis fell short of expectations last year and though Cairns impressed he will have to impress more often.

In Paul Johnson, Paul Pollard and Graham Archer, not to mention Robinson, the batting has some measure of class, but then a lack of ability has not been the problem at Trent Bridge recently. Between them the manager and captain have still got some sorting-out to do. (Michael Henderson)

CHAMPIONSHIP RATING: three bats, 3½ balls.
PREDICTED POSITION: 7th.

Overseas player: CHRIS CAIRNS
Becoming the overseas pro at Trent Bridge is particularly intimidating. The list of old boys includes a pair of knights, Garfield Sobers and Richard Hadlee, and two more fine all-rounders, Clive Rice and Franklyn Stephenson. If the offer goes out to a 21–year-old, as it did to Chris Cairns two summers ago, it could be interpreted as an invitation to fail.

Sobers was the greatest of all-rounders. Rice transformed the club, taking them to Championships with the help of Hadlee. Stephenson, who was on a hiding to nothing himself when he followed the New Zealander, promptly achieved the 'double' of 1,000 runs and 100 wickets in his first season. Cairns's father, Lance, moreover, not only took 130 wickets for New Zealand, second behind Hadlee, but was also the seamer whose seven wickets at Leeds 10 years ago brought his country their first Test win in England. How does a callow Kiwi follow that?

There is no doubting Cairns's independence. Tim Robinson found it out when Cairns waved his bat towards the dressing room in a display of frustration when an assumed declaration did not materialise. He has plenty of talent to go with it. Last year's return of 984 runs at 41 and 56 wickets at 35 hint at it, no more. His pace is medium to fast and he generates movement and nip off the pitch. A watchful effort at Colchester showed he could be methodical at the crease, and the way he struck the ball during a century against Gloucestershire at Worksop suggested a young Ted Dexter. It is to be trusted that a recent kidney operation does not prevent him from building on that impression. (Michael Henderson)

PLAYING STAFF 1993:

*AFFORD John Andrew b Crowland, Lincs, 12/5/64; RHB SLA; HS 22 not out; BB 6–68; 50w 3; 5w/i 9; 10w/m 2. England A cap.

ARCHER Graeme Francis b Carlisle, 26/9/70; RHB RAS; HS 117; 100s 1.

BATES Richard Terry b Stamford, Lincs, 17/6/72; RHB OS. Yet to make fc debut.

BRAMHALL Stephen b Warrington, 26/11/67; RHB WK; HS 37 not out; Ct 16; St 3.

i*CAIRNS Christopher Lance b Picton, New Zealand, 13/6/70; RHB RFM; HS 110 (for Northern Districts), 107 (for Notts); BB 7–34 (for Canterbury); 6–70 (for Notts); 100s 3; 50w 1; 5w/i 6; 10w/m 2. Tests 5.

CHAPMAN Robert James b Nottingham, 28/7/72; RHB RFM; HS O; BB 1–38.

CRAWLEY Mark Andrew b Newton-le-Willows, Lancs, 16/12/67; RHB RAS; HS 160 not out; BB 6–92 (for Oxford U), 3–18 (v Cambridge U), 3–38 (BAC); 100s 7; 1000r 1. Brother of J. P. (Lancs). Previous county: Lancashire (1990).

DESSAUR Wayne Anthony b Nottingham, 4/2/71; RHB RAS; HS 148 (v Cambridge U), 5 (BAC).

*EVANS Kevin Paul b Calverton, Nottingham, 10/9/63; RHB RAS; HS 104; BB 5–27; 100s 2; 5w/i 3.

FIELD-BUSS Michael Gwyn b Malta, 23/9/64; RHB OS; HS 34; BB 4–33. Previous county: Essex (1987).

*FRENCH Bruce Nicholas b Warsop, 13/8/59; RHB WK; HS 105 not out; 100s 1; Ct 767; St 85. Tests 16.

HINDSON James Edward b Huddersfield, 13/9/73; RHB SLA; BB 5–42 (v Cambridge U); 5w/i 1. Yet to make BAC debut.

*JOHNSON Paul b Newark, 24/4/65; RHB RAS; HS 165 not out; BB 1–9; 100s 22; 1000r 5. England A cap.

LEWIS Clairmonte Christopher b Georgetown, Guyana, 14/2/68; RHB RFM; HS 189 not out (for Leics), 134 not out (for Notts); BB 6–22 (for Leics v Oxford

U), 6–55 (for Leics, BAC), 6–90 (for Notts, BAC). 50w 2; 5wi 13; 10w/m 3. Tests 14. Previous county: Leicestershire (1987–91).

MIKE Gregory Wentworth b Nottingham, 14/7/66; RHB RAS; HS 61 not out; BB 3–48.

*NEWELL Michael b Blackburn, 25/2/65; RHB LS; HS 203 not out; BB 2–38 (v Sri Lanka), 1–0 (BAC).

PENNETT David Barrington b Leeds, 26/10/69; RHB RAS; HS 29; BB 4–58.

*PICK Robert Andrew b Nottingham, 19/11/63; LHB RFM; HS 63; BB 7–128; 50w 3; 5w/i 11; 10w/m 3. England A cap.

*POLLARD Paul Raymond b Carlton, 24/9/68; LHB RAS; HS 153 (v Cambridge U), 145 (BAC); BB 1–46; 100s 6; 1000r 2.

*RANDALL Derek William b Retford, 24/2/51; RHB RAS; HS 237; BB 3–15 (v MCC), 3–43 (BAC); 100s 52; 1000r 13. Tests 47.

†*ROBINSON Robert Timothy b Sutton-in-Ashfield, 21/11/58; RHB RAS; HS 220 not out; BB 1–22; 100s 46; 1000r 10. Captain since 1988. Tests 29.

SAXELBY Mark b Worksop, 4/1/69; LHB RM; HS 73 (v Cambridge U), 6 (BAC); BB 3–41.

WILEMAN Jonathan Ritchie b Sheffield, 19/8/70; RHB; HS 109 (v Cambridge U); 100s 1. Yet to make BAC debut.

Beneficiary '93: D. W. Randall.

In: R. J. Chapman, J. E. Hindson, D. B. Pennett, J. R. Wileman.
Out: B. C. Broad (Gloucs), K. E. Cooper (Gloucs), E. E. Hemmings (Sussex).

Colt to follow: G. F. Archer.

NOTTINGHAMSHIRE BAC AVERAGES 1992

BATTING	M	I	NO	Runs	HS	Av	100	50
R. T. Robinson	18	31	5	1510	189	58.08	4	8
C. C. Lewis	10	15	3	591	134*	49.25	2	3
G. F. Archer	6	11	2	424	117	47.11	1	3
P. Johnson	15	24	3	963	107*	45.86	2	7
B. C. Broad	13	25	3	1000	159*	45.45	5	0
C. L. Cairns	20	29	6	983	107*	42.74	2	6
D. W. Randall	18	27	3	865	133*	36.04	1	5
M. Saxelby	7	12	1	389	66	35.36	0	4
M. A. Crawley	22	39	7	1115	160*	34.84	3	4
P. R. Pollard	18	32	3	828	75	28.55	0	4
G. W. Mike	4	5	1	102	61*	25.50	0	1
K. P. Evans	18	22	4	419	104	23.28	1	2
E. E. Hemmings	7	11	5	132	52*	22.00	0	1
R. A. Pick	9	10	4	117	52	19.50	0	1
S. Bramhall	6	9	3	113	37*	18.83	0	0
B. N. French	16	18	3	246	55	16.40	0	1
D. B. Pennett	11	11	1	69	29	6.90	0	0
M. G. Field-Buss	7	7	2	27	13	5.40	0	0
J. A. Afford	15	15	5	33	12	3.30	0	0

Also batted: W. A. Dessaur (1 match) 1, 15. R. J. Chapman played in one match but did not bat.

BOWLING	O	M	R	W	Av	BB	5i	10m
C. C. Lewis	370.3	67	991	40	24.78	6–90	2	1
J. A. Afford	445.1	111	1434	43	33.35	6–68	1	1
E. E. Hemmings	259.5	95	602	18	33.44	4–30	0	0
G. W. Mike	68.2	9	276	8	34.50	3–48	0	0
C. L. Cairns	576.3	104	1945	54	36.02	6–70	2	0
D. B. Pennett	272.2	48	924	25	36.96	4–58	0	0
M. A. Crawley	206	52	601	16	37.56	3–38	0	0
K. P. Evans	558.5	123	1633	43	37.98	5–27	1	0
R. A. Pick	234.1	46	784	15	52.27	3–33	0	0
M. G. Field-Buss	159	24	571	10	57.10	4–71	0	0

Also bowled: R. J. Chapman 13–1–77–2, P. Johnson 5–0–30–0, P. R. Pollard 4–0–33–0, D. W. Randall 1–0–8–0, R. T. Robinson 1–0–4–0.

HUNDREDS (21)
5 – B. C. Broad: 104 v Warwicks (Trent Bridge), 117 v Derbys (Derby), 159* v Northants (Trent Bridge), 120 v Yorks (Scarborough), 122 v Leics (Leicester).
4 – R. T. Robinson: 100 v Northants (Trent Bridge), 164* v Durham (Trent Bridge), 189 v Warwicks (Edgbaston), 129* v Surrey (Trent Bridge).
3 – M. A. Crawley: 160* v Derbys (Derby), 102* v Kent (Maidstone), 115 v Worcs (Trent Bridge).
2 – C. L. Cairns: 102* v Lancs (Trent Bridge), 107* v Gloucs (Worksop). P. Johnson: 107* v Surrey (Oval), 107* v Warwicks (Edgbaston). C. C. Lewis: 134* v Northants (Northampton), 107 v Durham (Trent Bridge).
1 – G. F. Archer: 117 v Derbys (Trent Bridge). K. P. Evans: 104 v Surrey (Trent Bridge). D. W. Randall: 133* v Lancs (Trent Bridge).

SOMERSET

BAC position last five seasons: 9th; 17th; 15th; 14th; 11th.
Club formed: 1875.
Honours: Champions 0 (best 3rd, 1892, 1985, 1963, 1966, 1981); NWTGC 2 (1979, 1983); B&H 2 (1981–82); SL 1 (1979).

Suddenly, or so it seems, the clouds over Taunton are dispersing. For the first time in eight seasons, Somerset clambered into the top half of the Championship table last summer. They also earned their highest Sunday League placing since 1988 and reached the semi-finals of the Benson & Hedges Cup. Not bad considering only Gloucestershire had fewer capped members of their regular XI and Richard Snell's inexperience made him the least distinguished of the imports attracted to the County Ground down the years.

That the club saw fit to release so many players bespokes confidence in youth. And why not. Andy Caddick, Mark Lathwell, Harvey Trump and Andrew Cottam comprise a foursome long on punch and possibility if short on ring experience. An even greater degree of anticipation surrounds the acquisition of Mushtaq Ahmed. The fall of the Botham-Garner-Richards dynasty, distastefully achieved though it was, may soon have the desired long-term effect.

For now, though, the gestation period continues. The shallowness of the batting order, it must be said, does not nurture realistic visions of that elusive first Championship title. Neither does the back-up seam. There should nevertheless be much to enjoy in the latest steps taken by a breezy, exciting side.

Which brings us back to Lathwell. Deservedly voted Young Player of the Year last summer by his peers and (mostly) elders on the Cricketers' Association, this irrepressible opener captivated all who sighted him as he took wing with such verve and assurance in his first full season. That daring blade, wielded to impressive effect for England A in Australia will naturally provoke questions about application, but Somerset, to their eternal credit, seem quite happy to give him his head. Not that Lathwell, thankfully, seems too disposed to change his spots. Long may he reign.

The ability of Richard Harden to build on the advances of 1992 while cementing his claims to succeed Chris Tavaré as captain will also have a major say in the tenor of the season, and if Nick Folland's decision to trade teaching for runmaking works as well for him as his bravery warrants, last term's 64 batting points, second only to Lancashire's 75, could be exceeded.

The onus of translating bonuses into victories falls squarely into the laps of spin twins Mushtaq and Trump and the new ball team of Caddick and Neil Mallender. If the latter's belated and all-too-brief flirtation with the world of representative cricket – one that might easily have been extended to England's advantage in India – seems unlikely to develop into a meaningful romance, his county are unlikely to protest too much about that. But if Caddick's undoubted goods are not to be damaged by overwork Somerset sorely need Graham Rose to relocate his zip and Adrianus Van Troost to be less variable. That, though, may prove a common complaint for another season or so. The spirit of adventure should suffice while we wait.

CHAMPIONSHIP RATING: 2½ bats, three balls.
PREDICTED POSITION: 9th.

Overseas player: MUSHTAQ AHMED
Chubby cheeked, extremely competitive and remarkably self-assured for one so young, the precocious leg-spin and googly exponent who did so much to win the World Cup for Pakistan could provide as good a reason as any for setting foot inside a county ground this summer.

One glance at Mushtaq Ahmed's bubbly prance to the wicket and you can spot the brushstrokes of the old master, Abdul Qadir, a valued tutor. The variety of googlies at his fingertips – conventional leggies are shock rather than stock weapons – constitute another link with the best wrist-spinner of the post-Packer era.

In all other aspects Mushtaq is his own man. He was born in Sahiwal, far from Karachi and Lahore, a disadvantage best gauged by the fact that, until 1987, the ocean of land separating Pakistan's two principal cricketing centres had produced no more than seven Test representatives in 33 years. Like Waqar and Inzamam-ul-Haq, however, Mushtaq belongs to a new order. That is not to say he is entirely underprivileged. As a stocky 17–year-old schoolboy he took 6 for 81 against England in 1987, a feat which brought a job offer from United Bank. Instead of learning a trade, he was paid to practise his art.

Not for another five years would Mushtaq be ready, yet the timing of the entrance was exquisite. Armed with a CV detailing four wickets in three Tests, he set off for the Antipodes and enchanted the world. The World Cup's leading spinner and second highest wicket-taker – evidence of a mature command of line and length – then proceeded to England, where he mesmerised Robin Smith in particular and confused just about everyone else. And to think his best years are in front of him . . .

PLAYING STAFF 1993:

*BURNS Neil David b Chelmsford, 19/9/65; LHB WK; HS 166; 100s 4; Ct 275; St 28. Previous county: Essex (1986).

*CADDICK Andrew Richard b Christchurch, New Zealand, 21/11/68; RHB RFM; HS 54 not out; BB 6–52; 50w 1; 5w/i 3; 10w/m 1. England A cap.

COTTAM Andrew Colin b Northampton, 14/4/73; RHB SLA; HS 31; BB 1–1.

FLETCHER Ian b Sawbridgeworth, Herts, 31/8/71; RHB RAS; HS 56.

FOLLAND Nicholas Arthur b Bristol, 17/9/63; LHB LAS; HS 82 not out.

HALLETT Jeremy Charles b Yeovil, 18/10/70; RHB RAS; HS 15; BB 3–154.

*HARDEN Richard John b Bridgwater, 16/8/65; RHB LAS; HS 187; BB 2–7 (for Central Districts), 2–24 (BAC); 100s 15; 1000r 3.

*HAYHURST Andrew Neil b Davyhulme, Manchester, 23/11/62; RHB RAS; HS 172 not out; BB 4–27 (for Lancs) 3–27 (for Som); 100s 4; 1000r 2. Previous county: Lancashire (1985–89).

KERR Jason Ian Douglas b Bolton, 7/4/74; RHB RAS. Yet to make fc debut.

*LATHWELL Mark Nicholas b Bletchley, Bucks, 261271; RHB RAS; HS 114; BB 1–9. England A cap.

*MALLENDER Neil Alan b Kirk Sandall, Yorks, 13/8/61; RHB RAS; HS 100 not out (for Otago), 87 not out (for Som); BB 7–27 (for Otago), 7–41 (for North), 7–61 (for Som); 100s 1; 50w 6; 5w/i 33; 10w/m 5. Tests 2. Previous county: Northamptonshire (1980–86).

¡MUSHTAQ AHMED b Sahiwal, Pakistan, 28/6/70; RHB LS; HS 75 (for Multan); BB 9–93 (for Multan); 5w/i 7; 10w/m 2. Tests 8. Yet to make debut for Somerset.

PARSONS Keith Alan b Taunton, 2/5/73; RHB RAS; HS 1 (v Pakistan). Yet to make BAC debut.

PARSONS Kevin John b Taunton, 2/5/73; RHB. Identical twin to K. A. Parsons. Yet to make fc debut.

PAYNE Andrew b Rossendale, Lancs, 20/10/73; RHB RAS; HS 51 not out; BB 1–71.

*ROSE Graham David b Tottenham, London, 12/4/64: RHB RAS; HS 132; BB 6–41 (for Middx), 6–47 (for Som); 100s 3; 1000r 1; 50w 2; 5w/i 4. Previous county: Middlesex (1985–86).

†*TAVARE Christopher James b Orpington, Kent, 27/10/54; RHB RAS; HS 219; BB 1–3 (for Kent); 100s 47; 1000r 16. Captain since 1990. Previous county: Kent (1974–88, captain 1983–84).

TRESCOTHICK Marcus b Bristol, 25/12/75; RHB. Yet to make fc debut.

TRUMP Harvey Russell John b Taunton, 11/10/68; RHB OS; HS 48; BB 7–52; 50w 1; 5w/i 6; 10w/m 1; hat-trick 1.

TURNER Robert Julian b Malvern, Worcs, 25/11/67; RHB WK; HS 101 not out; 100s 1; Ct 42; St 12.

VAN TROOST Adrianus Pelrus b Schiedam, Netherlands, 2/10/72; RHB RAS; HS 12; BB 6–48; 5w/i 2.

WHITE Giles William b Barnstaple, 23/3/72; RHB LS; HS 42 (v Sri Lanka); BB 1–30 (v Sri Lanka). Yet to make BAC debut.

In: Mushtaq Ahmed.
Out: R. J. Bartlett, R. P. Lefebvre (Glamorgan), K. H. MacLeay, M. F. Robinson, R. P. Snell, G. T. J. Townsend.

Player of the Year 1992: M. N. Lathwell.
Colt to follow: H. R. J. Trump.

SOMERSET BAC AVERAGES 1992

BATTING	M	I	NO	Runs	HS	Av	100	50
R. J. Turner	7	10	5	286	101*	57.20	1	1
R. J. Harden	19	31	5	1321	187	50.81	3	6
C. J. Tavaré	21	32	2	1157	125	38.57	3	6
M. N. Lathwell	19	33	1	1176	114	36.75	1	11
N. D. Burns	21	31	11	709	73*	35.45	0	4
A. N. Hayhurst	22	36	2	1167	102	34.32	1	9
G. D. Rose	21	32	4	925	132	33.04	1	6
R. J. Bartlett	7	11	0	327	72	29.73	0	2
K. H. MacLeay	11	17	3	386	74	27.57	0	3
R. P. Snell	16	20	4	436	81	27.25	0	3
G. T. J. Townsend	6	11	1	252	49	25.20	0	0
A. R. Caddick	19	17	5	246	54*	20.50	0	1
R. P. Lefebvre	3	4	0	70	36	17.50	0	0
H. R. J. Trump	17	16	7	142	28	15.78	0	0
A. P. van Troost	10	7	5	30	12	15.00	0	0
N. A. Mallender	15	18	5	182	29*	14.00	0	0
A. C. Cottam	6	8	1	43	31	6.14	0	0

Also batted: N. A. Folland (1 match) 22, 82*, A. Payne (1) 51*.

BOWLING	O	M	R	W	Av	BB	5i	10m
R. P. Lefebvre	41	11	96	5	19.20	2–33	0	0
N. A. Mallender	361.4	74	1067	45	23.71	5–29	3	0
A. R. Caddick	558.2	94	1797	64	28.08	6–52	2	1
K. H. MacLeay	107	27	286	9	31.78	2–33	0	0
H. R. J. Trump	553	133	1558	49	31.80	7–52	2	1
A. P. van Troost	155.4	17	695	18	38.61	6–48	2	0
R. P. Snell	339.1	60	1194	27	44.22	3–29	0	0
A. C. Cottam	116.1	25	280	6	46.67	1–1	0	0
G. D. Rose	373	77	1179	24	49.13	4–59	0	0
A. N. Hayhurst	137	28	403	8	50.38	3–27	0	0

Also bowled: R. J. Harden 3–0–31–0, M. N. Lathwell 64–14–224–4, A. Payne 27–8–71–1, C. J. Tavaré 3.2–0–33–0, R. J. Turner 2.1–0–26–0.

HUNDREDS (10)
3 – R. J. Harden: 166* v Derbys (Taunton), 126 v Durham (Taunton), 187 v Notts (Taunton). C. J. Tavaré: 115 v Hants (Weston-super-Mare), 124 v Durham (Taunton), 125 v Notts (Taunton).
1 – A. N. Hayhurst: 102 v Durham (Taunton). M. N. Lathwell: 114 v Surrey (Bath). G. D. Rose: 132 v Surrey (Oval). R. J. Turner: 101* v Notts (Taunton).

SURREY

BAC position last five seasons: 13th; 5th; 9th; 12th; 4th.
Club formed: 1845.
Honours: Champions 18 (1864, 1887–88, 1890–92, 1894–95, 1899, 1914, 1952–58, 1971) plus 1 shared (1950); NWTGC 1 (1982); B&H 1 (1974); SL 0 (best: 4th, 1992).

Like near-neighbours Crystal Palace FC in another field of sporting expertise, Surrey were supposed to be the Team of the Nineties. Unlike their footballing counterparts they are still in with a shout of proving the prophets right. 1993, furthermore, figures prominently in the tea leaves.

One has to go back four decades to trace the last Oval side to strike fear into the opposition. Mind you, it was not so much fear as dread while Bedser was swinging, Laker was turning and May was marching. Seven consecutive Championship titles were claimed between George VI's final year on the throne and the crowning of Pope John XXIII. Save for Micky Stewart's 1971 combination, no successor has managed to throw off the yoke of expectation. How appropriate, then, that Stewart Junior, now perhaps the most self-assured cricketer England possesses outside Botham, should be leading a side capable of doing just that.

Should this summer usher in a new period of prosperity, we can take it as read that the return of the rich man's Rudi Bryson, Waqar Younis, will feature strongly in the credits. Yet Alec Stewart will be conducting an orchestra strong on able soloists. Question marks, however, linger over the opening spot Graham Clinton vacated in 1990, while seam resources are not ideal, even if there is more quality than width. Should Martin Bicknell's shoulder go, never mind Waqar's back, the loss could be irreparable. Surrey would have gone a lot closer to the 1991 pennant had the former not sat out a third of the season.

The best-case scenario for the batting sees Stewart making hay before he goes away, sturdy foundations being dug by Graham Thorpe, David Ward and Darren Bicknell (one of only four players to make 1,000 one-day runs in 1992), then over to Monte Lynch and Alistair Brown to plug in the electricity. Light of foot and heavy of clout, the impish Brown gives the ball an even heartier lash than Lathwell. He may lack the poise of the Somerset opener, but there was enough rousing fare in his first half-season to give notice of fun and games to come.

The Kennington faithful have been awaiting the new Lock and Laker for a generation, yet while Neil Kendrick and James Boiling have a way to go, they do appear to have what it takes to evolve into the best slow left-arm offspin duo the county have fielded since the hell-raising days of the L-Force. If anything, Kendrick was unlucky not to receive the A-team summons dispatched to Boiling when Ian Salisbury was kept on in India. The more aggressive and outwardly confident of the two, Kendrick has a lot of the Edmonds and Tufnell about him, which is, of course, virtually a guarantee of stardom and notoriety. Both bat capably, and few edges elude Boiling in the gully. All in all, there is a whole team coming nicely to the boil behind the Hobbs Gates.

CHAMPIONSHIP RATING: four bats, four balls.
PREDICTED POSITION: Champions.

Overseas player: WAQAR YOUNIS
First there was confusion over the name. Younis or Younus? Then came the age debate, just as it always does when the subcontinent contributes a new star to the constellation. How could anyone so young be so good? Then the ball-tampering furore. Only Curtly Ambrose, however, can seriously contest the assertion that Waqar Younis is currently the world's most dangerous bowler.

From the top of that long, scampering run to the flurry of limbs at the point of delivery, left arm pointing straight to the heavens, there is a blend of the bestial and the celestial about Waqar. True, he has none of Holding's effortlessness, nor the diversity of Lillee and Marshall, but when your holster contains the most lethal swinging yorker the game has ever known, who cares?

Not since Andy Roberts harvested 119 wickets at 13.62 runs apiece for Hampshire in 1974 has anyone taken as many wickets in one summer for so little cost as the 113 Waqar grabbed for 14.65 a throw in 1991. At his best, such as that Saturday at Leeds last July when he sent England slithering from 292 for 2 to 320 all out, he is simply irresistible. At 21 (officially), his count was 102 wickets in 20 Tests, most of them with the old ball, when Pakistan appointed him vice-captain for their recent Caribbean tour.

Perhaps the most pertinent statistic of all is the number of times he has done the job alone. Of those first 102 Test victims, 34 had their stumps scattered and 30 failed to remove their feet from harm's way. Only another Surrey destroyer of a bygone age, Tom Richardson, has ever bettered Waqar's proportion of bowleds and lbws, and he called it a day after 88 wickets. Back permitting, there is every chance that, by the time he is done, Waqar will have compelled the guardians of the record books to exhaust their supply of Tipp-Ex.

PLAYING STAFF 1993:

ALIKHAN Rehan Iqbal b Westminster, London, 28/12/62; RHB RAS; HS 138; BB 2-19 (for Sussex), 2-43; 100s 2; 1000r 1. Previous county: Sussex (1986-88).

ATKINS Paul David b Aylesbury, Bucks, 11/6/66; RHB OS; HS 114 not out (v Cambridge U), 99 (BAC); 100s 1.

BAINBRIDGE Mark Robert b Isleworth, Middx, 11/5/73; RHB SLA. Yet to make fc debut.

BENJAMIN Joseph Emmanuel b Christ Church, St Kitts, 2/2/61; RHB RFM; HS 42; BB 6-30; 5w/i 6. Previous county: Warwickshire (1988-91).

*BICKNELL Darren John b Guildford, 24/6/67; LHB LAS; HS 186; BB 2-62; 100s 17; 1000r 4. England A cap.

*BICKNELL Martin Paul b Guildford, 14/1/69; RHB RFM; HS 88; BB 9-45 (v Cambridge U), 7-52 (BAC); 50w 4; 5w/i 13. Brother of D. J. England A cap.

BOILING James b New Delhi, India, 8/4/68; RHB OS; HS 29; BB 6-84; 5w/i 1. England A cap.

BROWN Alistair Duncan b Beckenham, Kent, 11/2/70; RHB LS; HS 175; 100s 3.

BUTCHER Mark Alan b Croydon, 23/8/72; LHB RAS; HS 47; BB 1-95. Son of A. R. (Essex) and brother of G. P. (Glamorgan).

HOLLIOAKE Adam John b Melbourne, Australia, 5/9/71. RHB RM. Yet to make fc debut.

KELLEHER Daniel John Michael b Southwark, London, 5/5/66; RHB RAS; HS 53 not out (for Kent); BB 6-109 (for Kent); 5w/i 2. Previous county: Kent (1987-91). Yet to make Surrey debut.

KENDRICK Neil Michael b Bromley, 11/11/67; RHB SLA; HS 55; BB 6–61; 5w/i 5; 10w/m 1.

KERSEY Graham James b Plumstead, London, 19/5/71; RHB WK; HS 27 not out; Ct 14; St 1.

*LYNCH Monte Alan b Georgetown, Guyana, 21/5/58; RHB OS; HS 172 not out; BB 3–6; 100s 34; 1000r 9.

MURPHY Anthony John b Manchester, 6/8/62; RHB RAS; HS 38; BB 6–97; 50w 1; 5w/i 5. Previous county: Lancashire (1985–88).

SARGEANT Neil Fredrick b Hammersmith, London, 8/11/65; RHB WK; HS 49; Ct 91; St 16.

SMITH Andrew William b Cheam, 30/5/69; RHB OS. Yet to make fc debut.

†*STEWART Alec James b Merton, 8/4/63; RHB WK; HS 206 not out; BB 1–7; 100s 23; 1000r 7; Ct 278; St 6. Captain since 1992. Tests 22.

*THORPE Graham Paul b Farnham, 1/8/69; LHB RAS; HS 216, BB 2–31; 100s 10; 1000r 3. England A cap.

*i*WAQAR YOUNIS b Burewala, Punjab, 16/11/71; RHB RF; HS 31; BB 7–64 (for United Bank), 7–73 (for Surr); 100w 1; 50w 2; 5w/i 32; 10w/m 8. Tests 19.

*WARD David Mark b Croydon, 10/2/61; RHB OS WK; HS 263; BB 2–66; 100s 14; 1000r 2.

WARD Ian b Plymouth, 30/9/72; LHB RM.

Testimonial '93: H. T. Brind (head groundsman).
In: Waqar Younis (returning), D. J. M. Kelleher, I. J. Ward.
Out: R. E. Bryson, M. A. Feltham (Middlesex), I. A. Greig (retired), D. G. C. Ligertwood, K. T. Medlycott, J. D. Robinson.

Player of the Year 1992: G. P. Thorpe.
Colt to follow: A. D. Brown.

SURREY BAC AVERAGES 1992

BATTING	M	I	NO	Runs	HS	Av	100	50
A. D. Brown	11	16	1	740	175	49.33	3	3
G. P. Thorpe	22	39	3	1749	216	48.58	2	13
M. A. Lynch	22	39	6	1404	107	42.55	3	7
A. J. Stewart	13	24	3	766	140	36.48	1	5
D. J. Bicknell	22	40	5	1176	120*	33.60	1	7
D. M. Ward	17	28	5	756	138	32.87	2	1
M. A. Feltham	12	17	5	392	50	32.67	0	1
P. D. Atkins	7	14	0	382	99	27.29	0	2
J. D. Robinson	9	17	5	307	65*	25.58	0	2
M. P. Bicknell	18	25	8	426	88	25.06	0	2
R. E. Bryson	10	13	2	257	76	23.36	0	1
J. Boiling	18	21	11	190	29	19.00	0	0
N. M. Kendrick	16	20	4	300	55	18.75	0	2
A. J. Murphy	5	5	2	45	32	15.00	0	0
N. F. Sargeant	14	19	4	176	30	11.73	0	0
J. E. Benjamin	18	18	8	116	42	11.60	0	0
D. G. C. Ligertwood	4	7	0	63	28	9.00	0	0

Also batted: M. A. Butcher (2 matches) 5*, 47; I. J. Ward (1) 0.

BOWLING	O	M	R	W	Av	BB	5i	10m
M. P. Bicknell	597.5	107	1734	67	25.88	6–107	4	0
J. D. Robinson	93.4	14	341	13	26.23	3–22	0	0
N. M. Kendrick	557.1	161	1464	48	30.50	6–61	3	0
J. Boiling	557.2	143	1506	41	36.73	6–84	1	1
J. E. Benjamin	582.2	94	1780	45	39.56	6–30	2	0
M. A. Feltham	310.1	57	1071	23	46.57	4–75	0	0
A. J. Murphy	178.4	34	531	11	48.27	3–97	0	0
R. E. Bryson	305.4	36	1165	17	68.53	5–117	1	0

Also bowled: D. J. Bicknell 9.2–0–90–0, A. D. Brown 16–1–78–0, M. A. Butcher 44–10–115–1, M. A. Lynch 21–4–85–1, A. J. Stewart 7–1–14–0, G. P. Thorpe 17.4–5–79–0, D. M. Ward 4–0–16–0, I. J. Ward 8–0–35–0.

HUNDREDS (12)

3 – A. D. Brown: 111 v Notts (Oval), 175 v Durham (Durham Univ), 129 v Somerset (Oval). M. A. Lynch: 107 v Worcs (Oval), 106 v Leics (Oval), 102 v Essex (Colchester).

2 – G. P. Thorpe: 216 v Somerset (Oval), 100 v Notts (Trent Bridge). D. M. Ward: 103* v Northants (Oval), 138 v Glam (Neath).

1 – D. J. Bicknell: 120* v Lancs (Lytham). A. J. Stewart: 140 v Sussex (Oval).

SUSSEX

BAC position last five seasons: 7th; 11th; 17th; 10th; 16th.
Club formed: 1839.
Honours: Champions 0 (best: 2nd, 1902–03, 1932–34, 1953, 1981); NWTGC 4 (1963–64, 1978, 1986); B&H 0 (best: semi-finals, 1982); SL 1 (1982).

With the exception of Somerset, Sussex had dwelt longer in the bottom half of the table than any other county until 1992. The last time they occupied such a relatively lofty perch, in fact, was in 1985, a season that ended in a blaze of resignations and sackings. Nearly a decade on, the rebuilding, overseen by the sagacious England A coach, Norman Gifford, is not that far off completion.

Think of Hove these days and one name springs instantly to mind: Ian Salisbury. Here is that glorious anachronism, a good English leg-spinner. Mike Atherton was limbering up promisingly until his back problems started, but up to last June the only specialist to represent Queen and country for three decades had been Robin Hobbs, and the Essex man's Test career was done and dusted by 1971. To the romantically-inclined, therefore, Salisbury's debut at Lord's last year was one to cherish. The 87 first-class wickets, 23 of which came in the final two Championship fixtures, set the seal on an *annus mirabilis*. Although he has yet to acquire Mushtaq's range of googlies, the repertoire is enlarging as self-belief takes root. A fine fielder and dogged bat, the boy Northamptonshire let go is poised to stamp a lasting mark on his chosen profession.

Martin Speight adds further splashes of colour. Often too reckless for his own good – let alone that of his team – this Durham University graduate experienced a radical transformation last year, one entirely for the better. In each of the past two seasons he has reached fifty on five occasions, but whereas in 1991 he fell short of three figures every time, 1992 saw him go all the way every time. A shade less impetuosity and a dash more concentration could work wonders. In fact, he could do worse than take a tutorial or two from his captain, Alan Wells, whose first year at the helm was an object lesson in riding two horses with one behind.

Plagued by injury, the elder Wells, Colin, may not play that active a part in his benefit year now that Franklyn Stephenson has assumed the all-rounder's mantle, but the rest of the batting is sound enough. Jamie Hall and David Smith are a versatile opening pair with a good understanding, wicketkeeper Peter Moores is fresh from his most productive season, and Neil Lenham is coming into his own. Bill Athey, captured after much to-ing and fro-ing with the TCCB registration committee, has long come into his, and may prove a canny short-term investment even if his sell-by date is not that far off.

Undermined by a similar lack of youth, the bowling raises more doubts. A fit Adrian Jones and a few old tricks from Eddie Hemmings – now, incidentally, the most venerable player on the circuit at 44 – will make a sizeable difference, but for all the zest Ed Giddins brought to it towards the end of last summer, the attack could be rather lightweight should its focal point, Salisbury, be yanked away for national service.

With Salisbury on tap, Stephenson on fire and Speight and Wells junior on a roll, Sussex have a crew able to test the Championship-chasing fleet. Like Somerset, however, they appear to have too many holes for a successful pursuit of their Holy Grail.

CHAMPIONSHIP RATING: three bats, 2½ balls.
PREDICTED POSITION: 10th.

Overseas player: FRANKLYN STEPHENSON

Whatever else he does as a cricketer, Franklyn Stephenson seems destined for immortality. In 1988, during his first season at Trent Bridge, he completed the 'double' of 1,000 runs and 100 wickets by rattling up a century in each innings of the final match. Not a bad way to step into the shoes of Richard Hadlee, the only other man to accomplish this once commonplace feat since the reduction of the Championship programme in 1969 cut the number of opportunities for innings and overs. Now that they have tumbled even further, Stephenson's landmark looks as secure as the Bank of England once did.

At 34, this enormous bearded Bajan is fast approaching the unsaddling enclosure as a full-time all-rounder. Yet although sustaining pace can be problematic, and that legendary slower ball is becoming a mite predictable, Stephenson demonstrated last season that he can still make batsmen hop about and bowlers cower, as illustrated by an 11–wicket bag at Worcester and a blistering 133 when Somerset came to Hove.

He could, and should, have been a Test player. Acclaimed in some quarters as a potential new Sobers, the pretender opted to take the rand and run to South Africa, for which he earned a 'lifetime' ban. Even when it was lifted the call never came. That the gap remains, leaving the present West Indies tail both long and limp, may or may not console him. Knowing that he has enriched the county game ought to.

PLAYING STAFF 1993:

ATHEY Charles William Jeffrey b Middlesbrough, 27/9/57; RHB RAS; HS 184 (for England B), 171 not out (for Gloucs); BB 3–3 (for Gloucs); 100s 42; 1000r 10. Tests 23. Previous counties: Yorkshire (1976–83), Gloucestershire (1984–92, captain 1989). Yet to make debut for Sussex.

DEAN Jacob Winston b Cuckfield, 23/8/70; RHB SLA. Yet to make fc debut.

DONELAN Bradleigh Thomas b Park Royal, Middx, 3168; RHB OS; HS 68 not out; BB 6–62; 5w/i 3; 10w/m 1.

GIDDINS Edward Simon Hunter b Eastbourne, 20/7/71; RHB RFM; HS 14 not out; BB 5–32; 5w/i 2.

GREENFIELD Keith b Brighton 6/12/68; RHB RAS; HS 127 not out (v Cambridge U), 64 (BAC). 100s 1.

*HALL James William b Chichester, 30/3/68; RHB OS; HS 140 not out; 100s 4; 1000r 2.

HEMMINGS Edward Ernest b Leamington Spa, 20/2/49; RHB OS; HS 127 not out for Notts; BB 10–175 (for International XI), 7–23 (for Notts); 100s 1; 50w 14; 5w/i 66; 10wm 14. Tests 16. Previous counties: Warwickshire (1966–78), Nottinghamshire (1979–92). Yet to make debut for Sussex.

HUMPHRIES Shaun b Horsham, 11/1/73; RHB WK. Yet to make fc debut.

*JONES Adrian Nicholas b Woking, Surrey, 22/7/61; LHB RFM; HS 43 not out (for Som), 35 (for Suss); BB 7–30 (for Som), 5–29 (for Suss); 50w 5; 5w/i 12; 10w/m 1. Previous counties: Sussex (1981–86), Somerset (1987–90).

LAW Danny b London, 15/7/75; RHB RFM. Yet to make fc debut.

*LENHAM Neil John b Worthing, 17/12/65; RHB RAS; HS 222 not out; BB 4–85; 100s 13; 1000r 3.

*MOORES Peter b Macclesfield, Cheshire, 18/12/62; RHB WK; HS 116; 100s 4; Ct 270; St 34. Previous county: Worcestershire (1983–84).

NEWELL Keith b Crawley, 25/3/72; RHB RAS. Yet to make fc debut.

NORTH John Andrew b Slindon, 19/11/70; RHB RAS; HS 63 not out; BB 4–47 (v Sri Lanka), 3–51 (BAC).

PEIRCE Toby b Maidenhead, 14/6/73; LHB SLA. Yet to make fc debut.

*PIGOTT Anthony Charles Shackleton b London, 4668; RHB RFM; HS 104 not out; BB 7–74; 100s 1; 50w 5; 5w/i 23; 10w/m 1; hat-trick 1 (first fc wkts). Tests 1.

REMY Carlos Charles b Castries, St Lucia, 24/7/68; RHB RAS; HS 47; BB 4–63 (v Cambridge U), 3–27 (BAC).

ROBSON Andrew George b Boldon, Co Durham, 27/4/71; RHB RFM; HS 3 (for Surr), 0 not out (for Suss); BB 4–37. Previous county: Surrey (1991).

*SALISBURY Ian David Kenneth b Northampton, 21/1/70; RHB LS; HS 68; BB 7–54; 50w 1; 5wi 9; 10wm 2. Cricket Writers' Club Young Player of the Year 1992. Tests 2.

*SMITH David Mark b Balham, London, 9/1/56; LHB RAS; HS 213; BB 3–40 (for Surr); 100s 7; 1000r 27. Tests 2. Previous counties: Surrey (1973–83 and 1987–88), Worcestershire (1984–86).

*SPEIGHT Martin Peter b Walsall, 24/10/67; RHB WK; HS 179; 100s 8; 1000r 1.

*i*STEPHENSON Franklyn Dacosta b St James, Barbados, 8/4/59; RHB RFM; HS 165 (for Barbados), 133 (for Suss); 100s 6; 1000r 1; 50w 4; 5w/i 33; 10w/m

8. Achieved 'double' of 1000r and 100w in 1988, last player to do so. Previous counties: Gloucestershire (1982–83), Nottinghamshire (1988–91).

†*WELLS Alan Peter b Newhaven, 2/10/61; RHB RAS; HS 253 not out; BB 3–67; 100s 26; 1000r 7. Captain since 1992. Brother of CM.

*WELLS Colin Mark b Newhaven, 3/3/60; RHB RAS; HS 203; BB 7–42; 100s 20; 1000r 6; 50w 2; 5w/i 7. Brother of AP.

Beneficiary '93: C. M. Wells.

In: C. M. J. Athey (Gloucs), E. E. Hemmings (Notts), S. Humphries, D. Law, K. Newell, T. Peirce.
Out: R. Hanley, A. R. Hansford.

Player of the Year 1992: F. W. Stephenson.
Colt to follow: M. P. Speight.

SUSSEX BAC AVERAGES 1992

BATTING	M	I	NO	Runs	HS	Av	100	50
A. P. Wells	22	35	5	1465	165*	48.83	5	4
J. W. Hall	20	34	5	1125	140*	38.79	1	8
M. P. Speight	20	33	2	1180	179	38.06	5	0
N. J. Lenham	20	34	2	1173	222*	36.66	4	3
D. M. Smith	19	33	2	1076	213	34.71	2	5
P. Moores	21	30	5	851	109	34.04	1	3
F. D. Stephenson	18	25	4	680	133	32.38	1	2
K. Greenfield	6	10	2	205	48	25.63	0	0
C. M. Wells	6	7	1	133	39	22.17	0	0
B. T. P. Donelan	16	25	6	421	68*	22.16	0	2
C. C. Remy	7	9	0	192	47	21.33	0	0
A. C. S. Pigott	17	19	7	191	27*	15.92	0	0
A. J. North	5	7	1	81	53*	13.50	0	1
A. N. Jones	10	9	4	56	17	11.20	0	0
I. D. K. Salisbury	17	18	2	177	42	11.06	0	0
E. S. H. Giddins	11	8	6	15	10*	7.50	0	0
A. G. Robson	5	4	3	0	0*	0.00	0	0

Also batted: R. Hanley (1 match) 1; A. R. Hansford (1) 1.

BOWLING	O	M	R	W	Av	BB	5i	10m
I. D. K. Salisbury	678.3	169	2135	79	27.03	7–54	6	2
E. S. H. Giddins	247.5	52	857	31	27.65	5–32	2	0
J. A. North	96.3	14	331	11	30.09	3–51	0	0
C. M. Wells	119	26	323	10	32.30	3–26	0	0
F. D. Stephenson	467.2	93	1375	40	34.38	7–29	1	1
A. C. S. Pigott	363	74	1063	27	39.37	3–34	0	0
B. T. P. Donelan	404	85	1323	28	47.25	6–77	1	0
A. G. Robson	119	24	405	8	50.63	4–37	0	0
C. C. Remy	96.2	12	36	6	56.00	3–27	0	0
N. J. Lenham	120.1	28	362	6	60.33	2–61	0	0
A. N. Jones	161.5	17	745	11	67.73	3–76	0	0

Also bowled: K. Greenfield 17–0–84–0, J. W. Hall 2–1–14–0, A. R. Hansford 29–5–81–3, D. M. Smith 4–1–18–0, M. P. Speight 3–0–30–1, A. P. Wells 29–7–94–0.

HUNDREDS (19)
5 – M. P. Speight: 166 v Notts (Trent Bridge), 119* v Lancs (Hove), 122 v Somerset (Taunton), 179 v Glam (Eastbourne), 126 v Essex (Hove). A. P. Wells: 144 v Kent (Hove), 165* v Surrey (Oval), 115 v Warwicks (Hove), 103 v Somerset (Taunton), 143 v Lancs (Old Trafford).
4 – N. J. Lenham: 222* v Kent (Hove), 118 v Durham (Horsham), 136 v Lancs (Old Trafford), 135 v Yorks (Hove).
2 – D. M. Smith: 213 v Essex (Southend), 105 v Lancs (Hove).
1 – J. W. Hall: 140* v Lancs (Hove). P. Moores: 109 v Essex (Southend). F. D. Stephenson: 133 v Somerset (Hove).

WARWICKSHIRE

BAC position last five seasons: 6th; 2nd; 5th; 8th; 6th.
Club formed: 1882.
Honours: Champions 3 (1911, 1951, 1972); NWTGC 3 (1966, 1968, 1989); B&H 0 (best: finalists, 1984); SL 1 (1980).

Over the past five seasons Warwickshire's Championship record has been second only to that of Essex, no mean feat given so few runs in the bank and so little breadth to the attack. Their debt to Allan Donald, Tim Munton and Gladstone Small extends beyond the 815 wickets accumulated since 1988 by the country's most incisive strike trio.

It is, to be honest, a slightly unhealthy dependence. Last term, the invigorating if erratic Paul Smith afforded glimpses of his true ability – with ball if not bat – and the county will have been relieved to hang on to him after all the rumours of a move back to his native north-east. But unless Roger Twose continues to make a mockery of his journeyman image, the main seamers are likely to have to do it all, again. Neil Smith is a more than useful exponent of the one-day game but his brand of spin is too plain for more leisurely contests, as is Paul Booth's. One 'five-fer' each in a combined total of 92 first-class appearances does not augur well. Should Donald or Munton break down, the entire engine may cut out.

Without undergoing any changes of personnel, the batting will have greater substance about it now that Trevor Penney has a first-class season under his belt. An athletic fielder and strident bat, this slender young Zimbabwean completed his residential qualification period in 1991 and did enough to suggest he can emulate Graeme Hick. How his country must regret not attaining Test status earlier. Had they done so after the 1983 World Cup, as many felt was their due, they might have taken on India and New Zealand with Hick, Penney and Curran playing alongside Traicos, Houghton, Rawson and the Flower brothers. Makes you weep.

So does the treatment meted out to Andy Lloyd, relieved as captain with two games of 1992 to go. The man with the shortest Test career of all – 33 minutes – has been released yo concentrate on his business interests. Twose and the ever-improving Dominic Ostler, should keep the runs ticking over but this could be a make-or-break year for opener Jason Ratcliffe. The Warwickshire order has delivered only a dozen individual centuries in the last two summers and the new format looks like being a stern test of fibre. If the going gets tough, the choice between Keith Piper's superior gloves and Piran Holloway's broader bat could provide an intriguing sub-plot behind the stumps.

Acceleration, less important in the four-day game, will revolve once more around the new captain, Dermot Reeve. Kowloon's sole contribution to Test cricket probably does not quite have enough to offer as either batsman or bowler to be among the first 11 names to pop into the selectors' heads. What he does peddle is infectious energy, flair, an endearing swagger and an inspirational air, best suited to the shorter course. He leads a side with hope of higher things, if not quite the wherewithal for fulfilment.

CHAMPIONSHIP RATING: three bats, 3½ balls.
PREDICTED POSITION: 5th.

Overseas player: ALLAN DONALD
One benefit of the arguably premature decision to welcome South Africa back to the International Cricket Council was that it enabled Allan Donald to become a hero in his own land. Throughout English cricket his name is held in reverence; he is the fastest white bowler in the business, according to the world and his wife. In the Republic, strange to report, he was merely a reasonably well-known fast bowler from Bloemfontein until last winter.

At that point Donald had already collected 546 first-class wickets at barely 23 runs apiece, right up there with Wasim, Waqar and Curtly. It was clear, moreover, that this comparative anonymity would alter dramatically once Test matches returned to Newlands and Cape Town. Sure enough, by the end of South Africa's first Test series for 23 long years, Donald was as famous back home as his quacking namesake. The dominant figure of a drab rubber and the most successful bowler on either side, his 20 wickets (at 19.70) included 12 for 139 at Port Elizabeth to engineer the only conclusive result. Eliciting a fair degree of movement from that scrupulously good length, he also helped wicketkeeper David Richardson to two-thirds of his national Test record collection of nine catches. Above all, the fourth best analysis by a South African at this level confirmed the sheer speed of the manufacturer. As assets go, what more – bar good health – can a 26–year-old fast bowler ask for?

PLAYING STAFF 1993:

*ASIF DIN Mohamed b Kampala, Uganda, 21/9/60; RHB LS; HS 158 not out (v Cambridge U), 140 (BAC); BB 5–100; 100s 2; 1000r 2; 5w/i 1.

BELL Michael Anthony Vincent b Birmingham, 19/12/67; LAS; HS 5; BB 3–78.

BOOTH Paul Antony b Huddersfield, 5/9/65; LHB SLA; HS 62; BB 5–98 (for Yorks), 4–29 (for Warw): 5w/i 1. Previous county: Yorkshire (1982–89).

BROWN Douglas Robert b Stirling, Scotland, 29/10/69; RHB RAS; HS 44 not out (for Scotland), 5 not out (for Warw, v Cambridge U). Yet to make BAC debut.

BURNS Michael b Barrow-in-Furness, Lancs, 2/6/69; RHB WK; HS 78 (v Cambridge U), 4 (BAC). Ct 8.

ï*DONALD Allan Anthony b Bloemfontein, South Africa, 20/10/66; RHB RF; HS 46 not out (for Orange Free State), 41 (for Warw); BB 8–37 (for OFS), 7–37 (for Warw); 5w/i 30; 10w/m 3. Tests 1.

GILES Ashley b Ripley, Surrey, 19/3/73; RHB SLA. Yet to make fc debut.

HOLLOWAY Piran Christopher Laity b Helston, Cornwall, 11070; LHB WK; HS 102 not out; 100s 1; Ct 25; St 1.

KHAN Wasim Gulzar b Birmingham, 26/2/71, LHB LS. Yet to make fc debut.

*MOLES Andrew James b Solihull, 12/2/61; RHB RAS; HS 230 not out (for Griqualand West), 224 not out (BAC); BB 3–21 (v Oxford U), 3–50 (BAC).

MULRAINE Charles b Leamington Spa, 24/12/73; LHB. Yet to make fc debut.

*MUNTON Timothy Alan b Melton Mowbray, Leics, 30/7/65; RHB RAS; HS 47; BB 8–89; 50w 4; 5w/i 14; 10w/m 3. Tests 2.

*OSTLER Dominic Piers b Solihull, 15/7/70; RHB RAS; HS 192; 100s 4; 1000r 2.

PENNEY Trevor Lionel b Harare, Zimbabwe, 12/6/68; RHB LS; HS 151. 100s 3.

*PIPER Keith John b Leicester, 18/12/69; RHB WK; HS 111; BB 1–57; 100s 1; Ct 155; St 7.

RATCLIFFE Jason David b Solihull, 19/6/69; RHB RAS; HS 127 not out (v Cambridge U), 94 (BAC); 100s 2.

†*REEVE Dermot Alexander b Kowloon, Hong Kong, 2/4/63; RHB RAS; HS 202 not out; BB 7–37 (for Suss), 6–73 (for Warw); 100s 5; 1000r 2; 50w 2; 5w/i 6. Appointed captain for 1993. Tests 3. Previous county: Sussex (1983–87).

ROBINSON Matthew b Cardiff, 2/4/73; RHB RAS. Yet to make fc debut.

*SMALL Gladstone Cleophas b St George, Barbados, 18/10/61; RHB RAS; HS 70; BB 7–15; 50w 6; 5w/i 27; 10w/m 2. Tests 17.

SMITH Neil Michael Knight b Solihull, 27/7/67; RHB OS; HS 161; BB 5–61: 100s 1; 5w/i 1.

*SMITH Paul Andrew b Jesmond, 15/4/64; RHB RAS; HS 140; BB 6–91; 100s 4; 1000r 2; 5w/i 6; hat-tricks 2.

*TWOSE Roger Graham b Torquay, 7/4/68; LHB RAS; HS 233; BB 6–63; 100s 3; 1000r 1.

WELCH Graeme b Durham, 21/3/72; RHB RAS. Yet to make fc debut.

Out: T. A. Lloyd (retired), B. C. Usher.

Player of the Year 1992: R. G. Twose.
Colt to follow: T. L. Penney.

WARWICKSHIRE BAC AVERAGES 1992

BATTING	M	I	NO	Runs	HS	Av	100	50
P. C. L. Holloway	2	3	1	133	102*	66.50	1	0
T. L. Penney	15	23	6	802	151	47.18	2	4
R. G. Twose	22	37	3	1368	233	40.24	1	10
A. J. Moles	22	39	3	1292	122	35.89	1	11
D. A. Reeve	17	28	4	833	79	34.71	0	7
D. P. Ostler	21	35	1	1172	192	34.47	3	4
M. Asif Din	2	3	0	103	40	34.33	0	0
T. A. Lloyd	22	38	2	914	84*	25.39	0	5
N. M. K. Smith	12	20	2	454	67	25.22	0	1
K. J. Piper	19	25	8	345	72	20.29	0	2
A. A. Donald	21	22	10	234	41	19.50	0	0
P. A. Smith	18	25	4	394	45	18.76	0	0
J. D. Ratcliffe	6	12	0	219	50	18.25	0	1
G. C. Small	17	17	6	181	31*	16.45	0	0
T. A. Munton	15	17	6	123	47	11.18	0	0
P. A. Booth	7	10	4	64	22*	10.67	0	0
M. A. V. Bell	3	5	2	10	5	3.33	0	0

Also batted: M. Burns (1 match) 3, 4.

BOWLING	O	M	R	W	Av	BB	5i	10m
A. A. Donald	576.2	139	1647	74	22.26	7–37	6	0
M. A. V. Bell	79.2	17	247	8	30.88	3–78	0	0
P. A. Smith	364	55	1334	42	31.76	6–91	4	0
R. G. Twose	221.3	37	735	23	31.96	6–63	1	0
T. A. Munton	570.2	145	1389	42	33.07	7–64	3	1
G. C. Small	367.2	83	1003	30	33.43	3–43	0	0
P. A. Booth	231.4	60	723	16	45.19	4–29	0	0
D. A. Reeve	267	80	632	13	48.62	2–4	0	0
N. M. K. Smith	332.3	63	1178	24	49.08	5–61	1	0
T. A. Lloyd	68.5	8	295	6	49.17	3–7	0	0

Also bowled: A. J. Moles 42–8–167–2, D. P. Ostler 9–0–54–0, T. L. Penney 5–0–35–0, K. J. Piper 4.4–0–57–1.

HUNDREDS (8)
3 – D. P. Ostler: 102 v Notts (Trent Bridge), 108 v Sussex (Hove), 192 v Surrey (Guildford).
2 – T. L. Penney: 100* v Northants (Northampton), 151 v Middx (Lord's).
1 – P. C. L. Holloway: 102* v Worcs (Edgbaston). A. J. Moles: 122 v Sussex (Hove). R. G. Twose 233 v Leics (Edgbaston).

WORCESTERSHIRE

BAC position last five seasons: 17th; 6th; 4th; Champions; Champions.
Club formed: 1865.
Honours: Champions 5 (1964–65, 1974, 1988–89); NWTGC 0 (best: finalists 1963, 1966, 1988); B&H 1 (1991); SL 3 (1971, 1987–88).

This being the Year of the Rooster, Dave 'Rooster' Roberts, the Worcestershire and England physio, may well be reassuring his colleagues that New Road is destined for a change of luck in 1993. For the county champions of 1988 and 1989 to reclaim their standing as cocks of the walk, however, they will need more than that.

The slump Tim Curtis presided over in his first season as captain was sorry and dispiriting, and was rendered all the more poignant by his own upstanding form. Compared with the 35 Championship victories gleaned over the previous four seasons, the three obtained last year was an alarming drop, greasing a perturbing slide of 11 places that would have been good enough to bring home the county's first wooden spoon since 1928 but for Durham's late arrival at the table.

The causes were not hard to detect. Historymaker 12 months earlier when he struck gold with his very first Test delivery, never mind a vital part of the England attack in the World Cup final, Richard Illingworth tossed the ball up and slid down the greasy pole with indecent haste. Prolific in the past, Tom Moody's bat was fitful. Stuart Lampitt, a fringe candidate for England A, averaged less than two wickets per match. Graeme Hick made a hatful when available but, the dedicated, painstaking Curtis aside, runs were scarce. David Leatherdale made a hash of his first extended opportunity, missing only one match but still averaging under 27. Neal Radford and Phil Newport shared 118 Championship wickets, twice the aggregate output of the other eight seamers used. All this and Graham Dilley, sadly, finally, giving up the ghost. So long to the unluckiest English fast bowler since Alan Ward, farewell to the salad days.

Insult then compounded injury when Richard Stemp's desire for a full-time position led him to Yorkshire, depriving Illingworth of a foil. Kenny Benjamin had just signed on, promising pace and bounce, but Chris Broad's return to Bristol dashed murmurs about hiring an experienced hand to open. Curtis probably can't recall when he last had the luxury of a regular partner. Happily, Philip Weston, the former England Under-19 captain, bears the hallmark of quality. Sufficiently ambitious to turn down a place at Oxford, this composed batsman from Durham should prove a valuable aide in protecting a fragile middle order. Martin Weston, fitness willing, and Damian D'Oliveira will look to stiffen it in their joint benefit year and, who knows, they could even end up celebrating with the county's first 60-over title, a possibility that the restoration of Illingworth and Lampitt to normal service can only enhance. For all Hick's new-found glory with his adopted country, New Road may require an infusion of new blood if its team's Britannic performances are to regain the assurance of the Phil Neale era.

CHAMPIONSHIP RATING: two bats, three balls.
PREDICTED POSITION: 13th.

Overseas player: KENNETH BENJAMIN
When the England A batsmen first bumped into Kenneth Charlie Griffith Benjamin in Trinidad last spring, they had been forewarned. The attendant press corps were sure this muscular Leeward Islander would be quick. How could he be otherwise with *those* middle names, recalling as they did one of the most ferocious of fast bowlers?

Forewarned, though, did not mean forearmed. Only Courtney Walsh outdid Benjamin's hoard of 33 wickets during the 1992 Caribbean season, and, of these, 17 came against England A. Difficult to pick up owing to a deceptive late release, the latest addition to county cricket's expanding clan of Benjamins brandished a nasty yorker and picked off six of the tourists' seven specialist batsmen at least once – Mark Ramprakash, Paul Johnson and John Stephenson twice – during a series that silenced whispers about the home pace factory shutting down.

So taken was one pressman that he embarked upon a personal crusade to stir up interest in Yorkshire. Benjamin's initial prize was even grander: a late bugle call to the Test against South Africa, one he answered by dispatching Peter Kirsten and Andrew Hudson. Yorkshire ignored their spy's advice and, with Graham Dilley about to hang up his boots, Worcestershire stepped in, nudged, no doubt, by their A team representative, Steve Rhodes. Still a relatively unknown quantity despite his recent trek round Australia, Benjamin may take time to blossom on the slower pitches here. He may also take time to recover from a troublesome knee injury. Worcestershire, nevertheless, look to have made one of the more astute investments of the close season.

PLAYING STAFF 1993:

iBENJAMIN Kenneth Charlie Griffith b Antigua, 8/4/67; RHB RF; HS 52 not out (for Leeward Islands); BB 7–51 (for Leeward Islands); 5w/i 2. Yet to make debut for Worcestershire.

†*CURTIS Timothy Stephen b Chislehurst, Kent, 15/1/60; RHB LS; HS 248; BB 2–17 (v Oxford U), 2–72 (BAC); 100s 27; 1000r 9. Captain since 1992. Tests 5.

*D'OLIVEIRA Damian Basil b Cape Town, South Africa, 19/10/60; RHB OS; HS 237 (v Oxford U), 155 (BAC); BB 2–17; 100s 10; 1000r 4.

EDWARDS Tim b Penzance, 24/6/74; RHB WK. Yet to make fc debut.

HAYNES Gavin Richard b Stourbridge, 29/9/69; RHB RAS; HS 66.

*HICK Graeme Ashley b Harare, Zimbabwe, 23/5/66; RHB OS; HS 405 not out (highest score in UK fc cricket in the 20th century, second-highest ever); BB 5–37; 100s 67; 1000r 8; 5w/i 4; 10w/m 1. Tests 11.

*ILLINGWORTH Richard Keith b Bradford, 23/8/63; RHB SLA; HS 120 not out; BB 7–50 (v Oxford U); 5–23 (BAC); 100s 3; 50w 3; 5w/i 19; 10w/m 4. Tests 2.

*LAMPITT Stuart Richard b Wolverhampton, 29/7/66; RHB RAS; HS 93; BB 5–32; 50w 2; 5w/i 8.

LEATHERDALE David Anthony b Bradford, 26/11/67; RHB RAS; HS 157; BB 1–12; 100s 2.

*NEWPORT Philip John b High Wycombe, 11/10/62; RHB RAS; HS 98 (v New Zealand), 96 (BAC); BB 8–52; 50w 5; 5w/i 27; 10w/m 3. Tests 3.

*RADFORD Neal Victor b Luanshya, Zambia, 7/6/57; RHB RAS; HS 76 not out (for Lancs), 73 not out (for Worcs); BB 9–70; 50w 6; 5w/i 45; 10w/m 6. Tests 3. Previous county: Lancashire (1980–84).

*RHODES Steven John b Bradford, 17/6/64; RHB WK; HS 116 not out; 100s 3; Ct 488; St 57. Previous county: Yorkshire (1981–84). England A cap.

SEYMOUR Adam Charles Hylton b Royston, Cambs, 7/12/67; LHB RAS; HS 157 (for Essex), 133 (for Worcs, v Cambridge U), 62 (for Worcs, BAC); 100s 2. Previous county: Essex (1988–91).

SOLANKI Vikram b Udaipur, India, 1/4/76: RHB OS. Yet to make fc debut.

SPIRING Reuben b Southport, 13/11/74; RHB. Yet to make fc debut.

TOLLEY Christopher Mark b Kidderminster, 30/12/67; RHB LAS; HS 37; BB 4–69 (v Sri Lanka), 3–38 (BAC).

*WESTON Martin John b Worcester, 8/4/59; RHB RAS; HS 145 not out; BB 4–24; 100s 3.

WESTON William Philip Christopher b Durham, 16/6/73; LHB LAS; HS 66 not out.

WYLIE Alex b Tamworth, Staffs, 20/2/73; LHB RAS. Yet to make fc debut.

Beneficiary '93: (Joint) D. B. D'Oliveira and M. J. Weston.

In: K. C. G. Benjamin, T. Edwards, V. Solanki, R. Spiring.
Out: S. R. Bevins, M. Dallaway, G. R. Dilley (retired), R. D. Stemp (Yorks).

Player of the Year 1992: P. J. Newport.
Colt to follow: W. P. C. Weston.

WORCESTERSHIRE BAC AVERAGES 1992

BATTING	M	I	NO	Runs	HS	Av	100	50
G. A. Hick	11	19	2	1179	213*	69.35	4	4
T. S. Curtis	21	37	4	1622	228*	49.15	4	5
T. M. Moody	10	18	1	624	178	36.71	3	1
R. D. Stemp	11	6	4	70	16*	35.00	0	0
W. P. C. Weston	13	21	3	579	66*	32.17	0	4
S. J. Rhodes	21	29	7	703	116*	31.95	2	2
D. B. D'Oliveira	12	17	1	502	100	31.38	1	2
D. A. Leatherdale	21	36	3	882	112	26.73	1	4
P. A. Neale	2	3	0	79	38	26.33	0	0
G. R. Haynes	9	13	2	288	66	26.18	0	2
P. J. Newport	20	24	6	463	75*	25.72	0	3
S. R. Lampitt	18	28	5	562	71*	24.43	0	4
A. C. H. Seymour	9	17	0	373	62	21.94	0	1
R. K. Illingworth	18	19	6	282	43	21.69	0	0
N. V. Radford	20	18	7	195	73*	17.73	0	1
C. M. Tolley	12	10	4	89	27	14.83	0	0

Also batted: G. R. Dilley (1 match) 18,4*; M. J. Weston (2) 17*, 8*, 1*.

BOWLING	O	M	R	W	Av	BB	5i	10m
P. J. Newport	576.1	121	1655	61	27.13	5–45	3	0
N. V. Radford	497.2	91	1553	57	27.25	6–88	4	1
T. M. Moody	67	12	235	8	29.38	4–50	0	0
S. R. Lampitt	356	39	1239	33	37.55	4–57	0	0
R. D. Stemp	331.5	80	1054	28	37.64	6–67	3	1
C. M. Tolley	217	52	650	17	38.24	3–38	0	0
R. K. Illingworth	570.3	170	1420	36	39.44	4–43	0	0
G. A. Hick	104.3	33	304	7	43.43	3–32	0	0
D. B. D'Oliveira	153.4	29	536	10	53.60	2–44	0	0

Also bowled: T. S. Curtis 24–2–116–2, G. R. Dilley 11–3–34–0, G. R. Haynes 45.2–13–128–0, D. A. Leatherdale 10–2–33–0, M. J. Weston 19–3–58–1, W. P. C. Weston 46–6–125–0.

HUNDREDS (15)
4 – T. S. Curtis 228* v Derbys (Derby), 140* v Kent (Tunbridge Wells), 124 v Glam (Worcester), 197 v Yorks (Worcester). G. A. Hick: 131 v Sussex (Worcester), 213* v Notts (Trent Bridge), 168 v Middx (Uxbridge), 146 v Warwicks (Worcester).
3 – T. M. Moody: 118 v Gloucs (Gloucester), 100 v Kent (Tunbridge Wells), 178 v Essex (Kidderminster).
2 – S. J. Rhodes: 116* v Warwicks (Worcester), 107 v Hants (Southampton).
1 – D. B. D'Oliveira: 100 v Essex (Kidderminster). D. A. Leatherdale: 112 v Notts (Trent Bridge).

YORKSHIRE

BAC position last five seasons: 16th; 14th; 10th; 16th; 13th.
Club formed: 1863.
Honours: Champions 31 (1867, 1870, 1893, 1896, 1898, 1900–02, 1905, 1908, 1912, 1919, 1922–25, 1931–33, 1935, 1937–39, 1946, 1959–60, 1962–63, 1966–68) plus 2 shared (1869, 1949); NWTGC 2 (1965, 1969); B&H 1 (1987); SL 1 (1983).

After the revolutionary measure of importing a star batsman from India Yorkshire began the 1992 season with expectations that could hardly have been greater. At the end of the summer they would undoubtedly have traded Sachin Tendulkar's runs for the wickets Craig McDermott would have taken had he been fit enough to become Yorkshire's first overseas player.

Tendulkar did not fail. In breaching the county's common law he established a bridgehead which will benefit those who follow. Yet, judged by strict professional standards, his performance of 1,070 runs at an average of 46 was moderate fare after Yorkshire's declining membership had been promised a banquet.

This season Richie Richardson assumes the 'pro's' role. Gifted, popular, and – at least as important – proven, the West Indies captain will disappoint no one except those who would prefer Yorkshire to go for a bowler who can win matches. No-one can possibly rely on Paul Jarvis, the physio's friend, to dig the county out of a ditch.

At last the club is moving towards reformation. From this year the committee will comprise 12 members only, with no more than one former player from each of the four regions – and no Boycott. As Yorkshire's problems in camera have been identified with the sort of provincial squabbles which would shame a Sicilian village, this is thought to be 'a good thing'.

After years of incompetence in handling their affairs Yorkshire also appear to be making financial progress. When Sir Lawrence Byford was invited to become the club chairman as well as president, two years ago, the situation could hardly have been worse. A profit of £100,000 this year comes after several dispiriting annual reports which put the club's future in peril.

The selection of Jarvis and Richard Blakey for the winter tour of India was two picks more than any sensible Yorkshireman could imagine. Jarvis, a modern day Shirley Temple, had bowled as many overs in anger in two years as could be counted on the fingers of a hand; Blakey was the beneficiary of a selection policy which favours wicketkeepers who can bat a bit. Of the two, Jarvis had by far the better trip.

Martyn Moxon led the team splendidly last season, after an injury-scarred start. In other ages he would possibly have become an established Test batsman. Now there is nothing to do except acquaint the cricket-watching public with Yorkshire's birthright. They can certainly do a lot better than 16th place. (Michael Henderson)

CHAMPIONSHIP RATING: 2½ bats, 2½ balls.
PREDICTED POSITION: 15th.

Overseas player: RICHIE RICHARDSON

Richie Richardson's maroon sunhat, suited to warmer days in other places, will not, sadly, become a feature of the Headingley summer. In all other senses, however, its owner will, and everyone should feel better for it. At 31, the West Indies captain is in his batting prime, as fine a strokeplayer as any in the world, at his best – the matchwinning 182 against Australia in Georgetown two springs ago – the finest entertainer anywhere.

The West Indian selectors were gambling only slightly when they invited Richardson to succeed his fellow islander, Viv Richards, as the captain instead of Desmond Haynes, who had the edge in experience. But the Antiguan had proved himself to be the best batsman in the side and was thought to have the better temperament.

When he first came to England in 1984, Richardson failed to dispel fears about his ability to adjust to native conditions, where the ball moves about more. Even in 1988, during another West Indian summer of conquest, he found the transition hard to make. In 1991, though, he came through, centuries at Edgbaston and The Oval, one in victory, the other with Caribbean backs to the wall, helping him total 495 runs in the Test series, more than any friend or foe. In Australia during the winter his growing assurance as captain kept West Indian nerves cool in that frantic finish at Adelaide, dragging them back into a series that was all but lost. After a poor start to the tour the authority at the crease returned, though there was still talk about the responsibility affecting his form.

Tendulkar, for all his promise, and everyone's best wishes, made a single first-class century last year. Richardson comes to Yorkshire as an established cricketer. Batting at first wicket down he ought to illuminate the summer. (Michael Henderson)

PLAYING STAFF 1993:

BARTLE Steven b Shipley, 5/8/71; LHB RFM. Yet to make fc debut.

BATTY Jeremy David b Bradford, 15/5/71; RHB OS; HS 51 (v Sri Lanka), 49 (BAC); BB 6–48; 5w/i 2.

*BLAKEY Richard John b Huddersfield, 15/1/67; RHB WK; HS 221 (for England A), 204 not out (BAC); BB 1–68; 100s 9; 1000r 4. England A cap.

BROADHURST Mark b Barnsley, 20/6/74; RHB RFM; HS 1 (v Sri Lanka); BB 3–61 (v Oxford U). Yet to make BAC debut.

*BYAS David b Kilham, 26/8/63; LHB RAS; HS 153; BB 3–55; 100s 8; 1000r 1.

*CARRICK Phillip b Leeds, 16752; RHB SLA; HS 131 not out; BB 8–33 (v Cambridge U), 8–72 (BAC); 100s 3; 50w 11; 5w/i 47; 10w/m 5. Captain 1987–89.

CHAPMAN Colin Anthony b Bradford, 8/6/71; RHB WK; HS 20; Ct 3.

FOSTER Michael James b Leeds, 17/9/72; RHB RFM; Yet to make fc debut.

GOUGH Darren b Barnsley, 18/9/70; RHB RAS; HS 72; BB 5–41; 5w/i 1.

GRAYSON Adrian Paul b Ripon, 31/3/71; RHB SLA; HS 57; BB 1–3 (v Oxford U), 1–55 (BAC).

*HARTLEY Peter John b Keighley, 18/4/60; RHB RAS; HS 127 not out; BB 8–111; 50w 3; 5w/i 11. Previous county: Warwickshire (1982).

*JARVIS Paul William b Redcar, 29/6/65; RHB RFM; HS 80; BB 7–55; 50w 3; 5wi 18; 10w/m 3. Tests 6.

*KELLETT Simon Andrew b Mirfield, 16/10/67; RHB RAS; HS 125 not out; 100s 2; 1000r 2.

KETTLEBOROUGH Richard Allan b Sheffield, 15/3/73; LHB RAS. Yet to make fc debut.

*METCALFE Ashley Anthony b Horsforth, Leeds, 25/12/63; RHB OS; HS 216 not out; BB 2–18; 100s 23; 1000r 6.

MILBURN Stuart Mark b Harrogate, 29/9/72; RHB RAS; HS 5; BB 1–54.

†*MOXON Martyn Douglas b Barnsley, 4/5/60; RHB RAS; HS 218 not out; BB 3–24; 100s 33; 1000r 8. Captain since 1990. Tests 10.

PARKER Bradley B Mirfield, 23/6/70; RHB RAS; HS 30.

¡RICHARDSON Richard Benjamin b Five Islands, Antigua, 12/1/62; RHB RAS. HS 194 (for West Indies); BB 5–40 (for Leeward Islands); 100s 29. Yet to make Yorkshire debut.

*ROBINSON Mark Andrew b Hull, 23/11/66; RHB RAS; HS 19 not out (for Northants), 12 (for Yorks); BB 6–57; 50w 1; 5w/i 3; 10w/m 1. Previous county: Northamptonshire (1987–90), for whom he created an unwanted world record in 1990 by failing to score in 11 successive innings.

STEMP Richard David, b Erdington, Birmingham, 11/12/67; RHB SLA; HS 16 not out (for Worcs); BB 6–67 (for Worcs); 5w/i 3; 10w/m 1. Previous county: Worcestershire (1990–92).

VAUGHAN Michael Paul b Manchester, 29/10/74; RHB OS. Yet to make fc debut.

WHITE Craig b Morley, 161269; RHB OS; HS 79 not out; BB 5–74; 5wi 1.

Beneficiary '93: M. D. Moxon. Colt to follow: R. D. Stemp.

In: M. J. Foster, R. A. Kettleborough, S. M. Milburn, R. B. Richardson, R. D. Stemp (Worcs), M. P. Vaughan.
Out: S. Bethel, I. J. Houseman, C. S. Pickles, K. Sharp, S. R. Tendulkar.

YORKSHIRE BAC AVERAGES 1992

BATTING	M	I	NO	Runs	HS	Av	100	50
M. D. Moxon	18	27	2	1314	183	52.56	5	4
C. White	19	26	8	859	79*	47.72	0	7
S. R. Tendulkar	16	25	2	1070	100	46.52	1	7
R. J. Blakey	21	32	9	1065	125*	46.30	2	5
S. A. Kellett	22	36	1	1326	96	37.89	0	9
P. W. Jarvis	15	14	4	374	80	37.40	0	3
D. Byas	20	30	4	784	100	30.15	1	6
A. A. Metcalfe	11	17	1	422	73	26.38	0	1
A. P. Grayson	6	6	0	116	57	19.33	0	1
P. J. Hartley	20	23	3	353	69	17.65	0	2
C. S. Pickles	6	9	1	131	49	16.38	0	0
J. D. Batty	18	15	4	155	49	14.09	0	0
P. Carrick	19	25	5	261	46	13.05	0	0
D. Gough	11	12	4	72	22*	9.00	0	0
M. A. Robinson	17	12	5	31	12	4.43	0	0

Also batted: C. A. Chapman (1 match) 8*; S. M. Milburn (1) 2*, 5; B. Parker (1) 7, 30.

BOWLING	O	M	R	W	Av	BB	5i	10m
M. A. Robinson	413.5	79	1134	50	22.68	6–57	3	1
C. S. Pickles	120.1	27	387	14	27.64	4–40	0	0
P. W. Jarvis	393.4	89	1164	40	29.10	4–27	0	0
P. Carrick	630.1	202	1375	47	29.26	6–58	1	0
P. J. Hartley	549.5	101	1690	56	30.18	1–111	3	0
D. Gough	255.1	53	910	25	36.40	4–43	0	0
J. D. Batty	426	87	1408	33	42.67	4–34	0	0

Also bowled: A. P. Grayson 50–5–186–1, S. M. Milburn 28–2–115–1, M. D. Moxon 3–0–7–0, S. R. Tendulkar 62.3–10–195–4, C. White 3–0–22–0.

HUNDREDS (8)
5 – M. D. Moxon: 141 v Surrey (Oval), 117 v Somerset (Middlesbrough), 183 v Gloucs (Cheltenham), 103 v Glam (Cardiff), 101* v Northants (Scarborough).
1 – R. J. Blakey: 125* v Glam (Cardiff). D. Byas: 100 v Northants (Scarborough). S. R. Tendulkar: 100 v Durham (Durham Univ).

ENGLAND TEST BATTING AVERAGES 1992–93
(series v NZ, PAK, I, SL)

	M	I	NO	R	HS	Av	100	50	Ct	St
D. I. Gower	3	5	2	150	73	50.00	–	1	1	–
A. J. Lamb	5	8	0	392	142	49.00	1	2	2	–
A. J. Stewart	12	21	1	939	190	46.95	3	5	13	2
R. A. Smith	12	21	1	836	128	41.80	2	5	15	–
G. A. Hick	11	18	0	641	178	35.61	1	3	19	–
G. A. Gooch	10	17	0	589	135	34.65	2	2	1	–
M. W. Gatting	4	8	0	266	81	33.25	–	2	3	–
R. C. Russell	6	8	3	191	36	31.85	–	–	14	2
C. C. Lewis	11	18	0	513	117	28.50	1	2	4	–
N. H. Fairbrother	3	6	0	155	83	25,83	–	1	–	–
T. A. Munton	2	2	1	25	25*	25.00	–	–	–	–
D. A. Reeve	3	5	0	124	59	24.80	–	1	1	–
J. E. Emburey	2	4	1	73	59	24.33	–	1	–	–
M. A. Atherton	5	9	0	208	76	23.11	–	2	8	–
I. D. K. Salisbury	4	7	0	136	50	19.43	–	1	2	–
P. C. R. Tufnell	7	11	7	38	22*	9.50	–	–	2	–
D. R. Pringle	5	7	1	55	41	9.17	–	–	2	–
M. R. Ramprakash	3	5	1	31	17	9.75	–	–	1	–
I. T. Botham	3	4	0	24	15	6.00	–	–	3	–
P. A. DeFreitas	6	8	1	37	12	5.29	–	–	2	–
D. E. Malcolm	6	11	3	31	13	3.87	–	–	1	–
P. W. Jarvis	3	6	0	23	8	3.83	–	–	2	–
N. A. Mallender	2	3	0	8	4	2.67	–	–	–	–
R. J. Blakey	2	4	0	7	6	1.75	–	–	2	–

Played in one Test: D. V. Lawrence 6; J. P. Taylor 17, 17*.

ENGLAND TEST BOWLING AVERAGES 1992–93

	O	M	R	W	Av	BB	5w/i	10w/m
G. A. Gooch	51	15	94	5	18.30	3–39	–	–
N. A. Mallender	74.5	20	215	10	21.50	5–50	1	–
D. A. Reeve	24.5	8	60	2	30.00	1–4	–	–
P. A. J. DeFreitas	185.4	57	489	15	32.60	4–62	–	–
P. C. R. Tufnell	341.2	93	870	24	36.25	7–47	1	1
P. W. Jarvis	94.1	16	257	7	36.71	3–76	–	–
C. C. Lewis	406	83	1103	30	36.76	5–31	1	–
G. A. Hick	191.5	50	451	12	37.06	4–126	–	–
D. E. Malcolm	187.5	33	621	16	38.81	5–94	1	–
D. R. Pringle	128	26	389	10	38.90	3–66	–	–
I. T. Botham	46	13	137	3	45.67	2–23	–	–
T. A. Munton	67.3	15	200	4	50.00	2–22	–	–
J. E. Emburey	107	22	309	6	51.50	2–48	–	–
I. D. K. Salisbury	122.1	9	536	8	67.00	3–49	–	–
D. V. Lawrence	29.1	8	71	1	71.00	1–67	–	–
J. P. Taylor	22	3	74	1	74.00	1–65	–	–
M. R. Ramprakash	1.1	0	8	0	–	–	–	–
R. A. Smith	4	2	6	0	–	–	–	–

TEST CAREER RECORDS
(up to 1993 BAC season)

BATTING	M	I	NO	R	HS	Av	100	50	Ct	St
M. A. Atherton	23	43	1	1374	151	32.71	3	9	23	–
R. J. Blakey	2	4	0	7	6	1.75	–	–	2	–
I. T. Botham	101	161	6	5200	208	33.54	14	22	120	–
P. A. J. DeFreitas	32	48	4	550	55*	12.50	–	1	8	–
J. E. Emburey	62	93	19	1613	75	21.79	–	9	33	–
N. H. Fairbrother	10	15	1	219	83	15.64	–	1	4	–
M. W. Gatting	72	125	14	4136	207	37.26	9	20	54	–
G. A. Gooch	101	183	6	7617	333	43.03	17	41	95	–
D. I. Gower	117	204	18	8231	215	44.25	18	39	74	–
G. A. Hick	15	25	0	716	178	28.64	1	3	27	–
P. W. Jarvis	9	15	2	132	29*	10.15	–	–	2	–
A. J. Lamb	79	139	10	4656	142	36.09	14	18	75	–
D. V. Lawrence	5	6	0	60	34	10.00	–	–	–	–
C. C. Lewis	18	27	1	719	117	27.65	1	3	13	–
M. A. Mallender	2	3	0	8	4	2.66	–	–	–	–
D. E. Malcolm	23	35	11	130	15	5.42	–	–	3	–
T. A. Munton	2	2	1	25	25*	25.00	–	–	–	–
D. R. Pringle	30	50	4	695	63	15.11	–	1	10	–
M. R. Ramprakash	9	15	1	241	29	17.21	–	–	5	–
D. A. Reeve	3	5	0	124	59	24.80	–	1	1	–
R. C. Russell	31	49	10	1060	128*	27.17	1	3	80	8
I. D. K. Salisbury	4	7	0	136	50	19.43	–	1	2	–
R. A. Smith	40	74	14	2954	148*	49.23	8	20	29	–
A. J. Stewart	26	48	4	1705	190	38.75	4	8	32	2
J. P. Taylor	1	2	1	34	17*	34.00	–	–	–	–
P. C. R. Tufnell	13	19	11	53	22*	6.63	–	–	4	–

BOWLING	O	R	W	Av	BB	5w/i	10w/m
M. A. Atherton	61	282	1	282.00	1–60	–	–
I. T. Botham	3635.5	10878	383	28.40	8–34	27	4
P. A. J. DeFreitas	1124.4	3091	93	33.24	7–70	3	–
J. E. Emburey	2478.1	5414	144	37.59	7–78	6	–
N. H. Fairbrother	2	9	0	–	–	–	–
M. W. Gatting	125.2	317	4	79.25	1–14	–	–
G. A. Gooch	382.3	894	22	40.63	3–39	–	–
D. I. Gower	6	20	1	20.00	1–1	–	–
G. A. Hick	215.5	546	14	39.00	4–126	–	–
P. W. Jarvis	319	965	21	45.95	4–107	–	–
A. J. Lamb	5	23	1	23.00	1–6	–	–
D. V. Lawrence	181.3	676	18	37.55	5–106	1	–
C. C. Lewis	634	1830	50	36.60	6–111	2	–
D. E. Malcolm	888.3	2914	77	37.84	6–77	4	1
N. A. Mallender	74.5	215	10	21.50	5–50	1	–
T. A. Munton	67.3	200	4	50.00	2–22	–	–
D. R. Pringle	881.1	2518	70	35.97	5–95	1	–
M. R. Ramprakash	1.1	8	0	–	–	–	–
D. A. Reeve	24.5	60	2	30.00	1–4	–	–
I. D. K. Salisbury	122.1	536	8	67.00	3–49	–	–
R. A. Smith	4	6	0	–	–	–	–
J. P. Taylor	22	74	1	74.00	1–65	–	–
P. C. R. Tufnell	583.2	1507	45	33.49	7–47	4	1

DIGEST

Tests played (June 1992 to March 1993): 12
Record: Won 3   Lost 6   Drawn 3
Players used: 26
New caps: 5
100s: 10
50s: 28
Five wkts/inns: 4
10 wkts/match: 1

Total runs: For 6,018; Against 6,049
Average runs per wicket: For 30.55; Against 37.57
Total wickets: Taken 161; Lost 197
Overs: Bowled 2173.3; Faced 2098.4
Runs per over: For 2.87; Against 2.78
Strike rate (balls per wicket): For 81; Against 63.92

MODES OF DISMISSAL

Bowled: 26
Caught: 99
Caught-and-bowled: 5
Stumped: 4
Run outs: 7
Lbw: 20
Total: 161

HIGHLIGHTS

Highest score (team): 580–9 dec v New Zealand (Christchurch)
Highest score (individual): A. J. Stewart 190 v Pakistan (Edgbaston)
Highest stand: R. A. Smith/ A. J. Stewart 227 for 3rd wicket v Pakistan (Edgbaston)
Most runs: A. J. Stewart 939
Best bowling (innings): P. C. R. Tufnell 7–47 v New Zealand (Christchurch)
Best bowling (match): P. C. R. Tufnell 11–147 v New Zealand (Christchurch)
Most wickets: C. C. Lewis 30
Most catches (outfield): G. A. Hick 19

A TO Z OF CRICKET
BY MICHAEL HENDERSON

A: THE ASHES. Ostensibly these are up for grabs every two years, when England and Australia play on a home and away basis. In reality they belong at Lord's which has housed them since 1927. In 1883 ladies in the Surrey household of Sir William Clarke, the president of MCC, incinerated some bails in memory of the 'death' of English cricket. The Hon Ivo Bligh's England side had just been beaten by the colonials. The tiny urn remains a symbol of the oldest international fixture. Australia are the clear leaders, having won 104 Tests out of 274 to England's 88. The Ashes currently reside with Australia, who visit England this summer, extending international cricket's longest feud by another six Tests.

B: BALL-TAMPERING. Like date rape and ethnic cleansing this is a modern term for an old problem. Former cricketers were not slow to observe at the height of the diplomatic row involving Allan Lamb and the Pakistan management last summer that 'tampering' with the ball was as old as the hills. Like much else its seriousness is a matter of degree. Picking the seam, to give the ball a sharper edge and therefore a greater indentation on the pitch, used to be the trick. Now, apparently, the thing is to soak one side of the ball with a human or man-made 'conditioner' and scratch the other side. If done properly the old ball can swing like billy-o. If caught, the bowler faces expulsion from the attack and, the ruling International Cricket Council threatens, much else besides.

C: CAPTAIN. In no other sport is the function and aptitude of the captain so important. Calling correctly on the toss is merely the most visible demonstration of his leadership. Afterwards he is responsible for deciding the priority and necessity of changes in bowling and fielding which can win or lose a match. In limited-overs cricket those switches have become ever more important. Captains can lead by example, like Allan Border, the record runscorer in Test cricket; by nous, like Ray Illingworth; or by precept, like Mike Brearley who, according to John Arlott, 'brought to captaincy a dimension which had not hitherto been perceived' and who wrote a fascinating book on the subject, *The Art of Captaincy*, which had a resonance beyond the game which inspired it.

D: DELOITTE (Coopers & Lybrand) RATINGS. This form of international ranking, which was introduced in 1987 with marks from 0 to 1,000, helps to determine a cricketer's world ranking by assessing any performance according to the state of the game and pitch and the strength of the opposition, after he has completed 15 innings or taken 40 wickets. A fifty against Pakistan, therefore, weighs more heavily than a century against Sri Lanka. Performances are updated after every Test match and they should be taken more as indicators than as perfect mirrors of ability. BBC Television, who flash the rankings on the screen between balls, should be particularly wary. Statistics, after all, can only reveal so much. What sort of system comes up with the information that Imran Khan is a 'better' batsman than Javed Miandad?

E: EXTRAS. Extras (sundries in Australia) refer to all runs credited to the batting side which do not come off the bat. The umpires are responsible for calling no-balls and wides, which cost the bowler runs, and signalling byes and leg byes, which do not. They can be particularly significant in one-day cricket. From this season a no-ball, which penalises a bowler who breaks the crease with his entire front foot or chucks the ball, will cost two runs instead of one. Umpires are less tolerant in determining wides in limited-overs games where any ball more than 18 inches outside the off-stump is liable to be called. Extra runs can also be earned – or donated – if the ball strikes a fielder's helmet, but the five-run award is credited to the batsman, as are overthrows, perversely. Leg byes, incidentally, are given when the ball strikes any part of the batsman's body (including his helmet) other than his hand or wrist.

F: FAST. Fast is both an absolute and a relative term. The genuinely fast bowlers produced by English cricket can probably be counted on the fingers of two hands, although the term has come to embrace all shades of fast-medium. In last year's *Playfair* annual the description RF (right-arm fast) was allocated to four English bowlers: Graham Dilley and Norman Cowans (who both ceased to be fast long ago), Devon Malcolm and David Lawrence. David Millns of Leicestershire, who was at times more hostile last summer than any Englishman, was rated RMF (which is why this guide has sought to simplify matters by dispensing with RM – right-arm medium – and RMF, and introducing RAS, right-arm seam). By getting more bounce than others who are less quick, the fast bowler will get wickets they won't. But, as the outstanding ones from Fred Trueman to Malcolm Marshall have shown, there is much more to being a fast bowler than just being fast.

G: DAVID GOWER and GRAHAM GOOCH. From the civil war onwards English history can be interpreted as the conjunction of two strands, the cavalier and the roundhead. The careers and public perceptions of David Gower and Graham Gooch maintain that tradition. On the one hand is Gower, whose refinement would be rare in any age; on the other is Gooch, a fine enough player in his own right who, by dedication, has developed into a genuinely great batsman, arguably England's finest since Len Hutton. Gooch has always been committed to his cricket in a way that Gower, who has the wider range of interests beyond the boundary, would find restricting. This summer, as Gooch takes on Australia for the last time and contemplates a winter at home, Gower may retire altogether.

H: HAMBLEDON. The power of myth, as Wagner and others have proved, is inexhaustible. It provides a constant opportunity for people to define, reform or idealise external events. So it is that Hambledon, a tiny Hampshire village, is forever associated with the game of cricket. It is the world of blacksmiths and farmers trading hits, of the village green and pub, the kind of game that comes to mind when one imagines Tom Jones cavorting over the 18th century landscape. Never mind that cricket was first played in Kent and on the Sussex Downs, 'little' Hambledon, by staging games against All England under the captaincy of Richard Nyren from 1760, pushed a rural recreation towards the professional game which emerged a century later.

I: INTIMIDATORY BOWLING. The fast bowler has never been an altruistic chap. An important part of his armoury has always been intimidation and, effective as glares and snarls can be, they tend to be more effective when accompanied by a ball which singes the batsman's whiskers. However, the unwillingness of umpires to intervene when bowlers infringed the spirit of the law (the ability of the batsman is the most important consideration) led the International Cricket Council to amend Law 42. Bowlers can now be no-balled for intimidatory bowling and, if they persist, ordered out of the attack. But there is unease, even among genuine batsmen, that a bowler is permitted to bowl only one bouncer at a specific batsman in a single over. No one ever pretended there was an ideal balance.

J: JOURNALISTS. If every sport gets the coverage it deserves, cricket does pretty well. It is fair to say that no other game has been so well, or so extensively, written about in newspapers, magazines and books. One man is responsible. Neville Cardus, the illegitimate son of a Rusholme courtesan, may be too precious for modern taste but he bequeathed to more recent generations the idea that cricket was worth writing about decently. The torch has passed through the likes of Robertson-Glasgow and Jack Fingleton to E. W. Swanton and John Woodcock and, latterly, to Matthew Engel, Scyld Berry and Martin Johnson. If the cricket-lover feels inadequately served by the newspapers, he or she is not looking.

K: KNIGHTS. The elevation of Colin Cowdrey to the knighthood made a round dozen cricketing knights, far more than any other sport. Cowdrey has been both a distinguished player and an experienced administrator, becoming president of MCC and chairman of the International Cricket Council. He follows Francis Lacey, Frederick Toone, Pelham Warner, Donald Bradman, Henry Leveson Gower, Jack Hobbs, Len Hutton, Frank Worrell, Garfield Sobers, Gubby Allen and Richard Hadlee. If Neville Cardus is included, for services to journalism, there are 13 of them. 'Should you be offered a knighthood, accept it,' Sir Thomas Beecham once advised him. 'It makes booking tables at the Savoy so much easier.'

L: LIMITED OVERS. Back in the early 1960s, when the world was shedding its postwar skin, cricket had to change too if it was to survive. Since then the balance between 'proper' cricket and the instant variety has become increasingly hard to strike. The Gillette Cup, a 60–over competition, was established in 1963, joined by the Sunday League (which goes up from 40 overs to 50 this year) in 1969 and the Benson & Hedges Cup (55 overs) in 1972. Internationally the one-day game has grown out of all proportion. England is now the only Test-playing country which insists on the primacy of five-day cricket between World Cups, staged four years apart.

M: MCC. Until the Test and County Cricket Board was established in 1968 Marylebone Cricket Club governed the English game, to the point of having responsibility for the selection of the Test team. Since then it has come to regard itself as cricket's House of Lords, with the accrued wisdom of the venerable and venerated. Its presidents have included prime ministers, dukes and earls and it remains the custodian of the game's laws, providing the secretariat for the International Cricket Council, although this situation is about to change. With 19,000 members, and a waiting list for full membership of up to 20 years, it is far and away the most exclusive club in the world.

N: NEW BALL. A new cricket ball, red and gleaming, is a wondrous thing – except for the batsman who watches a fast bowler pawing the turf, waiting to propel it towards him. The ball's hardness and shine gives the fast bowler the quality of bounce which disconcerts the batsman and should, if used properly, be good for a wicket or two. It is 'available', never due, after 100 overs in Championship cricket and, in Tests, after 85. The counties choose from two makes of ball, Duke and Reader.

O: OVERSEAS PLAYERS. There have always been non-indigenous players in English cricket. Ted McDonald was a vivid Australian presence in Neville Cardus's reminiscences of the Lancashire side of the 1920s. Bill Alley and Bruce Dooland followed him over 20 years later, and Roy Marshall came to Somerset in the 1950s. The modern overseas player was a creation of the 1960s. First of all came Garfield Sobers, then the likes of Clive Lloyd, Rohan Kanhai and Lance Gibbs, all proven players, plus the occasional starlet like Greg Chappell. South Africans have proved the best: Mike Procter revitalised Gloucestershire, Eddie Barlow did much the same for Derbyshire and Clive

Rice (assisted by Richard Hadlee) transformed Nottinghamshire from rubbing-rags to champions. Sensibly, counties are now limited to one each.

P: PITCH. Frequently and misleadingly called the wicket, the pitch is the single most important feature of any game. Cardus thought that no report of a day's play could be considered complete unless it made reference to the condition of the pitch. Whether pitches should be covered or not is an annual debate. Many cricketers of yesteryear, who grew up playing on pitches open to the weather, believe their successors have been pampered by the change of rules regarding the covering of pitches. Generally speaking the more grass is left on the pitch, the livelier it will be and the longer a game lasts, the more help will be given to the spin bowler. Although, as Shaw once noted in *Man and Superman*, the golden rule is that there are no golden rules.

Q: QUOTE . . . UNQUOTE. 'Like poets, cricketers spend unimaginable numbers of hours doing something as near pointless as possible, trying to dig an elusive perfection out of themselves in the face of an infinite number of variables, and as a result a large proportion of their lives belongs to the realm of the mystical. Like poets their faces are deeply engraved by introspection – all cricketers seem prematurely lined – because they are as deeply locked in a struggle with themselves as they are with the opposition. But they look happier than poets.' P. J. Kavanagh, poet, in his essay, *The Mystery of Cricket*.

R: REFEREE. With the behaviour of Test cricketers becoming coarser the International Cricket Council has instituted a code of conduct which the players are honour-bound to uphold. As part of the agreement a match referee from a neutral country observes each Test equipped with powers to enforce Law 42, in other words to punish players who breach the code, and generally to maintain the spirit of the game. Those of a traditional bent have suggested that a more thorough application by captains and umpires would have saved the ICC this burden. Other have noted that if the ICC is genuinely concerned about declining standards the referees should be keener to wield the big stick. After a meek start, the suspension during the winter of Pakistan's Aqib Javed, a first, plus fines for Australian and West Indian players – Allan Border among them – suggest they are coming to grips with a thorny issue.

S: SEAM AND SWING. Unless he is genuinely fast the quicker bowler relies for effect on two methods of deceiving the batsman. By cutting his fingers across the seam he can assist the ball's movement once it has pitched, although the ball's newness and the grassiness of the pitch determine the ball's purchase on the surface. This is seam bowling: lbw and bowled are common methods of dismissal. Alternatively he can keep the shine on one side of the ball and, by some unwritten law of aerodynamics which has never been properly explained, swing the ball through the air so that the batsman, playing down 'the wrong line', nicks it to the wicketkeeper or slip cordon.

T: TEST MATCH SPECIAL. This radio programme is held by its many admirers to be an example of British public service broadcasting at its best. Every ball of every Test match and one-day international is described by a team of commentators and summarisers of whom the best are Christopher Martin-Jenkins and Trevor Bailey. More than anything TMS owes its special place in British folk memory to John Arlott's vivid imagery and, give or take the waffle, it remains a 'good listen'. It is, however, in danger of forfeiting the accumulated fund of goodwill through an editorial reluctance to stifle the golly-gosh-isn't-it-fun? excess of an Old Etonian who has seen better days and the drudgery of a great cricketer whose fast bowling was more thrilling than his sullen expertise.

U: UNIVERSITY CRICKET. By tradition the universities of Oxford and Cambridge play around nine matches apiece against the county sides each year, which are designated first-class, before ending their summer term with another hardy perennial, the Varsity Match, at Lord's. Strictly speaking the standards of play ceased to be first-class some years ago, although in Michael Atherton, who played Test cricket within a month of coming down, and the emerging John Crawley, Cambridge are having a good run. Of the great and good May, Sheppard and Dexter passed through Cambridge, Cowdrey and M. J. K. Smith through Oxford. In recent years Durham has supplied more players to the first-class game and some have gone on to play for England. Accordingly, the Combined Universities team which takes part in the Benson & Hedges Cup is now open to cricketers from universities other than Oxbridge.

V: VERBALS. Or 'sledging', as the modern world prefers it. Like other aspects of cricket it is something that has always happened, brought to prominence in recent years by the needs of image-conscious television and newspapers with back pages to splash. 'It's not cricket' is one of life's more enduring, and misleading, thoughts. Though essentially played by men of good character no one should ever pretend that it is all sweetness and light. Sending a batsman on his way with a few well-chosen words has always been part of the bowler's repertoire, although they used to be more discreet about it.

W: WISDEN. One hundred and 30 years old this year, *Wisden* is commonly regarded as the Bible of cricket although, since it deals mainly with facts, it is prone to fewer interpretations. Published each April to a fanfare of trumpets, the Editor's Notes amount to a reflection on the state of the game: Matthew Engel has written them for the first time this year. There are also, whenever relevant, profiles of the achievers and features relating to significant events and records. The editor's prerogative is to select Five Cricketers of the Year, a once-in-a-career accolade – a veritable feather in any player's cap.

X: THE X FACTOR. Talent is only part of it. In cricket, as in any public undertaking, temperament is the X factor, the quality without which even the gifted performer can feel naked. Particularly in cricket, it might be said, because in no other sport is the individual's skill so rigorously tested, as is a batsman's, by 11 opponents.

Y: YORKSHIRE. No matter how poorly the team performs, and in recent years they have performed very poorly indeed, Yorkshire CCC remains the most talked-about club in the world. Down the years they have won more Championships (31 outright, two shared, none since 1968), supplied more great players to the Test side and perpetrated more howlers than any other county. The list of personalities is formidable, from Hawke to Bairstow by way of Sutcliffe, Leyland, Hutton, Verity, Wardle, Trueman, Close, Illingworth and Boycott. There have been revolutions (though not of a velvet shade), counter revolutions and reformation. No one has yet lost his head, but give them time.

Z: Zzzz. By turns dramatic and poetic, cricket can sometimes be as turgid an entertainment as devised by man. There is a famous story of Groucho Marx who, on being taken to a Test match at Lord's, observed the first hour before wondering, 'It's fine so far but when does the game start?' Archbishop Temple put it another way. His phrase, 'organised loafing', may not carry the echo of boredom but it does not have the ring of action either. There are those who fear that with the arrival of four-day cricket the County Championship will see more strokeless batsmen and medium-pace trundlers, and less assertive play.

1993 Fixtures

* includes Sunday play

APRIL

14	Cambridge University v Derbyshire	Fenner's (Wed, 3 days)
	Oxford University v Durham	The Parks
17	Cambridge University v Yorkshire*	Fenner's (Sat, 3 days)
	Oxford University v Lancashire	The Parks
20	Rapid Cricketline Champions (Surrey 2nd XI) v England Under-19	(Tues, 4 days) The Oval
21	Cambridge University v Kent	Fenner's (Wed, 3 days)
	Oxford University v Glamorgan	The Parks
22	TETLEY BITTER SHIELD Essex v England A*	(Thur, 4 days) Chelmsford
24	Combined Universities v Middlesex	Fenner's (Sat, 1–day)
25	Combined Univ. v Northamptonshire	Fenner's (Sun, 1–day)
27	BENSON & HEDGES CUP (Preliminary Round)	(Tue)
	Durham v Minor Counties	Hartlepool
	Gloucestershire v Derbyshire	Bristol
	Hampshire v Combined Univ.	Southampton
	Kent v Glamorgan	Canterbury
	Scotland v Essex	Forfar
29	BRITANNIC ASSURANCE CHAMPIONSHIP	(Thur)
	Glamorgan v Sussex*	Cardiff
	Gloucestershire v Middlesex*	Bristol
	Hampshire v Somerset*	Southampton
	Leicestershire v Surrey*	Leicester
	Nottinghamshire v Worcestershire*	Trent Bridge
	Warwickshire v Northamptonshire*	Edgbaston
29	OTHER MATCH Yorkshire v Lancashire*	(Thur, 4 days) Headingley
30	TOURIST MATCH England Amateur XI v Australians	(Fri, 1–day) Radlett

MAY

1	OTHER MATCH Cambridge University v Essex*	Fenner's (Sat, 3 days)
2	TOURIST MATCH Lavinia Duchess of Norfolk's XI v Australians	(Sun, 1–day) Arundel

3	TOURIST MATCH Middlesex v Australians	(Mon, 1–day) Lord's
5	TETLEY BITTER CHALLENGE Worcestershire v Australians	(Wed, 3 days) Worcester
5	OTHER MATCHES Cambridge University v Glamorgan Oxford University v Hampshire	(Wed, 3 days) Fenner's The Parks
6	BRITANNIC ASSURANCE CHAMPIONSHIP Essex v Yorkshire Lancashire v Durham Leicestershire v Nottinghamshire Middlesex v Kent Northamptonshire v Gloucestershire Sussex v Surrey Warwickshire v Derbyshire	(Thur) Chelmsford Old Trafford Leicester Lord's Northampton Hove Edgbaston
8	TETLEY BITTER CHALLENGE Somerset v Australians*	(Sat, 3 days) Taunton
9	AXA EQUITY & LAW LEAGUE Essex v Yorkshire Lancashire v Durham Leicestershire v Nottinghamshire Middlesex v Kent Northamptonshire v Gloucestershire Sussex v Surrey Warwickshire v Derbyshire	(Sun) Chelmsford Old Trafford Leicester Lord's Northampton Hove Edgbaston
11	BENSON & HEDGES CUP (First Round) Durham or Minor Counties v Hampshire or Combined Univ. Gloucestershire or Derbyshire v Middlesex Kent or Glamorgan v Sussex Leicestershire v Warwickshire Nottinghamshire v Somerset Surrey v Lancashire Worcestershire v Scotland or Essex Yorkshire v Northamptonshire	(Tue) Stockton or Jesmond Bristol or Derby Canterbury or Cardiff Leicester Trent Bridge The Oval Worcester Headingley
13	BRITANNIC ASSURANCE CHAMPIONSHIP Derbyshire v Glamorgan Durham v Hampshire Kent v Warwickshire Middlesex v Nottinghamshire Somerset v Lancashire Surrey v Essex Yorkshire v Worcestershire	(Thur) Derby Stockton Canterbury Lord's Taunton The Oval Bradford
13	TETLEY BITTER CHALLENGE Sussex v Australians*	(Thur, 3 days) Hove

15	OTHER MATCHES	(Sat)
	Cambridge Univ. v Leicestershire*	Fenner's
	Oxford Univ. v Northamptonshire	The Parks
16	AXA EQUITY & LAW LEAGUE	(Sun)
	Derbyshire v Glamorgan	Derby
	Durham v Hampshire	Stockton
	Kent v Warwickshire	Canterbury
	Middlesex v Nottinghamshire	Lord's
	Somerset v Lancashire	Taunton
	Surrey v Essex	The Oval
	Yorkshire v Worcestershire	Headingley
16	TOURIST MATCH	(Sun, 1–day)
	Northamptonshire v Australians	Northampton
19	TEXACO TROPHY	
	ENGLAND v AUSTRALIA	(Wed)
	(First One-Day International)	Old Trafford
19	OTHER MATCHES	(Wed, 3 days)
	Cambridge University v Lancashire	Fenner's
	Oxford University v Middlesex	The Parks
20	BRITANNIC ASSURANCE	
	CHAMPIONSHIP	(Thur)
	Essex v Derbyshire	Chelmsford
	Glamorgan v Northamptonshire	Swansea
	Gloucestershire v Durham	Bristol
	Hampshire v Yorkshire	Southampton
	Nottinghamshire v Kent	Trent Bridge
	Sussex v Leicestershire	Horsham
	Worcestershire v Somerset	Worcester
21	TEXACO TROPHY	
	ENGLAND v AUSTRALIA	(Fri)
	(Second One-Day International)	Edgbaston
23	TEXACO TROPHY	
	ENGLAND v AUSTRALIA	(Sun)
	(Third One-Day International)	Lord's
23	AXA EQUITY & LAW LEAGUE	(Sun)
	Essex v Derbyshire	Chelmsford
	Glamorgan v Northamptonshire	Pentrych
	Gloucestershire v Durham	Bristol
	Hampshire v Yorkshire	Southampton
	Nottinghamshire v Kent	Trent Bridge
	Sussex v Leicestershire	Horsham
	Worcestershire v Somerset	Worcester
25	BENSON & HEDGES CUP	(Tue, 3 days)
	Quarter-finals	
25	TETLEY BITTER CHALLENGE	(Tue, 3 days)
	Surrey or Yorkshire† v Australians	The Oval or Headingley
	(†Northants or Notts if both are involved in B&H QFs)	

27	BRITANNIC ASSURANCE CHAMPIONSHIP	(Thur)
	Derbyshire v Hampshire	Derby
	Durham v Kent	Darlington
	Gloucestershire v Worcestershire	Gloucester
	Lancashire v Warwickshire	Liverpool
	Middlesex v Sussex	Lord's
	Somerset v Glamorgan	Taunton
29	TETLEY BITTER CHALLENGE	(Sat, 3 days)
	Leicestershire v Australians*	Leicester
29	OTHER MATCH	(Sat, 3 days)
	Oxford University v Nottinghamshire	The Parks
30	AXA EQUITY & LAW LEAGUE	(Sun)
	Derbyshire v Hampshire	Derby
	Durham v Kent	Darlington
	Gloucestershire v Worcestershire	Gloucester
	Lancashire v Warwickshire	Old Trafford
	Middlesex v Sussex	Lord's
	Somerset v Glamorgan	Taunton

JUNE

3	FIRST CORNHILL INSURANCE TEST MATCH	(Thur)
	ENGLAND v AUSTRALIA*	Old Trafford
3	BRITANNIC ASSURANCE CHAMPIONSHIP	(Thur)
	Essex v Somerset	Chelmsford
	Kent v Gloucestershire	Tunbridge Wells
	Leicestershire v Durham	Leicester
	Middlesex v Derbyshire	Lord's
	Norhamptonshire v Worcestershire	Northampton
	Nottinghamshire v Hampshire	Trent Bridge
	Surrey v Lancashire	The Oval
	Warwickshire v Sussex	Edgbaston
	Yorkshire v Glamorgan	Middlesbrough
6	AXA EQUITY & LAW LEAGUE	(Sun)
	Essex v Somerset	Chelmsford
	Kent v Gloucestershire	Tunbridge Wells
	Leicestershire v Durham	Leicester
	Middlesex v Derbyshire	Lord's
	Northamptonshire v Worcestershire	Northampton
	Nottinghamshire v Hampshire	Trent Bridge
	Surrey v Lancashire	The Oval
	Warwickshire v Sussex	Edgbaston
	Yorkshire v Glamorgan	Middlesbrough
8	BENSON & HEDGES CUP	(Tue)
	Semi-finals	

9	TETLEY BITTER CHALLENGE	(Wed, 3 days)
	Warwickshire or Nottinghamshire† v Australians	Edgbaston or Trent Bridge
	(†Somerset to play if both are involved in B&H SFs)	

- 9 **TETLEY BITTER CHALLENGE** (Wed, 3 days)
  Warwickshire or Nottinghamshire† v Australians — Edgbaston or Trent Bridge
  (†Somerset to play if both are involved in B&H SFs)

- 10 **BRITANNIC ASSURANCE CHAMPIONSHIP** (Thur)
  - Derbyshire v Yorkshire — Chesterfield
  - Durham v Middlesex — Gateshead Fell
  - Hampshire v Kent — Basingstoke
  - Lancashire v Essex — Old Trafford
  - Surrey v Glamorgan — The Oval
  - Sussex v Northamptonshire — Hove
  - Worcestershire v Leicestershire — Worcester

- 12 **TETLEY BITTER CHALLENGE** (Sat, 3 days)
  - Gloucestershire v Australians* — Bristol

- 12 **OTHER MATCHES** (Sat, 3 days)
  - Cambridge Univ. v Nottinghamshire* — Fenner's
  - Oxford University v Warwickshire — The Parks
  - Ireland v Scotland* — Eglinton

- 13 **AXA EQUITY & LAW LEAGUE** (Sun)
  - Derbyshire v Yorkshire — Chesterfield
  - Durham v Middlesex — Gateshead Fell
  - Hampshire v Kent — Basingstoke
  - Lancashire v Essex — Old Trafford
  - Surrey v Glamorgan — The Oval
  - Sussex v Northamptonshire — Hove
  - Worcestershire v Leicestershire — Worcester

- 17 **SECOND CORNHILL INSURANCE TEST MATCH** (Thur)
  - ENGLAND v AUSTRALIA* — Lord's

- 17 **BRITANNIC ASSURANCE CHAMPIONSHIP** (Thur)
  - Glamorgan v Durham — Colwyn Bay
  - Kent v Derbyshire — Canterbury
  - Lancashire v Sussex — Old Trafford
  - Northamptonshire v Hampshire — Northampton
  - Nottinghamshire v Essex — Trent Bridge
  - Somerset v Middlesex — Bath
  - Warwickshire v Surrey — Edgbaston
  - Yorkshire v Gloucestershire — Sheffield

- 18 **OTHER MATCH** (Fri, 3 days)
  - Worcestershire v Oxford University* — Worcester

- 20 **AXA EQUITY & LAW LEAGUE** (Sun)
  - Glamorgan v Durham — Colwyn Bay
  - Kent v Derbyshire — Canterbury
  - Lancashire v Sussex — Old Trafford
  - Northamptonshire v Hampshire — Northampton
  - Nottinghamshire v Essex — Trent Bridge
  - Somerset v Middlesex — Bath

	Warwickshire v Surrey	Edgbaston
	Yorkshire v Gloucestershire	Sheffield
22	**NATWEST BANK TROPHY**	(Tue)
	(First Round)	
	Buckinghamshire v Leicestershire	Marlow
	Cheshire v Nottinghamshire	Warrington
	Devon v Derbyshire	Exmouth
	Glamorgan v Oxfordshire	Swansea
	Gloucestershire v Hertfordshire	Bristol
	Kent v Middlesex	Canterbury
	Norfolk v Warwickshire	Lakenham
	Northamptonshire v Lancashire	Northampton
	Scotland v Worcestershire	Edinburgh (Myreside)
	Shropshire v Somerset	Telford (St Georges)
	Staffordshire v Hampshire	Stone
	Suffolk v Essex	Bury St Edmunds
	Surrey v Dorset	The Oval
	Sussex v Minor Counties Wales	Hove
	Wiltshire v Durham	Trowbridge
	Yorkshire v Ireland	Headingley
23	**TOURIST MATCH**	(Wed, 3 days)
	Combined Univ. v Australians	The Parks
24	**BRITANNIC ASSURANCE CHAMPIONSHIP**	(Thur)
	Derbyshire v Lancashire	Derby
	Durham v Worcestershire	Stockton
	Essex v Warwickshire	Ilford
	Glamorgan v Nottinghamshire	Swansea
	Leicestershire v Gloucestershire	Leicester
	Middlesex v Surrey	Lord's
	Northamptonshire v Somerset	Luton
	Yorkshire v Kent	Headingley
26	**TETLEY BITTER CHALLENGE**	(Sat, 3 days)
	Hampshire v Australians*	Southampton
26	**OTHER MATCH**	(Sat, 3 days)
	Sussex v Cambridge University*	Hove
27	**AXA EQUITY & LAW LEAGUE**	(Sun)
	Derbyshire v Lancashire	Derby
	Durham v Worcestershire	Stockton
	Essex v Warwickshire	Ilford
	Glamorgan v Nottinghamshire	Swansea
	Leicestershire v Gloucestershire	Leicester
	Middlesex v Surrey	Lord's
	Northamptonshire v Somerset	Luton
	Yorkshire v Kent	Headingley
30	**VARSITY MATCH**	(Wed, 3 days)
	Oxford Univ. v Cambridge Univ.	Lord's

JULY

1	THIRD CORNHILL INSURANCE TEST MATCH	(Thur)	
	ENGLAND v AUSTRALIA	Trent Bridge	

1 BRITANNIC ASSURANCE
   CHAMPIONSHIP   (Thur)
   Glamorgan v Middlesex   Cardiff
   Gloucestershire v Hampshire   Bristol
   Kent v Essex   Maidstone
   Leicestershire v Lancashire   Leicester
   Northamptonshire v Nottinghamshire   Northampton
   Somerset v Sussex   Taunton
   Surrey v Durham   The Oval
   Warwickshire v Yorkshire   Edgbaston
   Worcestershire v Derbyshire   Kidderminster

4 AXA EQUITY & LAW LEAGUE   (Sun)
   Glamorgan v Middlesex   Cardiff
   Gloucestershire v Hampshire   Bristol
   Kent v Essex   Maidstone
   Leicestershire v Lancashire   Leicester
   Northamptonshire v Nottinghamshire   Northampton
   Somerset v Sussex   Taunton
   Surrey v Durham   The Oval
   Warwickshire v Yorkshire   Edgbaston
   Worcestershire v Derbyshire   Worcester

7 NATWEST BANK TROPHY   (Wed)
   (Second Round)
   Buckinghamshire or Leicestershire   Marlow or
    v Surrey or Dorset   Leicester
   Cheshire or Nottinghamshire   Warrington or
    v Shropshire or Somerset   Trent Bridge
   Glamorgan or Oxfordshire   Cardiff or
    v Wiltshire or Durham   Oxford
   Gloucestershire or Hertfordshire   Bristol or
    v Yorkshire or Ireland   Hitchin
   Norfolk or Warwickshire   Lakenham or
    v Kent or Middlesex   Edgbaston
   Scotland or Worcestershire   Edinburgh or
    v Devon or Derbyshire   Worcester
   Suffolk or Essex   Bury St Edmunds
    v Northamptonshire or Lancashire   or Chelmsford
   Sussex or Minor Counties Wales   Hove or
    v Staffordshire or Hampshire   Colwyn Bay

8 TOURIST MATCH   (Thur, 1–day)
   Minor Counties v Australians   Stone

10 BENSON & HEDGES CUP FINAL   (Sat)
   (Reserve days – Sunday and Monday)   Lord's

10 TOURIST MATCH   (Sat, 1–day)
   Ireland v Australians   Dublin (Clontarf)

11	AXA EQUITY & LAW LEAGUE	(Sun)
	Glamorgan v Sussex	Llanelli
	Gloucestershire v Middlesex	Moreton-in-Marsh
	Hampshire v Somerset	Southampton
	Leicestershire v Surrey	Leicester
	Nottinghamshire v Worcestershire	Trent Bridge
	Warwickshire v Northamptonshire	Edgbaston
	(Matches involving B&H Cup Finalists to be played on July 13)	
12	OTHER MATCH	(Mon, 3 days)
	Tilcon Trophy	Harrogate
13	TETLEY BITTER CHALLENGE	(Tue, 3 days)
	Derbyshire v Australians	Derby
13	OTHER MATCHES	(Tue, 1-day)
	England XI v Rest of the World XI	Jesmond
14	England XI v Rest of the World XI	Jesmond (Wed, 1-day)
15	BRITANNIC ASSURANCE CHAMPIONSHIP	(Thur)
	Essex v Leicestershire	Southend
	Hampshire v Worcestershire	Portsmouth
	Lancashire v Glamorgan	Old Trafford
	Nottinghamshire v Somerset	Trent Bridge
	Surrey v Gloucestershire	Guildford
	Sussex v Kent	Arundel
	Warwickshire v Middlesex	Edgbaston
	Yorkshire v Northamptonshire	Harrogate
17	TETLEY BITTER CHALLENGE	(Sat, 3 days)
	Durham v Australians*	Durham University
18	AXA EQUITY & LAW LEAGUE	(Sun)
	Essex v Leicestershire	Southend
	Hampshire v Worcestershire	Portsmouth
	Lancashire v Glamorgan	Old Trafford
	Nottinghamshire v Somerset	Trent Bridge
	Surrey v Gloucestershire	Guildford
	Sussex v Kent	Hove
	Warwickshire v Middlesex	Edgbaston
	Yorkshire v Northamptonshire	Headingley
22	FOURTH CORNHILL INSURANCE TEST MATCH	(Thur)
	ENGLAND v AUSTRALIA*	Headingley
22	BRITANNIC ASSURANCE CHAMPIONSHIP	(Thur)
	Derbyshire v Sussex	Derby
	Essex v Durham	Chelmsford
	Lancashire v Nottinghamshire	Old Trafford
	Leicestershire v Warwickshire	Leicester
	Middlesex v Hampshire	Lord's
	Northamptonshire v Surrey	Northampton
	Somerset v Kent	Taunton
	Worcestershire v Glamorgan	Worcester

25	AXA EQUITY & LAW LEAGUE	(Sun)
	Derbyshire v Sussex	Derby
	Essex v Durham	Chelmsford
	Lancashire v Nottinghamshire	Old Trafford
	Leicestershire v Warwickshire	Leicester
	Middlesex v Hampshire	Lord's
	Northamptonshire v Surrey	Northampton
	Somerset v Kent	Taunton
	Worcestershire v Glamorgan	Worcester
27	NATWEST BANK TROPHY	(Tue)
	Quarter-finals	
28	TETLEY BITTER CHALLENGE	(Wed, 3 days)
	Northamptonshire or Lancashire v Australians	Northampton or Old Trafford
29	BRITANNIC ASSURANCE CHAMPIONSHIP	(Thur)
	Durham v Sussex	Durham University
	Essex v Worcestershire	Chelmsford
	Gloucestershire v Derbyshire	Cheltenham
	Hampshire v Warwickshire	Southampton
	Kent v Leicestershire	Canterbury
	Somerset v Yorkshire	Taunton
	Surrey v Nottinghamshire	The Oval
31	TETLEY BITTER CHALLENGE	(Sat, 3 days)
	Glamorgan v Australians*	Neath

AUGUST

1	AXA EQUITY & LAW LEAGUE	(Sun)
	Durham v Sussex	Durham University
	Essex v Worcestershire	Chelmsford
	Gloucestershire v Derbyshire	Cheltenham
	Hampshire v Warwickshire	Southampton
	Kent v Leicestershire	Canterbury
	Somerset v Yorkshire	Taunton
	Surrey v Nottinghamshire	The Oval
1	OTHER MATCH	(Sun, 1–day)
	Women's World Cup Final	Lord's
5	FIFTH CORNHILL INSURANCE TEST MATCH	(Thur)
	ENGLAND v AUSTRALIA*	Edgbaston
5	BRITANNIC ASSURANCE CHAMPIONSHIP	(Thur)
	Durham v Derbyshire	Durham University
	Glamorgan v Warwickshire	Cardiff
	Gloucestershire v Lancashire	Cheltenham
	Kent v Surrey	Canterbury
	Middlesex v Leicestershire	Lord's
	Northamptonshire v Essex	Northampton

	Nottinghamshire v Yorkshire	Trent Bridge
	Sussex v Worcestershire	Hove
5	OTHER MATCHES	(Thur)
	England U-19 v West Indies U-19	Leicester
	(First Youth One-Day International)	
7	England U-19 v West Indies U-19	(Sat)
	(Second Youth One-Day International)	Chelmsford
8	AXA EQUITY & LAW LEAGUE	(Sun)
	Durham v Derbyshire	Durham University
	Glamorgan v Warwickshire	Neath
	Gloucestershire v Lancashire	Cheltenham
	Kent v Surrey	Canterbury
	Middlesex v Leicestershire	Lord's
	Northamptonshire v Essex	Northampton
	Nottinghamshire v Yorkshire	Trent Bridge
	Sussex v Worcestershire	Hove
10	NATWEST BANK TROPHY	(Tue)
	Semi-finals	
11	TETLEY BITTER CHALLENGE	(Wed, 3 days)
	Kent v Australians	Canterbury
	(A one-day game will be played on Friday,	
	August 13 if Kent involved in NWT SFs)	
12	BRITANNIC ASSURANCE	
	CHAMPIONSHIP	(Thur)
	Derbyshire v Somerset	Derby
	Hampshire v Lancashire	Southampton
	Leicestershire v Glamorgan	Leicester
	Northamptonshire v Durham	Northampton
	Sussex v Nottinghamshire	Eastbourne
	Warwickshire v Gloucestershire	Edgbaston
	Worcestershire v Surrey	Worcester
	Yorkshire v Middlesex	Scarborough
12	OTHER MATCH	(Thur, 4 days)
	England U-19 v West Indies U-19*	Trent Bridge
	(First Youth Test Match)	
14	TETLEY BITTER CHALLENGE	(Sat, 3 days)
	Essex v Australians*	Chelmsford
15	AXA EQUITY & LAW LEAGUE	(Sun)
	Derbyshire v Somerset	Derby
	Hampshire v Lancashire	Southampton
	Leicestershire v Glamorgan	Leicester
	Northamptonshire v Durham	Northampton
	Sussex v Nottinghamshire	Eastbourne
	Warwickshire v Gloucestershire	Edgbaston
	Worcestershire v Surrey	Worcester
	Yorkshire v Middlesex	Scarborough
16	OTHER MATCH	(Mon or Tue, 1-day)
17	Bain Clarkson Trophy Semi-finals	

19	SIXTH CORNHILL INSURANCE TEST MATCH ENGLAND v AUSTRALIA*	(Thur) The Oval
19	BRITANNIC ASSURANCE CHAMPIONSHIP	(Thur)
	Derbyshire v Surrey	Derby
	Durham v Warwickshire	Darlington
	Glamorgan v Hampshire	Swansea
	Gloucestershire v Essex	Bristol
	Lancashire v Yorkshire	Old Trafford
	Middlesex v Northamptonshire	Lord's
	Somerset v Leicestershire	Weston-super-Mare
	Worcestershire v Kent	Worcester
22	AXA EQUITY & LAW LEAGUE	(Sun)
	Derbyshire v Surrey	Derby
	Durham v Warwickshire	Darlington
	Glamorgan v Hampshire	Swansea
	Gloucestershire v Essex	Bristol
	Lancashire v Yorkshire	Old Trafford
	Middlesex v Northamptonshire	Lord's
	Somerset v Leicestershire	Weston-super-Mare
	Worcestershire v Kent	Worcester
26	BRITANNIC ASSURANCE CHAMPIONSHIP	(Thur)
	Essex v Middlesex	Colchester
	Glamorgan v Gloucestershire	Abergavenny
	Hampshire v Sussex	Portsmouth
	Lancashire v Kent	Lytham
	Northamptonshire v Leicestershire	Northampton
	Nottinghamshire v Derbyshire	Trent Bridge
	Surrey v Somerset	The Oval
	Warwickshire v Worcestershire	Edgbaston
	Yorkshire v Durham	Headingley
26	OTHER MATCH England U-19 v West Indies U-19* (Second Youth Test Match)	(Thur, 4 days) Hove
27	League Cricket Conference v Zimbabwe	(Fri, 1-day) Haslingden
29	AXA EQUITY & LAW LEAGUE	(Sun)
	Essex v Middlesex	Colchester
	Glamorgan v Gloucestershire	Ebbw Vale
	Hampshire v Sussex	Portsmouth
	Lancashire v Kent	Old Trafford
	Northamptonshire v Leicestershire	Northampton
	Nottinghamshire v Derbyshire	Trent Bridge
	Surrey v Somerset	The Oval
	Warwickshire v Worcestershire	Edgbaston
	Yorkshire v Durham	Headingley
29	OTHER MATCH Rothmans Village Cricket Championship Final	(Sun, 1-day) Lord's

| 30 | President's XI v Zimbabwe (McCain Challenge) | (Mon, 1-day) Scarborough |

31	BRITANNIC ASSURANCE CHAMPIONSHIP	(Tue)
	Durham v Nottinghamshire	Chester-le-Street
	Kent v Northamptonshire	Canterbury
	Leicestershire v Yorkshire	Leicester
	Somerset v Gloucestershire	Taunton
	Surrey v Hampshire	The Oval
	Sussex v Essex	Hove
	Worcestershire v Lancashire	Worcester

SEPTEMBER

| 1 | President's XI v Zimbabwe (Tesco International) | (Wed, 3 days) Scarborough |

4	NATWEST BANK TROPHY FINAL (Reserve days Sunday and Monday)	(Sat)
	OTHER MATCH	
	Yorkshire v Durham (1-day) (Northern Electric Trophy)	Headingley

5	AXA EQUITY & LAW LEAGUE	(Sun)
	Durham v Nottinghamshire	Chester-le-Street
	Kent v Northamptonshire	Canterbury
	Leicestershire v Yorkshire	Leicester
	Somerset v Gloucestershire	Taunton
	Surrey v Hampshire	The Oval
	Sussex v Essex	Hove
	Worcestershire v Lancashire	Worcester
	(Matches involving NWT Finalists to be played on Tuesday, September 7).	

6	OTHER MATCHES	(Mon)
	Bain Clarkson Trophy Final (1–day)	Lord's
	Joshua Tetley Festival Trophy (3 days)	Scarborough

| 7 | Warwickshire v Zimbabwe (1-day) | (Tue) Edgbaston |

| 8 | Surrey v Zimbabwe (3 days) | (Wed) The Oval |

9	BRITANNIC ASSURANCE CHAMPIONSHIP	(Thur)
	Derbyshire v Northamptonshire	Derby
	Glamorgan v Essex	Cardiff
	Gloucestershire v Nottinghamshire	Bristol
	Hampshire v Leicestershire	Southampton
	Middlesex v Lancashire	Lord's
	Warwickshire v Somerset	Edgbaston
	Yorkshire v Sussex	Scarborough

10	OTHER MATCH England U-19 v West Indies U-19* (Third Youth Test Match)	(Fri, 4 days) Old Trafford
11	Kent v Zimbabwe (3 days)	(Sat) Canterbury
12	AXA EQUITY & LAW LEAGUE Derbyshire v Northamptonshire Glamorgan v Essex Gloucestershire v Nottinghamshire Hampshire v Leicestershire Middlesex v Lancashire Warwickshire v Somerset Yorkshire v Sussex	(Sun) Derby Cardiff Bristol Southampton Lord's Edgbaston Scarborough
16	BRITANNIC ASSURANCE CHAMPIONSHIP Durham v Somerset Essex v Hampshire Kent v Glamorgan Lancashire v Northamptonshire Leicestershire v Derbyshire Nottinghamshire v Warwickshire Surrey v Yorkshire Sussex v Gloucestershire Worcestershire v Middlesex	(Thur) Hartlepool Chelmsford Canterbury Old Trafford Leicester Trent Bridge The Oval Hove Worcester
19	AXA EQUITY & LAW LEAGUE Durham v Somerset Essex v Hampshire Kent v Glamorgan Lancashire v Northamptonshire Leicestershire v Derbyshire Nottinghamshire v Warwickshire Surrey v Yorkshire Sussex v Gloucestershire Worcestershire v Middlesex	(Sun) Hartlepool Chelmsford Canterbury Old Trafford Leicester Trent Bridge The Oval Hove Worcester